Modern Critical Views

Chinua Achebe
Henry Adams
Aeschylus
S. Y. Agnon
Edward Albee
Raphael Alberti
Louisa May Alcott
A. R. Ammons
Sherwood Anderson
Aristophanes
Matthew Arnold
Antonin Artaud
John Ashbery
Margaret Atwood
W. H. Auden
Jane Austen
Isaac Babel
Sir Francis Bacon
James Baldwin
Honoré de Balzac
John Barth
Donald Barthelme
Charles Baudelaire
Simone de Beauvoir
Samuel Beckett
Saul Bellow
Thomas Berger
John Berryman
The Bible
Elizabeth Bishop
William Blake
Giovanni Boccaccio
Heinrich Böll
Jorge Luis Borges
Elizabeth Bowen
Bertolt Brecht
The Brontës
Charles Brockden Brown
Sterling Brown
Robert Browning
Martin Buber
John Bunyan
Anthony Burgess
Kenneth Burke
Robert Burns
William Burroughs
George Gordon, Lord
  Byron
Pedro Calderón de la Barca
Italo Calvino
Albert Camus
Canadian Poetry: Modern
  and Contemporary
Canadian Poetry through
  E. J. Pratt
Thomas Carlyle
Alejo Carpentier
Lewis Carroll
Willa Cather
Louis-Ferdinand Céline
Miguel de Cervantes

Geoffrey Chaucer
John Cheever
Anton Chekhov
Kate Chopin
Chrétien de Troyes
Agatha Christie
Samuel Taylor Coleridge
Colette
William Congreve & the
  Restoration Dramatists
Joseph Conrad
Contemporary Poets
James Fenimore Cooper
Pierre Corneille
Julio Cortázar
Hart Crane
Stephen Crane
e. e. cummings
Dante
Robertson Davies
Daniel Defoe
Philip K. Dick
Charles Dickens
James Dickey
Emily Dickinson
Denis Diderot
Isak Dinesen
E. L. Doctorow
John Donne & the
  Seventeenth-Century
  Metaphysical Poets
John Dos Passos
Fyodor Dostoevsky
Frederick Douglass
Theodore Dreiser
John Dryden
W. E. B. Du Bois
Lawrence Durrell
George Eliot
T. S. Eliot
Elizabethan Dramatists
Ralph Ellison
Ralph Waldo Emerson
Euripides
William Faulkner
Henry Fielding
F. Scott Fitzgerald
Gustave Flaubert
E. M. Forster
John Fowles
Sigmund Freud
Robert Frost
Northrop Frye
Carlos Fuentes
William Gaddis
Federico García Lorca
Gabriel García Márquez
André Gide
W. S. Gilbert
Allen Ginsberg
J. W. von Goethe

Nikolai Gogol
William Golding
Oliver Goldsmith
Mary Gordon
Günther Grass
Robert Graves
Graham Greene
Thomas Hardy
Nathaniel Hawthorne
William Hazlitt
H. D.
Seamus Heaney
Lillian Hellman
Ernest Hemingway
Hermann Hesse
Geoffrey Hill
Friedrich Hölderlin
Homer
A. D. Hope
Gerard Manley Hopkins
Horace
A. E. Housman
William Dean Howells
Langston Hughes
Ted Hughes
Victor Hugo
Zora Neale Hurston
Aldous Huxley
Henrik Ibsen
Eugène Ionesco
Washington Irving
Henry James
Dr. Samuel Johnson and
  James Boswell
Ben Jonson
James Joyce
Carl Gustav Jung
Franz Kafka
Yasonari Kawabata
John Keats
Søren Kierkegaard
Rudyard Kipling
Melanie Klein
Heinrich von Kleist
Philip Larkin
D. H. Lawrence
John le Carré
Ursula K. Le Guin
Giacomo Leopardi
Doris Lessing
Sinclair Lewis
Jack London
Robert Lowell
Malcolm Lowry
Carson McCullers
Norman Mailer
Bernard Malamud
Stéphane Mallarmé
Sir Thomas Malory
André Malraux
Thomas Mann

Modern Critical Views

Modern Critical Views

CHARLES DICKENS

Edited and with an introduction by
Harold Bloom
Sterling Professor of the Humanities
Yale University

CHELSEA HOUSE PUBLISHERS
New York ◇ Philadelphia

Library of Congress Cataloging-in-Publication Data

Charles Dickens.

—(Modern critical views)
  Bibliography: p.
  Includes index.
  Summary: A collection of critical essays on
Dickens and his works.
  1. Dickens, Charles, 1812–1870—Criticism and
interpretation. [1. Dickens, Charles, 1812–1870—
Criticism and interpretation. 2. English literature—
History and criticism] I. Bloom, Harold. II. Series.
PR4588.C358   1987   823'.8   86–29917
ISBN 0–87754–690–8

Contents

Editor's Note

This book brings together a representative selection of the best criticism devoted to the novels of Charles Dickens. The essays are reprinted here in the chronological order of their original publication. I am grateful to Jennifer Wagner for her erudition and judgment in helping me to edit this volume.

My introduction centers upon Dickens's staging of the will in *David Copperfield, Bleak House, Hard Times,* and *A Tale of Two Cities.* The chronological sequence of criticism begins with J. Hillis Miller, who can be said to have given a new turn to Dickens criticism, one that is ongoing. *Oliver Twist* is chronicled by Miller as a dialectical interplay of dark and bright visions of the world. Northrop Frye, our foremost living critic, explores the affinities between Dickens and Ben Jonson, both of them writers of "the comedy of humors."

A Tale of Two Cities is analyzed by Robert Alter as a hallucinated vision of a demonic history, which gives us a very different Dickens from the one presented by the eminent Marxist critic Raymond Williams, who sees *Dombey and Son* and some related Dickens novels as the great English instance of the social transformation from a folk culture to a new urban popular culture. Steven Marcus, revisiting *Pickwick Papers,* finds in it Dickens's "first and freest novel," with an extraordinary negativity at its dramatic center.

A Christmas Carol is examined by Harry Stone as an instance of Dickens's skill in utilizing fairy-tale elements for his own purposes, while Robert L. Caserio concentrates on the creative power of Dickens's language of plot reversals in *Barnaby Rudge* and *Nicholas Nickleby.*

The focus moves to *David Copperfield* and *Great Expectations* in Dianne F. Sadoff's exegesis of the author-as-father in Dickens. *Bleak House,* his authentic masterpiece, is analyzed by D. A. Miller as an intricate representation of "discipline in different voices," with a particular emphasis upon Dickens's juxtaposed visions of the police and the family.

Hard Times, Dickens's attack upon the Utilitarians, is found by Stephen J. Spector to be less a work of social prophecy and more a dramatization of its own futility as social vision, a dramatization that features acute social and intellectual honesty. Eve Kosofsky Sedgwick, fiercely reading *Our Mutual Friend,* brilliantly integrates images of misogyny and finance, as she investigates the pattern in which women were made to renounce the ownership of real property.

Freud's "moral masochism," our terrible need for punishment, is traced in *Great Expectations* by Shuli Barzilai, particularly in the character of Estella. Ned Lukacher comprehensively surveys streetwalking in Dickens's work, locating in it Dickens's "primal scene."

In this book's final essay, on *Little Dorrit,* Jeff Nunokawa analyzes figures of acquisitive activity which he shows are also Dickensian metaphors for aspects of the female body. Nunokawa's reading of *Little Dorrit,* like the essays of Eve Kosofsky Sedgwick and Ned Lukacher, is an instance of the application to Dickens of some of the most advanced ideas in contemporary literary criticism. Dickens, like Shakespeare, illuminates these ideas more powerfully than they elucidate him, which is only to repeat an insight already shared by Sedgwick, Lukacher, and Nunokawa.

Introduction

I

Courage would be the critical virtue most required if anyone were to attempt an essay that might be called "The Limitations of Shakespeare." Tolstoy, in his most outrageous critical performance, more or less tried just that, with dismal results, and even Ben Jonson might not have done much better, had he sought to extend his ambivalent *obiter dicta* on his great friend and rival. Nearly as much courage, or foolhardiness, is involved in discoursing on the limitations of Dickens, but the young Henry James had a critical gusto that could carry him through every literary challenge. Reviewing *Our Mutual Friend* in 1865, James exuberantly proclaimed that "*Bleak House* was forced; *Little Dorrit* was labored; the present work is dug out as with a spade and pickaxe." At about this time, reviewing *Drum-Taps,* James memorably dismissed Whitman as an essentially prosaic mind seeking to lift itself, by muscular exertion, into poetry. To reject some of the major works of the strongest English novelist and the greatest American poet, at about the same moment, is to set standards for critical audacity that no one since has been able to match, even as no novelist since has equalled Dickens, nor any poet, Walt Whitman.

James was at his rare worst in summing up Dickens's supposedly principal inadequacy:

> Such scenes as this are useful in fixing the limits of Mr. Dickens's insight. Insight is, perhaps, too strong a word; for we are convinced that it is one of the chief conditions of his genius not to see beneath the surface of things. If we might hazard a definition of his literary character, we should, accordingly, call him the greatest of superficial novelists. We are aware that this definition confines him to an inferior rank in the department of letters which he adorns; but we accept this consequence of our

1

proposition. It were, in our opinion, an offence against humanity to place Mr. Dickens among the greatest novelists. For, to
repeat what we have already intimated, he has created nothing
but figure. He has added nothing to our understanding of
human character. He is master of but two alternatives: he
reconciles us to what is commonplace, and he reconciles us to
what is odd. The value of the former service is questionable;
and the manner in which Mr. Dickens performs it sometimes
conveys a certain impression of charlatanism. The value of the
latter service is incontestable, and here Mr. Dickens is an honest, an admirable artist.

This can be taken literally, and then transvalued: to see truly the
surface of things, to reconcile us at once to the commonplace and the
odd—these are not minor gifts. In 1860, John Ruskin, the great seer of
the surface of things, the charismatic illuminator of the commonplace and
the odd together, had reached a rather different conclusion from that of the
young Henry James, five years before James's brash rejection:

The essential value and truth of Dickens's writings have been
unwisely lost sight of by many thoughtful persons merely because he presents his truth with some colour of caricature.
Unwisely, because Dickens's caricature, though often gross, is
never mistaken. Allowing for his manner of telling them, the
things he tells us are always true. I wish that he could think it
right to limit his brilliant exaggeration to works written only
for public amusement; and when he takes up a subject of high
national importance, such as that which he handled in *Hard
Times,* that he would use severer and more accurate analysis.
The usefulness of that work (to my mind, in several respects,
the greatest he has written) is with many persons seriously
diminished because Mr. Bounderby is a dramatic monster, instead of a characteristic example of a worldly master; and
Stephen Blackpool a dramatic perfection, instead of a characteristic example of an honest workman. But let us not lose the
use of Dickens's wit and insight, because he chooses to speak in
a circle of stage fire. He is entirely right in his main drift and
purpose in every book he has written; and all of them, but
especially *Hard Times,* should be studied with close and earnest
care by persons interested in social questions. They will find
much that is partial, and, because partial, apparently unjust;

but if they examine all the evidence on the other side, which Dickens seems to overlook, it will appear, after all their trouble, that his view was the finally right one, grossly and sharply told.

To say of Dickens that he chose "to speak in a circle of stage fire" is exactly right, since Dickens is the greatest actor among novelists, the finest master of dramatic projection. A superb stage performer, he never stops performing in his novels, which is not the least of his many Shakespearean characteristics. Martin Price usefully defines some of these as "his effortless invention, his brilliant play of language, the scope and density of his imagined world." I like also Price's general comparison of Dickens to the strongest satirist in the language, Swift, a comparison that Price shrewdly turns into a confrontation:

> But the confrontation helps us to define differences as well: Dickens is more explicit, more overtly compassionate, insisting always upon the perversions of feeling as well as of thought. His outrage is of the same consistency as his generous celebration, the satirical wit of the same copious extravagance as the comic elaborations. Dickens' world is alive with things that snatch, lurch, teeter, thrust, leer; it is the animate world of Netherlandish genre painting or of Hogarth's prints, where all space is a field of force, where objects vie or intrigue with each other, where every human event spills over into the things that surround it. This may become the typically crowded scene of satire, where persons are reduced to things and things to matter in motion; or it may pulsate with fierce energy and noisy feeling. It is different from Swift; it is the distinctive Dickensian plenitude, which we find again in his verbal play, in his great array of vivid characters, in his massed scenes of feasts or public declamations. It creates rituals as compelling as the resuscitation of Rogue Riderhood, where strangers participate solemnly in the recovery of a spark of life, oblivious for the moment of the unlovely human form it will soon inhabit.

That animate, Hogarthian world, "where all space is a field of force," indeed is a plenitude and it strikes me that Price's vivid description suggests Rabelais rather than Swift as a true analogue. Dickens, like Shakespeare in one of many aspects and like Rabelais, is as much carnival as stage fire, a kind of endless festival. The reader of Dickens stands in the midst of a festival, which is too varied, too multiform, to be taken in even by innumerable readings. Something always escapes our ken; Ben Jonson's sense of being "rammed with life" is exemplified more even by Dickens than by Rabelais, in that near-Shakespearean plenitude that is Dickens's peculiar glory.

Is it possible to define that plenitude narrowly enough so as to conceptualize it for critical use, though by "conceptualize" one meant only a critical metaphor? Shakespearean representation is no touchstone for Dickens or for anyone else, since above all modes of representation it turns upon an inward changing brought about by characters listening to themselves speak. Dickens cannot do that. His villains are gorgeous, but there are no Iagos or Edmunds among them. The severer, more relevant test, which Dickens must fail, though hardly to his detriment, is Falstaff, who generates not only his own meaning, but meaning in so many others besides, both on and off the page. Probably the severest test is Shylock, most Dickensian of Shakespeare's characters, since we cannot say of Dickens's Shylock, Fagin, that there is much Shakespearean about him at all. Fagin is a wonderful grotesque, but the winds of will are not stirred in him, while they burn on hellishly forever in Shylock.

Carlyle's injunction, to work in the will, seems to have little enough place in the cosmos of the Dickens characters. I do not say this to indicate a limitation, or even a limit, nor do I believe that the will to live or the will to power is ever relaxed in or by Dickens. But nothing is got for nothing, except perhaps in or by Shakespeare, and Dickens purchases his kind of plenitude at the expense of one aspect of the will. T. S. Eliot remarked that "Dickens's characters are real because there is no one like them." I would modify that to "They are real because they are not like one another, though sometimes they are a touch more like some of us than like each other." Perhaps the will, in whatever aspect, can differ only in degree rather than in kind among us. The aesthetic secret of Dickens appears to be that his villains, heroes, heroines, victims, eccentrics, ornamental beings, do differ from one another *in the kinds of will that they possess*. Since that is hardly possible for us, as humans, it does bring about an absence in reality in and for Dickens. That is a high price to pay, but it is a good deal less than everything and Dickens got more than he paid for. We also receive a great deal more than we ever are asked to surrender when we read Dickens. That may indeed be his most Shakespearean quality, and may provide the critical trope I quest for in him. James and Proust hurt you more than Dickens does, and the hurt is the meaning, or much of it. What hurts in Dickens never has much to do with meaning, because there cannot be a poetics of pain where the will has ceased to be common or sadly uniform. Dickens really does offer a poetics of pleasure, which is surely worth our secondary uneasiness at his refusal to offer us any accurately mimetic representations of the human will. He writes always the book of the drives, which is why supposedly Freudian readings of him always fail so tediously. The conceptual metaphor he suggests in his representations of character and personality is neither Shakespearean mirror nor Romantic lamp, neither Rabelaisian carnival nor Fieldingesque open country. "Stage fire" seems to me perfect, for "stage" removes something of the reality of the will, yet only as modifier. The substantive remains "fire." Dickens is the poet of the fire of the drives, the true celebrant of Freud's myth of frontier concepts, of that domain lying on the border between psyche and body, falling into matter, yet partaking of the reality of both.

II

If the strong writer be defined as one who confronts his own contingency, his own dependent relation on a precursor, then we can discover only a few writers after Homer and the Yahwist who are strong without that sense of contingency. These are the Great Originals, and they are not many; Shakespeare and Freud are among them and so is Dickens. Dickens, like Shakespeare and Freud, had no true precursors, or perhaps it might be more accurate to say he swallowed up Tobias Smollett rather as Shakespeare devoured Christopher Marlowe. Originality, or an authentic freedom from contingency, is Dickens's salient characteristic as an author. Since Dickens's influence has been so immense, even upon writers so unlikely as Dostoyevski and Kafka, we find it a little difficult now to see at first how overwhelmingly original he is.

Dickens now constitutes a facticity or contingency that no subsequent novelist can transcend or evade without the risk of self-maiming. Consider the difference between two masters of modern fiction, Henry James and James Joyce. Is not Dickens the difference? *Ulysses* comes to terms with Dickens, and earns the exuberance it manifests. Poldy is larger, I think, than any single figure in Dickens, but he has recognizably Dickensian qualities. Lambert Strether in *The Ambassadors* has none, and is the poorer for it. Part of the excitement of *The Princess Casamissima* for us must be that, for once, James achieves a Dickensian sense of the outward life, a sense that is lacking even in *The Portrait of a Lady,* and that we miss acutely (at least I do) amidst even the most inward splendors of *The Wings of the Dove* and *The Golden Bowl.*

The Personal History of David Copperfield, indeed the most personal and autobiographical of all Dickens's novels, has been so influential upon all subsequent portraits of the artist as a young man that we have to make a conscious effort to recover our appreciation of the book's fierce originality. It is the first therapeutic novel, in part written to heal the author's self, or at least to solace permanent anxieties incurred in childhood and youth. Freud's esteem for *David Copperfield* seems inevitable, even if it has led to a number of unfortunate readings within that unlikely compound oddly called "Freudian literary criticism."

Dickens's biographer Edgar Johnson has traced the evolution of *David Copperfield* from an abandoned fragment of autobiography, with its powerful but perhaps self-deceived declaration: "I do not write resentfully or angrily: for I know how all these things have worked together to make me what I am." Instead of representing his own parents as being David Copperfield's, Dickens displaced them into the Micawbers, a change that purchased astonishing pathos and charm at the expense of avoiding a personal pain that might have produced greater meaningfulness. But *David Copperfield* was, as Dickens said, his "favourite child," fulfilling his deep need to become his own father. Of no other book would he have said: "I seem to be sending some part of myself into the Shadowy World."

Kierkegaard advised us that "he who is willing to do the work gives birth to his own father," while Nietzsche even more ironically observed that "if one hasn't had a good father, then it is necessary to invent one." *David Copperfield* is more in the spirit of Kierkegaard's adage, as Dickens more or less makes himself David's father. David, an illustrious novelist, allows himself to narrate his story in the first person. A juxtaposition of the start and conclusion of the narrative may be instructive:

> Whether I shall turn out to be the hero of my own life, or whether that station will be held by anybody else, these pages must show. To begin my life with the beginning of my life, I record that I was born (as I have been informed and believe) on a Friday, at twelve o'clock at night. It was remarked that the clock began to strike, and I began to cry, simultaneously.
>
> In consideration of the day and hour of my birth, it was declared by the nurse, and by some sage women in the neighbourhood who had taken a lively interest in me several months before there was any possibility of our becoming personally acquainted, first, that I was destined to be unlucky in life; and secondly, that I was privileged to see ghosts and

spirits; both these gifts inevitably attaching, as they believed, to all unlucky infants of either gender, born towards the small hours on a Friday night.

I need say nothing here, on the first head, because nothing can show better than my history whether that prediction was verified or falsified by the result. On the second branch of the question, I will only remark, that unless I ran through that part of my inheritance while I was still a baby, I have not come into it yet. But I do not at all complain of having been kept out of this property; and if anybody else should be in the present enjoyment of it, he is heartily welcome to keep it.

And now, as I close my task, subduing my desire to linger yet, these faces fade away. But one face, shining on me like a Heavenly light by which I see all other objects, is above them and beyond them all. And that remains.

I turn my head, and see it, in its beautiful serenity, beside me.

My lamp burns low, and I have written far into the night; but the dear presence, without which I were nothing, bears me company.

O Agnes, O my soul, so may thy face be by me when I close my life indeed; so may I, when realities are melting from me, like the shadows which I now dismiss, still find thee near me, pointing upward!

No adroit reader could prefer the last four paragraphs of *David Copperfield* to the first three. The high humor of the beginning is fortunately more typical of the book than the sugary conclusion. Yet the juxtaposition does convey the single rhetorical flaw in Dickens that matters, by which I do not mean the wild pathos that marks the death of Steerforth, or the even more celebrated career of the endlessly unfortunate Little Em'ly. If Dickens's image of voice or mode of representation is "stage fire," then his metaphors always will demand the possibility of being staged. Micawber, Uriah Heep, Steerforth in his life (not at the end) are all of them triumphs of stage fire, as are Peggotty, Murdstone, Betsey Trotwood, and even Dora Spenlow. But Agnes is a disaster, and that dreadful "pointing upward!" is not to be borne. You cannot stage Agnes, which would not matter except that she does represent the idealizing and self-mystifying side of David and so she raises the question, Can you, as a reader, stage David? How much stage fire got into him? Or, to be hopelessly reductive, has he a will, as Uriah Heep and Steerforth in their very different ways are wills incarnate?

If there is an aesthetic puzzle in the novel, it is why David has and conveys so overwhelming a sense of disordered suffering and early sorrow in his Murdstone phase, as it were, and before. Certainly the intensity of the pathos involved is out of all proportion to the fictive experience that comes through to the reader. Dickens both invested himself in and withdrew from David, so that something is always missing in the self-representation. Yet the will—to live, to interpret, to repeat, to write—survives and burgeons perpetually. Dickens's preternatural energy gets into David, and is at some considerable variance with the diffidence of David's apparent refusal to explore his own inwardness. What does mark Dickens's representation of David with stage fire is neither the excess of the early sufferings nor the tiresome idealization of the love for Agnes. It is rather the vocation of novelist, the drive to tell a story, particularly one's own story, that apparels David with the fire of what Freud called the drives.

Dickens's greatness in *David Copperfield* has little to do with the much more extraordinary strength that was to manifest itself in *Bleak House*, which can compete with *Clarissa, Emma, Middlemarch, The Portrait of a Lady, Women in Love,* and *Ulysses* for the eminence of being the inescapable novel in the language. *David Copperfield* is of another order, but it is the origin of that order, the novelist's account of how she or he burned through experience in order to achieve the Second Birth, into the will to narrate, the storyteller's destiny.

III

Bleak House may not be "the finest literary work the nineteenth century produced in England," as Geoffrey Tillotson called it in 1946. A century that gave us *The Prelude* and Wordsworth's major crisis lyrics, Blake's *Milton* and *Jerusalem,* Byron's *Don Juan,* the principal poems of Shelley, Keats, Tennyson, and Browning, and novels such as *Pride and Prejudice, Emma, Middlemarch,* and Dickens's own *Hard Times* and *Our Mutual Friend,* is an era of such literary plenitude that a single choice is necessarily highly problematic. Yet there is now something close to critical agreement that *Bleak House* is Dickens's most complex and memorable single achievement. W. J. Harvey usefully sketches just how formidably the novel is patterned:

Bleak House is for Dickens a unique and elaborate experiment in narration and plot composition. It is divided into two inter-mingled and roughly concurrent stories; Esther Summerson's first-person narrative and an omniscient narrative told consis-tently in the historic present. The latter takes up thirty-four chapters; Esther has one less. Her story, however, occupies a good deal more than half the novel. The reader who checks the distribution of these two narratives against the original part issues will hardly discern any significant pattern or correlation. Most parts contain a mixture of the two stories; one part is narrated entirely by Esther and five parts entirely by the omni-scient author. Such a check does, however, support the view that Dickens did not, as is sometimes supposed, use serial publication in the interest of crude suspense. A sensational novelist, for example, might well have ended a part issue with chapter 31; Dickens subdues the drama by adding another chapter to the number. The obvious exception to this only proves the rule; in the final double number the suspense of Bucket's search for Lady Dedlock is heightened by cutting back to the omniscient narrative and the stricken Sir Leicester. In general, however, Dickens' control of the double narrative is far richer and subtler than this.

I would add to Harvey the critical observation that Dickens's own narrative will in "his" thirty-four chapters is a will again different in kind than the will to tell her story of the admirable Esther Summerson. Dick-ens's (or the omniscient, historical present narrator's) metaphor of repre-sentation is one of stage fire: wild, free, unconditioned, incessant with the force of Freud's domain of those grandly indefinite frontier concepts, the drives. Esther's mode of representation is certainly not flat or insipid; for all of her monumental repressions, Esther finally seems to me the most mysteriously complex and profound personage in *Bleak House*. Her narra-tive is not so much plain style as it is indeed repressed in the precise Freudian sense of "repression," whose governing metaphor, in Esther's prose as in Freud's, is flight from, rather than a pushing down or pushing under. Esther frequently forgets, purposefully though "unconsciously," what she cannot bear to remember, and much of her narrative is her strong defense against the force of the past. Esther may not *appear* to change as she goes from little girl to adult, but that is because the rhythm of her psyche, unlike Dickens's own, is one of unfolding rather than development. She is Dickens's Muse, what Whitman would have called his "Fancy," as in the great death-lyric "Goodbye, My Fancy!" or what Stevens would have called Dickens's "Interior Paramour."

Contrast a passage of Esther's story with one of Dickens's own narrative, from the end of chapter 56, "Pursuit," and towards the close of the next chapter, "Esther's Narrative":

> Mr. Jarndyce, the only person up in the house, is just going to bed; rises from his book, on hearing the rapid ringing at the bell; and comes down to the door in his dressing-gown.
>
> "Don't be alarmed sir." In a moment his visitor is confidential with him in the hall, has shut the door, and stands with his hand upon the lock. "I've had the pleasure of seeing you before. Inspector Bucket. Look at that handkerchief, sir, Miss Esther Summerson's. Found it myself put away in a drawer of Lady Dedlock's, quarter of an hour ago. Not a moment to lose. Matter of life or death. You know Lady Dedlock?"
>
> "Yes."
>
> "There has been a discovery there, to-day. Family affairs have come out. Sir Leicester Dedlock, Baronet, has had a fit—apoplexy or paralysis—and couldn't be brought to, and precious time has been lost. Lady Dedlock disappeared this afternoon, and left a letter for him that looks bad. Run your eye over it. Here it is!"
>
> Mr. Jarndyce having read it, asks him what he thinks?
>
> "I don't know. It looks like suicide. Anyways, there's more and more danger, every minute, of its drawing to that. I'd give a hundred pound an hour to have got the start of the present time. Now, Mr. Jarndyce, I am employed by Sir Leicester Dedlock, Baronet, to follow her and find her—to save her, and take her his forgiveness. I have money and full power, but I want something else. I want Miss Summerson."
>
> Mr. Jarndyce, in a troubled voice, repeats "Miss Summerson?"
>
> "Now, Mr. Jarndyce"; Mr. Bucket has read his face with the greatest attention all along: "I speak to you as a gentleman of a humane heart, and under such pressing circumstances as don't often happen. If ever delay was dangerous, it's dangerous now; and if ever you couldn't afterwards forgive yourself for causing it, this is the time. Eight or ten hours, worth, as I tell you, a hundred pound a-piece at least, have been lost since Lady

Dedlock disappeared. I am charged to find her. I am Inspector Bucket. Besides all the rest that's heavy on her, she has upon her, as she believes, suspicion of murder. If I follow her alone, she, being in ignorance of what Sir Leicester Dedlock, Baronet, has communicated to me, may be driven to desperation. But if I follow her in company with a young lady, answering to the description of a young lady that she has a tenderness for—I ask no question, and I say no more than that—she will give me credit for being friendly. Let me come up with her, and be able to have the hold upon her of putting that young lady for'ard, and I'll save her and prevail with her if she is alive. Let me come up with her alone—a harder matter—and I'll do my best; but I don't answer for what the best may be. Time flies; it's getting on for one o'clock. When one strikes, there's another hour gone; and it's worth a thousand pound now, instead of a hundred."

This is all true, and the pressing nature of the case cannot be questioned. Mr. Jarndyce begs him to remain there, while he speaks to Miss Summerson. Mr. Bucket says he will; but acting on his usual principle, does no such thing—following up-stairs instead, and keeping his man in sight. So he remains, dodging and lurking about in the gloom of the staircase while they confer. In a very little time, Mr. Jarndyce comes down, and tells him that Miss Summerson will join him directly, and place herself under his protection, to accompany him where he pleases. Mr. Bucket, satisfied, expresses high approval; and awaits her coming, at the door.

There, he mounts a high tower in his mind, and looks out far and wide. Many solitary figures he perceives, creeping through the streets; many solitary figures out on heaths, and roads, and lying under haystacks. But the figure that he seeks is not among them. Other solitaries he perceives, in nooks of bridges, looking over; and in shadowed places down by the river's level; and a dark, dark, shapeless object drifting with the tide, more solitary than all, clings with a drowning hold on his attention.

Where is she? Living or dead, where is she? If, as he folds the handkerchief and carefully puts it up, it were able, with an enchanted power, to bring before him the place where she found it, and the night landscape near the cottage where it covered the little child, would he descry her there? On the waste, where the brick-kilns are burning with a pale blue flare; where the straw-roofs of the wretched huts in which the bricks are made, are being scattered by the wind; where the clay and water are hard frozen, and the mill in which the gaunt blind horse goes round all day, looks like an instrument of human torture;—traversing this deserted blighted spot, there is a lonely figure with the sad world to itself, pelted by the snow and driven by the wind, and cast out, it would seem, from all companionship. It is the figure of a woman, too; but it is miserably dressed, and no such clothes ever came through the hall, and out at the great door, of the Dedlock mansion.

The transparent windows with the fire and light, looking so bright and warm from the cold darkness out of doors, were soon gone, and again we were crushing and churning the loose snow. We went on with toil enough; but the dismal roads were not much worse than they had been, and the stage was only nine miles. My companion smoking on the box—I had thought at the last inn of begging him to do so, when I saw him standing at a great fire in a comfortable cloud of tobacco—was as vigilant as ever; and as quickly down and up again, when we came to any human abode or any human creature. He had lighted his little dark lantern, which seemed to be a favourite with him, for we had lamps to the carriage; and every now and then he turned it upon me, to see that I was doing well. There was a folding-window to the carriage-head, but I never closed it, for it seemed like shutting out hope.

We came to the end of the stage, and still the lost trace was not recovered. I looked at him anxiously when we stopped to change; but I knew by his yet graver face, as he stood watching the ostlers, that he had heard nothing. Almost in an instant afterwards, as I leaned back in my seat, he looked in, with his lighted lantern in his hand, an excited and quite different man.

"What is it?" said I, starting. "Is she here?"

"No, no. Don't deceive yourself, my dear. Nobody's here. But I've got it!"

The crystallised snow was in his eyelashes, in his hair, lying in ridges on his dress. He had to shake it from his face, and get his breath before he spoke to me.

"Now, Miss Summerson," said he, beating his finger on the

apron, "don't you be disappointed at what I'm a going to do. You know me. I'm Inspector Bucket, and you can trust me. We've come a long way; never mind. Four horses out there for the next stage up! Quick!"

There was a commotion in the yard, and a man came running out of the stables to know "if he meant up or down?"

"Up, I tell you! Up! Ain't it English? Up!"

"Up?" said I, astonished. "To London! Are we going back?"

"Miss Summerson," he answered, "back. Straight back as a die. You know me. Don't be afraid. I'll follow the other, by G—."

"The other?" I repeated. "Who?"

"You called her Jenny, didn't you? I'll follow her. Bring those two pair out here, for a crown a man. Wake up, some of you!"

"You will not desert this lady we are in search of; you will not abandon her on such a night, and in such a state of mind as I know her to be in!" said I, in an agony, and grasping his hand.

"You are right, my dear, I won't. But I'll follow the other. Look alive here with them horses. Send a man for'ard in the saddle to the next stage, and let him send another for'ard again, and order four on, up, right through. My darling, don't you be afraid!"

These orders, and the way in which he ran about the yard, urging them, caused a general excitement that was scarcely less bewildering to me than the sudden change. But in the height of the confusion, a mounted man galloped away to order the relays, and our horses were put to with great speed.

"My dear," said Mr. Bucket, jumping up to his seat, and looking in again—"you'll excuse me if I'm too familiar—don't you fret and worry yourself no more than you can help. I say nothing else at present; but you know me, my dear; now, don't you?"

I endeavoured to say that I knew he was far more capable than I of deciding what we ought to do; but was he sure that this was right? Could I not go forward by myself in search of——I grasped his hand again in my distress, and whispered it to him—of my own mother.

"My dear," he answered, "I know, I know, and would I put

you wrong, do you think? Inspector Bucket. Now you know
me, don't you?"

What could I say but yes!

"Then you keep up as good a heart as you can, and you rely
upon me for standing by you, no less than by Sir Leicester
Dedlock, Baronet. Now, are you right there?"

"All right, sir!"

"Off she goes, then. And get on, my lads!"

We were again upon the melancholy road by which we had
come; tearing up the miry sleet and thawing snow, as if they
were torn up by a waterwheel.

Both passages are extraordinary, by any standards, and certainly
"Pursuit" has far more stage fire than "Esther's Narrative," but this time
her repressive shield, in part, is broken through, and a fire leaps forth out
of her. If we start with "Pursuit" however, we are likelier to see what it is
that returns from the repressed in Esther, returns under the sign of negation (as Freud prophesied), so that what comes back is primarily cognitive,
while the affective aspect of the repression persists. We can remember the
opening of *David Copperfield*, where Dickens, in his *persona* as David,
disavows the gift of second sight attributed to him by the wise women and
gossips. Inspector Bucket, at the conclusion of the "Pursuit" chapter, is
granted a great vision, a preternatural second sight of Esther's lost mother,
Lady Dedlock. What Bucket *sees* is stage fire at its most intense, the
novelist's will to tell become an absolute vision of the will. Mounting a
high tower in his mind, Bucket (who thus becomes Dickens's authorial
will) looks out, far and wide, and sees the truth: "a dark, dark, shapeless
object drifting with the tide, more solitary than all," which "clings with a
drowning hold on his attention." That "drowning hold" leads to the
further vision: "where the clay and water are hard frozen, and the mill in
which the gaunt blind horse goes round all day." I suspect that Dickens
here has a debt to Browning's great romance, "Childe Roland to the Dark
Tower Came," where another apparent instrument of human torture in a
deserted, blighted spot, is seen by a companionless figure as being in
association with a starving blind horse, cast out from the Devil's stud, who
provokes in Browning's narrator the terrible outcry that he never saw a
beast he hated so, because: "He must be wicked to deserve such pain."

The ensuing chapter of "Esther's Narrative" brilliantly evokes the
cognitive return of Esther's acknowledgment of her mother, under the sign
of a negation of past affect. Here the narrative vision proceeds, not in the

Sublime mode of Bucket's extraordinary second sight, but in the grave, meditative lyricism that takes us first to a tentative return from unconscious flight through an image of pursuit of the fleeing, doomed mother: "The transparent windows with the fire and light, looking so bright and warm from the cold darkness out of doors, were soon gone, and again we were crushing and churning the loose snow." That "crushing and churning" images the breaking of the repressive shield, and Dickens shrewdly ends the chapter with Esther's counterpart to Bucket's concluding vision of a Browningesque demonic water mill, torturing consciousness into a return from flight. Esther whispers to Bucket that she desires to go forward by herself in search of her own mother, and the dark pursuit goes on in the sinister metaphor of the sleet and thawing snow, shield of repression, being torn up by a waterwheel that recirculates the meaning of memory's return, even as it buries part of the pains of abandonment by the mother once more: "We were again upon the melancholy road by which we had come; tearing up the miry sleet and thawing snow, as if they were torn up by a waterwheel."

It is a terrifying triumph of Dickens's art that, when "Esther's Narrative" resumes, in chapter 59, we know inevitably that we are headed straight for an apocalyptic image of what Shakespeare, in *Lear*, calls "the promised end" or "image of that horror," here not the corpse of the daughter, but of the mother. Esther goes, as she must, to be the first to touch and to see, and with no affect whatsoever, unveils the truth:

> I passed on to the gate, and stooped down. I lifted the heavy head, put the long dank hair aside, and turned the face. And it was my mother, cold and dead.

IV

Hard Times is, for Dickens, a strikingly condensed novel, being about one-third of the length of *David Copperfield* and *Bleak House,* the two masterpieces that directly preceded it. Astonishing and aesthetically satisfying as it is, I believe it to be somewhat over-praised by modern criticism, or perhaps praised for some less than fully relevant reasons. Ruskin and Bernard Shaw after him admired the book as a testament to Dickens's conversion away from a commercialized and industrialized England and back towards a supposed juster and more humane society. But to like *Hard Times* because of its anti-Utilitarian ideology is to confuse the book with Carlyle and William Morris, as well as with Ruskin and Shaw. The most balanced judgment of the novel is that of Monroe Engel, who observes that "the greatest virtues of *Hard Times* are Dickens's characteristic virtues, but less richly present in the book than in many others." Gradgrind is poor stuff, and is not even an effective parody of Jeremy Bentham. The strength of the novel is indeed elsewhere, as we might expect in the theatrical Dickens.

And yet *Hard Times* is lacking in stage fire; compared to *Bleak House,* it possesses only a tiny component of the Sublime. Again, as an instance of the plain style, the mode of Esther Summerson's narrative, it is curiously weak, and has moreover such drab characterizations as Sissy Jupe and Stephen Blackpool. Indeed, the book's rhetoric is the most colorless in all of Dickens's work. Though, as Engel insisted, many of Dickens's authorial virtues are present, the book lacks the preternatural exuberance that makes Dickens unique among all novelists. Has it any qualities of its own to recommend our devotion?

I would suggest that the start of any critical wisdom about *Hard Times* is to dismiss every Marxist or other moral interpretation of the book. Yes, Dickens's heart was accurate, even if his notion of Benthamite social philosophy was not, and a great novelist's overt defense of imagination cannot fail to move us. Consider however the outrageous first chapter of *Hard Times,* "The One Thing Needful":

> "Now, what I want is, Facts. Teach these boys and girls nothing but Facts. Facts alone are wanted in life. Plant nothing else, and root out everything else. You can only form the minds of reasoning animals upon Facts; nothing else will ever be of any service to them. This is the principle on which I bring up my own children, and this is the principle on which I bring up these children. Stick to Facts, sir!"
>
> The scene was a plain, bare, monotonous vault of a schoolroom, and the speaker's square forefinger emphasized his observations by underscoring every sentence with a line on the schoolmaster's sleeve. The emphasis was helped by the speaker's square wall of a forehead, which had his eyebrows for its base, while his eyes found commodious cellarage in two dark caves, overshadowed by the wall. The emphasis was helped by the speaker's mouth, which was wide, thin, and hard set. The emphasis was helped by the speaker's voice, which was inflexible, dry, and dictatorial. The emphasis was helped by the speaker's hair, which bristled on the skirts of his bald head, a

plantation of firs to keep the wind from its shining surface, all covered with knobs, like the crust of a plum pie, as if the head had scarcely warehouse-room for the hard facts stored inside. The speaker's obstinate carriage, square coat, square legs, square shoulders—nay, his very neckcloth, trained to take him by the throat with an unaccommodating grasp, like a stubborn fact, as it was—all helped the emphasis.

"In this life, we want nothing but Facts, sir; nothing but Facts!"

The speaker, and the schoolmaster, and the third grown person present, all backed a little, and swept with their eyes the inclined plane of little vessels then and there arranged in order, ready to have imperial gallons of facts poured into them until they were full to the brim.

Gradgrind is doubtless Dickens's ultimate revenge upon his own school sufferings; Gradgrind might be called Murdstone run wild, except that Murdstone stays within the circle of caricature, whereas Gradgrind's will is mad, is a drive towards death. And that is where, I now think, the peculiar aesthetic strength of *Hard Times* is to be located. The novel survives as phantasmagoria or nightmare, and hardly as a societal or conceptual bad dream. What goes wrong in it is what Freud called "family romances," which become family horrors. Critics always have noted how really dreadful family relations are in *Hard Times,* as they so frequently are elsewhere in Dickens. A particular power is manifest if we analyze a passage near the conclusion of the penultimate chapter of the first book of the novel, chapter 15, "Father and Daughter":

"Louisa," returned her father, "it appears to me that nothing can be plainer. Confining yourself rigidly to Fact, the question of Fact you state to yourself is: Does Mr. Bounderby ask me to marry him? Yes, he does. The sole remaining question then is: Shall I marry him? I think nothing can be plainer than that?"

"Shall I marry him?" repeated Louisa, with great deliberation.

"Precisely. And it is satisfactory to me, as your father, my dear Louisa, to know that you do not come to the consideration of that question with the previous habits of mind, and habits of life, that belong to many young women."

"No, father," she returned, "I do not."

"I now leave you to judge for yourself," said Mr. Gradgrind. "I have stated the case, as such cases are usually stated among practical minds; I have stated it, as the case of your mother and myself was stated in its time. The rest, my dear Louisa, is for you to decide."

From the beginning, she had sat looking at him fixedly. As he now leaned back in his chair, and bent his deep-set eyes upon her in his turn, perhaps he might have seen one wavering moment in her, when she was impelled to throw herself upon his breast, and give him the pent-up confidences of her heart. But, to see it, he must have overleaped at a bound the artificial barriers he had for many years been erecting, between himself and all those subtle essences of humanity which will elude the utmost cunning of algebra until the last trumpet ever to be sounded shall blow even algebra to wreck. The barriers were too many and too high for such a leap. With his unbending, utilitarian, matter-of-fact face, he hardened her again; and the moment shot away into the plumbless depths of the past, to mingle with all the lost opportunities that are drowned there.

Removing her eyes from him, she sat so long looking silently towards the town, that he said, at length: "Are you consulting the chimneys of the Coketown works, Louisa?"

"There seems to be nothing there but languid and monotonous smoke. Yet when the night comes, Fire bursts out, father!" she answered, turning quickly.

"Of course I know that, Louisa. I do not see the application of the remark." To do him justice he did not, at all.

She passed it away with a slight motion of her hand, and concentrating her attention upon him again, said, "Father, I have often thought that life is very short."—This was so distinctly one of his subjects that he interposed.

"It is short, no doubt, my dear. Still, the average duration of human life is proved to have increased of late years. The calculations of various life assurance and annuity offices, among other figures which cannot go wrong, have established the fact."

"I speak of my own life, father."

"O indeed? Still," said Mr. Gradgrind, "I need not point out to you, Louisa, that it is governed by the laws which govern lives in the aggregate."

"While it lasts, I would wish to do the little I can, and the little I am fit for. What does it matter?"

Mr. Gradgrind seemed rather at a loss to understand the last four words; replying, "How, matter? What matter, my dear?"

"Mr. Bounderby," she went on in a steady, straight way, without regarding this, "asks me to marry him. The question I have to ask myself is, shall I marry him? That is so, father, is it not? You have told me so, father. Have you not?"

"Certainly, my dear."

"Let it be so. Since Mr. Bounderby likes to take me thus, I am satisfied to accept his proposal. Tell him, father, as soon as you please, that this was my answer. Repeat it, word for word, if you can, because I should wish him to know what I said."

"It is quite right, my dear," retorted her father approvingly, "to be exact. I will observe your very proper request. Have you any wish in reference to the period of your marriage, my child?"

"None, father. What does it matter?"

Mr. Gradgrind had drawn his chair a little nearer to her, and taken her hand. But, her repetition of these words seemed to strike with some little discord on his ear. He paused to look at her, and, still holding her hand, said:

"Louisa, I have not considered it essential to ask you one question, because the possibility implied in it appeared to me to be too remote. But perhaps I ought to do so. You have never entertained in secret any other proposal?"

"Father," she returned, almost scornfully, "what other proposal can have been made to *me*? Whom have I seen? Where have I been? What are my heart's experiences?"

"My dear Louisa," returned Mr. Gradgrind, reassured and satisfied. "You correct me justly. I merely wished to discharge my duty."

"What do *I* know, father," said Louisa in her quiet manner, "of tastes and fancies; of aspirations and affections; of all that part of my nature in which such light things might have been nourished? What escape have I had from problems that could be demonstrated, and realities that could be grasped?" As she said it, she unconsciously closed her hand, as if upon a solid object, and slowly opened it as though she were releasing dust or ash.

Caricature here has leaped into Ruskin's "stage fire." Gradgrind, quite mad, nevertheless achieves the wit of asking Louisa whether she is consulting the oracular vapors of the Coketown chimneys. Her magnificent, "Yet when the night comes, Fire bursts out, father!" is more than a prophecy of the return of the repressed. It prophesies also the exuberance of Dickens himself, which comes flooding forth in the obvious yet grand metaphor a page later, when poor Louisa closes her hand, as if upon a graspable reality, and slowly opens it to disclose that her heart, like that of Tennyson's protagonist in *Maud,* is a handful of dust.

That is the true, dark power of *Hard Times.* Transcending Dickens's social vision, or his polemic for imagination, is his naked return to the domain of the drives, Eros and Death. The novel ends with an address to the reader that necessarily is far more equivocal than Dickens can have intended:

> Dear Reader! It rests with you and me, whether, in our two fields of action, similar things shall be or not. Let them be! We shall sit with lighter bosoms on the hearth, to see the ashes of our fires turn grey and cold.

Presumably, our imaginative escape from Gradgrindism into poetry will lighten our bosoms, even as we watch the reality principle overtake us. But the power of Dickens's rhetoric is in those grey and cold ashes, handfuls of dust that gather everywhere in the pages of *Hard Times.* Gradgrind, or the world without imagination, fails as a satire upon Utilitarianism, but triumphs frighteningly as a representation of the drive beyond the pleasure principle.

V

Except perhaps for *Pickwick Papers, A Tale of Two Cities* always has been the most popular of Dickens's books, if we set aside also the annual phenomenon of *A Christmas Carol* and the other Christmas books. No critic however would rank it with such other later novels as *Great Expectations* and *Our Mutual Friend* or the unfinished *Edwin Drood,* or with the many earlier and middle period masterpieces. The harshest single judgment remains that of the now forgotten but formidably pungent reviewer, Sir James Fitzjames Stephen, who left Dickens nothing:

> The moral tone of the *Tale of Two Cities* is not more wholesome than that of its predecessors, nor does it display any

nearer approach to a solid knowledge of the subject-matter to which it refers. Mr. Dickens observes in his preface—"It has been one of my hopes to add something to the popular and picturesque means of understanding that terrible time, though no one can hope to add anything to the philosophy of Mr. Carlyle's wonderful book." The allusion to Mr. Carlyle confirms the presumption which the book itself raises, that Mr. Dickens happened to have read the History of the French Revolution, and, being on the look-out for a subject, determined off-hand to write a novel about it. Whether he has any other knowledge of the subject than a single reading of Mr. Carlyle's work would supply does not appear, but certainly what he has written shows no more. It is exactly the sort of story which a man would write who had taken down Mr. Carlyle's theory without any sort of inquiry or examination, but with a comfortable conviction that "nothing could be added to its philosophy." The people, says Mr. Dickens, in effect, had been degraded by long and gross misgovernment, and acted like wild beasts in consequence. There is, no doubt, a great deal of truth in this view of the matter, but it is such very elementary truth that, unless a man had something new to say about it, it is hardly worth mentioning; and Mr. Dickens supports it by specific assertions which, if not absolutely false, are at any rate so selected as to convey an entirely false impression. It is a shameful thing for a popular writer to exaggerate the faults of the French aristocracy in a book which will naturally find its way to readers who know very little of the subject except what he chooses to tell them; but it is impossible not to feel that the melodramatic story which Mr. Dickens tells about the wicked Marquis who violates one of his serfs and murders another, is a grossly unfair representation of the state of society in France in the middle of the eighteenth century. That the French *noblesse* had much to answer for in a thousand ways, is a lamentable truth; but it is by no means true that they could rob, murder, and ravish with impunity. When Count Horn thought proper to try the experiment under the Regency, he was broken on the wheel, notwithstanding his nobility; and the sort of atrocities which Mr. Dickens depicts as characteristic of the eighteenth century were neither safe nor common in the fourteenth.

The most palpable hit here is certainly at Dickens's extraordinary reliance upon Carlyle's bizarre but effective *French Revolution,* which is not the history it purports to be but rather has the design, rhetoric, and vision of an apocalyptic fantasy. No one now would read either Carlyle or Dickens in order to learn anything about the French Revolution, and sadly enough no one now reads Carlyle anyway. Yet Stephen's dismay remains legitimate; countless thousands continue to receive the only impressions they ever will have of the French Revolution through the reading of *A Tale of Two Cities.* The book remains a great tale, a vivid instance of Dickens's preternatural gifts as a pure storyteller, though except for its depiction of the superbly ghastly Madame Defarge and her Jacobin associates it lacks the memorable grotesques and driven enthusiasts that we expect from Dickens.

The most palpable flaw in the novel is the weakness as representations of Lucie and Darnay, and the relative failure of the more crucial Carton, who simply lacks the aesthetic dignity that Dickens so desperately needed to give him. If Carton and Darnay, between them, really were meant to depict the spiritual form of Charles Dickens, then their mutual lack of gusto renders them even more inadequate. When Madame Defarge dies, slain by her own bullet, we are very moved, particularly by relief that such an unrelenting version of the death drive will cease to menace us. When Carton, looking "sublime and prophetic," goes to execution, Dickens attempts to move us: we receive the famous and unacceptable, "It is a far, far better thing that I do, than I have ever done; it is a far, far better rest that I go to than I have ever known." Dickens owes us a far, far better rhetoric than that, and generally he delivers it.

The life of *A Tale of Two Cities* is elsewhere, centered upon the negative sublimity of Madame Defarge and her knitting, which is one of Dickens's finest inventions, and is clearly a metaphor for the storytelling of the novel itself. Dickens hardly would have said: "I am Madame Defarge," but she, like the author, remorselessly controls the narrative, until she loses her struggle with the epitome of a loving Englishwoman, Miss Pross. The book's penultimate chapter, in which we are rid of Madame Defarge, is shrewdly called "The Knitting Done."

Even Dickens rarely surpasses the nightmare intensity of Madame Defarge, her absolute command of stage fire, and his finest accomplishment in the book is to increase her already stark aura as the narrative knits onwards. Here is a superb early epiphany of the lady, putting heart into her formidable husband, who seems weak only in comparison to his wife, less a force of nature than of history:

The night was hot, and the shop, close shut and surrounded by so foul a neighbourhood, was ill-smelling. Monsieur Defarge's olfactory sense was by no means delicate, but the stock of wine smelt much stronger than it ever tasted, and so did the stock of rum and brandy and aniseed. He whiffed the compound of scents away, as he put down his smoked-out pipe.

"You are fatigued," said madame, raising her glance as she knotted the money. "There are only the usual odours."

"I am a little tired," her husband acknowledged.

"You are a little depressed, too," said madame, whose quick eyes had never been so intent on the accounts, but they had had a ray or two for him. "Oh, the men, the men!"

"But my dear!" began Defarge.

"But my dear!" repeated madame, nodding firmly; "but my dear! You are faint of heart to-night, my dear!"

"Well, then," said Defarge, as if a thought were wrung out of his breast, "it *is* a long time."

"It is a long time," repeated his wife; "and when is it not a long time? Vengeance and retribution require a long time; it is the rule."

"It does not take a long time to strike a man with Lightning," said Defarge.

"How long," demanded madame, composely, "does it take to make and store the lightning? Tell me."

Defarge raised his head thoughtfully, as if there were something in that too.

"It does not take a long time," said madame, "for an earthquake to swallow a town. Eh well! Tell me how long it takes to prepare the earthquake?"

"A long time, I suppose," said Defarge.

"But when it is ready, it takes place, and grinds to pieces everything before it. In the meantime, it is always preparing, though it is not seen or heard. That is your consolation. Keep it."

She tied a knot with flashing eyes, as if it throttled a foe.

"I tell thee," said madame, extending her right hand, for emphasis, "that although it is a long time on the road, it is on the road and coming. I tell thee it never retreats, and never stops. I tell thee it is always advancing. Look around and consider the lives of all the world that we know, consider the faces of all the world that we know, consider the rage and discontent to which the Jacquerie addresses itself with more and more of certainty every hour. Can such things last? Bah! I mock you."

"My brave wife," returned Defarge, standing before her with his head a little bent, and his hands clasped at his back, like a docile and attentive pupil before his catechist, "I do not question all this. But it has lasted a long time, and it is possible— you know well, my wife, it is possible—that it may not come, during our lives."

"Eh well! How then?" demanded madame, tying another knot, as if there were another enemy strangled.

"Well!" said Defarge, with a half-complaining and half-apologetic shrug. "We shall not see the triumph."

"We shall have helped it," returned madame, with her extended hand in strong action. "Nothing that we do, is done in vain. I believe, with all my soul, that we shall see the triumph. But even if not, even if I knew certainly not, show me the neck of an aristocrat and tyrant, and still I would—"

Then madame, with her teeth set, tied a very terrible knot indeed.

"Hold!" cried Defarge, reddening a little as if he felt charged with cowardice; "I too, my dear, will stop at nothing."

"Yes! But it is your weakness that you sometimes need to see your victim and your opportunity, to sustain you. Sustain yourself without that. When the time comes, let loose a tiger and a devil; but wait for the time with the tiger and the devil chained— not shown—yet always ready."

To be always preparing, unseen and unheard, is Madame Defarge's one consolation. Dickens has made her childless, somewhat in the mysterious mode of Lady Macbeth, since somehow we believe that Madame Defarge too must have nursed an infant. Her dialogue with Defarge has overtones of Lady Macbeth heartening Macbeth, keying up his resolution to treason and a kind of parricide. What Dickens has learned from Shakespeare is the art of counterpointing degrees of terror, of excess, so as to suggest a dread that otherwise would reside beyond representation. Macbeth, early doubting, seems weak in contrast to his wife's force, but we will see him at his bloody work, until he becomes an astonishing manifestation of tyranny. Similarly, Defarge seems little in juxtaposition to his implacable wife, but we will see him as a demon of courage, skill, and apocalyptic drive, leading the triumphant assault upon the Bastille.

In his final vision of Madame Defarge, Dickens brilliantly reveals his masochistic passion for her:

> Madame Defarge slightly waved her hand, to imply that she heard, and might be relied upon to arrive in good time, and so went through the mud, and round the corner of the prison wall. The Vengeance and the Juryman, looking after her as she walked away, were highly appreciative of her fine figure, and her superb moral endowments.
>
> There were many women at that time, upon whom the time laid a dreadfully disfiguring hand; but, there was not one among them more to be dreaded than this ruthless woman, now taking her way along the streets. Of a strong and fearless character, of shrewd sense and readiness, of great determination, of that kind of beauty which not only seems to impart to its possessor firmness and animosity, but to strike into others an instinctive recognition of those qualities; the troubled time would have heaved her up, under any circumstances. But, imbued from her childhood with a brooding sense of wrong, and an inveterate hatred of a class, opportunity had developed her into a tigress. She was absolutely without pity. If she had ever had the virtue in her, it had quite gone out of her.
>
> It was nothing to her, that an innocent man was to die for the sins of his forefathers; she saw, not him, but them. It was nothing to her, that his wife was to be made a widow and his daughter an orphan; that was insufficient punishment, because they were her natural enemies and her prey, and as such had no right to live. To appeal to her, was made hopeless by her having no sense of pity, even for herself. If she had been laid low in the streets, in any of the many encounters in which she had been engaged, she would not have pitied herself; nor, if she had been ordered to the axe to-morrow, would she have gone to it with any softer feeling than a fierce desire to change places with the man who sent her there.
>
> Such a heart Madame Defarge carried under her rough robe. Carelessly worn, it was a becoming robe enough, in a certain weird way, and her dark hair looked rich under her coarse red cap. Lying hidden in her bosom, was a loaded pistol. Lying

hidden at her waist, was a sharpened dagger. Thus accoutred, and walking with the confident tread of such a character, and with the supple freedom of a woman who had habitually walked in her girlhood, bare-foot and bare-legged, on the brown sea-sand, Madame Defarge took her way along the streets.

We can discount Dickens's failed ironies here ("her superb moral endowments") and his obvious and rather tiresome moral judgments upon his own creation. What comes through overwhelmingly is Dickens's desire for this sadistic woman, which is the secret of our desire for her also, and so for her nightmare power over us. "Her fine figure," "that kind of beauty . . . firmness and animosity," "a tigress . . . absolutely without pity," "a becoming robe enough, in a certain weird way," "her dark hair looked rich," "confident tread . . . supple freedom . . . bare-foot and bare-legged"—these are the stigmata of a dominatrix. Loaded pistol in her bosom, sharpened dagger at her waist, Madame Defarge is the ultimate phallic woman, a monument to fetishism, to what Freud would have called the splitting of Dickens's ego in the defensive process.

That splitting attains a triumph in the grand wrestling match, where Miss Pross, a Jacob wrestling with the Angel of Death, holds off Madame Defarge in what is supposed to be an instance of Love stronger than Death, but which is all the more effective for its sexual overtones:

> Madame Defarge made at the door. Miss Pross, on the instinct of the moment, seized her round the waist in both her arms, and held her tight. It was in vain for Madame Defarge to struggle and to strike; Miss Pross, with the vigorous tenacity of love, always so much stronger than hate, clasped her tight, and even lifted her from the floor in the struggle that they had. The two hands of Madame Defarge buffeted and tore her face; but, Miss Pross, with her head down, held her round the waist, and clung to her with more than the hold of a drowning woman.
>
> Soon, Madame Defarge's hands ceased to strike, and felt at her encircled waist. "It is under my arm," said Miss Pross, in smothered tones, "you shall not draw it. I am stronger than you, I bless Heaven for it. I'll hold you till one or other of us faints or dies!"
>
> Madame Defarge's hands were at her bosom. Miss Pross looked up, saw what it was, struck at it, struck out a flash and a crash, and stood alone—blinded with smoke.

The embrace of Miss Pross clearly has a repressed lesbian passion for Madame Defarge in it, so that more than a transcendent love for Lucie here endows the force of the good with its immovable tenacity. But for the pistol blast, Madame Defarge would have been held until one or the other lady fainted or died. Miss Pross had never struck a blow in her life, but then our father Jacob had been no warrior either. Dickens, master of stage fire, destroyed Madame Defarge in the grand manner, the only fate worthy of so vivid and so passionately desired a creation.

J. HILLIS MILLER

The Dark World of Oliver Twist

> *I wished to show, in little Oliver, the principle of Good surviving*
> *through every adverse circumstance, and triumphing at last.*
> —Preface to the third edition

At first Oliver Twist is not at all aware of himself or of his situation. He is simply a kind of animate object, inhabited by a will to live. He is a "millstone . . . round the parochial throat" (chap. 4), passed indifferently from institution to institution, "brought up by hand" (chap. 2), put out "To Let" (chap. 3) as though he were a piece of real estate.

But self-awareness does come to Oliver eventually, and it returns intermittently even in the midst of his life of animal-like suffering and abjection. When it does come it appears spontaneously in a form which is simple and all-embracing. It is a consciousness of his total solitude:

> a sense of his loneliness in the great wide world, sank into the child's heart for the first time.
>
> (chap. 2)

> "I am a very little boy, sir; and it is so — so — . . . lonely, sir! So very lonely!"
>
> (chap. 4)

> He was alone in a strange place; and we all know how chilled and desolate the best of us will sometimes feel in such a situation.
>
> (chap. 5)

From *Charles Dickens: The World of His Novels.* © 1958 by the President and Fellows of Harvard College, © 1986 by J. Hillis Miller. Harvard University Press, 1958.

Oliver's desolation is the absence of a primary human requirement, some relation to something human or material outside oneself. His interior life is, as a result, formless. It is nothing but the prolonged monotonous repetition of a moment which is simply emptiness. "Gloom and loneliness . . . [surround] him" (chap. 3), and nothing can be seen or experienced but this gloom and this loneliness.

Oliver's story begins and the moment of his becoming potentially human occurs when he becomes aware of his solitude and in the same moment becomes instinctively aware that it is intolerable to him. Oliver's experience of solitude is not posited upon a prior experience of its opposite. He has never known any other condition: "The boy had no friends to care for, or to care for him. The regret of no recent separation was fresh in his mind; the absence of no loved and well-remembered face sank heavily into his heart. But his heart *was* heavy, notwithstanding" (chap. 5). It is only because Oliver's heart *is* heavy notwithstanding, only because he has an awareness of his state which does not depend on anything outside himself, that he can turn now to the outside world and demand from it some form of that love which he feels to be his natural right as a human being.

But when he turns to the world he finds something very different from the first undifferentiated gloom. He finds that the world does not simply leave the outcast in the open to die. It aggressively addresses itself to the destruction of the helpless being to which it gives no place. Once the decision is made that the outcast has no reason for existing, the world sets about deliberately to fill up the vacuum it has created by a legislative fiat. For even the space he takes up is needed. The world rushes violently in to bury him away out of sight, to take back the volume he occupied, and even to consume the very substance of his body. The characters of *Oliver Twist* find themselves in a world in which they are from the first moment and at every moment in extreme danger. Not how to "succeed," how to "rise in the world," but how to live in this world at all, is their problem. Neither the social world nor the world of nature is willing to give them the means of life. The thieves would have starved to death either in or out of a workhouse if they had not turned to crime, and Oliver's most pressing need is not the status and comfort of a recognized place in society, but simply breathing room and food.

The outcast is likely to be starved or smothered or crushed to death by mere accident, for the world goes on as though he were not in it. So parish children are often "overlooked in turning up a bedstead, or inadvertently scalded to death when there [happens] to be a washing" (chap. 2). And so Oliver is in danger of being beaten or crushed to death. "Grind him to ashes!" says Monks (chap. 33). The board of the workhouse thinks of sending Oliver to sea, "the probability being, that the skipper would flog him to death, in a playful mood, some day after dinner, or would knock his brains out with an iron bar" (chap. 4).

Or, the outcast may be starved to death. The fame of the scene in which Oliver asks for "more" derives, one feels, from the way it expresses dynamically Oliver's revolt against the hostile social and material world. Oliver's request is total. He demands not simply more food, but recognition of his right to live. The workhouse authorities respond to his demand by imprisoning him in a "dark and solitary room." Later on, when Oliver revolts again, he is again assigned to a windowless underground room, the universal scene of his incarceration throughout the novel.

In the windowless room, one may suffocate. The fear of enclosure and the fear of choking to death are closely related motifs in the central imaginative complex of *Oliver Twist*. When Oliver is born there is "considerable difficulty in inducing [him] to take upon himself the office of respiration" (chap. 1). Parish children are, we have seen, often turned up in beds and smothered by accident, and Oliver is nearly apprenticed to Mr. Gamfield, a chimney sweep, who reluctantly admits that "young boys have been smothered in chimneys before now" (chap. 3).

But when the "gentleman in the white waistcoat" predicts of Oliver, "I know that boy will be hung" (chap. 2), we meet for the first time a version of the motif of suffocation which dominates the novel. Hanging is the inescapable destiny in *Oliver Twist* of all those who attempt to live outside the world of honest men. It is Oliver's destiny too if Fagin succeeds in making him a thief. The characters in *Oliver Twist* are obsessed with a fear of being hanged, a fear which is expressed with hallucinatory intensity in the description of Fagin's "last night alive" and is fulfilled in the death of Sikes (chaps. 52, 50). In the narration of both of these deaths the motif of hanging is merged with the image of a dark suffocating interior. Hanging is a frightening mixture of two fears which operate throughout *Oliver Twist*—the fear of falling and the fear of being crushed or suffocated. A man is hanged out in the open, in full view of the crowd, and the executioner drops him into the air. But beneath his black hood the victim is as completely alone, enclosed in the dark, as if he were in the depths of a dungeon. And what more proper symbol of the crushing, suffocating violence of the hostile world than the instantaneous tightening of the noose? Fagin and Sikes merely act out the death which has threatened Oliver from the beginning, and has, in his case too, been connected with the image of close imprisonment in a dark room. When Oliver is locked in the "dark and solitary room" after he has asked for "more," Dickens comments: "It appears, at first sight, not unreasonable to suppose, that, if he had entertained a becoming feeling of respect for the prediction of the gentleman in the white waistcoat, he would have established that sage individual's prophetic character, once and for ever, by tying one end of his pocket-handkerchief to a hook in the wall, and attaching himself to the other" (chap. 3).

But there are other striking passages in *Oliver Twist* which combine the contrary actions of falling and being crushed: "A great many of the tenements had shop-fronts; but these were fast closed, and mouldering away; only the upper rooms being inhabited. Some houses which had become insecure from age and decay, were prevented from falling into the street, by huge beams of wood reared against the walls, and firmly planted in the road" (chap. 5). Or, in another place, we see: "tottering house-fronts projecting over the pavement, dismantled walls that seem to totter . . . , chimneys half crushed half hesitating to fall" (chap. 50). These buildings seem inhabited with a will to fall, to plunge down and smash themselves to bits. It is not a question here, as one might expect, of a fear that the roof will cave in and crush one. The windowless prison, dark and seemingly underground like a cave or grave, is really suspended over a void, and is kept only by a few insubstantial props from plunging down with all its inhabitants. It is the upper rooms of these houses which are inhabited. However solid the prison appears from the inside, the bottom may at any moment drop out. It encloses, entombs, but offers no substantial support, and its most dangerous potentiality may be to fall *with* its prisoner, crushing him. Enclosure in an absolutely dark underground room is, paradoxically, not total imprisonment, immobilization. For if one is wholly alone in the dark and cannot even see the surrounding stone walls, it is as if there were no walls there and one were suspended in nothingness or even falling endlessly through an indistinguishable gloom. One reaches out to touch even the imprisoning walls. They are at least something solid, something which will support, however coldly, the isolated being: "when the long, dismal night came on, [he] spread his little hands before his eyes to shut out the darkness, and crouching in the corner, tried to sleep: ever and anon waking with a start and tremble, and drawing himself closer and closer to the wall, as if to feel even its cold hard surface were a protection in the gloom and loneliness which surrounded him" (chap. 3).

The image of the dark, dilapidated house which strives constantly to fall of its own weight is one of the recurrent configurations of the imagination of Dickens. It appears in the slum houses of Tom-all-Alone's in *Bleak*

House which come crashing down with no warning, killing the paupers within, and it reappears most strikingly as one of the central motifs of *Little Dorrit*: the gloomy, heavy, apparently solid house of the Clennams which is secretly mined from within and falls at the climax of the novel.

There is another variation of this destructive plunge, a variation which haunted Dickens throughout his life and of which *Oliver Twist* contains striking examples. The fall may be into the dirty, suffocating, rending water of the rapidly flowing river. Dickens was, as has often been observed, obsessed by the river Thames and by the daydream of death by drowning, a daydream which was both repulsive and attractive at the same time. But it has not been so often noticed that an important part of Dickens's imaginative landscape of the river was the image of a nook at the edge of the water or of a house towering over the river bank or built in the mud of its shores and in the process of sinking gradually into the shore:

> The old smoke-stained storehouses on either side, rose heavy and dull from the dense mass of roofs and gables, and frowned sternly upon water too black to reflect even their lumbering shapes.
>
> (chap. 46)

> a scattered little colony of ruinous houses . . . [was] erected on a low unwholesome swamp, bordering upon the river.
>
> (chap. 38)

Nancy tells the secrets of Fagin's gang at a midnight meeting with Rose Maylie and Mr. Brownlow in a "dark and dismal hole" (chap. 46) formed by the landing-stairs going down to the river from London Bridge on the Surrey bank. Behind them are the dark stones of the bridge, before them is the dark water, and concealed in an angle of the stairs is the watcher sent by Fagin whose report of her infidelity will cause Bill Sikes to murder her. The scene is like all the black, suffocating interiors in the novel except that the floor is formed by the dark water which, Nancy says, is her destined deathbed. Nancy is actually crushed to death, but Dickens has her die in imagination the death by water which so fascinated and repelled him: "Look at that dark water," says Nancy to Rose Maylie. "How many times do you read of such as I who spring into the tide, and leave no living thing, to care for, or bewail them! It may be years hence, or it may be only months, but I shall come to that at last" (chap. 46).

Death by drowning is not, for Dickens, a soft and easy death. The drowning man does not melt away fluidly into the water. The plunge into the dark river ends in the same violence as hanging or as the fall of the windowless room. The meeting between Monks and the Bumbles is held in a room high up in a large abandoned factory. The image of the tall unstable tenements is repeated, but this time it is the river into which the building might fall: "a considerable portion of the building had already sunk down into the water; while the remainder, tottering and bending over the dark stream, seemed to wait a favourable opportunity of following its old companion" (chap. 38). The imminent fall of the building is, however, only an analogue of the corresponding human fall. Through the secret trap door Monks shows the horrified Bumbles a glimpse of "the turbid water, swollen by the heavy rain, . . . rushing rapidly on below" (chap. 38). It is into this turbulent water, which will both swallow up its victim and "cut [him] to pieces" (chap. 38), that Monks throws the locket and ring which are the only evidence of Oliver's identity, the symbolic vessels of that selfhood Oliver seeks. (See Monks' boast: "the only proofs of the boy's identity lie at the bottom of the river.") And just as Oliver is in danger of being hanged, crushed, or suffocated, so he is in danger of being drowned. When Sikes is taking him through a dark misty night the boy hears "a dull sound of falling water not far off": "The water!" he thinks, "He has brought me to this lonely place to murder me!" (chap. 21).

Apparently there is no escape. One demands life from this world only to be met by even more determined hostility. Against this calculated effort to destroy him, Oliver has for defense only what Bumble calls his "artificial soul and spirit" (chap. 7). Only the "good sturdy spirit" "implanted" "in Oliver's breast" by "nature or inheritance" (chap. 2) will keep him alive. It is both nature *and* inheritance, both the self that Oliver has inherited from his unknown parents, and his "natural goodness." Both are necessary to keep Oliver alive at all.

But at the heart of the novel is the fear that this "good sturdy spirit" will seize by violence what belongs to it by right—status and the goods of this world—and thus transform its innocence into a guilt which no longer deserves approval and status. He is saved by the fact that he is naturally "grateful and attached" (chap. 32), as Rose Maylie calls him, and, far from planning to seize by force the goods and status he lacks, is simply looking for someone to whom he can be related as a child to the parents who seem to him the source of all value and the absolute judges of right and wrong.

There is little active volition in Oliver, no will to do something definite, to carve out for himself a place in the solid and hostile world, to choose a course oriented toward the future and follow it out without regard to the sacrifices necessary. No, all Oliver's volition is the volition of passive resistance. Oliver wills to live, and therefore resists violently all the attempts of the world to crush him or bury him or make him into a thief. But at the center of this fierce will there is passivity, the passivity of waiting, of expectation, of "great expectations." Oliver will not seize for himself a place in the world, nor will he join in the attempts of the thieves to create a society in the depths of the slums. But neither will he allow the world of honest men to destroy him. He resists the crushing walls of his prison because he expects that somehow they will turn into a soft protecting enclosure, into a cradle, a comfortable nook where he will be securely cared for.

But before this can happen Oliver must endure a long trial, a sequence of experiences which is essentially the detailed exploration of the world as it is for the outcast. And without any external evidence at all that he is other than he seems to be, gallows' bait, Oliver must act as if he were what he wants to be, a good boy, the son of a gentleman.

II

Apparently there is no escape. No novel could be more completely dominated by an imaginative complex of claustrophobia. No other novel by Dickens returns so frequently to images of dark dirty rooms with no apparent exit. At various times Oliver is imprisoned in "the coal-celler" (chap. 2), in a "dark and solitary room" (chap. 3), in a "little room by himself" (chap. 3), in a "cell" "in shape and size something like an area cellar, only not so light. It was most intolerably dirty" (chap. 11). He is almost apprenticed as a chimney sweep, and is finally taken on by an undertaker who begins by pushing him "down a steep flight of stairs into a stone cell, damp and dark: forming the ante-room to the coal-cellar" (chap. 4). He sleeps in the workshop among the coffins: "The shop was close and hot. The atmosphere seemed tainted with the smell of coffins. The recess beneath the counter in which his flock mattress was thrust, looked like a grave" (chap. 5).

When Oliver reaches London it is to live in a world of dark rooms, rooms which seem to be underground even though they may be high above the earth. These rooms are reached by unlighted staircases and narrow corridors, crooked passageways which make it impossible to orient the rooms to which they lead with the street one has just left. The rooms which Oliver enters are usually lit, if at all, by a single candle which burns dimly in the gloom, or lit and warmed at once by a fire over which crouches Fagin, the evil power of the London underworld, guarding his treasure like some fabled dragon. In London Oliver is introduced to an entire society which lives in the total exclusion he has experienced alone in Mr. Sowerberry's coal cellar.

The time of Oliver's passage from the street to these entombed interiors is of especial importance. Not only is it the time when he loses his sense of direction and his knowledge of the whereabouts of the open street; it is also the period when he has a special awareness of his plight and of his surroundings. Here, for a moment, several distinct entities can be distinguished: the street from which Oliver is being excluded, the room toward which he is going, and the dark passage which forms an absolutely impassable barrier between the room and the street. It is impassable at least by the mind, for it is a space of absolute unintelligibility between the street and the buried room. The two latter have no connection with one another because they are separated by a blank, but for a moment, in the midst of that blank, it is possible at least to juxtapose what one has just left and what one is entering. In one direction there is the street from which one is being shut out, but the place where one is now is totally obscure: "The passage was perfectly dark. . . . it was impossible to distinguish even the form of the speaker in the darkness" (chap. 16); "Look sharp with the light, or I shall knock my brains out against something in this confounded hole" (chap. 26); "Oliver, groping his way with one hand, and having the other firmly grasped by his companion, ascended with much difficulty the dark and broken stairs" (chap. 8). But in the other direction, at the end of the dark passage, the room toward which one is going can be dimly seen: "the light of a feeble candle gleamed on the wall at the remote end of the passage; and a man's face peeped out, from where a balustrade of the old kitchen staircase had been broken away" (chap. 8).

If the darkness of the passage gives way to light it is only to reveal a series of rooms which cut one off more and more completely from the open street, and lead one to feel more inextricably buried within, deep underground: "They looked into all the rooms; they were cold, bare, and empty. They descended into the passage, and thence into the cellars below. The green damp hung upon the low walls; the tracks of the snail and slug glistened in the light of the candle; but all was still as death" (chap. 26).

At last one enters the inner room itself, the interior of the interior, beyond which it is impossible to go further. At first this inner room appears merely as a place which is lighted rather than dark. It is hardly possible to distinguish anything more: "The room was illuminated by two gas-lights; the glare of which was prevented by the barred shutters, and

closely-drawn curtains of faded red, from being visible outside. The ceiling
was blackened, to prevent its colour from being injured by the flaring of
the lamps; and the place was so full of dense tobacco smoke, that at first it
was scarcely possible to discern anything more" (chap. 26, and see chap.
15). But finally one makes out in the dim light various objects, the debris
of civilization and communal living, perhaps "a smoky fire, two or three
broken chairs, a table, and a very old couch" (chap. 22), perhaps merely
"a broken arm-chair, and an old couch or sofa without covering" (chap.
26). Dickens's precise enumeration of the contents of these low dark
rooms only makes their essential desolation more apparent. These objects,
old and broken as they are, must be named because they are the only
things in sight except the blackened walls. They form the total world of
the inhabitant; he is by now psychologically so far removed from the open
street that it is as if nothing but this room and its battered furniture
existed.

Along with the light and furniture which make this room a parody of
a human habitation, Oliver sees, in some cases, the people who live there.
But the discovery of the underworld society is described as the transition
from an almost total obscurity to the perception of a crowd of people
which is merely confusing and unintelligible to the observer. It no more
relates itself to him or tells him anything about his place in the world than
do the broken chairs and tables of the empty rooms: "By degrees, however,
as some of [the smoke] cleared away through the open door, an assemblage of heads, as confused as the noises that greeted the ear, might be
made out; and as the eye grew more accustomed to the scene, the spectator
gradually became aware of the presence of a numerous company, male and
female, crowded round a long table: at the upper end of which, sat a
chairman with a hammer of office in his hand; while a professional
gentleman, with a bluish nose, and his face tied up for the benefit of a
toothache, presided at a jingling piano in a remote corner" (chap. 26). The
gloom clears only to reveal the interior landscape of a dream—a group of
people carrying on some mysterious ritual or revelry as though the spectator were not there at all. The spectator can see only that the inhabitants
are like the scene in which they live, and that the same taint, a taint which
is both physical and spiritual, covers in one way or another both animate
and inanimate objects: "for depravity, or poverty, or an habitual acquaint-
ance with both, had left a taint on all the animate matter, hardly less
unpleasant than the thick greasy scum on every inanimate object that
frowned upon it" (chap. 43).

This world is wholly incomprehensible to Oliver. The exterior confu-

sion of sights and sounds is matched by an interior bewilderment. Oliver's
state of mind as prisoner of the thieves in these underground interiors is
usually that of semi-conscious anxiety. He has little awareness or understanding of his plight. He has merely a vague knowledge that he is living in
a kind of earthly hell, not the least unpleasant part of which is the fact that
he does not comprehend most of what is going on around him. This failure
to understand actually protects Oliver from the complicity of too much
knowledge of the thieves' world. But this is another of the things he does
not know, and he remains aware only of the confusion itself and of his
failure to understand it:

> Oliver tried to reply, but his tongue failed him. He was deadly
> pale; and the whole place seemed turning round and round.
>
> (chap. 11)

> Oliver looked at Sikes, in mute and timid wonder; and drawing
> a stool to the fire, sat with his aching head upon his hands,
> scarcely knowing where he was, or what was passing around him.
>
> (chap. 22)

Over and over again we see Oliver simply falling asleep in these "foul
and frowsy dens, where vice is closely packed and lacks the room to turn"
(preface to the third edition). Cut off altogether form the past and the future,
enclosed in a narrow shadowy present which does not make sense, he
loses consciousness altogether, so exhausted is he by anxiety and by his failure
to comprehend what is happening to him. More precisely, he is reduced
to the simplest and most undifferentiated form of consciousness, sleep.

> he was sick and weary; and he soon fell sound asleep.
>
> (chap. 16)

> The boy was lying, fast asleep, on a rude bed upon the floor; so
> pale with anxiety, and sadness, and the closeness of his prison,
> that he looked like death.
>
> (chap. 19)

> Weary with watching and anxiety, he at length fell asleep.
>
> (chap. 20)

> quite overpowered by fatigue and the fumes of the tobacco,
> [he] fell asleep.
>
> (chap. 21)

But Oliver is unable always to escape by sleep or bewilderment. As he slowly becomes acclimated to his new environment he comes to recognize that, for its inhabitants, this underground world has a certain logic and a certain coherence. Even in his very first glimpse of this world there was visible, along with the dirt and closeness, another quality, a quality which makes life to some degree tolerable and even pleasant for these outcasts: "The walls and ceiling of the room were perfectly black with age and dirt. There was a deal table before the fire: upon which were a candle, stuck in a ginger-beer bottle, two or three pewter pots, a loaf and butter, and a plate. In a frying-pan, which was on the fire, and which was secured to the mantleshelf by a string, some sausages were cooking; and standing over them, with a toasting-fork in his hand, was a very old shrivelled Jew, whose villainous-looking and repulsive face was obscured by a quantity of matted red hair" (chap. 8). There are two contradictory values in this passage: Fagin's den is both a dungeon and a place of refuge. It is dark, dirty, and absolutely shut off from the outside world, but it is also a parody, at least, of a home, that place where one lives safely by one's own fireside, protected from the outer world, and where one has food, light, warmth, and a circle of other human beings with whom one feels at ease. Fagin's den is a "snug retreat" (chap. 43), and inside its walls we find a society leagued for common protection against the hostility of the outside world. It is a situation well imaged by the single candle which so often appears shining dimly in the gloom.

Fagin expounds the apparent philosophy of this hidden society within society to Noah Claypole: "you depend upon me. To keep my little business all snug, I depend upon you. The first is your number one, the second my number one. The more you value your number one, the more careful you must be of mine; so we come at last to what I told you at first—that a regard for number one holds us all together, and must do so, unless we would all go to pieces in company" (chap. 43).

But the life of Fagin's gang does not always recall its origin in a Hobbesian contract. Dickens shows Oliver discovering and being attracted in spite of himself by the cheerfulness and camaraderie of their existence. He and the other boys laugh until the tears run down their faces at Fagin's imitation of a prosperous old gentleman taking a walk, and when Fagin tells them comic stories of his robberies, "Oliver [cannot] help laughing heartily, and showing that he [is] amused in spite of all his better feelings" (chap. 18).

Fagin's gang is an authentic society and provides the security and sense of belonging to a community which Oliver has never before known, but these goods are not won without a price. The price is the permanent loss of the kind of life among honest men of which Oliver instinctively dreams: "the wily old Jew had the boy in his toils. Having prepared his mind, by solitude and gloom, to prefer any society to the companionship of his own sad thoughts in such a dreary place, he was now slowly instilling into his soul the poison which he hoped would blacken it, and change its hue for ever" (chap. 18). Oliver among the thieves is, in fact, totally excluded from the life of protected security he desires. He is as truly outcast as if he were starving in the open, however warm and comfortable and even cheerful the interior of Fagin's den may be. Oliver's situation in the world is to be at once "hedged round and round" (chap. 20) and abandoned in the open. His relation to the thieves leads him inevitably to the moment when, left behind by Sikes after the failure of a robbery, he lies unconscious in a ditch in the rain (chap. 28).

But it is in Dickens's treatment of the lives of the thieves themselves rather than in his treatment of Oliver that we can see most clearly why he rejects the attempt by the outcasts to create an autonomous society of their own.

In the first place, the thieves' society is unstable. It is built on the principle of internal treason, and it is constantly threatened by destruction from the outside. If the least chink in the walls lets the beams of the hidden candle out into the night, the society of the "upper world" will rush in and destroy the hidden society of outcasts. The two qualities of disloyalty and danger from without are causally related. It is because the thieves live through raids on the world of honest men that they are, ultimately, disloyal to one another. They are inevitably disloyal because only by caring more for their own individual safety than for their common safety can they survive. It is Fagin who lives most deliberately by a philosophy of "every man for himself," and it is Fagin, consequently, who lives longest.

Fagin's apparent philosophy of one for all hides an actual philosophy which sacrifices all for one. He lives only by condemning others to death. If he does not do this, they will turn *him* in. Just as he moves from den to den, so he must constantly replace the members of his gang. A society defining itself as evil, that is, as the denial of all social laws, can only live by perpetual metamorphosis. Fagin is accordingly a shape-changer, a master of disguise, but his best disguise is the constantly changing membership of his gang. He can only survive by being nothing and by doing nothing himself, that is, by committing his crimes only by proxy and remaining himself the empty center of all this crime, the void of evil itself. For positive evil in this world is inevitably punished; the man who sets himself up against society always comes to be hanged. The periphery around Fagin, all the boys and adult thieves who work for him, are one by one plucked away and hanged or transported. It is only by maintaining this solid wall of active evil committed by others between himself and the world of good that Fagin can continue to live at the center of his dark hollow den.

The true relation of the thieves to one another is given not by the image of a mutually loyal group crouching around their single candle in an underground room, but by the recurrent motif of spying. Fagin himself spies on Oliver and on other members of his gang; Nancy finds out the secrets of Oliver's birth by spying on Fagin and Monks; Nancy herself is spied on by Fagin's representative. Her betrayal of the thieves is thus discovered and her death brought about. And Oliver is spied on by Fagin and Monks as he dwells in what he assumes to be the total security of Mrs. Maylie's country home. All the thieves are in constant fear not only that someone in the outside world will observe and identify them but that they will be observed and betrayed by one of their own number. Oliver's share in this general fear of the unseen look that steals one's secret is a measure of the degree of his participation, in spite of himself, in the thieves' psychology. For the world of honest men the thieves' world is invisible. When Oliver takes Dr. Losberne to the house where he has been with the thieves, everything is changed. They are met by "a little ugly hump-backed man" whom Oliver has never seen before, and when they enter the house "not an article of furniture; not a vestige of anything, animate or inanimate; not even the position of the cupboards; [answers] Oliver's description" (chap. 32). Only Oliver, with his unwilling complicity in the underworld, sees the dwarf's "glance so sharp and fierce and at the same time so furious and vindictive, that, waking or sleeping, he could not forget it for months afterwards" (chap. 32).

The thieves, then, are constantly threatened, within and without, by the possibility that their secret will be revealed. But the attempt to assume one's isolation publicly and thereby make it the source of one's identity is equally unsuccessful. The Artful Dodger attempts to achieve selfhood by assuming the alienation forced upon him by society: "I wouldn't go free, now, if you was to fall down on your knees and ask me," says the Dodger to his captors. "Here, carry me off to prison! Take me away!" (chap. 43). But the Dodger realizes that this defiance is hollow. It is a kind of comic role he plays: "I'm an Englishman, ain't I?" he asks. "Where are my priwileges?" But he knows, and everyone else knows, that he has no privileges, that he has no attorney "a-breakfasting this morning with the

Wice President of the House of Commons." All his defiance and all his pretense that he wills his punishment do not hide the fact that he has been caught by the law and will be treated as his captors wish. His attempt to will defiantly to be a thief does not permit him to escape from the process whereby society imposes upon him whatever identity it chooses, once it has dragged him out into the daylight.

But if the attempt to escape from isolation through a relationship to the world of good men is a failure, so equally is the attempt to establish relationships inside the underworld. The tragic end of the Sikes-Nancy liaison is final judgment on the futility of the attempt to keep love alive within a society which is excluded from the daylight of law and convention. Within such a society all voluntary relationships are evil. They are evil because there is nothing outside of themselves which justifies them. They cannot be other than illicit. Sikes and Nancy are inevitably destroyed by their guilty love, a love that is guilty because it is outside social sanctions. The only alternatives for them are death or separation and reintegration into the honest world: "Bill," pleads Nancy a moment before Sikes murders her, "the gentleman and that dear lady, told me to-night of a home in some foreign country where I could end my days in solitude and peace. Let me see them again, and beg them, on my knees, to show the same mercy and goodness to you; and let us both leave this dreadful place, and far apart lead better lives, and forget how we have lived, except in prayers, and never see each other more" (chap. 47).

Dickens, at this stage of his career, is willing to sacrifice all, even faithfulness in love, to the need to escape from social ostracism. For the outcast, it seems, is in an impossible dilemma. He is now nothing, because society has chosen to reject him utterly. But if he tries to take a place he will be even more certainly defined as an outlaw and all the more surely destroyed. Oliver's only hope is somehow to escape from the underground society altogether. But this seems impossible.

III

It was a very dirty place. The rooms up-stairs had great high wooden chimney-pieces and large doors, with panelled walls and cornices to the ceilings; which, although they were black with neglect and dust, were ornamented in various ways. From all of these tokens Oliver concluded that a long time ago, before the old Jew was born, it had belonged to better people, and had perhaps been quite gay and handsome: dismal and dreary as it looked now.

   ... and often, when it grew dark, and he was tired of wandering from room to room, he would crouch in the corner of the passage by the street-door, to be as near living people as he could.

(chap. 18)

   This passage marks Oliver's transition to an active search in the *external* world for the meaning of his plight and for the identity and security he obscurely seeks. He has been recaptured by Fagin and locked all alone in an empty house. He has had a brief glimpse of the world of honest people, and has been strangely moved by the sight of a picture which is, although he does not know it, a portrait of his mother, who died when he was born. Apparently his new prison is merely a repetition of all the interiors he has already known, interiors which offer no avenue of escape and which contain no clue whatsoever as to the meaning of his suffering. Oliver studies his new surroundings with a child's wonder. Everything seems larger than life-size. The chimney-pieces are high, the doors large, and the perspective is that of someone looking upward. But this interior is different. Oliver is no longer at the very center of the darkness. He can watch from the outside as the mice "scamper across the floor, and run back terrified to their holes" (chap. 18). It is as though he were a good man watching the thieves run for cover in their secret dens. Moreover, his new prison is not only dirty and enclosed. It also contains the decayed signs, almost the archeological remains, of another way of life. Oliver sees unmistakable evidence of a happy existence once lived within the very walls of his prison. And this prison is more than a single room reached by a dark corridor or by a series of rooms of increasing interiority. He can wander from room to room and explore each one for signs of the past happiness it seems indistinctly to reveal. The present is no longer wholly enclosed in itself. In the very midst of the present in all its dirt and darkness there are indications of a past that was wholly different. Perhaps if the present world is wholly intolerable there was nevertheless once in the past a "gay" life. All Oliver's life is oriented, without his knowing it, toward the discovery of a world anterior to his life, a life where he can, it may be, recover his lost identity and the happiness he has never known.

   Moreover, the life which existed in the past may exist also in the present outside the walls. Oliver crouches in the corner, as near to the outside world as he can get, but he has a new awareness of what this outside world might contain. And the present itself, perhaps because of this very discovery of the past and of an outside life very different from his own, ceases to be the blind endurance of a moment which simply repeats those which precede or follow. Now it has become a real duration. At least there is an awareness of the passage of time and of its emptiness: Oliver "would remain [crouching by the street door], listening and counting the hours" (chap. 18). Furthermore, this prison, unlike the others, lets in a little light from the outside. It has a tiny aperture through which Oliver may dimly descry the world of freedom and study it:

> In all the rooms, the mouldering shutters were fast closed: the bars which held them were screwed tight into the wood; the only light which was admitted, stealing its way through round holes at the top: which made the rooms more gloomy, and filled them with strange shadows. There was a back-garret window with rusty bars outside, which had no shutter; and out of this, Oliver often gazed with a melancholy face for hours together; but nothing was to be descried from it but a confused and crowded mass of house-tops, blackened chimneys, and gable-ends. Sometimes, indeed, a grizzly head might be seen, peering over the parapet-wall of a distant house: but it was quickly withdrawn again; and as the window of Oliver's observatory was nailed down, and dimmed with the rain and smoke of years, it was as much as he could do to make out the forms of the different objects beyond, without making any attempt to be seen or heard,—which he had as much chance of being, as if he had lived inside the ball of St. Paul's Cathedral.
>
> (chap. 18)

If there is any single image which we remember longest from *Oliver Twist* it is the picture of the lost boy, deprived of all knowledge of his forebears, imprisoned all alone in a labyrinthine ruin of a house, peering "with a melancholy face for hours together" through a high clouded window at a world he cannot understand, and with which he has seemingly no chance of making direct contact. Oliver's exploration of the outside world is here only that of passive and detached observation. There is an obscuring veil, the deposited layers of "the rain and smoke of years," between him and the world outside, so that he can hardly distinguish one object from another. What has cut him off from the past, the years of which he has no knowledge and cannot break through, cuts him off also from the outside world by depositing a veil of dust and cobwebs on the window. And, if the inside world is dark and unintelligible, if it offers to his gaze merely the same blank walls, black with age and dirt, or glistening with subterranean moisture, the outside world is unintelligible because of its jumbled multiplicity. Oliver sees only a "confused and crowded mass of house-tops, blackened chimneys, and gable-ends." There seems to be no order in this confusion, and it seems to be related in no significant way to himself. It is simply there before him, a bewildering collection of objects in the midst of which the figure of another human being makes a brief and mysterious appearance only to be "quickly withdrawn again." But, even though Oliver has no chance at all of being seen or heard, of making contact with this world, he is at least aware now that he is not buried deep underground out of all proximity to the outside world. He is as near to it, as close and yet as far, as if he were enclosed not underground but high in the air—as if he were enclosed in the ball of St. Paul's Cathedral. He spends long hours studying this disordered world, as if he had some faint chance of forcing it to yield up its secret, a secret which might be *his* secret too, the secret of his identity and the meaning of his life.

More than once Oliver does escape and is able to explore the external world, to make an active search for its meaning. Does this world have the same hostility that the walls of the dark interior world possessed? The windowless room corresponded to Oliver's interior darkness, to the semi-conscious stupor which was his initial condition. Perhaps the exterior world may be controlled by understanding it. Perhaps it may be held at arm's length, may be comprehended, may even be forced to correspond exactly to his inner state and thus to offer an escape from the total separation between inner and outer worlds imaged in Oliver's melancholy gaze out the back garret-window at the "confused and crowded mass of house-tops, blackened chimneys, and gable-ends."

At first the exterior world seems as dark and indistinct as the interior one. The image of a cold dark foggy night, a night in which no object can be clearly seen, is repeated again and again in *Oliver Twist*. In this obscurity, one is aware that what one sees is as much a projection of one's fear as an accurate perception of objects in the external world: "Every object before him, substance or shadow, still or moving, took the semblance of some fearful thing" (chap. 48, and see chap. 21). But the mist may be simply opaque and impenetrable, and perhaps this is even more frightening. The fog simply mirrors back to the lost boy his own lostness, his total inability to understand where he is or who he is or what is the meaning of the objects which surround him: "The night was dark and foggy. The lights in the shops could scarcely struggle through the heavy mist, which thickened every moment and shrouded the streets and houses in gloom; rendering the strange place still stranger in Oliver's eyes; and making his uncertainty the more dismal and depressing" (chap. 16, and see chaps. 19, 28, 46).

But when the obscurity gives way somewhat to light, when "the objects which had looked dim and terrible in the darkness, [grow] more and more defined, and gradually [resolve] into their familiar shapes" (chap. 28), the hero can look around him for the first time. The first thing he observes is that he is apparently totally alone in a world of objects which are closed to him or which exist statically at an unattainable distance:

> It was a cold, dark night. The stars seemed, to the boy's eyes, farther from the earth than he had ever seen them before; there was no wind; and the sombre shadows thrown by the trees upon the ground, looked sepulchral and death-like, from being so still.
>
> (chap. 7)

> the windows of the houses were all closely shut; and the streets through which they passed, were noiseless and empty.
>
> (chap. 21)

> The window-shutters were closed; the street was empty; not a soul had awakened to the business of the day. The sun was rising in all its splendid beauty; but the light only served to show the boy his own lonesomeness and desolation.
>
> (chap. 8)

This new state of isolation is in a way more desperate than the first. The walls of Oliver's prison were at least close to him and were a kind of comfort in themselves. And the outcast can no longer be consoled by the idea that everything will be all right if only he can escape from his prison. The outside world is revealed as simply the opposite extreme from the inside world. Instead of being close and suffocating it is absolutely open. And what can be seen at a distance in the clear light forms a kind of solid barrier just as hostile as the damp walls within which Oliver has been immured. It is now a hostility of withdrawal and silence rather than of active violence against Oliver. The world constitutes itself still as a solid wall, but it is now a wall of indifference rather than of hate. In the distance between himself and the closed shutters or the cold stars Oliver can see for the first time his total isolation. It is an isolation which is both material and social. He is cut off from the community behind the closed shutters as much as from the stars or the trees.

There is only one avenue of action left, only one thing the hero can do now that he could not do when he was locked in: he can run "hurrying through a labyrinth of streets" (chap. 45) seeking some escape from his exclusion: "They crossed from the Angel into St. John's Road; struck down the small street which terminates at Sadler's Wells Theatre; through Exmouth Street and Coppice Row; down the little court by the side of the workhouse; across the classic ground which once bore the name of Hockley-in-the-Hole; thence into Little Saffron Hill; and so into Saffron Hill the Great" (chap. 8). The labyrinth at first reveals itself as simply the repetition of the scene of empty desolation which had appeared when the fog cleared away. Now, however, this desolation has a geography. There are paths marked out in it, and walls at the sides which limit the indefiniteness of space, and indicate specific directions to be taken. But the careful precision with which Dickens names the streets of these itineraries only serves to emphasize the fact that each of these streets is merely a different version of the first. It is Dickens himself, or the detached narrator of the story, who knows the names of the streets, not Oliver. He has no idea where the Dodger is taking him. And the place names are simply superficial facts; they do not serve to relate Oliver to his environment.

The urban labyrinth turns out to be nothing more than an endless daedal prison. As in a dream, Oliver wanders through intricate streets which are different but which do not seem to lead anywhere. And the darkness, narrowness, muddiness, crookedness of this maze make it difficult to distinguish it from the underground prison in which the hero first found himself. The hero and his avatars are as much lost and as much enclosed outside as they were inside, and there is repeated over and over the sequence of a rapid walk, sometimes a flight, through streets which get narrower and narrower and dirtier and dirtier and more and more intricate and finally lead to the doors of one of the subterranean interiors I have described:

> They walked on, for some time, through the most crowded and densely inhabited part of the town; and then, striking down a narrow street more dirty and miserable than any they had yet passed through, paused to look for the house which was the object of their search.
>
> (chap. 5)

To reach this place, the visitor has to penetrate through a maze of close, narrow, and muddy streets.

(chap. 50)

He kept on his course, through many winding and narrow ways, until he reached Bethnal Green; then, turning suddenly off to the left, he soon became involved in a maze of the mean and dirty streets which abound in that close and densely-populated quarter.

... He hurried through several alleys and streets, and at length turned into one, lighted only by a single lamp at the farther end. At the door of a house in this street, he knocked.

(chap. 19)

At the deepest imaginative level the London of *Oliver Twist* is no longer a realistic description of the unsanitary London of the thirties but is the dream or poetic symbol of an infernal labyrinth, inhabited by the devil himself: "The mud lay thick upon the stones, and a black mist hung over the streets; the rain fell sluggishly down, and everything felt cold and clammy to the touch. It seemed just the night when it befitted such a being as the Jew to be abroad. As he glided stealthily along, creeping beneath the shelter of the walls and doorways, the hideous old man seemed like some loathsome reptile, engendered in the slime and darkness through which he moved: crawling forth, by night, in search of some rich offal for a meal" (chap. 19). Fagin is as much dream as reality. He is often called the devil (chaps. 19, 44), or shown in a pose that recalls the devil: crouching over a fire with a toasting fork (chap. 8), or other implement (chaps. 20, 25), or gloating over his hidden treasure (chap. 9). Dickens had been reading Defoe's *History of the Devil* with great interest while he was writing *Oliver Twist,* but his reading, it seems evident, only reinforced the image of the archetype of evil which was already present in his imagination. Fagin is imagined too vividly in his combination of supernatural and animal qualities to be the mere copy of traditional and literary representa- tions of the devil: "Fagin sat watching in his old lair, with face so distorted and pale, and eyes so red and bloodshot, that he looked less like a man, than like some hideous phantom, moist from the grave, and worried by an evil spirit. . . . and as, absorbed in thought, he bit his long black nails, he disclosed among his toothless gums a few such fangs as should have been a dog's or rat's" (chap. 47).

At the center of the labyrinth, then, is Fagin, the personified principle of the world cut off altogether from the light and the good. There he crouches, greedy to possess Oliver altogether by making him a thief, but hiding, perhaps, the secret that will make possible Oliver's permanent escape from the labyrinth. The only escape from the prison, it may be, is to descend into its very heart and to wrest from the darkness its secret. Oliver does not know this, of course. He only knows that there is a centripetal force which seems to pull him toward the center of the labyrinth, however hard he tries to escape. When Oliver flees from his living grave at Sowerberry's it is not outward through the maze to freedom, but into the intricacy of London, toward the dark center of the labyrinth—Fagin's den. And when Oliver's rescuer sends Oliver out on an errand he has only to turn down a bystreet by accident (chap. 15) to be plunged back into the labyrinth and recaptured by Fagin.

The true meaning of the labyrinth image is perhaps revealed in a phrase Dickens uses about Nancy: "Fagin . . . had led her, step by step, deeper and deeper down into an abyss of crime and misery, whence was no escape" (chap. 44). Movement in the Dickensian labyrinth is always inward and downward toward the center, and never outward toward freedom. The labyrinth is really an abyss, a bottomless pit of mud and darkness in which one can be lost forever, forever separated from the world of light and freedom. And the labyrinth is also a moral abyss. It is the world into which Oliver will be permanently plunged if the thieves succeed in hardening him and making him into one of themselves.

But thus far the labyrinth has seemed to be entirely uninhabited, or at least there has been no direct contact with its inhabitants. Its walls have been, so to speak, blank—simply endless repetitions of the same muddy, damp, featureless stones or planks. There have appeared neither people to whom the frantically searching wanderer might relate himself nor objects which he might separate out from the whole and scrutinize for their possible meaning. But there are several labyrinthine progressions in *Oliver Twist* which replace the journey through intricate streets to a gravelike interior with a journey through the obscurity of fog into streets that are at first empty but are then gradually filled up with a great crowd, a crowd either of distinct objects or of human beings. The blank walls take on distinct features and the visual field becomes a heterogeneous mass of details rather than a single homogeneous blur:

> In . . . filthy shops are exposed for sale huge bunches of second-hand silk handkerchiefs, of all sizes and patterns. . . . Hundreds of these handkerchiefs hang dangling form pegs out-

side the windows or flaunting from the door-posts; and the
shelves, within, are piled with them. . . . Here . . . stores of old
iron and bones, and heaps of mildewy fragments of woollen-
stuff and linen, rust and rot in the grimy cellars.

(chap. 26)

To reach this place [Jacob's Island], the visitor has to penetrate
through a maze of close, narrow, and muddy streets, thronged
by the roughest and poorest of waterside people, and devoted
to the traffic they may be supposed to occasion. The cheapest
and least delicate provisions are heaped in the shops; the coars-
est and commonest articles of wearing apparel dangle at the
salesman's door, and stream from the house-parapet and
windows.

(chap. 50)

These scenes present a world in chaotic action, a world in which the
undifferentiated fog has resolved itself into a mass of perceptible objects,
into multitudinous motion and cacophonous noise. But it is still a world
which does not relate itself to the spectator. He remains a passive observer
who takes no part in all this action and is ignored by all the people he sees.
The "drunken men and women" "wallowing in filth" (chap. 8) pay no
more attention to him than do the crowd of handkerchiefs which wave in
the wind. The inanimate and animate objects seen are strictly equivalent
and remain at a distance as pure spectacle. This spectacle is simply a great
swirl of mingled sense perceptions, of things seen, heard, and smelled.
Everything is in the plural, and multiplies itself inexhaustibly. Not only
are there innumerable distinct objects, there also seems to be an endless
supply of each species. The cellars are stuffed with "stores" and "heaps"
more of what is displayed outside; each house seems to contain enough
unseen drunkards to fill the streets even if all the visible ones were cleared
away; and the "commonest articles of wearing apparel" "stream from the
house-parapet and windows" as though flowing from a bottomless reser-
voir. These are scenes of profusion and excess, of the endless accumulation
of heteroclite details. But in the end this multiplicity gives way to a fluidity
in which everything seems to be surging liquidly up from the interior. Since
each detail is multiplied indefinitely it appears to be constantly replaced by
its fellows, and the entire series forms a continuous "stream" in which
what had been hidden a moment ago makes its momentary appearance
only to be replaced without transition by the next in line. It is conse-

quently a world which is inside out. All that should be secret is out in the open; wearing apparel, the evidence of lawbreaking, unseemly behavior, all is revealed. And yet the spectator finds that he is no nearer the real secret than he was before.

Even if the chaotic crowd remains harmlessly at a distance, its effect is malign. When Sikes takes Oliver off in the early morning to try to make a thief of him, at first the streets are empty. Gradually, though, the streets begin to fill with a motley crowd of men and women. Oliver and Sikes move toward the center of the city, toward the dense source of all this multiplicity and movement. At the center of it all, Smithfield, the distinct sounds are so numerous that they begin to blur and "swell" "into a roar of sound and bustle" (chap. 21). Each sound and each sight is still distinct, but each has become exactly the equivalent of all the others and thus, in the end, fuses into a single indistinguishable blur or roar. The multitudes of distinct sense perceptions destroy one another by their very abundance, and the spectator is left face to face with a single vertiginous cacophony in which nothing can be distinguished clearly because all the thresholds of clear sense perception have been exceeded: "the whistling of drovers, the barking of dogs, the bellowing and plunging of oxen, the bleating of sheep, the grunting and squeaking of pigs, the cries of hawkers, the shouts, oaths, and quarrelling on all sides; the ringing of bells and roar of voices, that issued from every public-house; the crowding, pushing, driving, beating, whooping, and yelling; the hideous and discordant din that resounded from every corner of the market; and the unwashed, unshaven, squalid, and dirty figures constantly running to and fro, and bursting in and out of the throng; rendered it a stunning and bewildering scene, which quite confounded the senses" (chap. 21).

At first the "tumult of discordant sounds" had filled Oliver "with amazement" (chap. 21), but in the end he is "stunned," "bewildered," his senses are "confounded." He is, in fact, reduced by his exploration of the exterior world to exactly the same state he was in when he lay in a half-conscious stupor in the darkness and solitude of his prison. And the world of distinct objects mingled together in an unintelligible mass is shown to be in the end the exact equivalent of the world of total darkness. A light too bright is invisible, and a world of sheer multiplicity is shown to be the same as a world in which nothing at all exists or in which nothing at all is perceptible. Both worlds mirror back to the alienated hero his own subjective confusion, his own bewildered inability to tell where he is or who he is.

Until the very end of the novel all the characters are living in the midst of experiences which have the total opacity of the present and cannot yet be seen in retrospect as having the logical structure of a destiny. The mystery, the unintelligibility, of the present is perfectly expressed by these scenes of multiplicity in a state of rapid, aimless agitation. The exterior scene is exactly matched by the state of mind of the inhabitants of this world of bewildering uncertainty and unpredictable change. Rose Maylie's interview with Nancy "had more the semblance of a rapid dream than an actual occurrence." She sinks into a chair and endeavors "to collect her wandering thoughts" (chap. 40). Fagin's violent thoughts when he learns he has been betrayed follow "close upon each other with rapid and ceaseless whirl" (chap. 47). At a crisis in the story Mr. Losberne and Mr. Brownlow hastily separate "each in a fever of excitement wholly uncontrollable" (chap. 49), and we see Oliver "in a flutter of agitation and uncertainty, which [deprives] him of the power of collecting his thoughts" (chap. 51).

But there is one case in *Oliver Twist* in which a character seeks out such a scene, and succeeds in losing his self-consciousness by identifying himself with the violent agitation of the world. When Sikes, after the murder of Nancy, has wandered through the countryside attempting to lose himself and his past, but lingering obsessively "about the same spot," he succeeds for a few hours in forgetting himself and his crime at the scene of a great fire (chap. 48). Sikes can forget himself momentarily because he has found an external scene which corresponds exactly to his inner state and can be intermingled with it. The objective fire is matched by Sikes's internal fever, and at the height of his "ecstacy" he is as much inside the fire as the fire is inside him: "in every part of that great fire was he" (chap. 48). Only if a person is in a state of self-destructive disintegration, consuming himself with some inner conflict, will the multitudinousness of the world be an appropriate projection of the self. Only then will self-forgetfulness be possible. And even this transcendence of the subject-object cleavage is only momentary: "This mad excitement over, there returned, with tenfold force, the dreadful consciousness of his crime" (chap. 48). The external fire is burned to "smoke and blackened ruins," but Sikes's inner fire burns on, and would be satisfied not by any mere chaotic swirling of the world such as bewildered Oliver at Smithfield, but by a gigantic holocaust which would consume the whole world in consuming him.

But perhaps the seemingly chaotic world can be kept at a distance and its details studied carefully for the meaning they may reveal. The spectator can, it may be, achieve a kind of detachment, put the world in brackets, and study it as pure phenomenon. So Fagin in the courtroom where he is on trial for his life: "He looked up into the gallery again. Some of the people were eating, and some fanning themselves with handkerchiefs; for the crowded place was very hot. There was one young man sketching his face in a little note-book. He wondered whether it was like, and looked on when the artist broke his pencil-point, and made another with his knife, as any idle spectator might have done. In the same way, when he turned his eyes towards the judge, his mind began to busy itself with the fashion of his dress, and what it cost, and how he put it on.... [He] pursued this train of careless thought until some new object caught his eye and roused another" (chap. 52). However, this detached study of events in the external world only shows that as pure phenomena they are utterly meaningless. To study the world in detachment is to study it *idly,* and to be led at best to a "train of careless thought" which is inconsequential speculation about the sheer facts of its mechanical operation. If this speculation goes behind the superficial appearances of things it is only to imagine more of the same absurd details: "He wondered within himself whether this man had been to get his dinner, what he had had, and where he had had it" (chap. 52). The real relationship of the world to Fagin, the relationship he is vaguely aware of even as he studies the scene from the point of view of a detached spectator, is the relationship of executioner to victim: "Not that, all this time, his mind was, for an instant, free from one oppressive overwhelming sense of the grave that opened at his feet; it was ever present to him, but in a vague and general way, and he could not fix his thoughts upon it. Thus, even while he trembled, and turned burning hot at the idea of speedy death, he fell to counting the iron spikes before him, and wondering how the head of one had been broken off, and whether they would mend it, or leave it as it was. Then, he thought of all the horrors of the gallows and the scaffold—and stopped to watch a man sprinkling the floor to cool it—and then went on to think again" (chap. 52). There is an extraordinary alternation here between Fagin's vague awareness that he is involved and threatened, and the clear vision of detached observation. At one moment Fagin sees things as if he were not part of them, as if he had all the time in the world and could watch forever the slow or rapid changing of the perceptible scene. At the next moment he remembers that he is involved in time and in the world, involved in them in the specifically human way, by reason of his awareness of his own inevitable death. His vision of the world as something separate and harmless, something which may be safely studied in its trivial detail for the satisfaction of mere idle curiosity, is false. The world is in reality hostile. Fagin can read in no face that stares at him "the faintest sympathy with himself, or any feeling but one of all-absorbing interest that he should be condemned" (chap. 52). The faces are, in fact, the exact equivalent of the stone walls of a prison: "He could glean nothing from their faces; they might as well have been of stone" (chap. 52). The human world is as inhuman as stone or as distant stars. For the solid opaque enmity of blank walls is substituted a world which is an infinitely repeated *look,* a look which pitilessly devours Fagin with its glance, now that he has been dragged at last from his den into the light of day: "The court was paved, from floor to roof, with human faces. Inquisitive and eager eyes peered from every inch of space. From the rail before the dock, away into the sharpest angle of the smallest corner in the galleries, all looks were fixed upon one man—Fagin. Before him and behind: above, below, on the right and on the left: he seemed to stand surrounded by a firmament, all bright with gleaming eyes" (chap. 52).

The search through the labyrinth, then, has come face to face with the absolute impasse of a world which, hovering at a distance, regards one with an implacable stare. It is a universe which has become all eyes, eyes which see into every corner of one's soul, and do not leave any recess which is free or secret. But worse is to follow. Three times in the novel for three different characters the direction of the labyrinth changes, the seeker becomes the sought, he who had rushed frantically through endless crooked streets seeking some escape now flees even more frantically from the active enmity of the mob. The labyrinth is turned into a hostile crowd which, no longer remaining at a distance, turns on the protagonist and hunts him down:

> "Stop thief! Stop thief!" The cry is taken up by a hundred voices, and the crowd accumulate at every turning. Away they fly, splashing through the mud, and rattling along the pavements: up go the windows, out run the people, onward bear the mob, a whole audience desert Punch in the very thickest of the plot, and, joining the rushing throng, swell the shout, and lend fresh vigour to the cry, "Stop thief! Stop thief!"
>
> "Stop thief! Stop thief!" There is a passion *for hunting something* deeply implanted in the human breast. One wretched breathless child, panting with exhaustion; terror in his looks; agony in his eyes; large drops of perspiration streaming down his face; strains every nerve to make head upon his pursuers; and as they follow on his track, and gain upon him every instant, they hail his decreasing strength with still louder shouts, and whoop and scream with joy.
>
> (chap. 10)

Here the entire world seems to have turned animate and to be chasing Oliver down the endless dreamlike corridors of the London labyrinth. And the aim of the mob is not simply to catch him, but to "crowd" him to death. The crowd "jostles" and "struggles" centripetally toward Oliver, and will suffocate him or crush him if it can: " 'Give him a little air!' 'Nonsense! he don't deserve it' " (chap. 10). In the same way the crowd tries to tear Fagin to pieces like a pack of wild animals when once he is dragged out of his den into the light of day (chap. 50), and another crowd, beside itself with rage and hatred, presses like a "strong struggling current of angry faces" around the house where Sikes is at bay, "to curse him" and kill him if they can (chap. 50).

The similarity of these three passages impresses upon us forcibly the kinship between Oliver and the thieves. Fagin dies "for" Oliver the death he would have died. The embodiment of all the evil in the novel, he is the scapegoat whose death, even more than Sikes's, destroys all that evil, and makes it possible for Oliver to "live happily ever after." The description of his "last night alive" and of Oliver's visit to the condemned man forms the penultimate chapter of the novel, coming just before the account of Oliver's subsequent happiness and preparing for it. In this scene, Fagin says, quite correctly, that Oliver has betrayed him and caused his death: "He has been the—the—somehow the cause of all this" (chap. 52). In the delirium of his fear Fagin claims a secret friendship and even kinship with Oliver, tells him where the papers containing the clue to the mystery of his life are hidden, and tries to get Oliver to smuggle him out of the prison. The few steps toward the gallows Oliver and Fagin take together testify to their profound consubstantiality. Oliver, by accepting the identity among honest men imposed upon him by the discovery of the secrets of his origin, has betrayed the identity as a pariah which was apparently his from birth. It is Oliver himself who is the real spy in the novel. Fagin dies the death Oliver would have died, but in choosing Mr. Brownlow's "little society" Oliver must betray and destroy the underground society which Fagin has created for protection against a world in which he and the other thieves are useless and despised, "the very scum and refuse of the land" (preface to the third edition).

Another kinship between Oliver and the thieves, the identity of their initial natures, is strongly implied in the preface to the third edition of *Oliver Twist*. Whereas Oliver is to represent "the principle of Good surviving through every adverse circumstance," the thieves are described not as initially evil, but as an original good which is, in the case of Sikes, finally destroyed, or is, in the case of Nancy, so corrupted that it remains only as "the last fair drop of water at the bottom of the dried-up weed-choked well." Sikes is one of those "insensible and callous natures that do become, at last, utterly and irredeemably bad." In the version of the preface for the Charles Dickens edition of 1856 this became "utterly and incurably bad," evidently to remove the theological implication of "irredeemably." Dickens did not want to deny God's power to redeem even those who are apparently hopelessly evil. But even in the earlier version he did not leave unqualified his assertion that all good is wholly dead in such people: "Whether every gentler human feeling is dead within such bosoms, or the proper chord to strike has rusted and is hard to find, I do not know." Moreover, the good feelings of Nancy are "emphatically God's truth, for it is the truth He leaves in such depraved and miserable breasts; the hope yet lingering behind." Whatever Dickens at this time felt to be the original source of human evil (and it is a crucial problem for him later on), it is clear that he did not believe the thieves were "naturally evil," just as Oliver was "naturally good." Though the world is fallen, evil is, initially, extrinsic to any individual. There is no acceptance of the doctrine of original sin in Dickens's anthropology. Each human creature comes pure and good from the hand of God and only *becomes* evil through the effects of an evil environment. Some are, however, like Oliver, paradoxically more naturally good than others, or more invulnerably so, "by nature or inheritance," and are thus able to withstand the pressure of evil surroundings, surroundings which slowly and inevitably taint, corrupt, and ultimately destroy all the others who are exposed to them. One might say that the fable of *Oliver Twist*, the father's will, the lost inheritance, and the lost identity, were devised to make this paradox plausible. But Oliver's special position does not prevent Dickens from sympathizing more or less openly with the thieves.

Indeed there is a good deal of covert sympathy even for Fagin, especially in the description of his capture and death. Fagin in jail is as much a figure to be pitied as hated (chap. 52), and it is clear that Dickens strongly identified himself with Fagin, and in writing of his death lived with intensity the death of the outcast, utterly cut off from society, hated by all the world, and implacably destroyed by it. It was, one feels, because he could imagine so vividly the life of the outcast that he strove so desperately in novel after novel to prove that the outcast was not really outcast, that there was a hidden identity waiting for him among the honest men who enjoy with complacency a secure status and the comforting sense that, like Dr. Losberne, they can act upon impulse and yet do no wrong because they are naturally and incorruptibly good (chap. 32).

Oliver, then, is in the same situation as Sikes or Fagin. For all three the human or material world is not simply unintelligible multiplicity in agitated motion. It is a great solid force which rushes in toward the isolated one at the center. There is escape neither underground nor out in the open for the outcasts. Both inside and out they are threatened by the remorselessly hostile wall of a world which converges on the central figure. "The great, black, ghastly gallows clos[es] up their prospects, turn them where they may" (preface to the third edition). They seek in vain for a tiny aperture through which they may escape.

The main axis of the nuclear structure of *Oliver Twist* is a fear of exclusion which alternates with a fear of enclosure. Between these two poles the novel oscillates. On the one hand there is the fear that one will be completely cut off from the world and from other men. Thrust into an empty world from which everything has receded to an unattainable distance, one is left only with a need, a lack, the need to be related to the world, to find a ground to stand on and a roof over one's head. On the other hand, there is the fear that the world will approach too near, that one will be buried alive, squeezed to death, or suffocated, that freedom and even life itself will be crushed out. At a level beneath the superficial coherence of narrated events, at a level where all the characters reduce themselves into isomorphic representations of a few basic possibilities, *Oliver Twist* is the search for a way of life which will escape from these two extremes. For the extremes of enclosure and exclusion come in the end to the same thing, from the point of view of individual existence. They are the failure to *be* someone, and to have that identity recognized by the outside world, to be someone in security and without guilt. The extreme of exclusion images that failure in a total evaporation of the self into a murky world where nothing can be distinguished clearly or where everything has retreated to an unattainable distance. The extreme of enclosure images the loss of identity in a narrowing down of the limits of selfhood until finally one ceases altogether to exist—like a snuffed candle flame. Oliver requires some firm ground to stand on and a warm protective covering, material or human, around him and above him. In a world in which there is nothing but himself and a dark unsubstantial mist he is nothing, and he would rather be related to the world as a slave among slaves than not be related at all. But on the other hand the world must not approach too close. It must be a protective and approving gaze, not a suffocating coercion, a secure foundation, not the solid enclosure of the prison, or the grave: "Mother! dear, dear mother, bury me in the open fields—anywhere but in these dreadful streets. I should like to be where you can see my grave, but not in these close crowded streets; they have killed me." The passage is from the *Sketches by Boz*, but there, as in *Oliver Twist,* the city is the place where one is crushed to death by the walls and the crowds or suffocated by the "closeness."

Oliver's search, then, is for a physical and social world which will offer support but not coercion, protection but not imprisonment, which will be tangibly *there,* but there at a certain safe distance. It is a world of which he has had no knowledge except in his dreams.

IV

Suddenly Oliver is extricated. He wakes to find himself in a kind of world he has never known. Both times when Oliver is transported into the good world there is an interval of unconsciousness between, followed by a period of serious illness. When he sinks into unconsciousness from the strain of his intolerable life there seems no possible escape. When he comes to his senses again he is in a transformed world. There is an absolute discontinuity between the two worlds. The movement from the bad world to the good one is as mysterious and as unpredictable as his initial incarceration in the dark world or as his redescent into the inferno when Fagin recaptures him. He simply finds everything suddenly changed. At first he does not know where he is, and the absolute transmutation of scene makes possible an absolute transmutation of self: "What room is this? Where have I been brought to? . . . This is not the place I went to sleep in." He has collapsed in the police office of the horrible Mr. Fang. He awakens to see "a motherly old lady, very neatly and precisely dressed" (chap. 12), sitting at needlework in an armchair by his curtained bed. All his past life seems a nightmare from which he has finally awakened to a life anterior to anything he has known in his actual life: "Weak, and thin, and pallid, he awoke at last from what seemed to have been a long and troubled dream" (chap. 12).

What are the characteristics of the new world in which Oliver so suddenly finds himself? Is it simply the opposite of the dark world of his initial interment? Is it freedom, openness, light, intelligible order rather than darkness, enclosedness, and incoherence?

At first it seems that the country world which is paradise on earth to Oliver is merely the diametrical opposite of the city world: "In the morning, Oliver would be a-foot by six o'clock, roaming the fields, and plundering the hedges, far and wide, for nosegays of wild flowers" (chap. 32). For the first time, Oliver is in a world where he can wander freely and without danger. There is even a passage which is a benign version of the frenzied race through the labyrinthine city streets: "Swiftly he ran across the fields, and down the little lanes which sometimes divided them: now almost hidden by the high corn on either side, and now emerging on an open field, where the mowers and haymakers were busy at their work" (chap. 33). Here all the narrowness and the threatening complexity of the city labyrinth have disappeared. The calm repose which is one leitmotiv of the country scenes seems caused simply by the openness they substitute for the suffocating narrowness of city streets or city interiors: "Who can describe the pleasure and delight, the peace of mind and soft tranquillity, the sickly boy felt in the balmy air, and among the green hills and rich woods, of an inland village! . . . It was a lovely spot to which they repaired. Oliver, whose days had been spent among squalid crowds, and in the midst of noise and brawling, seemed to enter on a new existence there. The rose and honeysuckle clung to the cottage walls; the ivy crept round the trunks of the trees; and the garden-flowers perfumed the air with delicious odours" (chap. 32). This seems simply to oppose the openness of the "balmy air, and . . . green hills and rich woods, of an inland village" to "crowded, pent-up streets." But what of the rose and honeysuckle which *cling* to the cottage walls, and the ivy which *creeps round* the trunks of the trees. Are not these images of protective enclosure rather than of complete openness? Are they not images which suggest domestic refuge rather than the empty sky and expansive landscapes of complete freedom?

Indeed, it soon becomes apparent that the country world is rather the reverse of the subterranean city world than its opposite. The country world combines the freedom Oliver had when he lay dying in the open with the enclosedness of the claustral interiors to produce a protected enclosure which is yet open to the outside and in direct contact with it. It is a paradise not of complete freedom but of a cosy security which looks out upon openness and enjoys it from the inside: "The little room in which he was accustomed to sit, when busy at his books, was on the ground-floor, at the back of the house. It was quite a cottage-room, with a lattice-window: around which were clusters of jessamine and honeysuckle, that crept over the casement, and filled the place with their delicious perfume. It looked into a garden, whence a wicket-gate opened into a small paddock; all beyond, was fine meadow-land and wood. There was no other dwelling near, in that direction; and the prospect it commanded was very extensive" (chap. 34, and see chap. 14). The ideal situation in *Oliver Twist*, then, is to be securely enclosed in a refuge which is yet open to the outside, in direct contact with the outside air and commanding an *extensive* view into the distance. Here Oliver possesses the entire surrounding world, *commands* it, by being able to see it, and yet he is secluded from view himself. He possesses intimacy, security, and expansion, openness, breadth of view: "The great trees . . . converted open and naked spots into choice nooks, where was a deep and pleasant shade from which to look upon the wide prospect, steeped in sunshine, which lay stretched beyond" (chap. 33).

The world of desirable enclosure differs from the subterranean interiors in being the place of tranquil repose and order rather than of anxious imprisonment. But this world is *like* the underground realm in being unintelligible. Oliver understands the world of the Brownlows and Maylies no more than he understood the world of Sikes and Fagin. He only knows that the walls have receded to a safe distance and that they now have apertures through which he can safely watch the outside world. But he is no more aware of having any right to enjoy this protected and modified enclosure than he felt that he was justly punished by incarceration in the scenes of entombment. The world remains unfathomable, opaque, in either case: "And thus the night crept slowly on. Oliver lay awake for some time, counting the little circles of light which the reflection of the rushlight-shade threw upon the ceiling; or tracing with his languid eyes the intricate pattern of the paper on the wall. The darkness and the deep stillness of the room were very solemn" (chap. 12).

Oliver imprisoned by Sowerberry, Bumble, or Fagin, or threatened by the crowd in the street, had no time to study so carefully the aspect presented to his eyes by the surrounding world. The world has ceased to push vertiginously upon the hero, and he can lie at his ease calmly studying the pattern it makes. But this pattern has no meaning for him. It is merely "intricate," and the number of little circles of light is merely a number. It has no significance for Oliver. Oliver is capable of being in the same state of bewilderment after he is saved as he was before: "[He] looked at the strangers without at all understanding what was going forward—in fact, without seeming to recollect where he was, or what had been passing" (chap. 31).

The image of Oliver languidly tracing the meaningless outlines of the world which presents itself to his vision is strangely like the passage quoted above in which Fagin, on trial for his life, is, so to speak, hypnotized by the very intensity of his fear into looking at what surrounds him with detachment and calm, as though it had nothing whatever to do with him. But just as Fagin is in fact about to be condemned to death, so Oliver is in great danger even in the midst of these scenes of protected repose. He is recaptured almost immediately by Fagin when Mr. Brownlow saves him, and his life with the Maylies is punctuated with appearances in the midst of his new environment of the dark world he was born in, appearances which only he can see. The vindictive glance of the hideous dwarf is glimpsed only by Oliver. He no sooner leaves the Maylies' cottage alone, than Monks starts up before him.

But the most important case of the appearance of the dark world in the midst of the good has a deeper significance.

Oliver falls asleep one evening in his little cottage room, sitting close by the lattice window from which he can see so much without being seen. There follows an experience which seems to prove the total insecurity of Oliver's present happy state. It is a passage which is, for Dickens, strangely deliberate and analytical. Apparently it is the statement of a doctrine about dreams, or, more precisely, about a certain state between sleep and waking in which the imaginary world of dreams is not cut off from the real situation of the sleeper but is mingled with it: "There is a kind of sleep that steals upon us sometimes, which, while it holds the body prisoner, does not free the mind from a sense of things about it, and enable it to ramble at its pleasure. So far as an overpowering heaviness, a prostration of strength, and an utter inability to control our thoughts or power of motion, can be called sleep, this is it; and yet, we have a consciousness of all that is going on about us, and, if we dream at such a time, words which are really spoken, or sounds which really exist at the moment, accommodate themselves with surprising readiness to our visions, until reality and imagination become so strangely blended that it is afterwards almost matter of impossibility to separate the two" (chap. 34). Earlier in the novel an almost exactly similar experience, defined in the same way—"There is a drowsy state, between sleeping and waking, when you dream more in five minutes . . . than you would in five nights with your eyes fast closed" (chap. 9)—had been explicitly defined as proof of the mighty power of the human mind to transcend its ordinary limitation to a single time and a single space. "At such times, a mortal knows just enough of what his mind is doing, to form some glimmering conception of its mighty powers, its bounding from earth and spurning time and space, when freed from the restraint of its corporeal associate" (chap. 9). For a moment, while such an experience lasts, a mortal is freed from his mortality and from his imprisonment in his body and in the present moment.

But the special interest of this state for Dickens is that it links an "imaginary" world to the actual present world, whereas an ordinary dream is entirely free, and has no direct relation whatever to the present.

Even if we are not at all aware through sensation of what is there in reality as a "mere silent presence," it will magically determine the nature of our dream: "It is an undoubted fact, that although our senses of touch and sight be for the time dead, yet our sleeping thoughts, and the visionary scenes that pass before us, will be influenced and materially influenced, by the *mere silent presence* of some external object; which may not have been near us when we closed our eyes: and of whose vicinity we have had no waking consciousness" (chap. 34).

Nevertheless, the most important peculiarity of this half-waking state is not, it turns out, that it links a real state to an imaginary state, but that it links a *present* state to a *past* state. In the earlier experience Oliver was perfectly aware of what was going on in the room around him and "yet the self-same senses were mentally engaged, at the same time, in busy action with almost everybody he had ever known" (chap. 9). In fact, what was perceived by Oliver's "half-closed eyes" was not only an immediate reality but a reality which seemed to contain, although Oliver was only vaguely aware of it, a hidden reminiscence, extending even prior to "everybody he had ever known." For what Oliver sees is Fagin gloating over his stolen jewels, and "poring long and earnestly" over a tiny trinket which may be a clue to his origin, and to his lost identity. This trinket functions as a magic talisman in whose presence the half-dreaming Oliver is put in touch with his past. But his mysterious sense that what he is doing or perceiving now is somehow a repetition of something from long ago is at this point wholly incomprehensible to Oliver.

In the second of such experiences the earlier time which the present repeats is definitely recognized: "Oliver knew, perfectly well, that he was in his own little room; that his books were lying on the table before him; that the sweet air was stirring among the creeping plants outside. And yet he was asleep. Suddenly, the scene changed; the air became close and confined; and he thought, with a glow of terror, that he was in the Jew's house again. There sat the hideous old man, in his accustomed corner, pointing at him, and whispering to another man, with his face averted, who sat beside him" (chap. 34).

Oliver wakes to find his dream reality: "There—there—at the window—close before him—so close, that he could have almost touched him before he started back: with his eyes peering into the room, and meeting his: there stood the Jew!" (chap. 34). The dream that is suggested by the "mere silent presence" of Fagin and Monks is not a free fantasy but is the total and exact reliving of Oliver's past as the prisoner of Fagin. The real theme of this striking passage is the possibility of that affective memory which forms, with many variations, a central theme of Romanticism. Here a peculiar psychological state caused by something directly present brings about the total recovery of a certain epoch of the past not as a faint memory but as an intimately relived experience. The past invades and altogether replaces a present which it is like. Or rather, the two times, past and present, are superimposed and inextricably mingled, and Oliver for a moment lives in a time which is neither past nor present but is somehow a universal and atemporal experience of being imprisoned by Fagin and subjected to his look. It is an experience which sums up his entire life since his birth.

But what Oliver endures is a very special variant of affective memory. He is perfectly aware that he is in his own little room, and suddenly he is in the Jew's house again. And yet when he wakes in terror he finds that Fagin and Monks are really there. What had seemed a fearful dream is literal actuality, and the present is in reality a reenactment of the past. The past has been recaptured. Here, though, there is no Proustian escape from the burden of an intolerable present through the ecstatic identification of a present moment and a past moment. Oliver has known no blissful infancy, and the past which comes back to dominate and to destroy his present happiness is the past of his subterranean life. Even though Oliver had thought himself secure in his new life with the Maylies, Fagin now reappears in the very midst of his most secure moment and invades his most secure place. Fagin comes as if to reclaim Oliver, as if to remind him that he really has belonged permanently to the dark underground world from his birth, and has never really escaped. A glance of "recognition" passes between Oliver and Fagin, like the look between Oliver and the dwarf, a look which seems to seal forever Oliver's secret identification with the world into which he was born, however completely he may seem to have left it behind: "It was but an instant, a glance, a flash, before his eyes; and they were gone. But they had recognised him, and he them; and their look was as firmly impressed upon his memory, as if it had been deeply carved in stone, and set before him from his birth" (chap. 34). (Compare: "the boy's eyes were fixed on his in mute curiosity; and although the recognition was only for an instant—for the briefest space of time that can possibly be conceived—it was enough to show the old man that he had been observed.") When Oliver's friends look for footprints in the garden where he has seen Fagin and Monks, they can find none. This may suggest that Fagin is the devil who leaves no footprints, but more importantly it shows that only Oliver is threatened by these sudden incursions into his happy present of a past from which he can never be free. Only Oliver is perpetually insecure because that past is "as firmly impressed upon his memory, as if it had been deeply carved in stone, and set before him from his birth." Oliver's past is permanently part of him and cannot be escaped by any movement into the future in the retrospectively oriented world of the novel.

Oliver knows now what he wants—a present which will be a protected repose combining freedom and enclosure. But he does not know how to possess this paradise on earth in permanent security. It seems to be in perpetual danger of being at any moment overrun and replaced by the dark past. The present, then, is altogether intolerable for Oliver, whether he is in the midst of a dark enclosed world which is accelerating toward his destruction, or whether he is in a calm protected world which may at any time be invaded and destroyed by the other world. The present in *Oliver Twist* is characterized by a failure to know who one is or to attain any acceptable identity. It is also characterized by a failure to understand the outside world. Oliver can only submit passively to a succession of present moments which do not relate coherently to one another. The world imposes a random rhythm of escape and capture. Oliver has only his "sturdy spirit" to defend himself, and because of the taboo against taking matters into his own hands he can use that spirit only to keep himself alive by passive resistance. Time in this unrelieved present either "steals tardily," slows down, coagulates, and freezes into an endless present of suffering, bewilderment, and interior emptiness, or, like a broken clock, it accelerates madly under the impulsion of fear toward the death that seems rushing out of the imminent future: "The day passed off. Day? There was no day: it was gone as soon as come—and night came on again; night so long, and yet so short; long in its dreadful silence, and short in its fleeting hours. . . . Eight—nine—ten. If it was not a trick to frighten him, and those were the real hours treading on each other's heels, where would he be, when they came round again! Eleven! Another struck, before the voice of the previous hour had ceased to vibrate. At eight, he would be the only mourner in his own funeral train; at eleven—" (chap. 52). The future then is a blank wall—an inevitable death by hanging. Only one dim hope appears. The present is able to be, through the phenomenon of affective memory, the reliving, the recapturing, of a past time.

V

Three distinct forms of repetition through memory of a past time may be distinguished in *Oliver Twist*.

First, there is the experience already described which links a present with a past moment in Oliver's own life. There is no escape here. Oliver is merely plunged back into the procession of enclosed and threatened moments which began with his birth and is carrying him implacably onward, even when he seems to have escaped, toward an outcast's death.

But there is another form of memory, a form which seems to connect the present with a supernatural paradise, a paradise which is anterior to all Oliver's present life, but which the present seems somehow to reveal. And it is revealed as a promise, the promise of an eventual escape out of this world of pain and suffering.

Oliver Twist abounds in intimations of immortality. In Mr. Brownlow's revery there were "faces that the grave had changed and closed upon, but which the mind, superior to its power, still dressed in their old freshness and beauty, . . . whispering of beauty beyond the tomb, changed but to be heightened, and taken from earth only to be set up as a light, to shed a soft and gentle glow upon the path to Heaven" (chap. 11). Rose Maylie's tears upon Oliver's forehead cause him to stir and smile in his sleep, "as though these marks of pity and compassion had awakened some pleasant dream of a love and affection he had never known" (chap. 30). But this dream is no mere fantasy; it is the recollection of a prenatal paradise, as "a strain of gentle music, or the rippling of water in a silent place, or the odour of a flower, or the mention of a familiar word, will sometimes call up sudden dim remembrances of scenes that never were, in this life; which vanish like a breath; which some brief memory of a happier existence, long gone by, would seem to have awakened; which no voluntary exertion of the mind can ever recall" (chap. 30). Memory, then, can be an intense sensation of *déjà vu*, a sensation which is no longer the reliving of a past moment in one's own earthly life, but is the faint apprehension of "some remote and distant time" which is not of this world at all and which seems to be one's real home: "The memories which peaceful country scenes call up, are not of this world, nor of its thoughts and hopes. . . . there lingers . . . a vague and half-formed consciousness of having held such feelings long before, in some remote and distant time, which calls up solemn thoughts of distant times to come" (chap. 32).

But this is not what Oliver wants. All the intimations of a supernatural state of bliss which Oliver receives from the earthly world only serve to accentuate the shortcomings of the latter. What Oliver wants is to possess his heaven on earth. The "memories" of a prior state of bliss called forth by "peaceful country scenes" only separate more radically the present real earthly world and the distant unattainable paradise. "Heaven is," as Oliver says, "a long way off; and they are too happy there, to come down to the bedside of a poor boy" (chap. 12). Graham Greene has spoken of the "Manicheanism" of the world of *Oliver Twist,* and indeed there does seem to be initially an absolute breach between heaven and the intolerable earthly world—which is a kind of hell. But the problem of the novel is precisely how to join these two apparently irreconcilable worlds, how to bring heaven to earth. It seems, though, that the only way to reach heaven is through death. Again and again any state of calm happiness, any beautiful landscape, and even any state of complete moral goodness is equated with death:

> he wished, as he crept into his narrow bed, that that were his coffin, and that he could be lain in a calm and lasting sleep in the church-yard ground, with the tall grass waving gently above his head, and the sound of the old deep bell to soothe him in his sleep.
>
> (chap. 5)

> Gradually, he fell into that deep tranquil sleep which ease from recent suffering alone imparts; that calm and peaceful rest which it is pain to wake from. Who, if this were death, would be roused again to all the struggles and turmoils of life; to all its cares for the present; its anxieties for the future; more than all, its weary recollections of the past!
>
> (chap. 12)

> He felt calm and happy, and could have died without a murmur.
>
> (chap. 30)

The city men go to the country to die; little Dick dies the death Oliver would have died and the news is brought to Oliver in the very moment when his happiness is at last secure (chap. 51); Dickens has no sooner got Oliver to the pleasant country cottage with the Maylies than he has Rose Maylie nearly die because she is too good for this world. The narrative of this event is characterized by that maudlin sentimentality of language which Dickens often slips into when he writes about either beautiful and pure young women or about heaven: " 'A creature,' continued the young man, passionately, 'a creature as fair and innocent of guile as one of God's own angels, fluttered between life and death. Oh! who could hope, when the distant world to which she was akin, half opened to her view, that she would return to the sorrow and calamity of this!' " (chap. 35). The falsity of the language here is a sign that Dickens rather wishes for the heavenly world than wholly believes in it. His real allegiance, it may be, is to the dark world, the world which he so fears is the real and only world that he writes novel after novel whose dramatic action is the attempt to escape from it.

But still Dickens can be caught up in the vision of a natural innocence which is brought into this world at birth from a prenatal heaven and which is regained at death after passing through a world which is predominantly evil: "Alas! How few of Nature's faces are left alone to gladden us with their beauty! The cares, and sorrows, and hungerings, of the world, change them as they change hearts; and it is only when those passions sleep, and have lost their hold for ever, that the troubled clouds pass off, and leave Heaven's surface clear. It is a common thing for the countenances of the dead, even in that fixed and rigid state, to subside into the long-forgotten expression of sleeping infancy, and settle into the very look of early life" (chap. 24). Heaven, then, is the place where all that has been lost in this fallen world is regained, and it is a place of which one may have glimpses momentarily athwart the almost totally unrelieved gloom of this world.

There seems no escape from this world but by death.

However, one final form remains of the repetition through memory of a past state: one may find signs in the present of a secret past life which existed *on this earth* before one was born. When those signs are understood, their revelations may be accepted as a definition of what one really is. Then it will be possible to live ever afterward in a kind of paradise on earth, a paradise regained which is the present lightened and spiritualized because it is a repetition of one's prenatal earthly past. if *Oliver Twist* is in one sense Oliver's procession through a sequence of opaque and meaningless present moments, it is in another sense the slow discovery, in the midst of that confusion, of a secret which will make all seem orderly and significant. As in all of Dickens's novels, there is a mystery at the center of apparently unrelated events which will make them turn out in retrospect to be orderly and intelligible. Here the mystery is the secret of Oliver's birth. When it is solved he can live happily ever after because now he knows who he *is*. He discovers his essence, his intrinsic nature, and with it acquires a place in society.

But the total dramatic pattern of *Oliver Twist* suggests that Oliver can have happiness so completely in the end only because he has lost it so completely at the beginning. If there had not been an absolute break in the chain of time which determines each person's present identity by an ineluctable series of causes and effects, and if there had not been an absolute break in the chain of community relationships by which parents

and adults own, control, and judge, as well as protect, their children,
would the secure life Oliver covets have been so desirable after all? Does
not Dickens secretly enjoy the situation of the outcast, with an enjoyment
nonetheless intense for being hidden far beneath the surface? If the outcast
is, in one sense, entirely coerced, in another sense he is entirely free,
entirely untrammeled by any direct ties to any other human being. Even if
Oliver secretly and almost unconsciously believes that he is something
other than the "bad 'un," destined for the gallows, which everyone names
him, that belief has no evident source in the external world. It depends
only on Oliver himself for its existence. And Oliver can claim his inheritance only after he has proved that he really is who he is in a world which
does not give him any reflection or recognition of that identity. Oliver can
only become himself by forming a relation between what he is initially, a
wholly independent self, depending on and sustained by nothing external,
and the self he discovers himself already to be. The distance between these
two selves is absolutely necessary. Hence the extreme importance of the
clause of Oliver's father's will providing that he shall inherit the money
"only on the stipulation that in his minority he should never have stained
his name with any public act of dishonour, meanness, cowardice, or
wrong" (chap. 51).

Dickens, then, in a manner contrives to have both his contradictory
needs simultaneously. Oliver is self-determining in that, without any knowledge of who he really is, he has had to defend his essence from the world
that tries to make him a thief. But in the end he is entirely the protégé of
the outside world, and submits without quarrel to a life under the approving eyes of Mr. Brownlow and the Maylies. Finally, when all the secrets
are out, having been wrested by force from the heart of the dark world,
Mr. Brownlow adopts Oliver "as his son," and Oliver has what he wants
at last as a member of "a little society, whose condition approached as
nearly to one of perfect happiness as can ever be known in this changing
world" (chap. 53). He has the landscape of reconciled enclosure and
freedom, now personified in Rose Maylie, literally his aunt, but in a way
mother and sister to him too, and described in language which identifies
her with the ideal scene of the novel: "I would show Rose Maylie in all
the bloom and grace of early womanhood, shedding on her secluded path
in life soft and gentle light, that fell on all who trod it with her, and shone
into their hearts" (chap. 53). And he has the selfhood he has sought, a
selfhood which he has not chosen or created, but which has been given to
him from the outside: "Mr. Brownlow went on, from day to day, filling
the mind of his adopted child with stores of knowledge, and becoming

attached to him, more and more, as his nature developed itself, and showed the thriving seeds of all he wished him to become— ... he traced in him new traits of his early friend, that awakened in his own bosom old remembrances, melancholy and yet sweet and soothing" (chap. 53).

Oliver has at last what he wants. He has reconciled freedom and the desire for self-determination with the desire not to choose what he is to be, to have the choice made for him, and then to be protected and accepted by society. Mr. Brownlow *fills* the empty spirit of Oliver with those "stores of knowledge" which will make him an authentic member of the middle class, but this education only reveals that Oliver has been all along potentially what Mr. Brownlow wants to make him in actuality. His selfhood is both made for him by Mr. Brownlow and yet prior to Mr. Brownlow's education of him. And this reconciliation of contradictory needs is possible because Oliver is willing to exist as the image of his father, willing to take as the definition of his essential selfhood those traits which are the repetition of his father's nature. He is willing to accept an identification of himself which does not derive, ultimately, from anything he has done, but only from what his parents were. In order to escape from the harsh world into which he has been born, a world in which the extreme of enclosedness combines with the extreme of isolation, Oliver is willing to live out his life facing backward into the past, spending with Rose Maylie "whole hours ... in picturing the friends whom they had so sadly lost" (chap. 53). He escapes from an intolerable present and a frightening future by making the present a reduplication of a past safely over and done with, and by turning his back altogether on the future and on autonomous action. He lives happily ever after, but only by living in a perpetual childhood of submission to protection and direction from without.

The ending of *Oliver Twist* is a resolution of Dickens's single great theme, the search of the outcast for status and authentic identity, but it is a resolution which is essentially based on self-deception and on an unwillingness to face fully his apprehension of the world. It is a resolution which will not satisfy him for long.

NORTHROP FRYE

Dickens and the Comedy of Humors

Dickens presents special problems to any critic who approaches him in the context of a "Victorian novelist." In general, the serious Victorian fiction writers are realistic and the less serious ones are romancers. We expect George Eliot or Trollope to give us a solid and well-rounded realization of the social life, attitudes, and intellectual issues of their time: we expect Disraeli and Bulwer-Lytton, because they are more "romantic," to give us the same kind of thing in a more flighty and dilettantish way; from the cheaper brands, Marie Corelli or Ouida, we expect nothing but the standard romance formulas. This alignment of the serious and the realistic, the commercial and the romantic, where realism has a moral dignity that romance lacks, intensified after Dickens's death, survived through the first half of the twentieth century, and still lingers vestigially. But in such an alignment Dickens is hard to place. What he writes, if I may use my own terminology for once, are not realistic novels but fairy tales in the low mimetic displacement. Hence there has grown up an assumption that, if we are to take Dickens seriously, we must emphasize the lifelike-ness of his characters or the shrewdness of his social observation; if we emphasize his violently unplausible plots and his playing up of popular sentiment, we are emphasizing only his concessions to an undeveloped public taste. This was a contemporary view of him, expressed very lucidly by Trollope in *The Warden*, and it is still a natural one to take.

A refinement of the same view sees the real story in Dickens's novels as a rather simple set of movements within a large group of characters. To

From *Experience in the Novel: Selected Papers from the English Institute*, edited by Roy Harvey Pearce. © 1968 by Columbia University Press.

this a mechanical plot seems to have been attached like an outboard motor to a rowboat, just to get things moving faster and more noisily. Thus our main interest, in reading *Little Dorrit*, is in the straightforward and quite touching story of Clennam's love for the heroine, of their separation through her suddenly acquired wealth, and of their eventual reunion through her loss of it. Along with this goes a preposterous melodrama about forged wills, identical twins, a mother who is not a mother, skulking foreigners, and dark mysteries of death and birth which seems almost detachable from the central story. Similarly, we finish *Our Mutual Friend* with a clear memory of a vast panoramic pageant of Victorian society, from the nouveau-riche Veneerings to Hexham living on the refuse of the Thames. But the creaky Griselda plot, in which John Harmon pretends to be dead in order to test the stability of his future wife, is something that we can hardly take in even when reading the book, much less remember afterwards.

Some works of fiction present a clearly designed or projected plot, where each episode seems to us to be logically the sequel to the previous episode. In others we feel that the episode that comes next does so only because the author has decided that it will come next. In stories with a projected plot we explain the episode from its context in the plot; in stories lacking such a plot, we are often thrown back on some other explanation, often one that originates in the author's wish to tell us something besides the story. This last is particularly true of thematic sequences like the "Dream Play" of Strindberg, where the succession of episodes is not like that of a projected plot, nor particularly like a dream either, but has to be accounted for in different terms. In Dickens we often notice that when he is most actively pursuing his plot he is careless, to the verge of being contemptuous, of the inner logic of the story. In *Little Dorrit*, the mysterious rumblings and creakings in the Clennam house, referred to at intervals throughout, mean that it is about to fall down. What this in turn means is that Dickens is going to push it over at a moment when the villain is inside and the hero outside. Similarly, Clennam, after a good deal of detective work, manages to discover where Miss Wade is living on the Continent. She did not expect him to ferret out her address, nor had she anything to say to him when he arrived; but, just in case he did come, she had written out the story of her life and had kept it in a drawer ready to hand to him. The outrage on probability seems almost deliberate, as does the burning up of Krook in *Bleak House* by spontaneous combustion as soon as the author is through with him, despite Dickens's protests about the authenticity of his device. Dickens's daughter, Mrs.

Pellegrini, remarked shrewdly that there was no reason to suppose that *The Mystery of Edwin Drood* would have been any more of an impeccable plot-structure than the novels that Dickens had already completed. But, because it is unfinished, the plot has been the main focus of critical attention in that story, usually on the assumption that this once Dickens was working with a plot which was not, like a fictional Briareus, equipped with a hundred arms of coincidence.

T. S. Eliot, in his essay on Dickens and Wilkie Collins, remarks on the "spurious fatality" of Collins's detective-story plots. This is no place to raise the question of why the sense of fatality in *The Moonstone* should be more spurious than in *The Family Reunion,* but we notice in Dickens how strong the impulse is to reject a logicality inherent in the story in favor of impressing on the reader an impatient sense of absolutism: of saying, in short, *la fatalité, c'est moi.* This disregard of plausibility is worth noticing, because everyone realizes that Dickens is a great genius of the absurd in his characterization, and it is possible that his plots are also absurd in the same sense, not from incompetence or bad taste, but from a genuinely creative instinct. If so, they are likely to be more relevant to the entire conception of the novel than is generally thought. I proceed to explore a little the sources of absurdity in Dickens, to see if that will lead us to a clearer idea of his total structure.

The structure that Dickens uses for his novels is the New Comedy structure, which has come down to us from Plautus and Terence through Ben Jonson, an author we know Dickens admired, and Molière. The main action is a collision of two societies which we may call for convenience the obstructing and the congenial society. The congenial society is usually centered on the love of hero and heroine, the obstructing society on the characters, often parental, who try to thwart this love. For most of the action the thwarting characters are in the ascendant, but toward the end a twist in the plot reverses the situation and the congenial society dominates the happy ending. A frequent form of plot-reversal was the discovery that one of the central characters, usually the heroine, was of better social origin than previously thought. This theme of mysterious parentage is greatly expanded in the late Greek romances, which closely resemble some of the plots of Menander. Here an infant of noble birth may be stolen or exposed and brought up by humble foster-parents, being restored to his original status at the end. In drama such a theme involves expounding a complicated antecedent action, and however skillfully done not all audiences have the patience to follow the unraveling, as Ben Jonson discovered to his cost at the opening of his *New Inn.* But in narrative forms, of course, it can have room to expand. Shakespeare gets away with it in *The Winter's Tale* by adopting a narrative-paced form of drama, where sixteen years are encompassed by the action.

Dickens is, throughout his career, very conventional in his handling of the New Comedy plot structure. All the stock devices, listed in Greek times as laws, oaths, compacts, witnesses, and ordeals, can be found in him. *Oliver Twist* and *Edwin Drood* are full of oaths, vows, councils of war, and conspiracies, on both benevolent and sinister sides. Witnesses include eavesdroppers like the Newman Noggs of *Nicholas Nickleby* or Morfin the cello-player in *Dombey and Son*. Ordeals are of various kinds: near-fatal illnesses are common, and we may compare the way that information is extracted from Rob the Grinder by Mrs. Brown in *Dombey and Son* with the maltreating of the tricky slave in Menander and Plautus. Many thrillers (perhaps a majority) use a stock episode of having the hero entrapped by the villain, who instead of killing him at once imparts an essential piece of information about the plot to him, after which the hero escapes, gaining his wisdom at the price of an ordeal of facing death. This type of episode occurs in *Great Expectations* in the encounter with Orlick.

Every novel of Dickens is a comedy (N.B.: such words as "comedy" are not essence words but context words, hence this means: "for every novel of Dickens the obvious context is comedy"). The death of a central character does not make a story tragic, any more than a similar device does in *The King and I* or *The Yeomen of the Guard*. Sydney Carton is a man without a social function who achieves that function by sacrificing himself for the congenial society; Little Nell's death is so emotionally luxurious that it provides a kind of muted festivity for the conclusion, or what *Finnegans Wake* calls a "funferall." The emphasis at the end of a comedy is sometimes thrown, not on the forming of a new society around the marriage of hero and heroine, but on the maturing or enlightening of the hero, a process which may detach him from marriage or full participation in the congenial group. We find this type of conclusion in Shaw's *Candida*: Dickens's contribution to it is *Great Expectations*. Again, there is usually a mystery in Dickens's stories, and this mystery is nearly always the traditional mystery of birth, in sharp contrast to the mystery of death on which the modern whodunit is based. In Dickens, when a character is murdered, we usually see it done, and if not the suspense is still perfunctory. A detective appears in *Bleak House* to investigate the murder of Tulkinghorn, but his task is easy: Lady Dedlock keeps a French maid, and French maids, being foreign, are emotionally unpredictable and morally insensitive. The problem is much less interesting than the problem of Lady

Dedlock's guilty secret, which involves a birth. Unless Edwin Drood was very unlike Dickens's other heroes, the mystery about him is much more likely to have been a mystery of how he got into the world than of how he disappeared from it.

The emergence of the congenial society at the conclusion of the story is presented in the traditional New Comedy terms of festivity. It usually holds several marriages; it dispenses money if it has money, and it dispenses a good deal of food. Such features have remained unchanged in the New Comedy tradition since Greek times. Dickens's predilection for feasting scenes needs no laboring: it may be significant that his last written words are "falls to with an appetite." This feature accounts for his relentless plugging of Christmas, always for him the central symbol of the congenial family feast. The famous sentimentality of Dickens is largely confined to demonstrations of family affection, and is particularly evident in certain set scenes that immediately precede the dénouement, where the affection of brother and sister, of father and daughter, or more rarely of mother and son, is the main theme. Examples are the housekeeping of Tom and Ruth Pinch in *Martin Chuzzlewit,* the dinner of Kit and his mother in *The Old Curiosity Shop,* the meetings of Bella Wilfer with her father in *Our Mutual Friend.* Such relationships, though occasionally described as marriages, are "innocent" in the technical Victorian sense of not involving sexual intercourse, and if they seem to post-Freudian readers to be emotionally somewhat overcharged, it is because they contribute to, and anticipate, the final triumph of Eros at the end of the story. The disregard of plausibility, already mentioned, is another traditional feature, being part of the violent manipulation of the story in the direction of a happy ending. Those who object to such endings on the grounds of probability are often put in the position of questioning the ways of divine providence, which uses the author as its agent for vindicating virtue and baffling vice.

Most of the people who move across the pages of Dickens are neither realistic portraits, like the characters of Trollope, nor "caricatures," so far as that term implies only a slightly different approach to realistic portraiture. They are humors, like the characters in Ben Jonson, who formulated the principle that humors were the appropriate characters for a New Comedy plot. The humor is a character identified with a characteristic, like the miser, the hypochondriac, the braggart, the parasite, or the pedant. He is obsessed by whatever it is that makes him a humor, and the sense of our superiority to an obsessed person, someone bound to an invariable ritual habit, is, according to Bergson, one of the chief sources of laughter. But it is not because he is incidentally funny that the humor is important in New Comedy: he is important because his obsession is the feature that creates the conditions of the action, and the opposition of the two societies. In *The Silent Woman*, everything depends on Morose's hatred of noise; covetousness and gullibility set everything going in *Volpone* and *The Alchemist* respectively. Thus it is only the obstructing society which is "humorous," in the Jonsonian sense, as a society. In Dickens we find humors on both sides of the social conflict, genial, generous, and lovable humors as well as absurd or sinister ones. But the humors in the congenial society merely diversify it with amiable and harmless eccentricities; the humors of the obstructing society help to build up that society, with all its false standards and values.

Most of the standard types of humor are conspicuous in Dickens, and could be illustrated from *Bleak House* alone: the miser in Smallweed; the hypocrite in Chadband; the parasite in Skimpole and Turveydrop; the pedant in Mrs. Jellyby. The braggart soldier is not much favored: Major Bagstock in *Dombey and Son* is more of a parasite. Agreeably to the conditions of Victorian life, the braggart soldier is replaced by a braggart merchant or politician. An example, treated in a thoroughly traditional manner, is Bounderby in *Hard Times*. Another Victorian commonplace of the braggart-soldier family, the duffer sportsman, whose pretensions are far beyond his performance, is represented by Winkle in *The Pickwick Papers*. There are, however, two Winkles in *The Pickwick Papers*, the duffer sportsman and the pleasant young man who breaks down family opposition on both sides to acquire a pleasant young woman. The duality reflects the curious and instructive way that *The Pickwick Papers* came into being. The original scheme proposed to Dickens was a comedy of humors in its most primitive and superficial form: a situation comedy in which various stock types, including an incautious amorist (Tupman), a melancholy poet (Snodgrass), and a pedant (Pickwick), as well as Winkle, get into one farcical predicament after another. This form is frequent in stories for children, and was represented in my childhood by now obsolete types of comic strip and silent movie comedies. It must have left some descendants in television, but my impression is that contemporary children are deficient in this vitamin. But although traces of the original scheme persist throughout *The Pickwick Papers*, it quickly turns inside out into a regular New Comedy story, which leads up in the regular way to a recognition scene and a reversal of direction in the plot at its most serious point, in the debtors' prison. The pedant becomes a man of principle, and the humor of pedantry is transferred to the law which entraps him. Thus the comedy of humors takes root in society, as Dickens sees society, instead of merely extending from one incident to another.

The simplest form of humor is the tagged humor, who is associated with the repetition of a set phrase. Thus we have Mrs. Micawber, whose tag is that she will never desert Mr. Micawber, and Major Bagnet in *Bleak House,* who admires his wife but asserts that he never tells her so because "discipline must be maintained." We notice that our sense of superiority to such characters is edged with antagonism: when the repeated trait is intended to be endearing we are more likely to find it irritating, as E. M. Forster does Mrs. Micawber's. Jarndyce with his "east wind" tag and Esther Summerson's constant bewilderment that other people should find her charming do not stick in our minds in the way that Chadband and Mrs. Jellyby do. The humor is, almost by definition, a bore, and the technical skill in handling him consists in seeing that we get just enough but not too much of him. The more unpleasant he is, the easier this problem is to solve. Repetition which is excessive even by Dickensian standards, like the emphasis on Carker's teeth in *Dombey and Son,* is appropriate for a villain, as its effect is to dehumanize and cut off sympathy. We cannot feel much concern over the fate of a character who is presented to us mainly as a set of teeth, like Berenice in Poe. The "lifelikeness" of a humor depends on two things: on the fact that we are all very largely creatures of ritual habit, and on the strength of a perverse tendency in most of us to live up to our own caricatures. Pecksniff may be a humbug, but that can hardly be the whole of our feeling about him when he begins to sound like a member of my own profession attempting to extract a discussion from a group of clammed-up freshmen:

> "The name of those fabulous animals (pagan, I regret to say) who used to sing in the water, has quite escaped me."
>
> Mr. George Chuzzlewit suggested "Swans."
>
> "No," said Mr. Pecksniff. "Not swans. Very like swans, too. Thank you."
>
> The nephew with the outline of a countenance, speaking for the first and last time on that occasion, propounded "Oysters."
>
> "No," said Mr. Pecksniff, with his own peculiar urbanity, "nor oysters. But by no means unlike oysters: a very excellent idea; thank you, my dear sir, very much. Wait! Sirens. Dear me! sirens, of course."

Humors are, at least dramatically, "good" if they are on the side of the congenial society, "bad" or ridiculous if on the side of the obstructing one. Thus the humor comedy has an easy and natural connection with the morality play. We notice this in the allegorical names that Dickens often gives some of his minor characters, like the "Pyke" and "Pluck" who are the satellites of Sir Mulberry Hawk in *Nicholas Nickleby,* or the "Bar," "Bishop," and "Physician" who turn up at Merdle's dinners in *Little Dorrit.* We notice it also in Dickens's tendency to arrange his humors in moral pairs, whether both are in the same novel or not. As just indicated, we have a "good" major in *Bleak House* and a "bad" one with a very similar name in *Dombey and Son;* we have a villainous Jew in *Oliver Twist* and a saintly Jew in *Our Mutual Friend,* and so on. Within *Dombey and Son* itself the "bad" major is paired against a "good" navy man, Captain Cuttle. If characters change sides, there may be a metamorphosis of character, which is not difficult in the humor technique, because it simply means putting on a different mask. Thus the generous Boffin pretends to be a miser for a while; Scrooge goes through the reverse process; Mercy Pecksniff changes roles from the feather-head to the faithful ill-used wife, and so on. Many humors are really chorus characters, who cannot do anything in the plot unless they step out of their roles: an example is Lord Frederick Verisopht in *Nicholas Nickleby,* who has to harden up a good deal to make his tragic end appropriate. The commonest form of this metamorphosis, and the most traditional one, is the release of the humor from his obsession at the end of the story: through the experience gained in the story, he is able to break through his besetting fault. At the end of *Martin Chuzzlewit* there is a whole series of these changes: the hero escapes from his selfishness, Mark Tapley from his compulsion to search for difficult situations in order to "come out strong," and Tom Pinch from an innocence that Dickens recognizes to be more obsessive than genuine innocence, and which we should now think of as a streak of masochism.

The rhetoric of the tagged humor consists mainly of variations of the stock identifying phrase or phrases. Some humors acquire a personal rhetorical rhythm of a strongly associative kind, which because it is associative gives the effect of being obsessive. The disjointed phrases of Jingle and the asyntactic babble of Mrs. Nickleby and Flora Finching are perhaps the most consistently successful examples. Closer to the single identifying phrase are Uriah Heep's insistence on his " 'umble" qualities, which reminds us a little of Iago's "honest" tag, and the repetitions that betray the hypocrisy of Casby, the squeezing landlord in *Little Dorrit.* Others develop parodies of standard types of oratory, like Chadband with his parsonical beggar's whine or Micawber with his Parliamentary flourishes.

More significant, for a reason that will meet us in a moment, is the humor of stock response, that is, the humor whose obsession it is to insist that what he or she has been conditioned to think proper and acceptable is in fact reality. This attitude gives us the Bouvard-et-Pécuchet type of humor, whose mind is confined within a dictionary of accepted ideas. Such humors, it is obvious, readily expand into cultural allegories, representatives of the kind of anxiety that caricatures an age. Thus our stereotypes about "Victorian prudery" are represented by Podsnap in *Our Mutual Friend* and Mrs. General (the prunes-and-prisms woman) in *Little Dorrit*. Martin Chuzzlewit finds that America is full of such humors: American shysters are no better and no worse than their British counterparts, but there is a more theoretical element in their lying, and bluster about their enlightened political institutions is much more used as a cover for swindling. In America, in other words, the complacent Podsnap and the rascally Lammle are more likely to be associated in the same person. The implication, which Dickens is not slow to press, is that American life is more vulnerable than British life to character assassination, personal attacks, charges of being un-American, and mob violence. A humor of this stock-response type is comic on Freudian principles: he often says what more cautious people would not say, but show by their actions that they believe. Thus Bumble's remarks about "them wicious paupers" are funny, not as typical of a Victorian beadle, but as revealing the hatred and contempt for the poor that official charity attempts to disguise.

Sometimes a humor's obsessed behavior and repetitive speech suggest a puppet or mechanical doll, whose response is invariable whatever the stimulus. We may feel with some of these characters that the mechanical quality is simply the result of Dickens's not having worked hard enough on them, but occasionally we realize that Dickens himself is encouraging us to see them as inanimate objects. Wemmick the postbox in *Great Expectations,* Pancks the "tug" in *Little Dorrit,* and several characters who are figuratively and to some extent literally wooden, like Silas Wegg, are examples. The Captain Cuttle of *Dombey and Son,* in particular, impresses us as an animated version of the Wooden Midshipman over the shop he so often inhabits. In *The Old Curiosity Shop,* after we have been introduced to Quilp, Little Nell and her grandfather set out on their travels and see a Punch and Judy show. It occurs to us that Quilp, who is described as a "grotesque puppet," who lies, cheats, beats his wife, gets into fistfights, drinks like a salamander, and comes to a sticky end in a bog, *is* Punch, brought to life as a character. Wyndham Lewis, in an essay on Joyce (another admirer of Ben Jonson), notes the Dickensian ancestry of Bloom's interior monologue in the speech of Jingle. He might have noted a similar connection between Flora Finching's unpunctuated harangues in *Little Dorrit* and the reverie of Molly Bloom. Lewis in his turn developed, mainly out of Bergson, a theory of satire as a vision of human behavior in mechanical terms, where his main predecessor, if not one he recognized, was Dickens. We notice also the reappearance of the Punch figure in the center of *The Human Age*.

We noted that, while there are humors on both sides of the social conflict in Dickens, it is only the obstructing society which is humorous as a society. This takes us back to the feature I mentioned at the beginning which distinguishes Dickens from his major contemporaries in fiction. In most of the best Victorian novels, apart from Dickens, the society described is organized by its institutions: the church, the government, the professions, the rural squirearchy, business, and the trade unions. It is a highly structured society, and the characters function from within those structures. But in Dickens we get a much more freewheeling and anarchistic social outlook. For him the structures of society, as structures, belong almost entirely to the absurd, obsessed, sinister aspect of it, the aspect that is overcome or evaded by the comic action. The comic action itself moves toward the regrouping of society around the only social unit that Dickens really regards as genuine, the family. In other Victorian novelists characters are regrouped within their social structures; in Dickens the comic action leads to a sense of having broken down or through those structures. Naturally there are limits to this: the same social functions have to continue; but the sense that social institutions have to reverse their relationship to human beings before society really becomes congenial is very strong.

The law, for instance, as represented by the Chancery suit in *Bleak House* and the Circumlocution Office in *Little Dorrit,* is a kind of social vampire, sucking out family secrets or draining off money through endless shifts and evasions. It is explicitly said in both novels that the legal establishment is not designed to be an instrument of society, but to be a self-perpetuating social parasite. Education, again, is usually presented in Dickens as a racket, a brutal and malignant racket with Squeers and Creakle, a force-feeding racket in the "fact" school of *Hard Times* and the classical cram school of Dr. Blimber in *Dombey and Son*. Dickens's view of the liberalizing quality of the Victorian classical training is perhaps symbolized in the grotesque scenes of Silas Wegg stumbling through Gibbon's *Decline and Fall* to the admiration of the illiterate Boffins: an unskillful performance which nobody understands. As for religion, even the respectable churches have little to do except marry the hero and heroine, and the spokesmen of the chapel, Chadband and Stiggins, are the same type of greasy lout as their ancestor in Ben Jonson, Zeal-of-the-Land Busy. Politics, from the Eatanswill election in *Pickwick* to the Parliamentary career of Veneering in *Our Mutual Friend,* is a farce, only tolerable when an amusing one. Industry is equally repulsive whether its spokesman is Bounderby or the labor organizer Slackbridge. The amassing of a fortune in the City, by Dombey, Ralph Nickleby, or Merdle in *Little Dorrit,* is an extension of miserliness: it is closely associated with usury; the debtor's prison is clearly the inseparable other side of it, and it usually blows up a bubble of credit speculation with no secured assets, ending in an appalling financial crash and endless misery. *Martin Chuzzlewit* carefully balances the swindling of American real estate speculators with the precisely similar activities of Montague's Anglo-Bengalee Company in London. In several of the novels there are two obstructing societies, one a social establishment and the other a criminal anti-establishment. When this occurs there is little if anything morally to choose between them. We find the Artful Dodger no worse than the respectable Bumble in his beadle's uniform, and Pip discovers a human companionship with the hunted convict on the marshes that the Wopsles and Pumblechooks of his Christmas dinner exclude him from.

It is perhaps in *Little Dorrit* that we get the most complete view of the obstructing society, a society which is shown to be a self-imprisoning society, locking itself in to the invariable responses of its own compulsions. At the beginning we are introduced to various types of prison: the Marseilles prison with Blandois, the quarantine prison with the discontented Tattycoram and her lesbian familiar Miss Wade, the prison-house of the paralyzed Mrs. Clennam, and finally the Marshalsea. As the story goes on these external prisons give place to internal ones. With the Circumlocution Office the prison image modulates to a maze or labyrinth, a very frequent sinister image in Dickens, and gradually a unified vision of the obstructing society takes shape. This society is symbolized by the Barnacles, who, as their name indicates, represent a social parasitism inherent in the aristocracy, and operating through the political and legal establishment. They are a family, but not a genuine family: their loyalties are class or tribal loyalties cutting across the real structure of society. One of their members, Mrs. Gowan, even goes so far as to speak of marriage as "accidental," and stresses the primary necessity of defending the position of her class, or rather of her private myth about her class. The fact that her son becomes the husband of the only child of the Meagles family gives a most ambiguous twist to the happy ending of the novel. We may compare the disaster wrought by Steerforth in *David Copperfield,* whose mother is similarly obsessed with making her son into a symbol of class arrogance. We begin to understand how consistent the pitiful pretense of aristocracy that old Dorrit tries to maintain, first in the prison, then in prosperity, is with the general scheme of the story. Miss Wade's autobiography, headed "The History of a Self-Tormentor," however arbitrarily introduced into the story, has a genuine symbolic relevance to it, and one of the most sharply observed passages in the novel is the moment of self-awareness when Fanny Dorrit realizes that her own selfishness is implacably driving her into an endless, pointless, pleasureless game of one-upmanship with Mrs. Merdle. Similarly in *Great Expectations* the "gentleman's" world which entraps Pip is symbolized by the decaying prison-house where all the clocks have been stopped at the moment of Miss Havisham's humiliation, the rest of her life consisting only of brooding on that moment.

The obstructing society in Dickens has two main characteristics: it is parasitic and it is pedantic. It is parasitic in the sense of setting up false values and loyalties which destroy the freedom of all those who accept them, as well as tyrannizing over many of those who do not. Dickens's implicit social vision is also radical, to an extent he hardly realized himself, in dividing society between workers and idlers, and in seeing in much of the leisure class a social sanctioning of parasitism. As for its pedantry, it is traditional in New Comedy to set up a pragmatic standard, based on experience, as a norm, and contrast it with the theoretical approaches to life typical of humors who cannot escape from their reflex responses. Like Blake, like every writer with any genuine radicalism in him, Dickens finds the really dangerous social evils in those which have achieved some acceptance by being rationalized. Already in *Oliver Twist* the word "experience" stands as a contrast to the words "experimental" and "philosophical," which are invariably pejorative. This contrast comes into Bumble's famous "the law is a ass" speech. In *Hard Times* the pedantry of the obstructing society is associated with a utilitarian philosophy and an infantile trust in facts, statistics, and all impersonal and generalized forms of knowledge. We may wonder why Dickens denounces this philosophy so earnestly and caricatures it so crudely, instead of letting its absurdities speak for themselves. But it is clear that *Hard Times,* of all Dickens's stories, comes nearest to being what in our day is sometimes called the dystopia, the book which, like *Brave New World* or *1984,* shows us the nightmare world that results from certain perverse tendencies inherent in society getting free play. The most effective dystopias are likely to be those in which the author isolates certain features in his society that most directly threaten his own social function as a writer. Dickens sees in the cult of facts and statistics a threat, not to the realistic novelist, and not only to a life based on concrete and personal relations, but to the unfettered imagination, the mind that can respond to fairy tales and fantasy and understand their relevance to reality. The insistence on the importance of fairy tales, nursery rhymes, and similar genres in education often meets us in Dickens, and implies that Dickens's fairy-tale plots are regarded by Dickens himself as an essential part of his novels.

The action of a comedy moves toward an identity which is usually a social identity. In Dickens the family, or a group analogous to a family, is the key to social identity. Hence his recognition scenes are usually genealogical, concerned with discovering unknown fathers and mothers or articulating the correct family relationships. There are often three sets of parental figures attached to a central character, with several doubles of each. First are the actual parents. These are often dead before the story begins, like the fathers of Nicholas Nickleby and David Copperfield, or stagger on weakly for a few pages, like David Copperfield's mother, or are mysterious and emerge at the end, sometimes as bare names unrelated to the story, like Oliver Twist's father or the parents of Little Nell. The father of Sissy Jupe in *Hard Times* deserts her without ever appearing in the novel; the first things we see in *Great Expectations* are the tombstones of Pip's parents. Pip himself is brought up by a sister who is twenty years older and (as we learn on practically the last page of the book) has the same name as his mother. Next come the parental figures of the obstructing society, generally cruel or foolish, and often descended from the harsh stepparents of folktale. Murdstone and his sister, Pip's sister, the pseudomothers of Esther Summerson and Clennam, belong to this group. One very frequent device which combines these two types of relationship is that of the preternaturally loving and hard-working daughter who is the sole support of a weak or foolish father. We have, among others, Little Dorrit, Little Nell, whose grandfather is a compulsive gambler, Jenny Wren in *Our Mutual Friend* with her drunken "child," Madeline Bray in *Nicholas Nickleby,* and, in a different way, Florence Dombey. Naturally the marriage of such a heroine, following on the death of the parent, transfers her to the more congenial society. Finally we have the parental or avuncular figures of the congenial society itself, those who take on a protective relation to the central characters as the story approaches its conclusion. Brownlow in *Oliver Twist,* who adopts the hero, Jarndyce in *Bleak House,* Abel Magwitch in *Great Expectations,* the Cheeryble brothers in *Nicholas Nickleby,* the Boffins in *Our Mutual Friend,* are examples. Abel Magwitch, besides being the ultimate father of Pip, is also the actual father of Estella, which makes Estella in a sense Pip's sister: this was doubtless one reason why Dickens so resisted the conventional ending of marriage for these two. The more realistic developments of New Comedy tend to eliminate this genealogical apparatus. When one of the girls in *Les Précieues ridicules* announces that being so interesting a girl she is quite sure that her real parents are much more interesting people than the ones she appears to have, we do not take her very seriously. But Dickens is always ready to cooperate with the lonely child's fantasies about lost congenial parents, and this marks his affinity with the romantic side of the tradition, the side related to classical romance.

I have used the word "anarchistic" in connection with Dickens's view of society, but it is clear that, so far as his comic structure leads to any sort of vision of a social ideal, that ideal would have to be an intensely paternalistic society, an expanded family. We get a somewhat naive glimpse of this with the Cheeryble brothers in *Nicholas Nickleby,* giving a party where the faithful servitors are brought in at the end for a drink of champagne, expressing undying loyalty and enthusiasm for the patronizing social arrangements. The reader gets the uneasy feeling that he is listening to the commercial. When in *Little Dorrit* Tattycoram runs away from the suffocating geniality of the Meagles family she has to be brought back repentant, though she may well have had much more of the reader's sympathy than Dickens intended her to have. Even the Dedlock ménage in *Bleak House,* hopeless social anachronism as Dickens clearly recognizes it to be, is still close enough to a family to gather a fair amount of the society of the novel around it at the end. In contrast, social parasites often assume the role of a false father. Examples include the Marquis in *A Tale of Two Cities* whose assassin is technically guilty of parricide, Sir Joseph Bowley, the Urizenic friend and father of the poor in *The Chimes,* and the elder Chester in *Barnaby Rudge.*

In New Comedy the obstructing humors absorb most of the character interest: the heroes and heroines are seldom individualized. Such characters as Bonario in *Volpone* or Valère in *Tartuffe* are only pleasant young men. In Dickens too the heroes and heroines resemble humors only in the fact that their responses are predictable, but they are predictable in terms of a norm, and they seldom if ever appear in the ridiculous or self-binding role of the humor. Such characters, who encourage the reader to identify with them, and who might be called norm-figures, could not exist in serious twentieth-century fiction, which belongs to the ironic mode, and sees all its characters as affected in some degree by hampering social forces. But they have some validity in nineteenth-century low mimetic conventions, which present only what is conventionally presentable, and whose heroes and heroines may therefore logically be models of presentability.

Comedy usually depicts the triumph of the young over the old, but Dickens is unusual among comic writers in that so many of his heroes and heroines are children, or are described in ways that associate them with childhood. Nobody has described more vividly than Dickens the reactions of a sensitive child in a Brobdingnagian world dominated by noisome and blundering adults. And because nearly all these children are predestined to belong to the congenial society, they can only be hurt, not corrupted, by the obstructing society. The one striking exception is Pip, whose detachment from the false standards of the obstructing group forms the main theme of *Great Expectations*. But David Copperfield is only superficially affected by his environment, and Oliver Twist escapes from the activities of the Fagin gang as miraculously as Marina does from the brothel in Shakespeare's *Pericles*. Usually this predestined child-figure is a girl. Many of the heroines, even when grown women, are described as "little" or are compared to fairies. A frequent central theme in Dickens is the theme of *Alice in Wonderland:* the descent of the invulnerable girl-child into a grotesque world. In the preface to *The Old Curiosity Shop* Dickens speaks of his interest in the beauty-and-beast archetype, of the girl-child surrounded by monsters, some of them amiable like Kit, others sinister like Quilp. Little Nell descends to this grotesque world and then rejoins the angels; the other heroines marry into the congenial society. The girl-child among grotesques recurs in Florence Dombey's protection by Captain Cuttle, in Little Dorrit's mothering of Maggie, and in many similar scenes. Sometimes an amiable grotesque, Toots or Kit or Smike or Chivery, will attach himself to such a girl-child figure, not good enough to marry her but protesting eternal devotion nonetheless, a kind of late farcical vestige of the Courtly Love convention. Nobody turns up in *The Old Curiosity Shop* good enough to marry Little Nell, which is doubtless one reason why she dies. We may also notice the role of the old curiosity shop itself: it plays little part in the story, but is a kind of threshold symbol of the entrance into the grotesque world, like the rabbit-hole and mirror in the Alice books. Its counterparts appear in the Wooden Midshipman shop in *Dombey and Son,* the Peggotty cottage in *David Copperfield,* the bone-shop of Venus in *Our Mutual Friend,* and elsewhere.

Many of the traditional features of romantic New Comedy reached their highest point of development in nineteenth-century Britain, making it the obvious time and place for a great genius in that form to emerge. One of these, already glanced at, is the domination of narrative genres, along with a moribund drama. Dickens had many dramatic interests, but his genius was for serial romance and not for the stage. Another is the Victorian assumption of moral standards shared between author and reader. This feature makes for melodrama, where the reader emotionally participates in the moral conflict of hero and villain, or of virtue and temptation. The rigidity, or assumed rigidity, of Victorian sexual mores is a great help to a nineteenth-century plot, as it enables an author, not only to make a Wagnerian noise about a woman's extramarital escapade, but to make the most frenzied activity on her part plausible as an effort to conceal the results of it. But the relation of melodrama to the foreground action is far more important than this.

A realistic writer in the New Comedy tradition tends to work out his action on one plane: young and old, hero and humor, struggle for power within the same social group. The more romantic the writer, the more he tends to set over against his humorous world another kind of world, with which the romantic side of his story is associated. In a paper presented to the English Institute nearly twenty years ago, I spoke of the action of romantic Shakespearean comedy as divided between a foreground world of humors and a background "green world," associated with magic, sleep and dreams, and enchanted forests or houses, from which the comic resolution comes. Dickens has no green world, except for a glint or two here and there (e.g., the pastoral retreats in which Smike and Little Nell end their days, Jenny Wren's paradisal dreams, the "beanstalk" abode of Tartar in *Edwin Drood,* and the like), but he does have his own way of dividing his action. I have spoken of the nineteenth-century emphasis on the presentable, on the world of public appearance to which the nineteenth-century novelist is almost entirely confined. Behind this world lies a vast secret world, the world of privacy, where there is little or no communication. For Dickens this world is associated mainly with dreams, memories, and death. He describes it very eloquently at the opening of the third "Quarter" of *The Chimes,* and again in the first paragraph of the third chapter of *A Tale of Two Cities,* besides referring frequently to it throughout his work.

Few can read Dickens without catching the infection of his intense curiosity about the life that lies in the dark houses behind the lights of his loved and hated London. We recognize it even at second hand: when Dylan Thomas's *Under Milk Wood* opens on a night of private dreams we can see an unmistakably Dickensian influence. For most of the ironic fiction of the twentieth century, this secret world is essentially the bedroom and bathroom world of ordinary privacy, as well as the world of sexual drives, perversions, repressions, and infantile fixations that not only complements the public world but conditions one's behavior in it at every point. Characters in twentieth-century fiction have no privacy: there is no distinction between dressing-room and stage. Dickens is by no means unaware of the importance of this aspect of the hidden world, but it is of little use to him as a novelist, and he shows no restiveness about being obliged to exclude it. This is because he is not primarily an ironic writer, like Joyce or Flaubert. What he is really curious about is a hidden world of *romantic* interest, not a world even more squalid and commonplace than the visible one. His detective interest in hidden life is comparable to other aspects of Victorian culture: one thinks of the Pre-Raphaelite paintings where we are challenged to guess what kind of story is being told by the picture and its enigmatic title, or of all the poems of Browning that appeal to us to deduce the reality hidden behind what is presented.

In following the main action of a Dickens novel we are frequently aware of a second form of experience being held up to it like a mirror. Sometimes this is explicitly the world of the stage. The kind of entertainment afforded by the Vincent Crummles troop in *Nicholas Nickleby* parallels the uninhibited melodrama of the main story: the dance of the savage and the Infant Phenomenon, in particular, mirrors the Dickensian theme of the girl-child in the monster-world. In *Hard Times,* where the relation is one of contrast, a circus company symbolizes an approach to experience that Gradgrind has missed out on. The Punch and Judy show in *The Old Curiosity Shop,* one of several popular dramatic entertainments in that book, has been mentioned, and in *Great Expectations* Pip, haunted by the ghost of a father, goes to see Mr. Wopsle in *Hamlet.* Then again, Dickens makes considerable use of the curious convention in New Comedy of the doubled character, who is often literally a twin. In *The Comedy of Errors* the foreground Ephesus and the background Syracuse, in *Twelfth Night* the melancholy courts of Orsino and Olivia, are brought into alignment by twins. Similarly, the foreground action of *Little Dorrit* is related to the background action partly through the concealed twin brother of Flintwinch. In *A Tale of Two Cities,* where the twin theme is at its most complicated, the resemblance of Darnay and Carton brings the two cities themselves into alignment. In *Dombey and Son* the purse-proud world of Dombey and the other social world that it tries to ignore are aligned by the parallel, explicitly alluded to, between Edith Dombey and Alice Brown. There are many other forms of doubling, both of characters and of action, that I have no space here to examine.

The basis for such a dividing of the action might be generalized as follows. There is a hidden and private world of dream and death, out of which all the energy of human life comes. The primary manifestation of this world, in experience, is in acts of destructive violence and passion. It is the source of war, cruelty, arrogance, lust, and grinding the faces of the poor. It produces the haughty lady with her guilty secret, like Lady Dedlock or Edith Dombey or Mrs. Clennam, the lynching mobs that hunt Bill Sikes to death or proclaim the charity of the Protestant religion in *Barnaby Rudge*, the flogging schoolmasters and the hanging judges. It also produces the courage to fight against these things, and the instinctive virtue that repudiates them. In short, the hidden world expresses itself most directly in melodramatic action and rhetoric. It is not so much better or worse than the ordinary world of experience, as a world in which good and evil appear as much stronger and less disguised forces. We may protest that its moods are exaggerated, its actions unlikely, its rhetoric stilted and unconvincing. But if it were not there nothing else in Dickens would be there. We notice that the mainspring of melodramatic action is, like that of humorous action, mainly obsession. We noticed too that Dickens's hair-raising descriptions, like that of Marseilles at the opening of *Little Dorrit* with its repetition of "stare," are based on the same kind of associative rhetoric as the speech of the humors.

From this point of view we can look at the foreground action of the humors in a new light. Humors are, so to speak, petrified by-products of the kind of energy that melodrama expresses more directly. Even the most contemptible humors, the miserly Fledgeby or the hypocritical Heep, are exuberantly miserly and hypocritical: their vices express an energy that possesses them because they cannot possess it. The world they operate in, so far as it is a peaceable and law-abiding world, is a world of very imperfectly suppressed violence. They never escape from the shadow of a power which is at once Eros and Thanatos, and are bound to a passion that is never satisfied by its rationalized objects, but is ultimately self-destructive. In the earlier novels the emotional focus of this self-destroying passion is usually a miser, or a person in some way obsessed with money, like Ralph Nickleby, Dombey, Little Nell's grandfather, or Jonas Chuzzlewit. The folktale association of money and excrement, which points to the psychological origin of miserliness, appears in the "Golden Dustman" theme of *Our Mutual Friend,* and is perhaps echoed in the names Murdstone and Merdle. In the later novels a more explicitly erotic drive gives us the victim-villain figures of Bradley Headstone and Jasper Drood. Food and animals are other images that Dickens often uses in sexual contexts, especially when a miser aspires to a heroine. Arthur Gride in *Nicholas Nickleby* speaks of Madeline Bray as a tasty morsel, and Uriah Heep is compared to a whole zoo of unpleasant animals: the effect is to give an Andromeda pattern to the heroine's situation, and suggest a demonic ferocity behind the domestic foreground. The same principle of construction causes the stock-response humors like Podsnap or Gradgrind to take on a peculiar importance. They represent the fact that an entire society can become mechanized like a humor, or fossilized into its institutions. This could happen to Victorian England, according to *Hard Times,* if it takes the gospel of facts and statistics too literally, and did happen to prerevolutionary France, as described in *A Tale of Two Cities,* dying of what Dickens calls "the leprosy of unreality," and awaiting the melodramatic deluge of the Revolution.

The obstructing humors cannot escape from the ritual habits that they have set up to deal with this disconcerting energy that has turned them into mechanical puppets. The heroes and heroines, however, along with some of the more amiable humors, have the power to plunge into the hidden world of dreams and death, and, though narrowly escaping death in the process, gain from it a renewed life and energy. Sometimes this plunge into the hidden world is symbolized by a distant voyage. The incredible Australia that makes a magistrate out of Wilkins Micawber also enables the hunted convict Magwitch to become an ambiguous but ultimately genuine fairy godfather. Walter Gay in *Dombey and Son* returns from the West Indies, remarkably silent, long after he has been given up for dead, and the reader follows Martin Chuzzlewit into a place, ironically called Eden, where he is confidently expected to die and nearly does die, but where he goes through a metamorphosis of character that fits him for the comic conclusion. Other characters, including Dick Swiveller, Pip, and Esther Summerson, go into a delirious illness with the same result. *Our Mutual Friend* has a complex pattern of resurrection imagery connected with dredging the Thames, reviving from drowning, finding treasure buried in dust-heaps, and the like; a similar pattern of digging up the dead in *A Tale of Two Cities* extends from the stately Dr. Manette to the grotesque Jerry Cruncher. We notice too that the sinister society is often introduced in a kind of wavering light between sleep and waking: the appearance of the faces of Fagin and Monks at Oliver Twist's window and the alleged dreams of Abbie Flintwinch in *Little Dorrit* are examples. The most uninhibited treatment of this plunge into the world of death and dreams occurs, as we should expect, in the Christmas Books, where Scrooge and Trotty Veck see in vision a tragic version of their own lives, and one which includes their own deaths, then wake up to renewed festivity. It seems clear that the hidden world, though most of its more direct expressions are destructive and terrible, contains within itself an irresistible power of renewing life.

The hidden world is thus, once again in literature, the world of an invincible Eros, the power strong enough to force a happy ending on the story in defiance of all probability, pushing all the obstructing humors out of the way, or killing them if they will not get out of the way, getting the attractive young people disentangled from their brothers and sisters and headed for the right beds. It dissolves all hardening social institutions and reconstitutes society on its sexual basis of the family, the shadowy old fathers and mothers being replaced by new and livelier successors. When a sympathetic character dies, a strongly religious projection of this power often appears: the "Judgment" expected shortly by Miss Flite in *Bleak House,* for instance, stands in apocalyptic contrast to the Chancery court. Dickens's Eros world is, above all, a designing and manipulating power. The obstructing humor can do only what his humor makes him do, and toward the end of the story he becomes the helpless pawn of a chess game in which black can never ultimately win.

The victorious hidden world is not the world of nature in the Rousseauistic context of that word. The people who talk about this kind of nature in Dickens are such people as Mrs. Merdle in *Little Dorrit,* Mrs. Chick in *Dombey and Son,* and Wackford Squeers—not an encouraging lot. Like most romancers, Dickens gives a prominent place to the fool or "natural"—Smike, Mr. Dick, Barnaby Rudge—whose instincts make up for retarded intelligence. But such people are privileged: elsewhere nature and *social* education, or human experience, are always associated. To say that Dora Copperfield is an unspoiled child of nature is also to say that she is a spoiled child. Dickens's nature is a human nature which is the same kind of thing as the power that creates art, a designing and shaping power. This is also true of Shakespeare's green world, but Dickens's Eros world is not the conserving force that the green world is, which revitalizes a society without altering its structure. At the end of a Shakespeare comedy there is usually a figure of authority, like Prospero or the various dukes, who represents this social conservation. We have nothing in Dickens to correspond to such figures: the nearest to them are the empty Santa Claus masks of the Cheerybles, Boffin, and the reformed Scrooge. For all its domestic and sentimental Victorian setting, there is a revolutionary and subversive, almost a nihilistic, quality in Dickens's melodrama that is post-Romantic, has inherited the experience of the French Revolution, and looks forward to the world of Freud, Marx, and the existential thriller.

I used the word "absurd" earlier about Dickens's melodramatic plots, suggesting that they were creatively and not incompetently absurd. In our day the word "absurd" usually refers to the absence of purpose or meaning in life and experience, the so-called metaphysical absurd. But for literary criticism the formulating of the theory of the absurd should not be left entirely to disillusioned theologians. In literature it is design, the forming and shaping power, that is absurd. Real life does not start or stop; it never ties up loose ends; it never manifests meaning or purpose except by blind accident; it is never comic or tragic, ironic or romantic, or anything else that has a shape. Whatever gives form and pattern to fiction, whatever technical skill keeps us turning the pages to get to the end, is absurd, and contradicts our sense of reality. The great Victorian realists subordinate their storytelling skill to their representational skill. Theirs is a dignified, leisurely vehicle that gives us time to look at the scenery. They have formed our stock responses to fiction, so that even when traveling at the much higher speed of drama, romance, or epic we still keep trying to focus our eyes on the incidental and transient. Most of us feel that there is something else in Dickens, something elemental, yet unconnected with either realistic clarity or philosophical profundity. What it is connected with is a kind of story that fully gratifies the hope expressed, according to Lewis Carroll, by the original of Alice, that "there will be nonsense in it." The silliest character in *Nicholas Nickleby* is the hero's mother, a romancer who keeps dreaming of impossible happy endings for her children. But the story itself follows her specifications and not those of the sensible people. The obstructing humors in Dickens are absurd because they have overdesigned their lives. But the kind of design that they parody is produced by another kind of energy, and one which insists, absurdly and yet irresistibly, that what is must never take final precedence over what ought to be.

ROBERT ALTER

The Demons of History
in Dickens's Tale

A *Tale of Two Cities* has probably given serious critics of Dickens more
trouble than any other of his novels. Written at the height of Dickens's
artistic maturity, it seems almost willfully to turn away from the very
modes of imagination that had made him great and to stress some of the
facile formulas that had merely made him popular. From the first, admirers of Dickens have sensed this book to be an uncharacteristic expression
of his genius, while Dickens's detractors have seized upon it as a transparent revelation of his general weakness as a novelist. The novel offers good
evidence for both views, though the former seems to me on the whole the
more cogent of the two. On the one hand, it is clear that Dickens was
attempting something new, as he himself confesses in his letters, in treating
this whole historical subject. The fact, on the other hand, that the general
strategy of this novel differs from that of his other fiction has the effect of
leaving certain regrettable conventional elements nakedly exposed which,
in the more typical novels, are submerged in the great swirl of brilliant
fantastication that can only be called Dickensian. In *Little Dorrit, Bleak
House, Great Expectations, Our Mutual Friend,* the teeming life of Dickensian
invention tends to draw our attention away from the imaginative thinness
of the heroes and heroines, the contrived coincidences, the strained notes
of melodrama, the moments of dewy-eyed, lip-serving religiosity, while the
more intently dramatic presentation of character and event in *A Tale of
Two Cities* frequently stresses just these qualities.

The *Tale,* then, is conspicuously the uneven work of a writer who, in

From *Novel: A Forum on Fiction* 2, no. 2 (Winter 1969). © 1969 by Novel Corp.

his greatest novels as well, persists in a kind of splendid, self-transcending unevenness. It is essential, however, to try to see just what he was aiming at in this uncharacteristic book, for his peculiar method of historical fiction here does enable him to make palpable to the imagination a realm of experience that is generally beyond the scope of his other novels. If Dickens's Two Cities in the age of revolution lack the vivid humor and warmth, the intimate feel of bizarre yet familiar British experience, associated with the contemporary England of his other novels, we should not dismiss the *Tale* for failing to be another *Pickwick* but should rather seek to understand why Dickens chose to restrict the role in it of just such appealing characteristics.

The term Dickens stresses in his correspondence to distinguish the technique of the *Tale* from that of his previous novels is "picturesque," and that will do nicely for the book if we extend its meaning beyond the limited sense of "dramatic immediacy" which Dickens seems to have had in mind. Most of Dickens's fiction is boldly visual, but the visualization typically concentrates on fascinating and eccentric details, wonderful gargoyles, to borrow George Orwell's happy metaphor, rather than architectural wholes. In *A Tale of Two Cities,* on the other hand, the visual elements are deployed panoramically, often in the compositional arrangements of a large painted canvas. As nowhere else in his writing, Dickens wants to generalize his subject, and so he repeatedly holds the novel—images, characters, events—at a long distance to be seen in broad overview, its materials arranged in manifestly formal patterns. This method might well be described as picturesque, or a little more precisely, as scenic, for the *Tale* is a novel where the scene is the real event. The individual human actors are frequently no more than secondary elements of the scenes of which they are part; and the episodes that focus merely on the personages, isolated from the vivid panorama which is more often foreground than background, frequently reveal the novel at its weakest.

The novels of Dickens's maturity, as modern criticism has made abundantly clear, convey much of their meaning through the elaborate evocation of symbolic atmosphere. This is true of the *Tale* as well, but with this difference: the symbolic atmosphere does not simply give larger resonance to what happens in the novel—ultimately, it *is* what happens in the novel, for the subject as Dickens conceives it can only be represented in large symbolic terms. The plane of symbolic generalization on which the action takes place is apparent from the first paragraph. The narrator begins not with his protagonists but with the times, surveying the state of civilization in France and England in the year 1775, at once fixing the contradictions of the age in an emphatic series of formally balanced contrasts—"it was the season of Light, it was the season of Darkness, it was the spring of hope, it was the winter of despair." The capitalization of Light and Darkness, perhaps an ironic allusion to the allegorical use of such capitalized nouns in eighteenth-century English poetry, is very much to the point of the whole novel, which one could say is really "about" Light and Darkness (though chiefly the latter) in all their traditional symbolic associations.

A dank, viscous murkiness pervades the first part of the novel, and, throughout, a clouded somberness of atmosphere is sustained in the most effective scenes, where the prevailing gloom is merely accentuated by the pale inadequate glimmerings of artificial illumination or the ominous glow of violent red fires. Most of the major scenes are set at night, and there is something uncannily nocturnal even about those that supposedly take place in the light of day.

The action begins with a mail-coach making its arduous way through a clammy and impenetrable mist. When Jarvis Lorry arrives at his destination, the obscurity in the room where he meets Lucie Manette is so thick that he can scarcely make her out as he stands amidst heavy dark tables that "had been oiled and oiled, until the two tall candles on the table in the middle of the room were gloomily reflected on every leaf; as if *they* were buried, in deep graves of black mahogany, and no light to speak of could be expected from them until they were dug out." This vigorous twist of visual fantasy binds darkness and light firmly to the novel's central themes of death and resurrection, imprisonment and liberation. A few pages later, when the setting shifts to France for the first time, darkness will be more explicitly associated with the forces through which the aristocracy smothers the life of the people: in the quarter of Saint Antoine, it becomes something that can be smelled and almost touched, the dense polluted atmosphere of a "steep dark shaft of dirt and poison" that is not only the stairway to Manette's garret but also the symbolic dwelling place, the prison-house, of the poor of France.

With this accumulation of imagery, Defarge's simple statement to the crazed shoemaker-doctor in his darkened attic has a special poignancy: "I want . . . to let in a little more light here. You can bear a little more?" And the vision later of the Marquis's gloomy chateau, a single flambeau "disturbing the darkness" within it, hints at the precarious ambiguity of the relationship of darkness to light—the Marquis and his kind, by interring the people in a black prison of oppression, finally transform the people itself into a terrible force of darkness.

What Dickens is ultimately concerned with in *A Tale of Two Cities* is not a particular historical event—that is simply his chosen dramatic setting—but rather the relationship between history and evil, how violent oppression breeds violent rebellion which becomes a new kind of oppression. His account of the *ancien régime* and the French Revolution is a study in civilized man's vocation for proliferating moral chaos, and in this one important regard the *Tale* is the most compellingly "modern" of his novels. He also tries hard, through the selfless devotion of his more exemplary characters, to suggest something of mankind's potential for moral regeneration; but he is considerably less convincing in this effort, partly because history itself offers so little evidence which the imagination of hope can use to sustain itself.

The most powerful imaginings of the novel reach out again and again to touch ultimate possiblities of violence, whether in the tidal waves of mass destruction or in the hideous inventiveness of individual acts of cruelty. In the first chapter we are introduced to France through the detailed description of an execution by horrible mutilation, and to England by a rapid series of images of murder, mob violence, and hangings. Throughout the novel, the English mob is in potential what the French revolutionary hordes are in bloody fact. At the English trial of the falsely accused Darnay, the "ogreish" spectators, eagerly awaiting the condemnation, vie with one another in their lip-smacking description of how a man looks being drawn and quartered. Again in France, the details of torture and savagery exercise an obscene fascination over the imagination of the characters (and perhaps of the writer as well)—nightmarish images of tongues torn out with pincers, gradual dismemberment, boiling oil and lead poured into gaping wounds, float through the darkness of the novel and linger on the retina of the memory.

The energy of destruction that gathers to such acts of concentrated horror pulses through the whole world of the novel, pounding at its foundations. It is conceived as an elemental force in nature which works through men as well. Dover Beach as Jarvis Lorry contemplates it near the beginning of the novel is a replica in nature of the revolution to come, the scene most strikingly serving as event: "the sea did what it liked, and what it liked was destruction. It thundered at the town, and thundered at the cliffs, and brought the coast down madly." The image of the revolutionary mob, much later in the novel, is simply the obverse of this vision of the ocean as chaos and darkness: "The sea of black and threatening waters, and of destructive upheaving of wave against wave, whose depths were yet unfathomed and whose forces were yet unknown. The remorseless sea of turbulently swaying shapes, voices of vengeance." These same pitiless forces are present in the rainstorm that descends upon the quiet Soho home of the Manettes as Lucie, Darnay, and Carton watch: the lightning, harbinger of revolution, that they see leaping from the stormy dark is the only light that can be born from the murky atmosphere of this world—the hot light of destruction. Later the revolution is also likened to a great earthquake, and when Madame Defarge adds to this her grim declaration—"Tell wind and fire where to stop . . . but don't tell me"—all four elements of the traditional world-picture have been associated with the forces of blind destruction, earth and water and fire and air.

There is, ultimately, a peculiar impersonality about this novel, for it is intended to dramatize the ways in which human beings become the slaves of impersonal forces, at last are made inhuman by them. In order to show the play of these elemental forces in history, Dickens adopts a generalizing novelistic technique which frequently approaches allegory, the mode of imagination traditionally used for the representation of cosmic powers doing battle or carrying out a destined plan. The Darkness and Light of the novel's first sentence are almost immediately supported by the introduction of two explicitly allegorical figures in the same chapter: the Woodman, Fate; and the Farmer, Death. In the action that follows, events and characters often assume the symbolic postures and formal masks of allegory.

The man seen clinging to the chains of the Marquis's carriage, "all covered with dust, white as a spectre, tall as a spectre," is no longer the flesh-and-blood father of the child murdered by the Marquis but has become a ghastly Messenger, sent to exact vengeance from the nobleman. The Marquis himself, always seen from an immense distance of implacable irony, is far more an allegorical representation of the French ruling classes than an individual character. The elaborate figure of a new face struck to stone by the Gorgon's head which is used to describe the Marquis's death is entirely appropriate, for his death is not a "realistic" murder but the symbolic acting out of the inexorable workings of retribution. In this novel, it is fitting that one Frenchwoman should actually be called The Vengeance, whom the narrator at the end will ironically bid by name to shout loud after a Thérèse Defarge who is forever beyond answering. It is equally fitting that Charles Darnay's French name, Evrémonde, should sound like an English name of a different sort: he is the Everyman who is drawn to the heart of destruction, virtually gives up his life there, in legal fact and physical appearance, to be reborn only through the expiatory death of another self, and so to return to his beloved, whose name means "light."

One of the most striking symbolic tableaux in the novel, the haunting scene of the four incendiaries setting out across the countryside to burn the castles of the aristocracy, is directly modeled on a great allegory of the New Testament, for the four revolutionaries become the Four Horsemen of the Apocalypse, spreading universal ruin: "four fierce figures trudged away, east, west, north, and south, along the night-enshrouded roads, guided by the beacon they had lighted, toward their next destination." When, on the other hand, the allegory moves in from such anonymous, symbolic figures to characters with whom we are more intimately acquainted, it tends to be somewhat less successful. The fatal confrontation, for example, at the end of the novel between Miss Pross and Madame Defarge is clearly presented as a battle between pitiless French savagery and staunch English humanity ("You shall not get the better of me," says Miss Pross, "I am an Englishwoman"), between Darkness and Light, evil and good, the power of hate and the power of love. Neither combatant can understand, literally or figuratively, the language of the other, and the struggle is one to the death. One senses an obtrusive neatness here in the symmetrically symbolic roles into which the characters have been pressed: if Madame Defarge, as the exemplary Woman of the Revolution in the novel, is an appropriate champion of Darkness in this final conflict, Miss Pross is enlisted as the champion of Light only with some strain on credence. Miss Pross, of course, prevails "with the vigorous tenacity of love, always so much stronger than hate," but her victory may seem a little contrived because the novel has demonstrated the energy and tenacity of hate so much more forcefully than it has shown the power of love.

In a world dominated by vast inexorable forces, it is understandable that human action should often take the form of ritual. Ritual, after all, involves the careful repetition of a series of prescribed gestures which serve as a means of placating the inhuman powers or of acting out man's fealty to them, his willing or coerced identity of purpose with them. On its lowest level, ritual expresses itself in purely obsessive action—Doctor Manette's desperate cobbling, the newly-imprisoned Darnay's compulsive counting of steps. Appropriately, the obsessive ritual must be countered by a conscious ritual of exorcism: Jarvis Lorry hacks the cobbler's bench to pieces while Miss Pross holds a candle for him, and then they burn and bury the pieces, with the uneasy feeling of complicity in some terrible crime. Other ritualistic acts in the novel have a compulsive aspect, but their main purpose, as is generally the case with ritual, is broadly symbolic. The grim knitting of the wives of the Revolution, led by Madame Defarge, expresses in regular nervous motion the irresistible impulse of vengeance working within the women, and, in the allegorical scheme of the novel, it is made clear that they are the Fates, knitting an irreversible pattern of doom.

In general, Dickens's imagination of the revolutionists is founded on an insight into the religious nature of their revolutionary fervor. The faith to which they adhere is a kind of anti-Christianity, and Dickens takes pains to note that a replica of the guillotine—the symbol of unpitying vengeance—replaces the cross—the symbol of redeeming love—on every breast. This is, of course, the final balanced antithesis of Light over against Darkness in the novel. Sydney Carton, who possesses the greatest love, to lay down his life for his friend, achieves an imitation of Christ in his death, and the novel's scheme of symmetric contrasts culminates—perhaps a little too neatly—in his ascent to the scaffold, the stage of the Revolution's central rite, reciting the words of Christ, "I am the Resurrection and the Life."

Some of the most compelling scenes in this scenic novel are at once allegorical tableaux and solemn sacraments of the Revolution. The wine-cask smashed outside the Defarge shop provides the opportunity for a sort of red mass in which the wine, tasted by all the people, smeared on their lips and faces, becomes blood; there is, pointedly, no bread of life—no body of Christ—for the hungry in this mass, and for that very reason the blood is solely a portent of destruction, not a promise of redemption. Much later, the ambiguity of wine and blood is recalled in another revolutionary rite, the horrendous thronging of the people to the grindstone to sharpen their blood-stained weapons, to renew themselves and their instruments for the holy purpose of slaughter.

The climactic ritual, however, in which the destructive spirit of the Revolution is celebrated, is the great frenzied dance, the Carmagnole. The movements of the dancers vividly show forth the satanic aspect of the revolutionary faith, its commitment to the elemental force of violence. Thus, the crowd of five thousand, with The Vengeance in the lead, appears before Lucie "dancing like five thousand demons, . . . keeping a ferocious time that was like a gnashing of teeth in unison." At first they seem "a mere storm" of red caps, but then Lucie sees them as "some ghastly apparition of a dance-figure gone raving mad." The dancers, that is, recapitulate scenic or symbolic events that have occurred earlier in the novel—the fierceness of the storm sweeping down on Soho, the madness of the sea pounding at Dover Beach, the various ghastly apparitions, victims of despotism and spirits of retribution alike. The Carmagnole is both an acting out of the meaning of the Revolution and a rite that inspires its celebrants with a strengthened dedication to the revolutionary cause—"a means of angering the blood, bewildering the senses, and steeling the heart." And as Dickens sums up the picture he has painted, the human figures in it are seen as representative "types"—that is, allegorical embodiments—of the movement of large forces through history: "The maidenly bosom bared to this, the pretty almost-child's head distracted, the delicate foot mincing in this slough of blood and dirt, were types of the disjointed time."

It is often claimed that the life of this novel is thin and meager because Dickens sets the major action away from the English world in which he was imaginatively at home. Quite to the contrary, it seems to me that the French scenes are the ones that really fire his imagination here, and that the most brilliantly realized character in the novel is the French revolutionary mob. The fact that a corporate entity—the many-headed monster which Dickens, like Shakespeare, saw in the mob—should so impose itself as a distinctive presence has, I think, a great deal to do with the large allegorical perspective to which the novel recurs, its habit of pulling back from the observation of particulars to see its whole subject in symbolic panorama.

The bold conception, to be sure, of an allegorical plan for the novel hardly guarantees the book's artistic success, and there is at least one very serious flaw in the execution of the plan. The symbolic conflict around which the novel is organized ultimately alludes, as I have noted, to an opposition between promised regeneration in Christ and threatened annihilation by the forces of the anti-Christ. The trouble is that while the threat of moral anarchy is as constant and close to Dickens as his own heartbeat, his imagination of resurrection, whether for individuals or for societies, is conventionally pious and little more. Nevertheless, the treatment of history in *A Tale of Two Cities* does possess a certain imaginative authority because it generally concentrates on history as the medium for the implementation of evil, which is, alas, what history has generally been, what it seems now more than ever to be.

In this connection, the emphasis placed in the novel on the idea of inevitability is worth noting. The essence of history, at least when we view it retrospectively, is inevitability, for history is before all else the record of what has already happened, which, because it has already happened, must forever be as it is and not otherwise. By dramatically translating this notion of inevitability into the irreversible progress of violence in the life of a nation, Dickens, who is usually anything but an austere writer, gives this novel a kind of oblique reflection of the stern grandeur of the Greek tragedies, where inexorable fate works itself out through human lives. "At last it is come," Defarge declares to his wife as the Revolution begins, the affirmation of an eternally destined decree ringing through his words. It is as though a law of moral physics were operating with mathematical certainty in the events of history: "Crush humanity out of shape once more, under similar hammers, and it will twist itself into the same tortured forms."

This sense of inevitability, I would suggest, is deliberately reinforced by the use of coincidence in the plot. After all, Dickens surely could have invented some credible subterfuge to get Carton into Darnay's cell without having Miss Pross discover her long-lost brother Solomon in the police-spy, Barsad, at the crucial moment, without the superfluous abundance of evidence against Barsad in the testimonies of Mr. Lorry, Carton himself, and even Jerry Cruncher, all conveniently present just when needed. In compounding the initial coincidence of physical similarity between Darnay and Carton with all these other coincidences, Dickens demonstrates not only his own habitual delight in mystification and manipulation but also how the lines of destiny imperceptibly converge on a single, inevitable point—in this case, the scaffold of the guillotine, where Sydney Carton will take the place of Charles Darnay on the day when fifty-two heads have been appointed to roll, as surely as there are fifty-two weeks in the fixed annual cycle.

Against this background of inexorable destiny, the "happy ending" of *A Tale of Two Cities* includes an element of unillusioned realism absent from the conclusions to Dickens's other books. In the world of this novel, expiation must be made—the phrase is invoked at the climax of Carton's final prophecy—both by individuals and by nations. The aristocracy must pay the price of the iniquities it has perpetrated, and the revolutionaries will pay the price of their own terrible violence. Charles Darnay, descendant of the Evrémondes, must die in the Place of the Revolution, if only vicariously, through his double. Nobody gets off scot-free from the encounter with history: curiously, a price is even exacted from the innocent Miss Pross for her conquest of Madame Defarge; the pistol-shot that destroys Thérèse Defarge leaves Miss Pross stone-deaf till her dying day.

I have been emphasizing how Dickens visualized history in a more or less ordered symbolic scheme, but it is important to add that his visualization reaches moments of intensity which have to be called visionary. Dickens, as criticism in the past two decades has amply recognized, was a hallucinated genius, fascinated and bedeviled by the imagined persons and events cast up from the depths of his own inner world. When he speaks in the preface to the *Tale* of the "complete possession" the book had over him while he wrote it, he uses that term in the sense of possession by spirits, or demons. What he says of the unforgettable vision of the revolutionary mob at the grindstone could easily be extended to his entire recreation of history in the novel: "All this was seen in a moment, as the vision of a drowning man, or of any human creature at any very great pass, could see a world as if it were there." Dickens in his mature years was in his own emotional life a drowning man, fiercely refusing to go under, creating out of his increasingly pained sense of life great and sometimes still exuberant fiction through a heroic exertion of will. In *A Tale of Two Cities* the drowning man's vision achieves piercing moments of prophetic comprehensiveness because it is focused on history itself and on the vast moral struggle he saw implicit in history. Whatever the faults of the book, there is still much in it that can speak to us in the very great pass to which our own history has come, with its recurrent premonitions of a universal drowning.

RAYMOND WILLIAMS

The Creation of Consciousness
and Dickens's Vision of the City

It is still widely believed that the traditional culture of the English people
was broken and disintegrated by the Industrial Revolution. What then
emerged, it is said, was on the one hand a debased synthetic commercial
culture—the world of the newspapers and popular entertainment; on the
other hand an increasingly threatened minority culture—an educated tradition within which the finest literature and thought of the time sought to
maintain and extend itself and to keep its connections, its continuities,
with the best work of the past. Each of these descriptions seems to me
partially true but when we have given them all the weight we can they still
do not, taken together, describe the whole situation in urban and industrial England, and above all in its culture; in the novel especially. What is
missing is that element of authentic popular response to the new conditions of life, through which in many ways—in new radical institutions and
beliefs, but also in the crowded many-voiced anonymous world of idioms,
stories, songs, jokes, parodies, sentiments, caricatures—people described
and responded to their unprecedented experiences.

We do not yet know nearly enough about either of these kinds. The
educated world has of course neglected them. In the last few years we have
been getting some preliminary accounts: both of the radical culture which
is so central an achievement, and in more fragmentary ways of the anonymous culture, which has a continuing, often oral, traditional strength. And
as we begin to see these more clearly we can see the condition of literature

From *The English Novel: From Dickens to Lawrence.* © 1970 by Raymond
Williams. Chatto & Windus, 1970.

in this rapidly changing society, and especially the condition of the novel, in some very new ways. We can especially realise our good fortune that at the most critical point in this history—at the time of the critical remaking of the novel and of the critical emergence of a new urban popular culture—we have a novelist of genius who is involved in both; we have Dickens.

The shift of emphasis involved here is of course very difficult. It extends its changes of viewpoint—some of them very radical—into a whole structure of critical and social beliefs. Dickens certainly is now more admired, more respected, more carefully studied than he has ever been, and especially within a minority critical public; the majority of readers he has of course always kept. But I do not think this would be happening in the way it now is if the other revaluation were not also going on, in what amounts to a recovery of some of the central history and culture of our own people: a history and a culture that had been excluded, set aside, by the rigidities of an old educated world. We are beginning to know now, with increasing substance and precision, our inherited popular culture; and to know its difference from a folk culture, which is perhaps the hardest point to grasp.

There are always eventual interactions, of a limited kind, between folk and polite culture. But characteristically each occurs in a relatively rigid and immobile society: in peasant communities and in courts; or in the country and in the city when these are relatively distinct. When the society becomes mobile, both internally and as a whole, these simpler kinds disappear in their old forms. Through many transitional stages we come to different cultures, where the terms that matter are not "folk" and "polite" (or "aristocratic"); but significantly, "popular" and "educated." In a class society of a modern kind these characteristically express a *relationship* rather than a distinction or separation. Thus when an "educated" culture is called, as so often, a "minority" culture, we have to see this as an indication of a social fact and relationship: the class limitation of education. "Popular culture" is similarly a fact of the whole society, not of a distinct and separate area as in "folk."

Each kind of culture, in a class society, is aware of the other: involved, critical, responsive, hostile. And "popular culture" is especially complicated, because it includes both what is provided *for* the majority and what is made *by* them. It would be simpler if these were wholly separable areas, but as the whole history of fiction (among many other cases) indicates, they are not and cannot be. When we say of Dickens that he draws on a popular culture, we do not mean that this is unaffected or that he is unaffected by the educated culture. Many serious ideas had been popularised, and there were earlier recognised artists who had expressed this popular life. No more can we say of George Eliot, who is the crucial contrasting case, that she draws on an educated culture (which is obviously true) but not on a popular culture (which especially in popular religion and rural life is as obviously part of her world). It is really the interaction, indeed the disturbance induced in her work by the changing relations between the "educated" and "popular" life and thought, that is decisive.

Similarly in popular culture, even before we get to Dickens's creative uses of it, we have to notice a range and a contradiction. It goes all the way from authentic popular response in idioms and values, through authentic popular demand for certain kinds of issue and story, through important earlier art and thought which had been based on or accepted into its sensibility, to exploitation and manipulation of popular response and demand (as in so much tendentious magazine fiction written to direct or deflect the interests of the majority) and finally to that most difficult area of all, in which certain adjustments, resignations, illusions, fantasies— born of the whole experience of the society—became popular and even self-generating. These are authentic enough in that they are widely represented, but they are also inauthentic in the sense that they are incapable of revealing, that they prevent others revealing, certain actual interests and truths. What is composed in particular (and this is very relevant to Dickens) is a self-defensive, alternately jolly or cynical tone and mood, which can take over and become very difficult to distinguish from the humorous or ironic popular observation of reality.

That is our central critical problem in Dickens. But it is masked by another which we had better deal with directly. By the standards of one kind of novel, which in England has been emphasised as the great tradition, Dickens's faults—what are seen as his faults—are so many and so central as to produce embarrassment. Almost every criterion of that other kind of novel—characteristically, the fiction of an educated minority— works against him. His characters are not "rounded" and developing but "flat" and emphatic. They are not slowly revealed but directly presented. Significance is not enacted in mainly tacit and intricate ways but is often directly presented in moral address and indeed exhortation. Instead of the controlled language of analysis and comprehension he uses, directly, the language of persuasion and display. His plots depend often on arbitrary coincidences, on sudden revelations and changes of heart. He offers not the details of psychological process but the finished articles: the social and psychological products.

Yet we get nowhere—critically nowhere—if we apply the standards of this kind of fiction to another and very different kind. We get nowhere if we try to salvage from Dickens what is compatible with that essentially alternative world, and then for the rest refer mildly and kindly to the great entertainer and to the popular tradition: not explaining but explaining away. The central case we have to make is that Dickens could write a new kind of novel—fiction uniquely capable of realising a new kind of reality— just because he shared with the new urban popular culture certain decisive experiences and responses. That he shared with it, also, certain adjustments and illusions is a significant but minor part of this case. Unless we acknowledge this new reality—essentially it is the reality of the new kind of city—we shall go on discussing his methods in abstract and marginal ways. Yet if we can grasp this new experience, we shall see how much of his method—his creative method—necessarily follows from it; that it is the only or at least the major way in which that unprecedented experience could be seen and valued; that it is a breakthrough in the novel from which those other novelists of cities—Dostoyevski and Kafka are the most immediate names—in their own ways learned. Not apology then. Not a slow resigned acceptance that he is not after all George Eliot. But emphasis— critical emphasis—that he is a new kind of novelist and that his method *is* his experience.

Of course we can acknowledge as a fact in itself his marvellous energy. But then the energy and the methods are in fact inseparable. It is through his very specific plots and characters and not in spite of them that he makes his intense and involving world. He takes and transforms certain traditional methods: not like George Eliot into more locally observed actions or more particularly known individuals or more carefully charted stages of growth of a relationship; but, in his own way, into a dramatic method which is uniquely capable of expressing the experience of living in cities.

As we stand and look back at a Dickens novel the general movement we remember—the decisive movement—is a hurrying seemingly random passing of men and women, each heard in some fixed phrase, seen in some fixed expression: a way of seeing men and women that belongs to the street. There is at first an absence of ordinary connection and development. These men and women do not so much relate as pass each other and then sometimes collide. Nor often in the ordinary way do they speak to each other. They speak at or past each other, each intent above all on defining through his words his own identity and reality; in fixed self-descriptions, in voices raised emphatically to be heard through and past other similar voices. But then as the action develops, unknown and unacknowledged relationships, profound and decisive connections, definite and committing recognitions and avowals are as it were forced into consciousness. These are the real and inevitable relationships and connections, the necessary recognitions and avowals of any human society. But they are of a kind that are obscured, complicated, mystified, by the sheer rush and noise and miscellaneity of this new and complex social order.

This creation of consciousness—of recognitions and relationships—seems to me indeed to be the purpose of Dickens's developed fiction. The need for it is at the centre of his social and personal vision:

> Oh for a good spirit who would take the housetops off, with a more potent and benignant hand than the lame demon in the tale, and show a Christian people what dark shapes issue from amidst their homes, to swell the retinue of the Destroying Angel as he moves forth among them. For only one night's view of the pale phantoms rising from the scenes of our too long neglect; and from the thick and sullen air where Vice and Fever propagate together, raining the tremendous social retributions which are ever pouring down, and ever coming thicker. Bright and blest the morning that should rise on such a night; for men, delayed no more by stumbling-blocks of their own making, which are but specks of dust on the path between them and eternity, would then apply themselves, like creatures of one common origin, owning one duty to the Father of one family, and tending to one common end, to make the world a better place. Not the less bright and blest would that day be for rousing some who have never looked out upon the world of human life around them, to a knowledge of their own relation to it, and for making them acquainted with a perversion of nature in their own contracted sympathies and estimates; as great, and yet as natural in its development, when once begun, as the lowest degradation known. But no such day had ever dawned for Mr. Dombey, or his wife; and the course of each was taken.

That potent and benignant hand, which takes off the housetops and shows the shapes and phantoms which arise from neglect and indifference; which clears the air so that people can see and acknowledge each other, overcoming that contraction of sympathy which is against nature: that hand is the hand of the novelist; it is Dickens seeing himself. And it's significant that this comes in a description of the city, in that same forty-seventh chapter of *Dombey and Son*. He is describing, in the image of a dense black cloud hanging over the city, the human and moral consequences of an indifferent and "unnatural" society. It is an image to which he often returns: the obscurity, the darkness, the fog that keeps us from seeing each other clearly and from seeing the relation between ourselves and our actions, ourselves and others.

And this is another aspect of Dickens's originality. He is able to dramatise those social institutions and consequences which are not accessible to ordinary physical observation. He takes them and presents them as if they were persons or natural phenomena. Sometimes as the black cloud or as the fog through which people are groping and looking for each other. Sometimes as the Circumlocution Office, or Bleeding Heart Yard, where a way of life takes on physical shape. Sometimes as if they were human characters, like Shares in *Our Mutual Friend,* and of course the Great Expectations. This connects with his moral naming of characters: Gradgrind, M'Choakumchild, Merdle. It connects also but in a less obvious way with a kind of observation which again belongs to the city: a perception, one might say, that the most evident inhabitants of cities are buildings, and that there is at once a connection and a confusion between the shapes and appearance of buildings and the real shapes and appearances of the people who live in them.

As in this passage from *Little Dorrit*:

> Upon that establishment of state, the Merdle establishment in Harley Street, Cavendish Square, there was the shadow of no more common wall than the fronts of other establishments of state on the opposite side of the street. Like unexceptionable society, the opposing rows of houses in Harley Street were very grim with one another. Indeed, the mansions and their inhabitants were so much alike in that respect, that the people were often to be found drawn up on opposite sides of dinner-tables, in the shade of their own loftiness, staring at the other side of the way with the dullness of the houses.
>
> Everybody knows how like the street, the two dinner-rows of people who take their stand by the street will be. The expressionless uniform twenty houses, all to be knocked at and rung at in the same form, all approachable by the same dull steps, all

fended off by the same pattern of railing, all with the same impracticable fire-escapes, the same inconvenient fixtures in their heads, and everything without exception to be taken at a high valuation—who has not dined with these? The house so drearily out of repair, the occasional bow-window, the stuccoed house, the newly-fronted house, the corner house with nothing but angular rooms, the house with the blinds always down, the house with the hatchment always up, the house where the collector has called for one quarter of an idea, and found nobody at home—who has not dined with these?

The house that nobody will take, and is to be had a bargain—who does not know her? The showy house that was taken for life by the disappointed gentleman, and which does not suit him at all—who is unacquainted with that haunted habitation?

This is a formal description which takes the analogy of houses and people right through, and in the end playfully. But it recurs in more local insights, where the house and the life being lived in it are indistinguishable (this is again from *Little Dorrit*):

The debilitated old house in the city, wrapped in its mantle of soot, and leaning heavily on the crutches that had partaken of its decay and worn out with it, never knew a healthy or a cheerful interval, let what would betide. You should alike find rain, hail, frost and thaw lingering in that dismal enclosure, when they had vanished from other places; and as to snow, you should see it there for weeks, long after it had changed from yellow to black, slowly weeping away its grimy life. The place had no other adherents. As to street noises, the rumbling of wheels in the lane merely rushed in at the gateway in going past, and rushed out again: making the listening mistress Affery feel as if she were deaf, and recovered the sense of hearing by instantaneous flashes. So with whistling, singing, talking, laughing, and all pleasant human sounds, they leaped the gap in a moment, and went upon their way.

Or again:

It was now summertime; a grey, hot, dusty evening. They rode to the top of Oxford Street, and there alighting, dived in among the great streets of melancholy stateliness, and the little streets that try to be as stately and succeed in being more melancholy, of which there is a labyrinth near Park Lane. Wildernesses of corner houses, with barbarous old porticoes and appurtenances, horrors that came into existence under some wrong-headed person in some wrong-headed time, still demanding the blind admiration of all ensuing generations and determined to do so until they tumbled down; frowned upon the twilight. Parasite little tenements, with the cramp in their whole frame, from the dwarf-hills in the mews, made the evening doleful. Rickety dwellings of undoubted fashion, but of a capacity to hold nothing comfortably except a dismal smell, looked like the last result of the great mansions breeding in-and-in; and, where their little supplementary bows and balconies were supported on thin iron columns, seemed to be scrofulously resting upon crutches. Here and there a Hatchment, with the whole science of Heraldry in it, loomed down upon the street, like an Arch-bishop discoursing on Vanity. The shops, few in number, made no show, for popular opinion was as nothing to them.

This method is very remarkable. It has its basis, of course, in certain properties of the language: perceptions of relations between persons and things. But in Dickens it is critical. It is a conscious way of seeing and showing. The city is shown as at once a social fact and a human landscape. What is dramatised in it is a very complex structure of feeling. Thus he can respond warmly to the miscellaneous bustle and colour of a mobile commercial life:

> Mr. Dombey's offices were in a court where there was an old-established stall of choice fruit at the corner: where peram-bulating merchants, of both sexes, offered for sale at any time between the hours of ten and five, slippers, pocket-books, sponges, dogs' collars, Windsor soap, and sometimes a pointer or an oil-painting.
>
> The pointer always came that way, with a view to the Stock Exchange, where a sporting taste (originating generally in bets of new hats) is much in vogue.

And it is characteristic that when Mr. Dombey arrives none of these passing commodities is offered to him. His kind of trade, reflected in his house—his "Home-Department"—has established itself in colder, more settled, more remote ways; and then another aspect of the city is evident:

Mr. Dombey's house was a large one, on the shady side of a tall, dark, dreadfully genteel street in the region between Portland Place and Bryanstone Square. It was a corner house, with great wide areas containing cellars frowned upon by barred windows, and leered at by crooked-eyed doors leading to dust-bins. It was a house of dismal state, with a circular back to it, containing a whole suite of drawing-rooms looking up a gravelled yard, where two gaunt trees, with blackened trunks and branches, rattled rather than rustled, their leaves were so smoke-dried. The summer sun was never on the street, but in the morning about breakfast time, when it came with the water-carts and the old-clothes men, and the people with geraniums, and the umbrella-mender, and the man who trilled the little bell of the Dutch clock as he went along. It was soon gone again to return no more that day; and the bands of music and the straggling Punch's shows going after it, left it a prey to the most dismal of organs, and white mice; with now and then a porcupine, to vary the entertainments; until the butlers whose families were dining out, began to stand at the house-doors in the twilight, and the lamp-lighter made his nightly failure in attempting to brighten up the street with gas. It was as blank a house inside as outside.

The contrast between the dismal establishment and the strolling variety of the streets is very clearly made. Again, the characteristics of houses and of people are consciously exchanged:

cellars frowned upon by barred windows, and leered at by crooked-eyed doors.

This transposition of detail can then be extended, again with some traditional support, to a way of seeing the city as a destructive animal, a monster, utterly beyond the individual human scale:

She often looked with compassion, at such a time, upon the stragglers who came wandering into London, by the great highway hard by, and who, footsore and weary, and gazing fearfully at the huge town before them, as if foreboding that their misery there would be but as a drop of water in the sea, or as a grain of sea-sand on the shore, went shrinking on, cowering before the angry weather, and looking as if the very elements rejected them. Day after day, such travellers crept past,

but always, as she thought in one direction—always towards
the town. Swallowed up in one phase or other of its immensity,
towards which they seemed impelled by a desperate fascination,
they never returned. Food for the hospitals, the churchyards,
the prisons, the rivers, fever, madness, vice, and death—they
passed on to the monster, roaring in the distance, and were
lost.

That is one way of seeing it: the rhetorical totalising view from outside.
But Dickens moves with still greater certainty into the streets themselves:
into that experience of the streets—the crowd of strangers—which many
of us now have got used to but which in Blake and Wordsworth was seen
as strange and threatening. Dickens recreates and extends this experience,
in a new range of feeling, when Florence Dombey runs away from her
father's dark house:

> The cheerful vista of the long street, burnished by the morning
> light, the sight of the blue sky and airy clouds, the vigorous
> freshness of the day, so flushed and rosy in its conquest of the
> night, awakened no responsive feelings in her so hurt bosom.
> Somewhere, anywhere, to hide her head! somewhere, anywhere,
> for refuge, never more to look upon the place from which she
> fled!
>
> But there were people going to and fro; there were opening
> shops, and servants at the doors of houses; there was the rising
> clash and roar of the day's struggle. Florence saw surprise and
> curiosity in the faces flitting past her; saw long shadows com-
> ing back upon the pavement; and heard voices that were strange
> to her asking her where she went, and what the matter was;
> and though these frightened her the more at first, and made her
> hurry on the faster, they did her the good service of recalling
> her in some degree to herself, and reminding her of the neces-
> sity of greater composure.
>
> Where to go? Still somewhere, anywhere! still going on; but
> where! She thought of the only other time she had been lost in
> the wide wilderness of London—though not lost as now—and
> went that way.

This street of the city is seen in very particular ways. It is a place of
everyday business, not frightening in itself but amounting in its combined
effect to a "wide wilderness." It is a place as difficult to relate to as her

"shut-up house." But another note is struck: a physical effect which is also a social fact, sharply seen: the same social fact against which Dickens's effort at recognition and kindness is consistently made:

the rising clash and roar of the day's struggle.

The only companion she finds is her dog, and she goes on with him:

> With this last adherent, Florence hurried away in the advancing morning, and the strengthening sunshine, to the City. The roar soon grew more loud, the passengers more numerous, the shops more busy, until she was carried onward in a stream of life setting that way, and flowing, indifferently, past marts and mansions, prisons, churches, market-places, wealth, poverty, good, and evil, like the broad river side by side with it, awakened from its dreams of rushes, willows, and green moss, and rolling on, turbid and troubled, among the works and cares of men, to the deep sea.

What is emphatic here is not only the noise and the everyday business; not only the miscellaneity—"prisons, churches"; but through all this the indifference, in an unwilled general sense:

a stream of life setting that way, and flowing, indifferently.

It is again not a matter of particular acts or characters. It is a general phenomenon—a stream, a way of life. It is what Arthur Clennam and his wife go down into, in *Little Dorrit,* having learned, painfully, a precarious but still inviolable human connection:

> They went quietly down into the roaring streets, inseparable and blessed; and as they passed along in sunshine and in shade, the noisy and the eager and the arrogant and the froward and the vain, fretted, and chafed, and made their usual uproar.

The individual moral qualities, still sharply seen, are heard as it were collectively, in the "roaring streets." This is again an advance in consciousness as it is very clearly a gain—now absorbed—in fictional method.

For we have to relate this view not simply to description—animated description—but to the power of dramatising a moral world in physical terms. The physical world is never in Dickens unconnected with man. It is of his making, his manufacture, his interpretation. That is why it matters so much what shape he has given it.

Dickens's method, in this, relates very precisely to his historical period. It was in just this capacity to remake the world, in the process we summarise as the Industrial Revolution, that men reached this crisis of choice; of the human shape that should underlie the physical creation. At one extreme Dickens can see this as comic:

> The earth was made for Dombey and Son to trade in, and the sun and moon were made to give them light. Rivers and seas were formed to float their ships; rainbows gave them promise of fair weather; winds blew for or against their enterprises; stars and planets circled in their orbits, to preserve inviolate a system of which they were the centre.

This is a mocking of a familiar commercial confidence but not at all in the name of an undisturbed nature. Rather it is a way of seeing the kind of system that is *imposed,* that is *made* central. It is qualified, precisely, by the other kinds of physical life and confidence in which men are making their own worlds, carrying them about with them through the noise and the crowding. It is not only that power is ambiguous—the power to create new worlds. There is also a choice: a choice of the human shape of the new physical environment. Or there *can* be a choice—we *can* be in a position to choose—if we see, physically and morally, what is happening to people in this time of unprecedented change:

> The first shock of a great earthquake had, just at that period, rent the whole neighbourhood to its centre. Traces of its course were visible on every side. Houses were knocked down; streets broken through and stopped; deep pits and trenches dug in the ground; enormous heaps of earth and clay thrown up; buildings that were undermined and shaking, propped by great beams of wood. Here, a chaos of carts, overthrown and jumbled together, lay topsy-turvy at the bottom of a steep unnatural hill; there, confused treasures of iron soaked and rusted in something that had accidentally become a pond. Everywhere were bridges that led nowhere; thoroughfares that were wholly impassable; Babel towers of chimneys, wanting half their height; temporary wooden houses and enclosures, in the most unlikely situations; carcasses of ragged tenements, and fragments of unfinished walls and arches, and piles of scaffolding, and wildernesses of bricks, and giant forms of cranes, and tripods straddling above nothing. There were a hundred thousand shapes and substances of incompleteness, wildly mingled out of their

places, upside down, burrowing in the earth, aspiring in the air, mouldering in the water and unintelligible as any dream. Hot springs and fiery eruptions, the usual attendants upon earthquakes, lent their contributions of confusion to the scene. Boiling water hissed and heaved within dilapidated walls; whence also, the glare and roar of flames came issuing forth; and mounds of ashes blocked up rights of way, and wholly changed the law and custom of the neighbourhood.

In short, the yet unfinished and unopened railroad was in progress; and from the very core of all this dire disorder, trailed smoothly away, upon its mighty course of civilisation and improvement.

This is the apprehension of direct disturbance, but Dickens goes on to see what in the end matters more: not the disorder of change, but the kind of new order that is made to emerge from it:

The miserable waste ground, where the refuse-matter had been heaped of yore, was swallowed up and gone; and in its frowsy stead were tiers of warehouses, crammed with rich goods and costly merchandise. The old by-streets now swarmed with passengers and vehicles of every kind; the new streets that had stopped disheartened in the mud and waggon-ruts, formed towns within themselves, originating wholesome comforts and conveniences belonging to themselves, and never tried nor thought of until they sprung into existence. Bridges that had led to nothing, led to villas, gardens, churches, healthy public walks. The carcasses of houses, and beginnings of new thoroughfares, had started off upon the line at steam's own speed, and shot away into the country in a monster train.

As to the neighbourhood which had hesitated to acknowledge the railroad in its struggling days, that had grown wise and penitent, as any Christian might in such a case, and now boasted of its powerful and prosperous relation. There were railway patterns in its drapers' shops, and railway journals in the windows of its newsmen. There were railway hotels, coffeehouses, lodging-houses, boarding-houses, railway plans, maps, views, wrappers, bottles, sandwich-boxes, and time-tables; railway hackney-coach and cabstands; railway omnibuses, railway streets and buildings, railway hangers-on and parasites, and flatterers out of all calculation. There was even railway time

observed in clocks, as if the sun itself had given in. Among the
vanquished was the master chimney-sweeper, whilom incredu-
lous at Staggs's Gardens, who now lived in a stuccoed house
three stories high, and gave himself out, with flourishes upon a
varnished board, as contractor for the cleansing of railway
chimneys by machinery.

To and from the heart of this great change, all day and night,
throbbing currents rushed and returned, incessantly like its
life's blood. Crowds of people and mountains of goods, depart-
ing and arriving scores upon scores of times in every four-and-
twenty hours, produced a fermentation in the place that was
always in action. The very houses seemed disposed to pack up
and take trips. Wonderful Members of Parliament, who, little
more than twenty years before, had made themselves merry
with the wild railroad theories of engineers, and given them the
liveliest rubs in cross-examination, went down into the north
with their watches in their hands, and sent on messages before
by the electric telegraph, to say that they were coming. Night
and day the conquering engines rumbled at their distant work,
or, advancing smoothly to their journey's end, and gliding like
tame dragons into the allotted corners grooved out to the inch
for their reception, stood bubbling and trembling there, making
the walls quake, as if they were dilating with the secret knowledge of great powers yet unsuspected in them, and strong
purposes not yet achieved.

The complexity of this feeling is a true complexity of insight. All the pride
of power—the new power of the Industrial Revolution—is felt in the
language: the circulation by railway is the "life's blood." But there is also
the recognition of this power overriding all other human habits and
purposes. It is the recognition confirmed, later, in

the power that forced itself upon its iron way—its own—defiant
of all paths and roads, piercing through the heart of every
obstacle, and dragging living creatures of all classes, ages and
degrees behind it.

The railway is at once the "life's blood" and "the triumphant monster,
Death." And in this dramatic enactment Dickens is responding to the real
contradictions—the power for life or death; for disintegration, order and
false order—of the new social and economic forces of his time. His

concern always was to keep human recognition and human kindness alive, through these unprecedented changes and within this unrecognisably altered landscape.

> The very houses seemed disposed to pack up and take trips.

That is the mobility, the critical mobility, which was altering the novel. It is also the altered, the critically altered relationship between men and things.

In this altered relationship the character of moral analysis is inevitably changed. Thus it is easy to see that *Dombey and Son* is a novel about pride. But we have to go on and make a more difficult distinction. I suggested [elsewhere] that there is a kind of moral analysis in which society is a background against which the drama of personal virtues and vices is enacted, and that there is another kind—increasingly important in the development of nineteenth-century literature—in which society is the creator of virtues and vices; its active relationships and institutions at once generating and controlling, or failing to control, what in the earlier mode of analysis could be seen as faults of the soul.

And then the important thing to realise about a novel like *Dombey and Son* is that Dickens uses and relies on both these kinds. Indeed *Dombey and Son* is the novel in which he makes a decisive transition from the first to the second, in his essential organisation.

> "I have dreamed," said Edith in a low voice, "of a pride that is all powerless for good, all powerful for evil; of a pride that has been galled and goaded, through many shameful years, and has never recoiled except upon itself; a pride that has debased its owner with the consciousness of deep humiliation, and never helped its owner boldly to resent it or avoid it, or to say, This shall not be! a pride that, rightly guided, might have led perhaps to better things, but which, misdirected and perverted, like all else belonging to the same possessor, has been self-contempt, mere hardihood, and ruin."
>
> She neither looked nor spoke to Florence now, but went on as if she were alone.
>
> "I have dreamed," she said, "of such indifference and callousness, arising from this self-contempt; this wretched, inefficient, miserable pride; that it has gone on with listless steps even to the altar, yielding to the old, familiar, beckoning finger,—oh mother, oh mother!—while it spurned it; and will-

ing to be hateful to itself for once and for all, rather than to be stung daily in some new form. Mean poor thing!"

And now with gathering and darkening emotion, she looked as she had looked when Florence entered.

"And I have dreamed," she said, "that in a first late effort to achieve a purpose, it has been trodden on, and trodden down by a base foot, but turns and looks upon him. I have dreamed that it is wounded, hunted, set upon by dogs, but that it stands at bay, and will not yield; no, that it cannot, if it would; but that it is urged on to hate him, rise against him, and defy him!"

Her clenched hand tightened on the trembling arm she had in hers, and as she looked down on the alarmed and wondering face, her own subsided. "Oh Florence!" she said, "I think I have been nearly mad to-night!" and humbled her proud head upon her neck, and wept again.

That is a traditional kind of individualised moral description. In the same spirit there is a traditional invocation to wake from error, in the description of Florence going in to her father's room:

Awake, unkind father! Awake now, sullen man! The time is flitting by; the hour is coming with an angry tread. Awake! Awake, doomed man, while she is near! The time is flitting by; the hour is coming with an angry tread; its foot is in the house, Awake!

But this is not the only way in which this destructive pride is seen. "House" in this civilisation has two meanings: the family home and the firm. In bringing their values into contradiction, in the single word, Dickens sets going his characteristic conflict of primary and secondary feelings. For the outlook of the firm—a social institution, trading in the confident spirit of its time—is seen from the beginning as the creator of a destructively indifferent pride. Here, characteristically, Dickens does not plead emotionally, but sets down ironically:

Common abbreviations took new meanings in his eyes, and had sole reference to them. A.D. had no concern with anno Domini, but stood for anno Dombei—and Son.

That is part of the observation—the satirical observation—that "the earth was made for Dombey and Son to trade in." It is the way in which social institutions, particular social purposes, reshape not only the physical but the moral world. And the question then arises: what is the nature, the human nature, by which this can be judged?

> Was Mr. Dombey's master-vice, that ruled him so inexorably, an unnatural characteristic? It might be worth while sometimes, to inquire what Nature is, and how men work to change her, and whether, in the enforced distortions so produced, it is not natural to be unnatural. Coop any son or daughter to one idea, and foster it by servile worship of it on the part of the few timid or designing people standing round, and what is Nature to the willing captive who has never risen up upon the wings of a free mind—drooping and useless soon—to see her in her comprehensive truth!
>
> Alas! are there so few things in the world, about us, most unnatural, and yet most natural in being so! Hear the magistrate or judge admonish the unnatural outcasts of society; unnatural in brutal habits, unnatural in want of decency, unnatural in losing and confounding all distinctions between good and evil; unnatural in ignorance, in vice, in recklessness, in contumacy, in mind, in looks, in everything. But follow the good clergyman, or doctor, who, with his life imperilled at every breath he draws, goes down into their dens, lying within the echoes of our carriage-wheels and daily tread upon the pavement stones. Look round upon the world of odious sights— millions of immortal creatures have no other world on earth—at the lightest mention of which humanity revolts, and dainty delicacy living in the next street, stops her ears, and lisps "I don't believe it!" Breathe the polluted air, foul with every impurity that is poisonous to health and life; and have every sense, conferred upon our race for its delight and happiness, offended, sickened and disgusted, and made a channel by which misery and death alone can enter. Vainly attempt to think of any simple plant, or flower, or wholesome weed, that, set in this foetid bed, could have its natural growth, or put its little leaves forth to the sun as God designed it. And then, calling up some ghastly child, with stunted form and wicked face, hold forth on its unnatural sinfulness, and lament its being, so early, far away from Heaven— but think a little of its having been conceived, and born and bred, in Hell!

It is interesting to see where this question has led Dickens. Beginning with Dombey's "master-vice," and its traditional reference to "Nature," he has gone on to describe a process in which men work to change nature and to produce "enforced distortions." The argument then slips imperceptibly to the strongest social feeling he then had: his horror in seeing the diseased slums of the city, produced by indifference and neglect: a Hell produced and maintained by men.

It is at this point, significantly in the course of trying to answer a traditional moral question, that Dickens reaches not only an indignant social description but the definition of purpose that I have already quoted:

Oh for a good spirit who would take the house tops off

—a way of seeing through the "dense black cloud." An individual moral question has become a social question and then, decisively, a creative intervention. This seems to me the essential pattern of all Dickens's work.

What do we mean, precisely, by "creative intervention?" What I mean, though it is hard to say, is that Dickens's morality, his social criticism, is in the form of his novels: a form based on ways of seeing people in their world and their society. Certainly these complicated ways of seeing are more important to his achievement than his separable attitudes to money, to poverty, to the family and to other known social questions. Nothing is clearer, when the treatment of any of these is examined by a method predicated by the assumption of "treatment," than that Dickens is often contradictory, often confused, and indeed often, to use fashionable terms, unenlightened and unintelligent. And I do not mean that any of these observations is negligible, but they are only critical responses when they are parts of a whole response.

Thus it has been argued (and I among others have felt the force of this) that he is curiously blind to the real forces in nineteenth-century society which were even then beginning to "reform the abuses against which he protested." This is where an initial wrong assumption returns to confuse us. Certainly Dickens saw abuses and wanted them reformed. But it is not only that he increasingly saw them as related to a general condition: a fact reflected in the more concentrated organisation of the novels from *Dombey and Son* onwards. This was in the best sense an intellectual perception, and Shaw was right when he described it as "declaring that it is not our disorder but our order that is horrible."

More deeply, however, from his whole experience, and underlying the intellectual formulations which—like popular radical culture itself—he picked up from so many and so different and such contradictory sources, the total vision, not so much drawn from his material as imposed on it, came through and was decisive. This human drama, rooted and acted through, is inescapably general, and its generality, its totality, is its strength rather than its weakness. If the general condition and the forces operating on it were as he felt them to be, then what others may see as the "real forces" can indeed seem incidental. Parliament, the trade unions, educational reform, public protective legislation of many kinds: outside the fiction Dickens can often see these as others saw them: now this opinion, now that. But the kinds of thing they were could not operate, at that level, in the fiction itself. We can say if we wish that this is blindness: an emotional overpowering of the ways in which the world has to be seen and changed. But it may be some check to our confidence, even now, to ask if the human and social condition as Dickens saw it has been much changed by the kind of work we call enlightened. The haunting isolation; the self-conscious neglect of the damned of the earth; the energy and despair of fixed public appearances, endlessly talking: these too are social facts and more resistible to reform than the institutions which they intersect.

To suppose that man as created by an immensely powerful society can be primarily affected by institutional amendments may not after all be very enlightened. This is why it is stupid of Orwell to dismiss Dickens as a "change-of-heart" man (though it is characteristic of his own persistently external vision). Reference to a "change of heart" is indeed now mainly known as a rationalisation of resistance to change, but this is clearly not Dickens. To see a change of heart and a change of institutions as alternatives is already to ratify an alienated society, for neither can be separated, or ever is, from the other; simply one or other can be *ignored*. The relevant question is still that of Marx: who educates the educators? Or, more generally, who legislates the legislators? Who mans the institutions?

In most important ways, Dickens has little in common with Marx. But they shared the sense of a general human condition:

> Human life is the true social life of man. As the irremediable exclusion from this life is much more complete, more unbearable, dreadful and contradictory, than the exclusion from political life, so is the ending of this exclusion, and even a limited reaction, a revolt against it, more fundamental, as man is more fundamental than the citizen, human life more than political life.

Marx is talking here of alienated labour but the vision is structurally similar to that of Dickens. Absolute human exclusion is more important than the relative kinds of exclusion which can be remedied by partial and piecemeal change. What Dickens saw as a redemption through love and innocence Marx saw as revolution, and that difference is crucial. But still, if this kind of total change is seen as the necessary response to a total condition, the consequent attitude to limited changes is governed by principle rather than by a kind of overlooking.

This is the key, surely, to Dickens's contradictions in the matter of character and environment. Consider this from *Nicholas Nickleby*:

> Now, when he thought how regularly things went on from day to day in the same unvarying round—how youth and beauty died, and ugly griping age lived tottering on—how crafty avarice grew rich, and manly honest hearts were poor and sad—how few they were who tenanted the stately houses, and how many those who lay in noisome pens, or rose each day and laid them down at night, and lived and died, father and son, mother and child, race upon race, and generation upon generation, without a home to shelter them or the energies of one single man directed to their aid—how in seeking, not a luxurious and splendid life, but the bare means of a most wretched and inadequate subsistence, there were women and children in that one town, divided into classes, numbered and estimated as regularly as the noble families and folks of great degree, and reared from infancy to drive most criminal and dreadful trades—how ignorance was punished and never taught—how jail-door gaped and gallows loomed for thousands urged towards them by circumstances darkly curtaining their very cradles' heads, and but for which they might have earned their honest bread and lived in peace—how many died in soul, and had no chance of life—how many who could scarcely go astray, be they vicious as they would, turned haughtily from the crushed and stricken wretch who could scarce do otherwise, and who would have been a greater wonder had he or she done well, than even they, had they done ill—how much injustice, and misery and wrong, there was—and yet how the world rolled on from year to year, alike careless and indifferent, and no man seeking to remedy or redress it:—when he thought of all this, and selected from the mass the one slight case on which his thoughts were bent, he felt indeed that there was little ground for hope, and little cause or reason why it should not form an atom in the

huge aggregate of distress and sorrow, and add one small and
unimportant unit to swell the great amount.

This deliberately generalising description, which it pleases some people to
call rant, is the general condition as Dickens quite consistently saw it.
Within it, certainly, there is determinism: circumstances create evil. To
that, inevitably, there is the humane response: help, where now no man
seeks to "remedy or redress"; teach, rather than punish, ignorance. But the
whole description is of a *system*: the numbering into classes; the careless-
ness and indifference; the aggregate of distress and sorrow.

It is then a social condition but seen at a level where it is also a human
condition. The complaint of beauty dying and ugliness surviving is what is
so often now seen, by men who think they have outgrown social criticism,
as "criticising life." But social criticism when it is most successful is always
and inescapably a criticism of life. If Dickens believed that not only
"noisome pens" and "stately houses" but the death of beauty and the
"griping" survival of ugliness were the products of the system, can we be
quite sure that he was wrong? It would be easy to show him falling into
confusion of unlike facts, in some "general mood" of indignation. But
death and survival, though they can be seen as absolutes, are almost
always related to a general condition of living. And to push social criticism
that far is to pass beyond what is ordinarily seen as social criticism but not
to pass beyond social experience. Moreover, if the "huge aggregate of
distress and sorrow" is seen as a human condition, in this way of living, it
is seen as a matter for response rather than for mere recognition. Nicholas,
after this vision, "gradually summoned up his utmost energy." It is what
Dickens manages to do, almost always, by way of intervening. He often
believed because he must try to believe that good circumstances would
produce good characters, and so help for the unfortunate. But already, in
this early novel, he cannot see it as a *general* fact. The comfortable turn
haughtily away, and from *Dombey and Son* onwards we see a social
system in which the turning away is as much a product of circumstances as
the distress. Indifference indeed, in the later novels, is a thing that the
system and its expectations actively teach.

Yet under the weight of this system, and from no demonstrable cause,
a turning towards also occurs. It is easy to show that having defined a
social condition as the cause of virtue and vice, Dickens then produces
virtue, almost magically as in *Little Dorrit,* from the same conditions
which in others bred vice; or produces charity by making an exceptional
and surprising benevolence flourish, overriding the determinism of the

system, or often by an arranged and unexplained withdrawal from the system, where charity can suddenly be afforded.

We may or may not believe in it, as social observation, but though it has the character of miracle it is the kind of miracle that happens: the flowering of love or energy which is inexplicable by the ways of describing people to which (usually under the influence of the same system) we have got used. There is no reason, that is to say, for love or innocence, except that almost obliterated by this general condition there is humanity. The exclusion of the human, which we can see operating in a describable system, is not after all absolute, or it would make no sense to call what is alienated human; there would otherwise be nothing to alienate. The inexplicable quality of the indestructible innocence, of the miraculously intervening goodness, on which Dickens so much depends and which has been casually written off as sentimentality is genuine *because* it is inexplicable. What is explicable, after all, is the system, which consciously or unconsciously has been made. To believe that a human spirit exists, ultimately more powerful than even this system, is an act of faith but an act of faith in ourselves. That this became more and more difficult for Dickens is not surprising, but to the end, under increasing pressure, it is what he is not only saying but making happen.

It is in this dimension that we must judge his creation of characters. There has been an important critical difficulty about what is called his reduction of people to caricatures and about what is called the "sentimentality" of his "impossibly pure" heroines. But Dickens was creating, openly and deliberately, a world in which people had been deprived of any customary identity and yet in which, paradoxically, the deprivation was a kind of liberation, in which the most fantastic and idiosyncratic kinds of growth could come about. People had to define themselves and their position in the world—it is his characteristic mode:

> "My present salary, Miss Summerson, at Kenge and Carboy's, is two pound a week. When I first had the happiness of looking upon you, it was one-fifteen, and had stood at that figure for a lengthened period. A rise of five has since taken place, and a further rise of five is guaranteed at the expiration of a term not exceeding twelve months from the present date."

> "When I offered to your sister to keep company, and to be asked in church, at such times as she was willing and ready to come to the forge, I said to her, 'And bring the poor little child. God bless the poor little child.' "

"But that's like me I run away with an idea and having none to spare I keep it, alas there was a time dear Arthur that is to say decidedly not dear nor Arthur neither but you understand me when one bright idea gilded the what's-his name horizon of et cetera but it is darkly clouded now and all is over."

"My friends, what is this which we now behold as being spread before us? Refreshment. Do we need refreshment then, my friends? We do. And why do we need refreshment, my friends? Because we are but mortal, because we are but sinful, because we are but of the earth, because we are not of the air. Can we fly, my friends? We cannot. Why can we not fly, my friends?"

The emphasis is often isolated, often absurd, but what runs through it is a paradoxical energy. It is a loss of customary settlement, though not of customary phrases, which in their abstract repetition can become ludicrous because misplaced. But at the same time it is a kind of release, which even at its most grotesque is irrepressible and above all various. It is in this paradoxical dimension that Dickens creates the ordinary human condition, in ways that are clearer and sharper, given his general vision, than any more normative characterisation could be. Many of the techniques for this kind of description came from popular journalism, including "police characters," from popular illustrations and cartoons, and from the theatre. It is from the theatre also and especially from melodrama that the counterweight is taken: the stabilising simple figures of innocence and purity. These are not the morality figures of an age of common belief, but the dramatic figures of an age in which individuality and growth are paradoxical and in which, as an emphasis and an intervention, the simplest human qualities of love and kindness must be deliberately sustained. It is a structure of feeling, in its strengths and weaknesses, which he shares with the popular culture of his time.

At the same time, by moving this structure into an extended action, Dickens ran into problems which are quite specific to his own art. There are times when the emotions can seem too large for the objects and situations through which they are released, and the line between intensity and absurdity is then often crossed, quite apart from those occasions when the dramatic structure fails, temporarily, to hold and is merely remembered and imitated. Where the failure is in the writing we can only note and consider it. But when there is overlapping of meaning it may be possible to avoid some of our own failures by analysis. Here is a mixed case:

> The mature young gentleman is a gentleman of property. He invests his property. He goes in a condescending amateurish way, into the City, attends meetings of directors, and has to do with traffic in Shares. As is well known to the wise in their generation, traffic in Shares is the one thing to have to do with in this world. Have no antecedents, no established character, no cultivation, no ideas, no manners; have Shares. Have Shares enough to be on Boards of Direction in capital letters, oscillate on mysterious business between London and Paris, and be great. Where does he come from? Shares. Has he any principles? Shares. What squeezes him into Parliament? Shares. Perhaps he never of himself achieved success in anything, never originated anything, never produced anything. Sufficient answer to all: Shares. O mighty Shares!

It is true that this passage would have "special force in the years just before the crisis of 1866, which saw the failure of Overend and Gurney," and that it is integrated into the novel by its reference to the careers of several of the characters. But we do not need to deny these points to remind ourselves that this power of making an abstraction into a dramatic force is, as we have seen, a major element in all Dickens's social vision. And it is just here that the problem of "exaggeration" is hardest. Traffic in shares is the *one* thing to have to do with the world? Do even the wise in their generation believe that? It is like "no man seeking to remedy or redress it," in the *Nickleby* passage, when the most casual observation would have turned up a thousand. Is Dickens then being unfair? Is such a character credible?

But the character here is Shares. And the question is not really whether share capital, as a technique, leads to economic prosperity or to the crash of Overend and Gurney. It is what quality of living, what kinds of relationships, Shares embody (the repeated capital letter is important, as is stressed again in "Boards of Direction"). It is not so much an isolated economic technique or an isolated aspect of character. It is more a free-acting force, separated from man though of course created by him. That it then in turns creates behaviour, principles, power: this is the whole point and the social observation is indeed fundamental—this is a *general* condition. The dramatic element, which Shares becomes, is like the dust-heaps and the river and the isolated colliding characters who live through and on them and who are brought to a willed and valued resolution. If you ask in detail how shares operate, this share and that, or how and why businesses flourish and fall, you are outside the drama, but what you have gained in one kind of contact with reality you have lost in another: learning the detailed workings but missing Dickens's dramatisation of what he saw as the total experience.

And this is of course very easy to do, quite apart from Overend and Gurney. For once he has got his dramatic figure, Dickens literally throws the book at it. The received phrases of aristocratic values—"antecedents, established character, cultivation, ideas, manners"—are hurled with the bourgeois values—"achieved success, originated, produced." Are these then to be set against Shares? Is that Dickens's meaning? But then which set of values, or both? From the primary feeling—that shares are replacing men as the active creators of the world—there is a rapid process of translation and overlapping, through the ordinarily available meanings. It is like the spectre attendant on Merdle addressing the high priests of the Circumlocution Office—"Are such the signs you trust and love to honour; this head, these eyes, this mode of speech, the tone and manner of this man?," for all the world as if it were Matthew Arnold. The spectre is the general vision; the words are from the book. And in a sense, any book will do, once the action is joined. Mainly Carlyle, of course, and the angry, sarcastic radicalism of Cobbett. But also, when it can help, a proposition about utility (as House has shown); a constructive suggestion from Robert Owen (character immediately alterable by change of circumstances); an appeal for organised charity and a tirade against it; a reminiscence of Scripture; a detail from a contemporary report; a statistic and a tirade against statistics. It wouldn't be difficult, picking up all these bits and pieces and seeing how often they are contradictory, to call Dickens merely irresponsible; indeed it has been done. But the responsibility, finally, is to the general vision, and in the end this is deep and remarkable. At the surface, there is the confusion of theory and the debris of phrases so characteristic of this period of English popular radicalism; and that the confusion persisted, that Dickens even propagated it, is historically very important. But still, the whole drama of values, the powerful way of seeing the world so that it cannot but be criticised and responded to: these, as substance, are more penetrating into the reality of nineteenth-century England than any of the systems which were in fact made clear and consistent.

Even the deepest contradictions are within this power. The vision of alienation has its own alienated elements: a child is destroyed, as in

Dombey and Son, by the subjection of a human being to a social role, but then Toodles or Cuttle are similarly subjected, by their author, who defines their whole reality in the jargon of their job, not only to show but in fact to minimise the pressures on them. The appeasing ventriloquism of the whining poor is only a step from the desperate inarticulacy of men subject to arbitrary economic power, but the step is taken. The aggregate of distress and sorrow has only to move, collectively, to be converted into its opposite and be seen as a howling mob. The trick played by Dombey on Polly, making her Richards for his convenience, is played by Meagles on Tattycoram, but the flow of feeling is now different. The good are *our* people, even when other people are different only because they are minor characters. Money corrupts, but it does not corrupt Sol Gills. The house of Dombey deserves to fall, but Walter can reestablish it. There are very many examples of this kind. The hurling of random ideas and the profoundly selective character of the moral action have certainly to be recognised. They are the problems of translation, but also the probable accompaniments of so single, intense, compulsive and self-involving a vision: the characteristic weaknesses where we have already recognised the strengths.

But the social criticism, giving that phrase its full value—not a set of opinions only, nor a series of reforms only, nor even habitual attitudes only, but a vision of the nature of man and the means of his liberation in a close and particular place and time—this social criticism is in the end marvellously achieved and still profoundly active. For indeed it is the kind of social criticism which belongs to literature and especially, in our own civilisation, to the novel. Sociology can describe social conditions more accurately, at the level of ordinary measurement. A political programme can offer more precise remedies, at the level of ordinary action. Literature can attempt to follow these modes, but at its most important its process is different and yet still inescapably social: a whole way of seeing that is communicable to others, and a dramatisation of values that becomes an action.

STEVEN MARCUS

Language into Structure:
Pickwick Revisited

Mysteries in real life exist in order to be solved, and literary mysteries exist in order to be consulted. As one who has already tried his hand in picking at the greatest of Dickens's mysteries—*Pickwick Papers*—I feel no need to apologize for frequenting these grounds again, nor for consulting the mystery in the hope that this time it will prove still more receptive and less resistant to critical interrogation. For the mystery has been and remains essentially a critical one: Where is the critical handle for such a work of genius to be found?

Let us begin then at the beginning. And, as it is only appropriate in such a perplexing context, we discover the beginning before the beginning and after the ending. I am referring to the advertisement that was published before the first number of *Pickwick Papers* appeared and to the prefaces that Dickens wrote after he had completed the novel. The advertisement begins as follows: "On the 31st of March will be published, to be continued Monthly, price One Shilling, the First Number of *The Posthumous Papers of the Pickwick Club;* containing a faithful record of the perambulations, perils, travels, adventures, and sporting transactions of the corresponding members. Edited by 'Boz.' And each Monthly Part embellished with Four Illustrations by Seymour." It is all thoroughly inauspicious and conventional. Amid these conventionalities, however, and indeed as part of them, three things persist in attracting the attention of the modern reader. First the papers are "posthumous"—but to what? To the club itself, presumably. But what does this mean, and why? It is not

From *Daedalus: Journal of the American Academy of Arts and Sciences* 101, no. 1 (Winter 1972). © 1972 by the American Academy of Arts and Sciences.

alive, it is not there, it is dead or has disappeared. It exists in a negative state or as a negation, in a condition of almost pure otherness. But the papers themselves may be posthumous as well in the sense that they are dead before they have ever come alive; they are being produced as a piece of hack work and will be or are dead as literature before they are even written.

Second, these papers are not "written" but "edited." This too was a convention of popular fiction and other writing, although Carlyle had recently made considerable creative play with it in *Sartor Resartus*. But it implies a statement similar to that contained in "posthumous." The agent behind this publication is as it were not yet the novelist; he exists again in a kind of negative or not-yet-appeared or absent state. He is not writing the work; he does not create it or own or possess it. Somehow it is written through him. But at the same time once more there is a sense of some slight distance and disavowal present and being communicated. And third, the editor is Boz, not Dickens. Boz who did "sketches," not Dickens who wrote novels. Moreover, we are to learn in the future that Boz was not even in the first place Dickens's pseudonym for himself. It was a nickname that he had given to a younger brother, so that his using it for himself is on one of its sides another form of a complex, inexplicit disavowal, though on another side it is a characteristic gesture of aggrandizement. Boz contains the suggestion—retrospectively to be sure—that Dickens so to speak is not yet here, that he has not yet been created as he will eventually be. And thus the novel announces itself beforehand in a cluster of negations, of othernesses and circumstances which are not there, or are not yet there.

If we turn next to the preface to the first edition, we come across a number of equally arresting phrases and formulations. This was written some year and a half later, at the conclusion of the work, and with that work figuratively present in its entirety before the writer. We all know what had happened to *Pickwick Papers* in that interval; and we know in addition that an occurrence of similar magnitude had taken place in the young writer, that he had undergone a transformation and become Charles Dickens. It is to be supposed, therefore, that he would undertake to communicate some part of this momentousness in his prefatory leavetaking. But he does nothing of the kind. The first sentence of that preface begins as follows: "The author's object in this work was to place before the reader a constant succession of characters and incidents." We should note in passing that although he has become "the author," he has continued speaking in the distant and distancing convention of the authorial or editorial third person rather than the first person which he subsequently adopted on such occasions. What stops us, however, is his formulation of his "object"—"a constant succession." There is some notion here of endless movement, of incessant motion, an idea that is elaborated along one line later on when he tells us that the only sport at which he was really good (the word he uses is "great") was "all kinds of locomotion." But that is only one line of development, and we shall return to this conception in due course.

He then goes on to describe the conditions of the imaginative inception of the work. "Deferring to the judgement of others in the outset of the undertaking," he writes, "he [Dickens] adopted the machinery of the club, which was suggested as that best adapted to his purpose." It is always interesting to find an occasion on which Dickens refers in public to some act of deference on his part; and it is not surprising that he should do so with a touch of ill-nature—the supererogatory double emphasis and quasi-circularity of phrasing make his annoyance sufficiently clear. He did not, he is saying, want this "machinery" there at the beginning; and, he continues, finding as he wrote "that it tended rather to his embarrassment than otherwise, he gradually abandoned it, considering it a matter of very little importance to the work." The implication seems virtually to be that he wanted no machinery at all; that had he had his own way he would have begun without any machinery—that is to say, he would have begun in some other and almost entirely unimaginable way. He cannot of course tell us what that way would have been, but he does remark that the form or "general design" of the work, owing to its mode of publication, had to be as "simple" as possible. And the linking between the separate events and numbers, if they were to "form one tolerably harmonious whole," had to follow "a gentle and not-unnatural progress of adventure." After having misspent a certain number of years contemplating this utterance, I find that my response to it is to say—"meaning what?" A progress in what "not-unnatural" sense? A progress that is pure succession? The one thing that is indisputably clear about this assertion is that Dickens was in no position to understand discursively what it was that he had done—which may in point of creative fact have been exactly the most advantageous position for him to have occupied.

These observations are supported by what follows shortly, a description in one sentence by Dickens of his manner of writing *Pickwick Papers*. "The following pages," he states, "have been written from time to time, almost as the periodical occasion arose." Again, it is the subdued uncertainty and unintended ambiguity that draw the attention of the reader. On the one hand Dickens seems to be describing an activity that occurred spontaneously, and almost at random; on the other he tends to represent himself as writing by order for the occasion, or as the occasion "arose," which introduces an uncertainty of another kind. The point about this ambiguity is that it happens to correspond to an actuality. The parts were written by the yard, to prearranged mechanical specifications; at the same time they were composed spontaneously. It was not only Dickens who stood in puzzlement over this circumstance.

Ten years later the occasion arose again, and Dickens took the opportunity of the publication of the First Cheap Edition of his works to write a new preface in which he described more fully the circumstances of the inception of the now legendary novel. He recalls how William Hall came to his rooms in Furnivall's Inn to propose "a something that should be published in shilling numbers." This something soon becomes a "monthly something," both of the ironic phrases suggesting Dickens's growing awareness of the extraordinarily unformed and unconscious character of what it was that—ten years before—was then about to happen to him and unfold out of him. He next describes how it was proposed to him that his writing should be the "vehicle" for Seymour's plates, how he objected to this view of the project and proposed successfully to reverse it. "My views being deferred to," he states, "I thought of Mr. Pickwick and wrote the first number." The deference of the preface to the first edition is now on the other foot. As for the famous statement about Mr. Pickwick, I have discussed its deceptive complexities elsewhere and there is no need to rehearse them here. But the second half of this sentence introduces still further difficulties, for after remarking that he "wrote the first number," Dickens goes on to add "from the proof-sheets of which, Mr. Seymour made his drawing of the club and that happy portrait of its founder, by which he is always recognized and which may be said to have made him a reality." Which may be said by whom? and in what sense? and for Dickens as well as for others? The confusion, however, was to be still worse confounded, for twenty years later Dickens revised the preface once again, took out the second half of that sentence, and substituted this: "from the proof sheets of which, Mr. Seymour made his drawing of the Club, and his happy portrait of its founder:—the latter on Mr. Edward Chapman's description of the dress and bearing of a real personage whom he had often seen." This revision had its origin in assertions that were made on Seymour's behalf, that had to do with the part he played in the primary imagination of the novel, and that cannot be discussed here. Dickens's "clarification," however, serves primarily to divert and distract one's attention. The sentence is still running in two directions—Seymour making his drawing now from both the proof sheets and Chapman's description of "a real personage" no less. Once more Dickens cannot withstand the impulse to introduce some such word as "real" or "reality." And each time that he does make such an introduction our sense of his permanent uncertainty about what it was that had happened to him is augmented. This observation holds for the well-known following paragraph about Mr. Pickwick's changing character as the novel develops, in which Dickens speaks about him as if he were a real and independent being from the very beginning and a complete invention at the same time.

What we are left with, then, after these extended prefatory marchings and countermarchings is a distinct conviction of how mysterious almost everything about *Pickwick Papers* remained to Dickens himself. We are therefore rather better off than we were when we began; we are still in darkness, but at least we have been joined there by the man who "may be said to have made [it] a reality." And if we can rely no further upon the teller, we have to turn to the tale, which begins thus:

The Pickwickians

The first ray of light which illumines the gloom, and converts into a dazzling brilliancy that obscurity in which the earlier history of the public career of the immortal Pickwick would appear to be involved, is derived from the perusal of the following entry in the Transactions of the Pickwick Club, which the editor of these papers feels the highest pleasure in laying before his readers, as a proof of the careful attention, indefatigable assiduity, and nice discrimination, with which his search among the multifarious documents confided to him has been conducted.

It opens with a title followed by a single epic sentence, a paragraph long, that closes in a dying fall. It is a parody, which later on and at length we learn is in part not a parody. It begins at the beginning, with the "creation" itself, with the Logos appearing out of "obscurity"—that is, the "earlier history . . . of the immortal Pickwick"—and into the light of creation. But it also dramatizes the fundamental activity of the Logos; it dramatizes the notion of cosmic creation as a word—which is how God, as the Logos, created the world: *fiat lux*, said God, when he was speaking Latin, and so it was. And here too, in this novel, we begin the creation with a word, with language; with Dickens's language on the one hand and the word "Pickwickians" on the other. Mr. Pickwick and Dickens are each of them the Logos as well, emerging brightly out of their immanence and creating. And each of them is in his separate, distinctive way the Word made flesh—as are those documents and papers mentioned by the "editor," which do not exist, or do not exist just yet, but will become another incarnation of language, a novel, a printed book. Thus we begin with a comic, cosmic creation in the form of the Logos, the word.

There follows the second sentence of the novel, which is the first sentence of the mythical papers, enclosed in quotation marks. "May 12, 1827. Joseph Smiggers, Esq., P.V.P.M.P.C.,* presiding." The work is set in the past. And although the date is not 4004 B.C., there appears to be something equally accidental and gratuitous about May 12, 1827; in addition readers of *Pickwick Papers,* like readers of the Bible, have encountered certain difficulties in keeping its chronology straight or consistent. But that date is not in actuality gratuitous, although we have to go outside of the book to find its significance: May 1827 was the date at which the fifteen-year-old Charles Dickens first went to work as a clerk in the law firm of Ellis and Blackmore. In the popular idiom of the time, it was the moment at which he "began the world." Then there are those funny letters that follow Smiggers's name. At the risk of appearing absurd, we may ask why they are there; and if we put to one side the simple comic intention and effect of the long set of initials (and the extravagant title to which they refer), we may observe that letters arranged in such a novel and quasi-arbitrary way sometimes form words, or suggest a code that is different from though related to the codes by which we ordinarily communicate. They are almost a kind of doodling, which may be a first clue for us to hold onto. (What I am suggesting is that in this instance the letters P.V.P.M.P.C. are more important than the words to which they refer. It is the letters themselves that make one laugh at first; the humor in the footnoted explanation of their reference and of the inflation in the title is certainly there, but it is secondary.)

There follows an account of the meeting of the club, which first records that Mr. Pickwick had read his celebrated paper entitled "Speculations on the Source of the Hampstead Ponds, with some Observations on the Theory of Tittlebats." Whatever the theory of tittlebats may be, the term itself is of interest. It is, the *Oxford English Dictionary* records, a variant form of stickleback; it comes into use in about 1820, and has its origin in "childish" pronunciation of the fish's name. Once again, as the novel feels about for its beginning, it presses itself and the reader back into words themselves, into matters connected with learning words and with some kind of fundamental or primitive relation to the language.

As for the meeting as a whole, it is conceived of at the outset as the mildest of burlesques upon the transactions of some scientific or scholarly association. It is that, but it is also a parody of a scene in heaven, a fanciful rendering of an unwritten episode of *Paradise Lost*. These comic-epic, immortally foolish creatures are going to visit the earth and report in their correspondence on what they see. And if Mr. Pickwick is the blandest of parodic imaginations of a traveler, explorer, observer, scientist, and scholar, he is just as much a parodic refraction of a god visiting his creation. There follows immediately upon the reading of the resolutions that assign their work of traveling and reporting to Mr. Pickwick and his companions a first description of this deity. "A casual observer, adds the secretary, . . . might possibly have remarked nothing extraordinary in the bald head, and circular spectacles, which were intently turned towards his (the secretary's) face, during the reading of the above resolutions: to those who knew that the gigantic brain of Pickwick was working beneath that forehead, and that the beaming eyes of Pickwick were twinkling behind those glasses, the sight was indeed an interesting one." The image of Pickwick's face is itself almost like a doodle: a number of blank circles to be filled in later—even the solid dots and lines of his "beaming eyes" are not there yet and have to be imagined.

Mr. Pickwick stands on a Windsor chair. His coat tails, tights, and gaiters are mentioned; Tupman, Snodgrass, and Winkle are cursorily sketched, while Dickens readies himself to do what comes next. What comes next is that Mr. Pickwick begins to speak; or more precisely the secretary begins to transcribe in the third person the speech of Mr. Pickwick. At once we see that a travesty parliamentary speech is in the course of being composed, and the best parliamentary reporter of his time is spitballing away in a Homeric doodle, letting the language improvisationally, incontinently, and inconsequentially run on. For example: "The praise of mankind was his [Mr. Pickwick's] Swing; philanthropy was his insurance office. (Vehement cheering) . . . Still he could not but feel that they had selected him for a service of great honour, and of some danger. Travelling was in a troubled state, and the minds of coachmen were unsettled. Let them look abroad and contemplate the scenes which were enacting around them. Stage coaches were upsetting in all directions, horses were bolting, boats were overturning, and boilers were bursting. (Cheers—a voice 'No.') No! (Cheers.)" It runs on until Blotton makes his objection, the altercation between him and Mr. Pickwick breaks out, he calls Pickwick a "humbug"—"Immense confusion, and loud cries of 'Chair,' and 'Order,' " and a compromise settlement is reached when Blotton asserts that he had used that word or expression "in its Pickwickian sense." At this point, of course, Dickens—and his readers—have hit upon something.

What is the Pickwickian sense? If we recall that the chapter begins with the Logos and with the word Pickwickians, we can begin by suggesting that it is a sense in which the word is seized creatively in the first instance almost as a kind of doodle, as a play of the pen, as a kind of verbal scribble or game. It is the word—or verbal expression—actively regarded not primarily as conscious imitation of either nature or preexistent models, but rather as largely unconscious invention, whose meaning is created essentially as it is spontaneously uttered or written down. It is the world, language, writing, as these exist in each other, as a complex process that is self-generating—so that beginning, so to say, either with the name Pickwick, or the word or title Pickwickian, the world, the language, and the writing implicit in or unfolded by such words appears to generate itself. It is language with the shackles removed from certain of its deeper creative powers, which henceforth becomes capable of a constant, rapid, and virtually limitless multiplication of its own effects and forms in new inventions and combinations and configurations. *Mutatis mutandis* it is the timely equivalent in written novelistic prose of the take-off into self-sustained growth. In *Pickwick Papers* the English novel becomes, as it were, airborne.

What we have, in short, is something rather new and spectacular. Such a breakthrough in literature would in the nature of the case have to be largely unconscious; it could not at first have been understood by the person who was the bearer of such a force. For Dickens has committed himself at the outset of *Pickwick Papers* to something like pure writing, to language itself. No novelist had, I believe, ever quite done this in such a measure before—certainly not Sterne. In addition, the commitment was paradoxically ensured and enforced by the circumstance of compelled spontaneity in which Dickens wrote, by the necessity he accepted of turning it out every month, of being regularly spontaneous and self-generatingly creative on demand. Dickens was, if it may be said, undertaking to let the writing write the book. There are several other ways of stating this notion and several explanatory means that may be applied to its elaboration—out of which I shall choose one. Dickens was able to abandon himself or give expression to what Freud called the primary process in a degree that was unprecedented in English fictional prose; he was able to let the fundamental and primitive mental processes of condensation, displacement, and equivalence or substitution find their way into consciousness with a minimum of inhibition, impedence, or resistance. These processes correspond to and are constituents of the deep nonlogical, the metaphoric and metonymic, processes of language—and it was these processes that Dickens allowed to have their run. It may be asked why such a development, in anything like a similar degree, had not occurred before in the English novel. Poets have, after all, often written in just such a way. Was it too frightening a prospect for novelists? Such a question inevitably involves historical circumstances of enormous complexity, and only a partial and provisional answer is possible here. In a sense the possibilities opened up by such an experience were too unnerving for most novelists. The novel had been built primarily on the secondary, logical processes, processes that develop ontogenetically at a later state of mental existence and form the essential structures of consciousness. The regression implied by this manner of composition, the threat of an ego overwhelmed by such regression and loss or abdication of control, must have appeared too alarming to English novelists hitherto. Or we can put it another way and state that before Dickens no English novelist had appeared with an ego of such imperial powers and with a sense of reality so secure that he could temporarily abandon those powers without fear of being overwhelmed or of their permanent loss. At the same time, such an abandonment, successfully carried through, marks the opening up of a new dimension of freedom for the English novel, if not for the human mind in general. Thus at the outset of *Pickwick Papers* Dickens has allowed the language to go into motion within him, and it is to the motion of that language, to its movement in writing, that we must first attend.

Chapter 2 opens with Mr. Pickwick about to begin experiencing the world, which is as yet unformed, undifferentiated, and uncreated, as he is himself. He has had almost no experience, but as we quickly learn the experience that he has not had is essentially linguistic experience. As his encounter with the cab man demonstrates at once:

> "How old is that horse, my friend?" inquired Mr. Pickwick, rubbing his nose with the shilling he had reserved for the fare.
> "Forty-two," replied the driver, eyeing him askant.
> "What!" ejaculated Mr. Pickwick, laying his hand upon his notebook. The driver reiterated his former statement. . . .
> "And how long do you keep him out at a time?" inquired Mr. Pickwick, searching for further information.
> "Two or three weeks," replied the man.
> "Weeks!" said Mr. Pickwick in astonishment—and out came the notebook again.

"He lives at Pentonwil when he's at home," observed the driver, coolly, "but we seldom takes him home, on account of his veakness."

"On account of his weakness!" reiterated the perplexed Mr. Pickwick.

"He always falls down when he's took out o' the cab," continued the driver, "but when he's in it, we bears him up werry tight, and takes him in werry short, so as he can't werry well fall down; and we've got a pair o' precious large wheels on, so ven he *does* move, they run after him, and he must go on—he can't help it."

What we learn from this meeting of minds is that the cab man is using language in the Pickwickian sense, but Mr. Pickwick is not. Mr. Pickwick's use of the language is literal, abstractly symbolic, and almost entirely denotative and normative, and as the novel continues this characteristic of his becomes increasingly pronounced. He does not yet understand language, and his innocence is primarily a linguistic innocence. And yet we recall that he is supposed to be the Logos as well, whose principal creation is language, the means of which comprise all other creation, including those utterances that are his self-creation. In this reversal and paradox, Dickens has erected for himself a problem whose multiple workings-out will occupy considerable space throughout the novel.

But Dickens is not yet ready for that, and the affray between the Pickwickians and the cab man is brought to an end by the entrance of Jingle who delivers them from the embraces of the crowd that surrounds them and into the equally vigorous embrace of volubility and verbiage with which he succeeds to envelop them.

"Heads, heads—take care of your heads!" cried the loquacious stranger, as they came out under the low archway, which in those days formed the entrance to the coach-yard. "Terrible place—dangerous work—other day—five children—mother—tall lady, eating sandwiches—forgot the arch—crash—knock—children look round—mother's head off—sandwich in her hand—no mouth to put it in—head of a family off—shocking, shocking! Looking at Whitehall, sir?—fine place—little window—somebody else's head off there, eh, sir?—he didn't keep a sharp look-out enough either—eh, sir, eh?"

At this point, it may be said, *Pickwick Papers* is off and running, it has really begun to find itself. Jingle is an approximation of uninflected linguistic energy. He seems incoherent but he is not; his speech proceeds rapidly and by associations; his syntactical mode is abbreviatory and contracted; his logic is elliptical, abstractly minimal, and apropositional. He brings us into closer touch with the primary process. He is, moreover, the first expression of the "constant succession" that Dickens mentions in his preface to the first edition; but the constant succession, as it first appears here and will persist throughout the novel, is the constant succession of writing, of characters rising up to speak in print in unending torrents of words, of language in incessant motion, of writing apparently and extraordinarily writing itself—through the no less extraordinary means of Dickens. It is almost as if in Jingle Dickens had hit upon or invented a way of dramatizing or embodying this unconscious apprehension or conception, that somehow language itself is spontaneously creating this novel— and it is that conception that provides the dramatic substructure of rather more than half the novel.

But Jingle's speech is something more than this. At a slightly later point Dickens refers to it as a "system of stenography," and here we arrive on closer grounds. For Dickens had of course been a stenographer, a writer of shorthand, the very best shorthand writer of his time. He started to learn it soon after he went to work as a clerk at Ellis and Blackmore's, before he was sixteen years old; he had written in it for years in his work in Doctor's Commons and other courts and as a parliamentary reporter; and he was never to forget it, as he reminded his audience in a memorable speech made in his later life. For a number of important formative years he had worked as a kind of written recording device for the human voice, for speech, for the English language. He had been a writing instrument for others, their language flowing through his writing. In one sense those written voices were all inside of him, wonderfully and instantaneously recorded on the most remarkable of all electronic tapes, and now were about to be played back and expressed—although the mechanical and electronic analogy is, I should forcibly state, far from being an adequate approximation to what it was that went on inside him. In another sense Dickens was acting as the stenographer of his characters and of the language itself as well as of its written form; he was transcribing writing, writing down what that particular mode of the language said to him and through him. And yet these notions of stenographic memory and transcription, however useful and suggestive they may be, are surely insufficient, for nothing is less mistakable about the writing of *Pickwick Papers* than its qualities of free inventiveness, of active, spontaneous creativity, of its movement in a higher imaginative order than that which is circumscribed by storage, memory, or recoverable transcriptions alone.

There is, however, another side to this experience that is relevant to our argument. Dickens describes what it was like to learn shorthand in a famous passage in *David Copperfield* (chap. 38). He had laid out the sum of half a guinea on "an approved scheme of the noble art and mystery of stenography"—it was Gurney's textbook, *Brachygraphy, or an Easy and Compendious System of Shorthand*—

> and plunged into a sea of perplexity that brought me, in a few weeks, to the confines of distraction. The changes that were rung upon dots, which in such a position meant such a thing, and in another position something else, entirely different; the wonderful vagaries that were played by circles; the unaccountable consequences that resulted from marks like flies' legs; the tremendous effects of a curve in a wrong place; not only troubled my waking hours, but reappeared before me in my sleep. When I had groped my way, blindly, through these difficulties, and had mastered the alphabet, which was an Egyptian Temple in itself, there then appeared a procession of new horrors, called arbitrary characters; the most despotic characters I have ever known; who insisted, for instance, that a thing like the beginning of a cobweb, meant expectation, and that a pen-and-ink sky-rocket stood for disadvantageous. When I had fixed these wretches in my mind, I found that they had driven everything else out of it; then, beginning again, I forgot them; while I was picking them up, I dropped the other fragments of the system.

He goes on to describe how after three or four months, when he first made an attempt to take down a speech at Doctor's Commons, the "speaker walked off from me before I began, and left my imbecile pencil staggering about the paper as if it were in a fit!" He turns to practicing at night with Traddles, who reads out speeches to him from "Enfield's Speaker or a volume of parliamentary orations," which the aspiring young writer faithfully takes down. "But, as to reading them after I had got them, I might as well have copied the Chinese inscriptions on an immense collection of tea-chests, or the golden characters on all the great red and green bottles in the chemists' shops!" In short, he concludes, he spent this period "making the most desperate efforts to know these elusive characters by sight whenever I met them." I should like to suggest that Dickens's prolonged experience as a shorthand writer had a significant effect on what for a writer must be the most important of relations, the relation between speech and writing. The brachygraphic characters, as he describes them in recollection, were themselves doodles—apparently random plays of the pen, out of which figures or partial figures would emerge and to which meaning could be ascribed. It was almost as if the nascent novelist had providentially been given or discovered another way of structurally relating himself to the language. Speech could now be rendered not only in the abstract forms of cursive or printed letters and units; it could be represented *graphically* as well—the two other forms of written transcription that he refers to are Egyptian hieroglyphics and Chinese ideograms (along with the written code of science, chemistry). What I am suggesting is that this experience of an alternative, quasi-graphic way of representing speech had among other things the effect upon Dickens of loosening up the rigid relations between speech and writing that prevail in our linguistic and cultural system. By providing him with an experience of something that closely resembled a hieroglyphic means of preserving speech, it allowed the spoken language to enter into his writing with a parity it had never enjoyed before in English fictional prose. Speech here was not the traditional subordinate of its written representation; it could appear now in writing with a freedom and spontaneity that made it virtually, if momentarily, writing's equal. And yet whenever a development of this magnitude takes place in writing, in literature, the capacities and possibilities of that written art are themselves suddenly multiplied and enhanced.

This kind of free, wild, inventive doodling language tends to break out in character after character in *Pickwick Papers,* even the most minor ones. The instances are almost limitless, and one more will have to stand for all the rest. After the Dingley Dell–Muggleton cricket match (at which, by the way, Jingle makes another sensational appearance with an account of his own epic match with Sir Thomas Blazo in the West Indies), little Mr. Staple arises to address the assembled company.

> But, sir, while we remember that Muggleton has given birth to a Dumkins and a Podder, let us never forget that Dingley Dell can boast a Luffey and a Struggles ... Every gentleman who hears me, is probably acquainted with the reply made by an individual, who—to use an ordinary figure of speech—"hung out" in a tub, to the emperor Alexander:—"If I were not Diogenes," said he, "I would be Alexander." I can well imagine

these gentlemen to say, "If I were not Dumkins I would be Luffey; if I were not Podder I would be Struggles." (Enthusiasm.) But . . . is it in cricket alone that your fellow-townsmen stand preeminent? Have you never heard of Dumkins and determination? Have you never been taught to associate Podder with prosperity? (Great applause.)

But this kind of language in which the primary process is having a field day (which does not mean that it is pure fantasy without reference to realities of every description, external as well as internal and linguistic) gets into Dickens's authorial prose as well. It is to be found particularly in his metaphoric figures. Here are two examples: "The evening grew more dull every moment, and a melancholy wind sounded through the deserted fields, like a distant giant whistling for his house-dog" (chap. 2). Or there is this from Dingley Dell and the courtship of Tupman and Miss Wardle. "It was evening . . . the buxom servants were lounging at the side-door, enjoying the pleasantness of the hour, and the delights of a flirtation, on first principles, with certain unwieldy animals attached to the farm; and there sat the interesting pair, uncared for by all, caring for none, and dreaming only of themselves; there they sat, in short, like a pair of carefully-folded kid gloves—bound up in each other" (chap. 8).

As the novel advances Dickens becomes increasingly preoccupied with what it is he is doing in this connection, and at a crucial juncture in its early development this preoccupation surfaces and begins consciously to inform the entire substance of an episode. I am referring to the stone and "Bill Stumps, his mark." Mr. Pickwick discovers the stone and its "fragment of an inscription," but although he can make out the markings and letters, he cannot decipher their meaning. Writing and language remain a secret, a puzzle, an arcanum to him. What he finds is a species of writing, a hieroglyphic, that for him does not reduce to ordinary sense. He thereupon writes a pamphlet ninety-six pages long that contains "twenty-seven different readings of the inscription," and achieves great renown among the learned societies of the civilized world. At this point the vicious Blotton turns up again with another of his poisonous accusations. He denies "the antiquity of the inscription," accuses Pickwick of being a mystifier or a fool, and produces the evidence of the man who sold the stone to Mr. Pickwick. Yet if Blotton is correct what has he found except writing that is precisely a kind of doodling. It was written or inscribed "in an idle mood," that is to say at random; it is writing apparently for the sake of writing alone. Moreover, it contains still another paradox within itself, since what is supposed to have been written down is the traditional formula that is used when an illiterate man makes his mark. Hence this is the utterly confounding riddle of writing by a man who appears to be *illiterate,* and so perhaps Mr. Pickwick is right after all. In any case, right or wrong, Pickwick or Blotton, what we are confronted with here is writing in the Pickwickian sense once more. And so at this juncture too the book reveals itself as being at some deep structural level about the act of its own coming into existence. It is writing about writing, and writing itself—as is "BILL STUMPS, HIS MARK." As a result, Dickens remarks, the stone is "an illegible monument" to Mr. Pickwick, something written but mysteriously unreadable, as in a sense is Dickens in *Pickwick Papers.*

The importance I attribute to this episode is supported by what comes immediately after it. In the very next chapter the novel takes its first really large swerve of development, which is in fact a double swerve. Mr. Pickwick does two things. He sends for Sam Weller, the great master of language and invention, who by virtue of that mastery is going to protect Mr. Pickwick from the world. But while he is doing so he gets into trouble with Mrs. Bardell precisely by being betrayed by the language, which, Mr. Pickwick will never be quite able to learn, has an ambiguous social life all its own. The sexual and linguistic plays and implications of the scene need only be touched upon. While Mr. Pickwick is begetting his only begotten son—it is one of the few truly immaculate conceptions in world history—he is having a conversation with Mrs. Bardell that is full of sexual double entendres, none of which are apparent or intelligible to him. Although he has not committed criminal conversation with Mrs. Bardell, he is going to be found guilty of a linguistic offense at law, for which he will be punished, namely breach of promise. His bafflement by language, by the inescapable form in which the experience of this novel (and he himself) is created, is going to lead to his suffering. This eventuality is, however, postponed to a later part of the book, for at this moment with the active entry of Sam Weller, the novel's proportions are altered again, and it has at last settled into its full course. From now on Mr. Pickwick will be explicitly represented as employing the language in an essentially innocent or single-minded sense, and out of this his moral innocence and goodness will inexorably grow. At the same time, in Sam, Dickens has invented a virtuoso of language, of both the primary and secondary processes; he is a master hand at managing means and ends, of actively engaging reality through rational, symbolic language as well as appreciating it and playing with it through the other kind. He is unmistakably Dickens's principal surrogate in the novel itself, the novelist-poet within the novel, and becomes from the moment of his effective entry its dominant creative center.

Hereafter the novel becomes even more clearly a "continuous succession" of language or writing in constant motion, moving itself. We pass directly on to Eatanswill where we have the language or diction of politics, generating its own obfuscation. Along with this there is Mr. Pott and his journalistic writings and style—in relation to which Mr. Pickwick remains the linguistic innocent. Pott asks Mr. Pickwick to read with him some of his leaders, upon which Dickens comments: "We have every reason to believe that he was perfectly enraptured with the vigour and freshness of the style; indeed . . . his eyes were closed, as if with excess of pleasure, during the whole time of their perusal" (chap. 13). And indeed one of the most charming moments in the entire novel is when Mr. Pickwick forgets how to speak altogether. Soon, however, everything is breaking into speech, including the furniture, as the chair does in "The Bagman's Tale" of Tom Smart. There naturally follows Mrs. Leo Hunter and her literary breakfasts—the subject of which is literature and writing, and we find again that the writing, the novel, takes itself for its subject in the very act of its creation. Pope gets into it under false pretenses—"feasts of reason, sir, and flows of soul," quotes Mr. Leo Hunter, who then adds "as somebody who wrote a sonnet to Mrs. Leo Hunter on her breakfasts, feelingly and originally observed"—as do language and writing in almost innumerable forms, some of them indescribable. Even foreigners are dragged into the act, as in the passages about Count Smorltork and his pursuit of English under difficulties, passages which Dickens was going to use again but to other effects almost thirty years later in *Our Mutual Friend*.

By this time it seems evident that Dickens was intermittently and fleetingly close to being aware of the extraordinary thing that was happening to him or that he was doing—it is never quite clear which. There are any number of instances that indicate such an oblique and partial awareness, out of which mass I shall choose but one. It occurs at the beginning of chapter 17, with Mr. Pickwick in bed with an attack of rheumatism brought on by his night spent outdoors in the damp. The bulk of the chapter consists of the tale of "The Parish Clerk," which Mr. Pickwick produces, "with sundry blushes . . . as having been 'edited' by himself, during his recent indisposition, from his notes of Mr. Weller's unsophisticated recital." This is a wonderful bit of play, and what we have is as follows: at this moment Pickwick is to Sam as Dickens is to Mr. Pickwick. Yet we know as well that Sam is in some closely intimate sense also Dickens. So Pickwick is to Dickens as Dickens is to Pickwick—that is, for an instant Pickwick is editing Dickens, or in other words writing his own book. Once again writing seems to be reflexively writing itself. Another embodiment of this circumstance begins to take shape with the increasing presence in the novel of the law, which is another kind of language and another kind of writing. Mr. Pickwick first becomes aware of its ominous presence when he receives a letter from Dodson and Fogg informing him "that a writ has been issued against you in this suit in the Court of Common Pleas" (chap. 18). The novel thus proceeds to make itself by this continuous succession of kinds of writing spontaneously introduced—and that for the most part is what constitutes its structure. It is a structure that is, like the events themselves, "a gross violation of all established rules and precedents," which may, for all I know, be what Dickens meant when he referred to "a gentle and not-unnatural progress of adventure." For it constitutes itself in the main by Dickens's repeatedly rising up in the form of one character after another and bursting irrepressibly "into an animated torrent of words" (chap. 20).

But that is by no means all *Pickwick Papers* is. There are, for example, those notorious interpolated tales. On this reading—as on others—they dramatically represent the obverse principle to that which informs the body of the novel. In them motion and movement of both language and event come to a dead halt. In almost every one of them, even the funny ones, someone is paralyzed, immobilized, or locked up and imprisoned in something. Their language is not the free, wild, astonishingly creative language of the balance of the novel. It tends almost uniformly to be obsessed, imprisoned, anal, caught in various immobile, repetitive modes—to be for the largest part unmastered. One passage will remind us adequately of the effect of the whole. It comes from the most important of those tales, "The Old Man's Tale about the Queer Client."

> That night, in the silence and desolation of his miserable room, the wretched man knelt down by the dead body of his wife, and called on God to witness a terrible oath, that from that hour, he devoted himself to revenge her death and that of his child; that thenceforth to the last moment of his life, his whole energies should be directed to this *one object;* that his revenge should be protracted and terrible; that his hatred should be undying and inextinguishable; and should hunt its *object* through the world [my italics].
>
> (chap. 21)

The object in question is the antithesis of that "constant succession" which Dickens asserted to be his overarching creative intention. The language in which that object is represented is itself as yet utterly unfree; and the tales of that language are accordingly encapsulated, stuck, encysted, and imbedded in the movement of the novel which moves about and around them.

As that movement proceeds it takes a still wilder turn with the introduction of Tony Weller. Tony is in some measure a representation in language of the energies and workings of the primary process itself; he is Sam without the rationality, the logic, the instrumental relation to the world. Much of him may be caught from this one interchange with Mr. Pickwick, on the nature of the "Wery queer life" led by turnpike keepers.

> "They's all on 'em men as has met vith some disappointment in life," said Mr. Weller senior.
>
> "Ay, ay?" said Mr. Pickwick.
>
> "Yes. Consequence of vich, they retires from the world, and shuts themselves up in pikes; partly vith the view of being solitary, and partly to rewenge themselves on mankind, by takin' tolls."
>
> "Dear me," said Mr. Pickwick, "I never knew that before."
>
> "Fact, sir," said Mr. Weller; "if they was gen'l'm'n you'd call them misanthropes, but as it is, they only takes to pike-keepin'."
>
> (chap. 22)

And Dickens proceeds to remark that Tony's conversation had "the inestimable charm" and virtue of "blending amusement with instruction," thus implying that he is in short literature itself. With Sam and Tony entering upon dialogue the novel finds its most creative moments, many of which are about its own mysterious nature, about the activity whereby it continues to bring itself into being. The *locus classicus*, of course, is chapter 33, which is about Sam's writing a valentine, and Mr. Weller "the elder" delivering "some Critical Sentiments respecting Literary Composition." Detail after detail is brought lightly to bear upon this fundamental preoccupation. There is, for example, the boy, who comes looking for Sam with a message from Tony—"young brockiley sprout" Sam calls him—who having delivered his message "walked away, awakening all the echoes in George Yard as he did so, with several chaste and extremely correct imitations of a drover's whistle, delivered in a tone of peculiar richness and volume." Then there is Sam, looking in a stationer's window and seeing a valentine, which Dickens thereupon describes:

The particular picture on which Sam Weller's eyes were fixed
... was a highly coloured representation of a couple of human
hearts skewered together with an arrow cooking before a cheerful fire, while a male and female cannibal in modern attire: the
gentleman being clad in a blue coat and white trousers, and the
lady in a deep red pelisse with a parasol of the same: were
approaching the meal with hungry eyes, up a serpentine gravel
path leading thereunto. A decidedly indelicate young gentleman, in a pair of wings and nothing else, was depicted as
superintending the cooking; a representation of the spire of the
church in Langham Place, London, appeared in the distance;
and the whole formed a "valentine," of which, as a written
inscription in the window testified, there was a large assort-
ment within, which the shopkeeper pledged himself to dispose
of, to his countrymen generally, at the reduced rate of one and
sixpence each.

Sam then walks on toward Leadenhall Market in search of the Blue Boar,
whence his father's summons had emanated. "Looking round him, he
there beheld a sign-board on which the painter's art had delineated something remotely resembling a cerulean elephant with an aquiline nose in lieu
of a trunk. Rightly conjecturing that this was the Blue Boar himself," he
steps inside and begins to compose his valentine while waiting for his
father. In due time Tony arrives and the immortal conversation about
"literary composition" takes place. "Lovely creetur," begins Sam's valentine.

> "Tain't in poetry, is it?" interposed his father.
> "No, no," replied Sam.
> "Werry glad to hear it," said Mr. Weller. "Poetry's unnat'ral;
> no man ever talked poetry 'cept a beadle on boxin' day, or
> Warren's blackin', or Rowland's oil, or some o' them low
> fellows; never you let yourself down to talk poetry, my boy.
> Begin agin, Sammy."

And he goes on in the course of this conversation to make similar magiste-
rial observations about words, style, metaphor, and writing in general.

In this chapter the young Dickens is writing at the very top of his
inventive bent, and what he is implicitly and covertly asserting is that there
is nothing he cannot capture and represent in his writing. He can gratuitously bring to life the sound of a drover's whistle, or even an extremely
correct imitation of that sound, if that is what is wanted. He can turn

pictures into writing which is more vivid, more graphic, more representational than the pictures themselves—as he does with the valentine. He can represent things more accurately and graphically than graphic art, as he does with the sign of the Blue Boar. His writing is superior even to poetry, both because it is more "natural" and because it can include all poetry, its agents and its objects, within its limitless range. It can even include Warren's blacking, and when we take note of this inclusion we understand that what Dickens is unconsciously asserting is that there is at this moment nothing he cannot overcome, there is nothing he cannot transcend, by writing about it, or through *writing it*. He genuinely feels free, for he is writing in freedom. He is perhaps the first novelist ever to have done so in such a degree.

It is very much to the point that it is at just this moment that Dickens chooses to emphasize that Sam, great poet and impresario of the language that he is, can hardly write. Dickens is the writer and Sam is what he is writing—that is, one brilliantly split off, deflected, and reorganized segment of himself. It was part of Dickens's genius as a writer to write Sam, or to tap that untapped resource of language in the near illiterate, and to get that speech and *its* genius into writing, into his writing. It was his genius, in other words, to be able *to write that as yet unwritten language*. It is at such a juncture that society and social change on the one hand and language and writing on the other all come richly together.

Correlative with this development, Dickens and Sam both become increasingly conscious of the meaning and value of Pickwick. At one point, it is asserted that Pickwick is a "magic word," and in a subsequent episode the cat is let entirely out of the bag. They are waiting in the travelers' room of the White Horse Cellar, when Sam emphatically draws his master's attention to a coach that is standing outside, and to what is written on its door: "and there, sure enough, in gilt letters of a goodly size, was the magic name of PICKWICK!" (chap. 35). At this moment both the magic and the reality that in collaboration go into the formation of creative originality are brought into active conjunction. For the name of Pickwick was clearly taken by Dickens from the actual man who ran the Bath coach. Moreover, as Sam does not fail indignantly to inform us, his first name was Moses. And at this point it becomes our turn to recall that "Boz" is a shortened version of Moses—and to realize again and in another way what we already know differently, that Boz and Pickwick are of course one. Even more, however, the real Pickwick was a coachman—and thus we realize once again that Mr. Pickwick and Tony are also in reality one, as in point of fact they were, both of them imaginative refractions and idealizations of John Dickens. It is Sam who voices Dickens's final comment on this nexus, saying something for once that is beyond his own enlarged understanding. To put the name Moses before Pickwick, he says, is what "I call addin' insult to injury, as the parrot said ven they not only took him from his native land, but made him talk the English langwidge arterwards" (chap. 35). The whole secret is in learning the English language; the secret lies in that primordial mystery that seems spontaneously to be creating out of itself, out of its own inherent resources, this marvelous work.

Finally there is the trial, which is a veritable mania of language in almost all the forms that have appeared before. There is the language, or languages, of the law itself; there is more court reporting on Dickens's part and more shorthand writing in an ideally transcribed form. There is the rhetoric of Buzfuz, and his masterful dealing with writing, with Mrs. Bardell's "written placard"—"I intreat the attention of the jury to the wording of this document. 'Apartments furnished for a single gentleman'!"—as well as with Mr. Pickwick's fatally compromising letters. There is the presiding judge, Mr. Justice Stareleigh, who wakening from the slumber in which he conducts almost all of the trial "immediately wrote down something with a pen without any ink in it," and whose questioning of Winkle follows a similar intelligible line.

> "What's your Christian name, sir?" angrily inquired the little judge.
> "Nathaniel, sir."
> "Daniel,—any other name?"
> "Nathaniel, sir—my Lord, I mean."
> "Nathaniel Daniel, or Daniel Nathaniel?"
> "No, my Lord, only Nathaniel; not Daniel at all."
> "What did you tell me it was Daniel for, then, sir?" inquired the judge.
> "I didn't, my Lord," replied Mr. Winkle.
> "You did, sir," replied the judge, with a severe frown. "How could I have got Daniel on my notes, unless you told me so, sir?"
> This argument was, of course, unanswerable.

Exactly. As are those arguments and circumstances through which Mr. Pickwick at length finds himself in prison, at which point, as everyone knows, the novel makes its final, momentous turn of development. Mr. Pickwick has in effect let himself be put in prison by the law, by its licentious abuse and misuse of language. And as he is thus confined within

the world or precincts of the law, Dickens's writing too becomes imprisoned and immobile, preoccupied again as it was in the tales with intensi-
ties and obsessions and closeness and deprivation and filth, bound in by
the law, by cases, by the past, by the accumulated weight of mold and dirt
and misery that the prison and the law represent. But the writing in these
crucial passages is not exactly the same as the writing in the interpolated
tales; it is harder and has a greater bite to it. That writing, which before was
free, has become like Mr. Pickwick himself engaged and involved, and
engaged and involved with society. For in the person of the law Pickwick
and Dickens have run into something which though it may seem at
first to be an unalloyed linguistic universe is in fact much more than a
world of words. It is and it represents society and its structures, in
particular those structures known as property and money, both of them
extralinguistic phenomena. Property and money are more than words, and
words cannot make you free of them. It is a matter of the very largest
moment for Dickens's development as a writer—and a testimony to his
exceptional inner integrity—that he should in the midst of his greatest
celebration of his freedom and transcendence as a genius of language,
engage himself imaginatively in those very conditions which were calculated most powerfully to nullify that freedom. His entire future development is contained by anticipation in that nullification.

In one of his later utterances, Hegel undertook to settle a long-
outstanding score between himself and Rousseau. As for the Rousseauian
idea of some original state of freedom, he declared bluntly, it simply makes
no sense. Hegel was a great genius, but he was an old man when he made
this remark and had long since forgotten his childhood and youth, let
alone his youthful writings. Dickens was also a great genius, who wrote
Pickwick Papers in the flush of his young manhood, as a celebration of the
positive sides of the childhood and youth that he yet remembered and as
an exercise of what may be the highest kind of freedom that an individual
person can enjoy, the freedom that consists in the exercise of one's native
powers and that has as its consequence the creation out of one's self of an
object that is of lasting value and that is at the same time an activity of
self-creation. What Hegel goes on next to say, however, is of larger
pertinence. It is true, he declares, that we are all unfree, that we all suffer
from a pervasive sense of limitation, confinement, and constraint; yet that
very constraint, he states, "is part of the process through which is first
produced the consciousness of and the desire for freedom in its true, that
is, its rational and ideal form." Indeed, he continues, every terrible limitation upon impulse, desire, and passion that we feel is itself "the very

condition leading to liberation; and society and the state are the very conditions in which freedom is realized." What Hegel in his prodigious austerity is saying is that freedom can only come about, can only be realized, in and through its negation. A truly human freedom, that freedom which is the one goal worthy of being the "destination" of men as the human species, can only be achieved through the most profound historical experience of negativity. It is, it seems to me, no accident that Dickens installed that negativity at the dramatic center of his first and freest novel, at the very moment when he was sustaining himself with a freedom that was virtually unexampled in the history of the novel. The consequences that such a creative act of courage had are known to us all—they are nothing less than Dickens's long and arduous subsequent development, a development that as the later novels make increasingly clear is in fact a search for a wider, a more general, and a truly human freedom.

HARRY STONE

A Christmas Carol:
"Giving Nursery Tales a Higher Form"

In the interval between the beginning of *Martin Chuzzlewit* and the completion of *Dombey and Son,* Dickens wrote five Christmas books: *A Christmas Carol* (1843), *The Chimes* (1844), *The Cricket on the Hearth* (1845), *The Battle of Life* (1846), and *The Haunted Man* (1848). *The Haunted Man,* the last of the Christmas books, straddles the later limits of this interval. *The Haunted Man* was conceived and partly written in the interval, but not finished until *Dombey* was completed. With the exception of *The Battle of Life,* which depends for its central mechanism on a straightforward analogy between life and an ancient battlefield, the Christmas books rely on fairy-tale machinery to gain their characteristic effects. But this puts the matter too restrictively. The Christmas books draw their innermost energies from fairy tales: they exploit fairy-tale themes, fairy-tale happenings, and fairy-tale techniques. Indeed the Christmas books *are* fairy tales. As Dickens himself put it, he was here taking old nursery tales and "giving them a higher form."

The pattern that Dickens traces in each of his Christmas books— always excepting *The Battle of Life*—is the pattern that he followed with "Gabriel Grub" in *Pickwick.* The design could hardly be simpler or more direct. A protagonist who is mistaken or displays false values is forced, through a series of extraordinary events, to see his errors. This familiar, almost pedestrian given is interfused with fairy-tale elements, a commingling that shapes and transfigures every aspect of the design. Storybook

From *Dickens and the Invisible World: Fairy Tales, Fantasy, and Novel-Making.*
© 1979 by Harry Stone. Indiana University Press, 1979.

signs set the mood, herald the onset of the action, and enforce the moral lessons. Magical happenings dominate the story. The crucial action takes place in a dream or vision presided over by supernatural creatures who control what goes on. The resolution occurs when the happenings of the vision—a magically telescoped survey of the protagonist's life, and a masquelike representation of the consequences of his false attitudes—force him to reassess his views. In the fashion of most fairy stories, the moral is strongly reiterated at the end.

This structure was of immense value to Dickens. It gave him a framework that provided an aesthetic justification for the legerdemain which in his earlier works, especially in his finales, had usually appeared, not as fairy-tale felicities, but as arbitrary fairy-tale wrenchings. He could now show misery and horror and yet do so in a context of joyful affirmation. He could depict evil flourishing to its ultimate flowering and still deny that flowering. He could introduce the most disparate scenes, events, and visions without losing the reader's confidence. He could manipulate time with no need to obey the ordinary laws of chronology. He could make his characters and events real when he wished them real, magical when he wished them magical. He could effect overnight conversions which could be justified aesthetically. He could teach by parable rather than exhortation. And he could deal with life in terms of a storybook logic that underscored both the real and the ideal.

These potentialities, fundamental ingredients in Dickens's mature narrative method (but there thoroughly assimilated to the dominant realism), are exploited with varying degrees of success in all the Christmas books. In *A Christmas Carol*, to take the first of the Christmas books, Dickens adapts fairy-tale effects and fairy-tale techniques with marvelous skill. All readers are aware of the ghosts and spirits that manipulate the story, but these supernatural beings are only the most obvious signs of a pervasive indebtedness to fairy stories. Dickens himself emphasized that indebtedness. He subtitled his novelette *A Ghost Story of Christmas,* and he followed this spectral overture with other magical associations. In the preface to the *Carol* he told potential readers that he had endeavored "in this ghostly little book, to raise the Ghost of an Idea." Then he went on: "May it haunt their houses pleasantly and no one wish to lay it!" The chapter headings continue this emphasis. Four of the five headings reinforce supernatural expectations: "Marley's Ghost," "The First of the Three Spirits," "The Second of the Three Spirits," and "The Last of the Spirits." With such signposts at the outset, we can expect the journey itself to be full of wondrous events. We are not disappointed, though the opening begins disarmingly enough. It insists on the deadness of Marley and then drifts into a long, facetious reference to the ghost of Hamlet's father. The narrator's attitude is worldly and commonsensical, but Marley's deadness and the ghost of Hamlet's father set the scene for the wild events that are about to take place.

Scrooge sets the scene too. He has much of the archetypal miser in him, but he is more of an ordinary man than his immediate prototypes, prototypes such as Gabriel Grub, Arthur Gride, Ralph Nickleby, and Jonas Chuzzlewit. Yet at the same time Scrooge is compassed round with supernatural attributes that cunningly suffuse his fundamental realism. One soon sees how this process works. The freezing cold that pervades his inner being frosts all his external features and outward mannerisms (nipped and pointed nose, shrivelled cheek, stiffened gait, red eyes, blue lips, grating voice), and this glacial iciness chills all the world without. "He carried his own low temperature always about with him; he iced his office in the dog-days; and didn't thaw it one degree at Christmas. . . . No warmth could warm, no wintry weather chill him." In this respect Scrooge is a prototype of Mr. Dombey. That cold gentleman freezes and congeals his small universe with haughty frostiness.

The story proper of *A Christmas Carol* begins with the traditional "Once upon a time." After this evocative opening Dickens quickly intensifies the storybook atmosphere. Scrooge lives in Marley's old chambers, and Marley died seven years ago on Christmas Eve, that is, seven years ago on the night the story opens. It is a foggy night. Nearby houses dwindle mysteriously into "mere phantoms"; ghostly forms loom dimly in the hazy mist. Out of such details, out of cold, fog, and frost, and out of brief touches of contrasting warmth, Dickens builds an atmosphere dense with personification, animism, anthropomorphism, and the like. The inanimate world is alive and active; every structure, every object plays its percipient role in the unfolding drama. Buildings and gateways, bedposts and door knockers become sentient beings that conspire in a universal morality. Everything is connected by magical means to everything else. Scrooge's chambers are a case in point. The narrator tells us that they are in a lonely, isolated building that must have played hide-and-seek with other houses in its youth, run into a yard where it had no business to be, forgotten its way out again, and remained there ever since. This lost, isolated, cutoff building, fit residence for a lost, isolated, cutoff man, has its own special weather and tutelary spirit. The fog and frost hang so heavy about the black old gateway of this building "that it seemed as if the Genius of the Weather sat in mournful meditation on the threshold."

Given a universe so magical and responsive, we are hardly surprised when Scrooge momentarily sees Marley's face glowing faintly in his front-door knocker, its "ghostly spectacles turned up on its ghostly forehead." When Scrooge sees an equally ghostly hearse on his staircase a few moments later, we know that he is in for a night of it. Thus we are fully prepared for Marley's ghost when it does appear, and we know how to interpret its every movement and accoutrement. Marley's ghost is a superb compound of social symbolism, wild imagination, realistic detail, and grisly humor. It moves in its own strange atmosphere, its hair and clothes stirring curiously, as though agitated by "the hot vapour from an oven"; it wears a bandage round its head, and when it removes this death cloth, its lower jaw drops down upon its breast. Like Blake's city-pent Londoner, Marley's ghost drags and clanks its "mind-forg'd manacles," the chain it "forged in life" and girded on of its "own free will"; like the ghost of Hamlet's father, it is doomed to walk the night and wander restlessly abroad. Scrooge is skeptical of this apparition, but he is no match for the ghost's supernatural power. Like the Ancient Mariner with the wedding guest, the ghost "hath his will." When Scrooge offers his last resistance, the ghost raises a frightful cry, shakes its chains appallingly, and takes the bandage from round its head. Scrooge falls on his knees and submits. Like the wedding guest, now Scrooge "cannot choose but hear." And as in the *Ancient Mariner,* where the wedding guest's struggle and reluctant submission help us suspend our disbelief, in *A Christmas Carol* Scrooge's struggle and submission help us to a like suspension. The ghost has accomplished its mission; the work of the three spirits, work that will culminate in Scrooge's redemption (and our enlightenment), can now begin.

The three spirits or ghosts (Dickens uses the terms interchangeably) are allegorical figures as well as supernatural agents. The Ghost of Christmas Past combines in his person and in his actions distance and closeness, childhood and age, forgetfulness and memory; in a similar fashion the Ghost of Christmas Present is a figure of ease, plenty, and joy—an embodiment of the meaning of Christmas; the Ghost of Christmas Yet to Come, on the other hand, a hooded and shrouded Death, bears implacable witness to the fatal course Scrooge has been pursuing. Each spirit, in other words, enacts a role and presides over scenes that befit its representation. But it is the scenes rather than the spirits that are all-important. The scenes embody Dickens's message in swift vignettes and unforgettable paradigms—Fezziwig's ball, the Cratchits' Christmas dinner, Scrooge's lonely grave. By means of the fairy-tale machinery Dickens can move instantaneously from magic-lantern picture to magic-lantern picture, juxtaposing, contrasting, commenting, and counterpointing, and he can do all this with absolute freedom and ease. He can evoke the crucial image, limn the archetypal scene, concentrate on the traumatic spot of time, with no need to sketch the valleys in between. Like Le Sage much earlier in *The Devil upon Two Sticks* (a boyhood favorite of Dickens), he can fly over the unsuspecting city, lift its imperturbable rooftops, and reveal swift tableaus of pathos and passion; like Joyce much later in the opening pages of *A Portrait of the Artist as a Young Man,* he can race through the years, linger here and there, and provide brief glimpses of the unregarded moments that move and shape us. The overall effect, however, is more like that of a richly colored Japanese screen. Amid swirling mists and dense clouds one glimpses prototypical scenes of serenity and turmoil, joy and nightmare horror.

Through Scrooge Dickens attempts to embody symbolic, social, psychological, and mythic truth. Scrooge is an outrageous miser and ogre, but he is also an emblem of more ordinary pathology: he is an epitome of all selfish and self-regarding men. In his latter aspect, he touches our lives. He allows us to see how self-interest—an impulse that motivates each one of us—can swell to monster proportions. He shows us how not to live, and then, at the end, he points us toward salvation. That lesson has social as well as symbolic ramifications. We are made to see that in grinding Bob Cratchit Scrooge grinds himself, that in letting Tiny Tim perish he perishes alive himself. All society is connected: individual actions are not self-contained and personal, they have social consequences; social evils are not limited and discrete, they taint the whole society. These ideas, of course, were not unique to Dickens. They were being preached by many Victorians, by two such different men—both friends of Dickens—as Douglas Jerrold and Thomas Carlyle, for example. But Dickens presents these ideas in a more seductive guise than any of his contemporaries. And he blends teaching with much else.

For one thing, he merges symbolic paradigms and social doctrines with psychological analysis. By means of a few swift childhood vignettes he gives us some notion of why Scrooge became what he is. The first spirit shows Scrooge an image of his early self: "a solitary child, neglected by his friends," and left alone in school at Christmas time. This scene of loneliness and neglect is mitigated by a single relief: the boy's intense reading. The reading is not simply referred to, it comes to life, a bright pageant of color and warmth in his drab isolation. The exotic characters from that reading troop into the barren room and enact their familiar adventures.

Scenes from *The Arabian Nights* flash before Scrooge, then images from *Valentine and Orson,* then vignettes from *The Arabian Nights* again, then episodes from *Robinson Crusoe*—all as of yore, all wonderfully thrilling and absorbing. Scrooge is beside himself with excitement. The long-forgotten memory of his lonely self and of his succoring reading softens him: he remembers what it was to be a child; he wishes that he had given something to the boy who sang a Christmas carol at his door the night before. A moment later Scrooge is looking at a somewhat older image of his former self, again alone in a school, again left behind at Christmas time. But now his sister Fan enters and tells him that he can come home at last, that father is kinder now and will permit him to return, that Scrooge is to be a man and "never to come back here" again. These memories also soften Scrooge.

The memories, of course, are versions of Dickens's own experiences: the lonely boy "reading as if for life," and saved by that reading; the abandoned child, left in Chatham to finish the Christmas term, while the family goes off to London; the banished son (banished while Fanny remains free), exiled by his father to the blacking warehouse and then released by him at last. These wounding experiences, or rather the *Carol* version of them, help turn Scrooge (and here he is very different from the outward Dickens) into a lonely, isolated man intent on insulating himself from harm or hurt. In a subsequent vignette, a vignette between him and his fiancée, Scrooge chooses money over love. He is the victim of his earlier wound. He seeks through power and aggrandizement to gird himself against the vulnerability that had scarred his childhood. But in making himself invulnerable, he shuts out humanity as well. This happens to Scrooge because, paradoxically, in trying to triumph over his past, he has forgotten it; he has forgotten what it is to be a child, he has forgotten what it is to be lonely and friendless, to cry, laugh, imagine, yearn, and love. The first spirit, through memory, helps Scrooge recover his past, helps him recover the humanness (the responsiveness and fellow feeling) and the imagination (the reading and the visions) that were his birthright, that are every man's birthright.

All this, and much more, is done swiftly and economically with the aid of Dickens's fairy-tale format. The rapid shifts from scene to scene, the spirits' pointed questions and answers, the telescoping, blurring, and juxtaposition of time, the fusion of allegory, realism, psychology, and fancy—all are made possible, all are brought into order and believability, by Dickens's storybook atmosphere and storybook devices. *A Christmas Carol* has a greater unity of effect, a greater concentration of thematic purpose, a greater economy of means towards ends, and a greater sense of integration and cohesiveness than any previous work by Dickens.

A Christmas Carol is the finest of the Christmas books. This preeminence results from its consummate melding of the most archetypal losses, fears, and yearnings with the most lucid embodiment of such elements in characters and actions. No other Christmas book displays this perfect coming together of concept and vehicle. The result is a most powerful, almost mythic statement of widely held truths and aspirations. Scrooge represents every man who has hardened his heart, lost his ability to feel, separated himself from his fellow men, or sacrificed his life to ego, power, or accumulation. The symbolic force of Scrooge's conversion is allied to the relief we feel (since we are all Scrooges, in part) in knowing that we too can change and be reborn. This is why we are moved by the reborn Scrooge's childlike exultation in his prosaic physical surroundings, by his glee at still having time to give and share. We too can exult in "Golden sunlight; Heavenly sky; sweet fresh air; merry bells"; we too can cry, "Oh, glorious. Glorious!"; we too can give and share. Scrooge assures us that we can advance from the prison of self to the paradise of community. The *Carol's* fairy-tale structure helps in that assurance. The structure evokes and objectifies the undefiled world of childhood and makes us feel that we, like Scrooge, can recapture it. Deep symbolic identifications such as these, identifications that stir us whether we are consciously aware of them or not, give *A Christmas Carol* its enduring grip on our culture. *A Christmas Carol* is a myth or fairy tale for our times, one that is still full of life and relevance. Its yearly resurrection in advertisement, cartoon, and television program, its reappearance in new versions (in Bergman's *Wild Strawberries,* to cite only one instance), testify to this.

Yet the vitality of *A Christmas Carol* raises other questions. Why is the *Carol,* which elaborates the central idea found in the Gabriel Grub story in *Pickwick,* so much better than its prototype? "Gabriel Grub" does not elicit the empathy of the *Carol.* This is so because Gabriel never ascends to universality; he is simply a mean man who is taught an idiosyncratic lesson. We see nothing of his childhood, of his development, of his future; we see nothing, in other words, of the shaping forces that would allow us to relate to his experiences. The story centers on his drunken vision; it scants his salvation and our enlightenment. Furthermore, "Gabriel Grub" lacks any rich social import. Unlike the *Carol,* there is virtually no intertwining of plot with social criticism: no ideas about ignorance and want, no anatomy of materialism, no criticism of relations between employer and employee, no effective demonstration of how to

live. Misanthropy is simply presented and then punished. I am not suggesting that a work of art must have a social message. I am simply affirming
that part of the *Carol*'s appeal comes from its powerful demonstration of
how a man should live—live in society—if he is to save his soul, a kind of
demonstration that is largely lacking in "Gabriel Grub."

By the same token, the supernatural machinery of "Gabriel Grub,"
despite successful local effects, is mechanical and abrupt. Unlike the *Carol*,
where Marley's ghost is the culmination of many signs and actions, in
"Gabriel Grub" the King of the Goblins appears with little preparation;
again, unlike the *Carol*, where Marley's ghost is a prototype of Scrooge,
and therefore deeply significant, in "Gabriel Grub" the King of the Goblins is simply an agency, a convenient manipulative device, a creature who
has no relevance to Gabriel's life and habits (other, perhaps, than being an
emanation of Gabriel's habitual drunkenness). Even the *Carol* equivalents
to the King of the Goblins, the three spirits, have an allegorical pertinence
that the King of the Goblins lacks. In part these differences in the two
stories are owing to differences in length, but more importantly they are
owing to differences in conception and execution. Obviously the preeminence of the *Carol*, its elevation to culture fable, comes not from the basic
ingredients—they can be found in "Gabriel Grub"—but from the perfect
blending of well-wrought theme and well-wrought form. *A Christmas
Carol* demonstrates how much more skilled Dickens had become in using
fairy-tale conceptions to achieve that virtuoso blending, how adept he had
become in using fairy-tale elements to integrate and convey his view of life.

ROBERT L. CASERIO

Plot and the Point of Reversal

> The descent
> made up of despairs
> and without accomplishment
> realizes a new awakening:
> which is a reversal
> —WILLIAM CARLOS WILLIAMS, Paterson

I have been gathering examples of story congenial to a negative or at least a wary sense of plot, barely illustrating an alternative sense or any grounds for an alternative. It is time to change direction. I have held back positive consideration of plot and story in the hope that their strengths will now become more apparent. Not that we are to be free of doubts about the truth, meaning, or usefulness of plot; but by turning to the function of *peripety* or *reversal* in story, we approach ground on which a confident sense of plot can trust the truth of narrative reason in both its intellectual and moral functions. We also approach ground on which narrative reason is shown to depend upon an alliance of significance or meaning with the featuring of action. But one might wonder how a focus on peripety can be an approach to a trusting sense of plot if reversal represents what Aristotle implies by peripety: the terrible, untrustworthy instability or mutability of experience. My answer is that, at least as Dickens—and his great predecessor Scott—use reversal, peripety's representation of the instability of life incites the clearest and most persuasive reasonings and moralizings of experience. At the same time, the earnest use of reversal in Scott and Dickens testifies to action as the origin of development, of novelty, and of

---

From *Plot, Story, and the Novel: From Dickens and Poe to the Modern Period.*
© 1979 by Princeton University Press.

creativity. Scott and Dickens make us feel that when in story—or in life—we experience reversal, even if this means the overthrow of the purposes of our heroes or of ourselves, we face in surprise and wonder the radical fact of a new difference in experience, a creative development. If reversal in Scott and Dickens annihilates one purposeful motion, another purpose appears in its place.

Thus, through these novelists we see the primacy of action at work in the world as both transformation and transforming force, not, we might add, in the way Carlyle views his version of peripety, the Revolution, as a chaotic static presence, but rather as a definable change. Peripety seems to define the transforming action it represents; where it is used to attenuate or confuse definition or difference or where it is used as mere narrative decor—as an artificial trick or "twist"—we shall find ourselves in the presence of story and plot doubting and undermining themselves. With reversal, as with any of story's elements, a negative sense of plot can work its own distrustful way. The distrust, of course, can issue in brilliant results, as is the case with Poe, whose power and originality depend upon the joining of story with a witty flaunting of peripety. This flaunting lends itself to a modern sense of plot far more than to a sense of plot like that of Dickens, and in this respect Poe is a playful ally of the hostile and wary senses of plot. Dickens and Poe are in fact great antagonistic contrasts as storytellers, and a focus on their use of plot-reversals best defines their implicit antagonism. Whereas Poe's brilliance results from his subversion of the dependence of plot on reversal, Dickens's brilliance results in large part from his cherishing of the experience of reversal and of its structural analogue in story, the point of peripety. The modern sense of plot, especially as it shows itself in the critical interpretation of literary storytelling, is strongly shaped by its response to peripety and is deeply implicated in the contrasting uses of reversal represented by Dickens and Poe.

In considering Dickens's use of reversal in the novel we are taking up issues of literary influence and critical evaluation. We cannot dissociate Dickensian story and its use of reversal from Scott; moreover, Scott's influence on Dickens and Victorian plotting reminds us of Orwell's description of the Victorian plot as "awful." All the "melodrama" and "machinery" Orwell associates with "the awful Victorian plot" derives from Scott, and Orwell's use of both words results from the effect of the continuously surprising and ensnaring peripeties upon which both Scott and Dickens base their stories. Does this indeed make their stories "awful," a complex mechanical muddle? I believe that Dickens plots badly only when he is attempting to prove his talent by resisting Scott's form. Indeed Carlyle's *The French Revolution* and Dickens's *Barnaby Rudge* ought to be understood as two examples of the sense of plot dominated by a jealous hostility to Scott. This means that they are texts dominated by a resistance to yoking together story and plot with the experience and the structural form of reversal. For Scott chooses for his subject, for the keystone of his stories, the fact of a great reversal in human consciousness and human affairs—the English Revolution and Civil War—and the effect it works for more than a hundred years on the daily lives of men and women. This historical reversal is for Scott "the thing in itself." According to Scott, what we are results from the fact and the understanding of the human transformations that have preceded us. The sense of actuality or reality that rules "the infinite arbitrariness of our inner cabalism" originates in reversal, which for Scott bears profoundly on the intelligibility of experience and on any considerations of morality. And of course for Scott's sense of plot, it takes the passing of time to both accomplish and understand reversal; indeed in Scott as in social revolution, time itself is reversal's essential medium. Hence, for example, in *The Heart of Midlothian* the turnings of time and experience represented by the plot finally give us the definitive moral measure, the sadly but inevitably diminished stature of Jeanie Deans's heroic effort to save her sister from death. Here reversal is the ultimate instructor of narrative moral reason. And along with its moral disclosures, reversal also reveals the purely intellectual coherence of the way Effie Deans's son, a follower of Rob Roy, finally kills his father and, fleeing to America, settles with Indians. For this fate of the son is no random and inexplicable melodramatic accident; it articulates in its own small way the continuing fortunes of the tribal life that the English Revolution began utterly to abolish. It is the English Revolution and *its* historical reversal that makes intelligible the only *apparently* wayward and insignificant life of the lost boy. These turnings make experience "tell" for Scott. And of course for Scott, men's actions, above all, bring them to telling points of reversal, just as the reversals of experience bring men to the point of their most telling acts. But when we look to *The French Revolution* and *Barnaby Rudge* we find both narratives stamped with resistance to Scott's assumptions about the instructive nature of peripeties.

Barnaby Rudge does indeed have an awful plot; Dickens's sense of plot, having built so brilliantly on Scott's in *Oliver Twist, Nicholas Nickleby,* and *The Old Curiosity Shop,* is undone temporarily when it competes with Scott in a representation of the era portrayed in *Guy Mannering.* It is undone because Dickens abuses reversal in *Barnaby Rudge,* especially when he attempts to divide his plot from his theme: he has written reversals resolving his plot's conflicts and events into his story, and at the same time has emphasized aspects of the story that leave crucial elements of his plot unexplored and inert. He is forcing a division between what happens and reasoning about what happens, requiring his story and his action to be merely an excuse, a convenience on which to string imaginations and contemplations that undergo no significant transformation or development. To modern criticism this divorce of theme and plot (which I see as a forcing of self-contradiction upon the perspectival functions of story and plot) is congenial. We find one of the most intelligent modern interpreters of *Barnaby Rudge* [Steven Marcus] stating that the novel's true theme is the unresolvable conflicts of fathers and sons, representing "contradictions which, continuing without resolution, make existence intolerable. . . . Nowhere in *Barnaby Rudge* do we find anything that genuinely suggests reconciliation." This is a way of saying that the conflicts of Dickens's plot do not tell us anything but that they are conflicts. In fact his plot tells us much more; but it is as if Dickens, as much as his critic, wants to ignore what the plot tells: he wants to thematize deadlock, even though his story tells of resolution. And the way Dickens can separate the theme from the plot's events, making the plot look like muddled machinery, is by misusing, or by not using at all, the experience and form of reversal.

Before we embroil ourselves in the complicity of modern criticism with its separation of theme and plot and its simultaneous evasion of reversal, let us look more closely at the absurdities occasioned by Dickens's abuse of reversal in *Barnaby Rudge.* This abuse I believe is the result of Dickens's attempt to fight off the influence of Scott's storytelling practice. One of Scott's principal uses of reversal lies in his placement of the wavering figure at the center of his novels (most of which are named generically for the figure who embodies "wavering"). The theme of all Scott's novels has been identified as the search for a way to balance the attractions and claims of differing historical forces when those differences appear in revolutionary conflict. For Scott's heroes, the way of achieving this balance is through their unstable mediocrity, their constant wavering. By his own instability the hero can find out which changing historical forces he should lend himself to and which to abandon in order in the end to achieve independent and balanced maturity (and relative modernity). The plot of this kind of hero's story must also be a continuous wavering, a constant reversing of expectation, allegiance, awareness. Together the wavering hero—and the complex wavering plot—finally enable history and the personal story to make intellectual and moral sense. Of course, the wavering of both hero and plot is a form of constant reversal: the plot fits the theme, its reversals eventually showing how it is that balance can be achieved by the hero's openness in fronting the turns and counterturns of experience and judgment. And the reader too must be kept wavering, so that when the plot reveals and articulates the character's final form and his final historical position, the revelation will seem the just result of all the story's elements and of Scott's disinterestedness.

Now Dickens, by transforming the wavering hero of Scott into Barnaby Rudge, gets rid of wavering altogether. Most of the plot takes its bearing from the fact of Barnaby's idiocy, which Dickens describes with relentless pathos. Barnaby does not have enough sense to waver. Insofar as he stands at the book's center, one cannot gauge with disinterested judgment the value or importance of what happens to or around him. Yet if Barnaby did have wavering sense, the reader could only be as bewildered as he is. For in this novel Dickens has not only banished reversal as constant wavering but he has gotten rid of the idea that history is significant as a turning point in human affairs. What significant reversal in human consciousness and action is represented by the Gordon Riots and 1780? Dickens does not know and cannot say. He uses the idiot Barnaby as a symbol of the urgent incoherent popular needs of England in the 1770s, but he cannot define those needs. In *Barnaby Rudge* history is the projection of private mania or personal hatred and spite; it is thus a tale signifying nothing, or a word masking a kind of noumenal inarticulateness or madness. If we ask if 1780 is for Dickens a turning point in Protestant and Catholic relations in England, we get no answer. Dickens can scarcely be dramatizing Protestantism through the shrewishness of Mrs. Varden, just as he can scarcely be dramatizing Catholicism through Lord Gordon's imbecility. The Catholic-Protestant donnée of the plot has no content after all: the Catholic Geoffrey Haredale works for the emancipation of his coreligionists only offstage; in the story itself his conflict with John Chester results not from religious differences but from the fact that Chester once stole Haredale's only love. Dickens writes the historical religious content into the plot, and almost immediately writes it out. Just as he will not use Scott's wavering hero to make his story tell, so he is not using any demonstrable historical turning point, any significant human reversal and transformation, to make his plot make sense.

In fact in the plot of *Barnaby Rudge* Dickens has imbedded reversals that *do* make sense of what happens, but since he wants to thematize an idea of unresolvable conflicts, he ignores the telling turning points of his story. Mrs. Varden does surrender her religious mania to the cause of domestic peace; the Chester-Haredale hatred reverses itself through the love of their children. Dickens seems merely to mention these turns, however. And the most significant reversal of all, made use of only to be brushed aside by the author, is Gabriel Varden's reversal of the sentence of execution handed down against Barnaby. The theme of "unreconcilable" contradictions and conflicts is built on the antagonism between Hugh "the centaur," the uncivilized man, and his unacknowledged father, John Chester, the civilized man. But by Gabriel's reversal of Barnaby's sentence, the plot tells us what Dickens does not want to consider—that the contradictions are resolvable. By reversing Barnaby's fate, Gabriel Varden, the middling man of the middle class, obviously stands for the possibility of enacting a reconciliation of the natural man (Barnaby and Hugh) to civilization, without suffering contamination by the unnatural diseases of civilization (typified by John Chester, Geoffrey Haredale, and Mrs. Varden). But Dickens in effect throws away his own tale, refusing to articulate what the plot's reversal accounts for. Thus the story of *Barnaby Rudge* seems to be a forced relation of fragments, events, and motives that make no sense. We never know, for example, the motive or meaning behind the murder committed by Barnaby's father. Does this murder also illustrate the "irreconcilable" conflicts? But Varden shows that the conflicts *are* reconcilable. Is the primal murder, which in fact causes Barnaby's idiocy, to highlight for us the inevitable bad effects of bad deeds? But Varden subverts such a logic of effects. The more we ask questions about the plot the more we feel the plot as an encumbrance. And this results from Dickens's rejection of the compositional logic of wavering. In the end one remembers *Barnaby Rudge,* as Orwell would have said, "statically": Hugh and Barnaby and Dennis the hangman have no development, they go on and on in a kind of eternity because Dickens cannot "bring his characters into action" without involving them in a story that, by virtue of his own neglect, looks a mechanical mess.

Yet the absence of narrative reason and of significant reversal in *Barnaby Rudge* is highly unusual for Dickens; I have been forced to explain the novel's uncharacteristic absurdity of plot by positing a competition with Scott that has bad effects on Dickens's form. Elsewhere Dickens plots brilliantly, does not separate story from theme, and makes reversal the heart of his narration. But while the Dickensian sense of plot is *not* represented by *Barnaby Rudge,* modern criticism has been willing not only to overlook this fact but to applaud and to justify Dickens for just the kind of bungling that is rare in his storytelling. The traditional charges against

Dickens's plots have always emphasized their absurdity, their artificial and implausible contrivances, their divagation from the way things happen in ordinary reality. Modern criticism takes these negative charges and writes them all positive: Dickens is great, it is said, because his sense of plot is absurd and because his kind of story has nothing to do with real happenings. It is especially important to our analysis that this kind of justification of Dickens during the last twenty years belongs to the guardians of the interpretation of literary plot and that theirs is a kind of interpretation that significantly undervalues—and in truth overlooks—the importance of peripety.

The criticism I speak of believes that all plot in literature is myth, that all narrative reasonings "displace," by means of a distorted repetition, a handful of archetypal mythic stories. This is the criticism of Northrop Frye and his school. We can see at once that just by its notion of "displacement" such criticism can easily lead to the separation of theme and plot: the author's plotted events may be treated as distortions of an archetypal story whose theme in turn may be read back into the fiction at issue with a kind of casual dismissal of the particular plot of the fiction as well as of any particular thematics in conflict with the alleged archetype. And there are other misleading results of the sense of plot belonging to this prestigious critical method: for example, it upholds our now apparently inveterate tendency to distinguish "eventfulness" or "external" incidents and something opposed to them, something "deeper" or more artful, a symbolic or purely speculative action rather than a literal one. Prestigious as this method is, since I believe it stands in the way of a genuine appreciation of Dickensian plot and action and since we are about to consider the successful waverings of *Nicholas Nickleby* as a marked contrast to those of *Barnaby Rudge,* let us consider what Northrop Frye tells us about plot and peripety in general and about Dickens and *Nicholas Nickleby* in particular.

In "Dickens and the Comedy of Humors" we find Dickensian plot justified because of its absurdity:

> We notice in Dickens how strong the impulse is to reject a logicality inherent in the story in favor of impressing on the reader an impatient sense of absolutism: of saying, in short, *la fatalité, c'est moi.* This disregard of plausibility is worth noticing, because everyone realizes that Dickens is a great genius of the absurd in his characterization, and it is possible that his plots are also absurd in the same sense, not from incompetence

or bad taste, but from a genuinely creative instinct. If so they
are likely to be more relevant to the entire conception of the
novel than is generally thought.

Frye goes on "to explore a little the sources of absurdity in Dickens, to see
if that will lead us to a clearer idea of his total structure." He shows how
a Dickens plot differentiates two embryonic societies, one characterized by
spontaneity and beneficence and the other by an insistent exercise of
pedantic and parasitic humors. At the end of a Dickens novel this second
society has consolidated itself and is blocking its rival. Then "a twist in the
plot reverses the situation." The genial, generous, and lovable humors
smash the blocking forces. "Once again in literature," Frye notes, "the
hidden world is the world of an invincible Eros, the power strong enough
to force a happy ending on the story in defiance of all probability."
Dickens's Eros is "a designing and manipulating power." And, Frye con-
tends, if Dickens's Eros-originated plotting seems absurd to us, we must
remember that

> in literature it is design, the forming and shaping power, that is
> absurd. Real life does not start or stop; it never ties up loose
> ends; it never manifests meaning or purpose except by blind
> accident; it is never comic or tragic, ironic or romantic, or
> anything else that has a shape. . . . The silliest character in
> *Nicholas Nickleby* is the hero's mother, a romancer who keeps
> dreaming of impossible happy endings for her children. But the
> story itself follows her specifications and not those of the
> sensible people. The obstructing humors in Dickens are absurd
> because they have overdesigned their lives. But the kind of
> design that they parody is produced by another kind of energy,
> and one which insists, absurdly and yet irresistibly, that what is
> must never take final precedence over what ought to be.

Of the two remarkable assumptions these excerpts evidence, the first
is Frye's assertion that "real" life is blind shapeless accident. Frye's sense
of plot differs from, say, Stein's or Orwell's, because it ostensibly delights
in narrative form, and it certainly believes story is true to what we may
imagine or desire; but it is also clearly a modern sense of plot in that it
divorces empirical reality from story's form or shape. No story *as story* is
true for Frye. The second assumption in the excerpts does not show itself
as clearly as the first. It is glimpsed in the claim that a Dickensian
dilemma is reversed by "a twist in the plot." What does it mean to speak

of reversal as "a twist"? It sounds like "the twist" is a convenience, a mechanical contrivance for the assertion of the absurd forming and shaping power that is invincibly there anyway, twist or no twist. For Frye "the twist" is implausible and does not grapple with or express any realities other than our imagination's desire.

When Dickens uses reversal as a convenient twist he plots badly, as in *Barnaby Rudge*. But in fact, unlike Frye, Dickens usually does not demean reversal to the status of a convenience because he believes in the power of reversal to focus the particular narrative reason and moral of a particular, undisplaced plot, and because he wants his readers to feel that the action pointed up by reversal is a hazardous, crucial, and "real" development for his readers as well as for his story's characters. It is not merely imagination or desire that are at issue. In his use of reversal Dickens is much closer to Aristotle than to Frye, who uses the terminology of the *Poetics* but then shortchanges peripety. When Aristotle speaks of reversal and recognition as the soul of plot and as the mark of the superior dramatist he is favoring the power of the turning point to engage the audience. They are engaged, thrilled with pity and fear, because the reversal ensnares them, making the audience believe that what is happening on stage is happening literally or "really," not just in imagination. Dickens wants his turning points to have the same effect; indeed he goes farther than Aristotle, for while Aristotle seems to consider drama finally as a deflecting substitute for action, Dickens seems to want to use novelistic story to incite readers to imitate and reproduce the acts he represents.

Whatever their differences, however, both Aristotle and Dickens appear to value peripety's potential for erasing the boundary between literature, imagination, and real life. Frye does not favor this. As *Anatomy of Criticism* puts it, literature's "relation to reality . . . is neither direct nor negative, but potential." If the emotional effect of peripety is to substitute a "direct" relation for a "potential" one and to thus break down the boundary between literature, imagination, and "real life," then criticism must reconstruct the boundary. For Frye calls "the sense of the sharply focused reproduction of life in fiction" the province of what he terms "critical naturalism," a criticism of " 'effects.' " "We need to move from a criticism of 'effects' to what we may call a criticism of causes, specifically the formal cause which holds the work together." Dickensian reversal is "effect," "twist"; but the formal cause, the unifying agent of the story and the true province of interpretation, is, apparently, the underlying plot-myth of the work. Dickens writes "not realistic novels, but fairy tales [or myths] in the low mimetic displacement." To make much of reversal is to make too much of Dickensian "effect."

Yet without reversal and its effect, Dickens seems to claim, we know or recognize nothing significant about our experience, nor do we even know that we are actors. Again like Aristotle, Dickens understands that reversal and significant recognition go hand in hand—though for Dickens "recognition" means far more than the literal recognizing of persons. Moreover, when Aristotle gives examples of peripety he uses the verb *mellein,* "to be on the point of doing something." Thus the reversal, as Dickens sees it and as I understand it, emphasizes "doing" as much as "point." Finally, what the reversal tells us as knowledge and as a featuring of act is generally for Dickens (and perhaps also for Aristotle) a thrilling and novel revelation, a recognition not available to us otherwise or before. Frye, on the other hand, transforms Aristotle's "point" of recognition into epiphany, "the symbolic presentation of the point at which the undisplaced apocalyptic world and the cyclical world of nature come into alignment." The epiphanic point reveals the mythic world—for example the paradise of absurdly designing Eros—but our recognition of this world is a discovery without surprise, without the shock of experiencing a novel turn. Because the mythic world is undisplaced and has its origin in imagination and desire and because it is a nonpragmatic human universal, the reader knows it before he sees it; and the revelation comes as a featuring of seeing, not of doing. According to Frye, no point of reversal inciting both novelty of awareness and action can be important for a nonnaturalistic criticism which believes that

> the profoundest experiences possible to obtain in the arts are available in the art already produced. . . . The culture of the past is not only the memory of mankind, but our own buried life, and study of it leads to a recognition scene, a discovery in which we see, not our past lives, but the total cultural form of our present life.

For Frye, revelation and recognition do not go hand in hand with any feeling of reversal. In contrast, I believe that a point of reversal suggests a radical overturning of expectations, a new awareness in time of a new fact in time, or of a fact so extraordinarily presented as to strike one as surprisingly and perennially new. From the point of view of archetypal criticism this idea apparently belongs to direct experience, to precritical naiveté, not to criticism and to literature more properly considered. It is apparently naive to treat the "twist" of a novel like *Nicholas Nickleby* as interesting in its own right, as offering surprising, perhaps as yet unrecognized human intelligence or news or as instancing the creativity of desire or imagination transformed into external, purposive, and pragmatic act.

Nevertheless, Dickens is guilty of this naiveté. He gives us the sense that a novel is new, that a novel's plot is new, because he believes human experience in some way is always new. This means he feels sharply the instability and inconsistency of experience, that he feels (pace Barnaby Rudge) life is always wavering, always at the point of peripety. Generally Dickens starts out plotting a story by reversing in some way the assurance we feel about what it is to be human or natural. He himself seems to feel "reversed": in each story he approaches daily life as if he were a stranger, having to find out where he is and what the people of the place are like. This approach issues in a new or freshly felt sense of humanity or nature. In response to such novelty the reader is likely to resist any reversal of his expectations. When *Nicholas Nickleby* begins with Squeers and Dotheboys Hall, the reader squirms: There are not people or institutions like this, are there? But to be insistently confident about human nature or reality may lead to just the lack of grasp on it that uneasy readers accuse Dickens of having. By leaving open the possibility of a deep, essential turn of awareness, one begins to see what Dickens is talking about and how authentic his perceptions are. But although he cultivates the surprising inconstancy and novelty of experience, Dickens uses reversal, both as phenomenon and as form of story, to make a clear narrative reasoning about life. In Dickens's major work the uncertainty of experience does not throw us into a permanent state of unknowing. Epiphany, recognition, cognition seem possible to him in the greater part of his practice only through and because of the use of the point of reversal. Moreover, for Dickens reversal significantly engages the reader's attention when Dickens does not attempt to separate plot and theme, when he does not assume that a particular story with its particular turns is ruled by an underlying extricable fairy tale or myth arbitrarily forcing the turns upon the story.

In one last preparatory step towards *Nicholas Nickleby,* let us consider what a genuinely Dickensian sense of plot makes of Dickens's storytelling, of mythic plots, and of points of reversal. In his introduction to a 1907 Everyman edition of *Nicholas Nickleby,* G. K. Chesterton finds it possible for "literary shape" and theme to come directly from the elements of the plot at hand and for critical naturalists to sort out the feeling of unity these elements express. For Chesterton (and for common sense?) unity is felt and known in literature and outside it without appeal to an underlying myth-cause. Moreover, the critical naturalist may comment on an art work's "sharply focused reproduction of life" and at the same time talk about a mythical pattern or force felt in and through the immediate "effects." Thus, Chesterton at once points out the romance plot of *Nicholas Nickleby* and goes on to identify the questing hero and the other characteristics of "every pure romance." But his penetration to the archetype results from his conviction of the presence of the archetype as a fact of life. His archetypal criticism is simultaneously naturalistic criticism. He thinks of romance, and he thinks of it as affecting a reader in an immediate way. This immediate and indeed urgent impact of romance on the reader has to do with its ability, as Chesterton says, to foreshorten existence and to bring it "to a point—to the point." He asserts this in the opening paragraph of his commentary on *Nicholas Nickleby:*

> Romance is perhaps the highest point of human expression, except indeed religion, to which it is closely allied. Romance resembles religion especially in this, that it is not only a simplification but a shortening of existence. Both romance and religion see everything in an abrupt and fantastic perspective, coming to a point. It is the whole essence of perspective that it comes quickly to a point—to the point. For instance, religion is always insisting on the shortness of human life. But it does not insist on the shortness of human life as the pessimists [do]. . . . Pessimism insists on the shortness of human life in order to show that life is valueless. Religion insists on the shortness of human life in order to show that life is frightfully valuable—is almost horribly valuable. Pessimism says that life is so short that it gives nobody a chance; religion says that life is so short that it gives everybody his final chance. In the first case the word brevity means futility. In the second case the word brevity means opportunity. . . . All this is equally true for romance. Romance is a shortening and sharpening of the human difficulty.

The description of Dickensian plot in this appeal to romance is especially faithful to Dickens's novels and to the experience of reading them because in the main Dickens makes use of his elaborate and complicated plots for the sake of a maximum of abrupt points and perspectives. The points that for Dickens are essential to narrative reason and that open up the romantic and religious perspectives are points of reversal. (And it is reversals that Chesterton is implicitly thinking of here—as we shall see later.) Just as the stories of Greek tragedy are for Aristotle most powerful when they shorten and sharpen the human difficulty by bringing experience to the turning point, so too are plot and story for Dickens. In Dickensian narration it seems as if men and women in story and in life cannot recognize themselves, each other, or the actions engaging them without experiencing peripety. The awful Victorian plot is the sort of plot that tells nothing because its turns, if it has any, are carelessly made to tell nothing. But the great Victorian plot—preeminently the great Dickensian plot—reverses the expectations of both the characters and of those reading or hearing the story because it assumes that knowledge, life's value, and the featuring of act are available only through the abrupt and fantastic perspective described by Chesterton.

Now that we have considered the bearing of Scott's reversal-filled stories on Dickens and narrative reasoning and the bearing of modern criticism's evasion of peripety on the understanding of Dickensian plot, we can look closely at Dickens's use of reversal in *Nicholas Nickleby*. It must first be noted that the reversals that develop Dickens's story do not separate the intellectual and moral aspects of narrative reason. And Dickens's characters, his delegated plotting agents, also move the story's development along by hazarding a series of moral ventures that stimulate some crucial turning point of action, which itself creates intellectual and moral recognitions. Dickens dramatizes recognitions that are literal and personal, but he usually combines reversal and recognition in another way. His plots create recognition scenes *for the reader* that are only secondarily the discovery of the literal relations among persons in the story. Primarily, recognition scenes in Dickens make the reader grasp the unity and relatedness of human experience and moral concern that bind the characters and their activity into one single narrative.

Dickens begins almost invariably with a mystery—with an unintelligible reversal, we might say—because he does not want the reader to ask who originally killed or abandoned whom but how the disparate persons and actions of the story interrelate—how they are coherently connected. The principle of coherent connection is what we refer to in common usage as theme, and it is also that theoretical part of narrative reason we have discussed [earlier]. As I have suggested earlier, theme is the theory whereby an author explains and accounts for what he is talking about, whereby a storyteller, as Henry James says, "prosecutes those generalizations in which alone consists the real greatness of art." Dickens insistently uses reversal to enable his readers to prosecute those generalizations with him; the reversals therefore usually precede—or are inextricably connected with—the gradual disclosure of the unifying theme. But for Dickens the theme is not just intellectual; it embodies a pressing moral insight. The reversals disclose this moral insight, and they do so aided by the moral choices and acts of the characters. Dickens's plots are a kind of curious moral allegory in which the turns of plot rather than the allegorical personifications move the intellectual and the moral design along. The design itself awaits the end of the story for its disclosure; some nearly final turning point of action signals the death of the story and reveals its intellectual and moral principle of life. The retardation of the disclosure results from the fact that almost up to the end of the story the characters have no certainty about what kind of willful exertion and what kind of moral action will ensure the achievement of happiness. Throughout the story, will and action and crucial points of peripety are moral experiments—the characters must gamble on which way to follow and which way to turn. When the reversals and their effects are sorted out, the plot amounts finally to a resolution of moral uncertainty. Thus, the moral and thematic perspectives of the plot, the actors' hazardous moral ventures, and the story's reversals are bound up together as an invariable condition of the sense of plot in Dickens.

Now the theme Dickens is most interested in exploring in *Nicholas Nickleby* concerns the contemporary state of marriage, which Dickens sees as his character Squeers sees nature. "It is a blessed thing . . . to be in a state o' natur," says Squeers, but "natur . . . is more easier conceived than described." Similarly, it may be a blessed thing to be in the state of matrimony, but in *Nicholas Nickleby* matrimony too "is more easier conceived than described." Indeed it is so difficult to describe that state, which seems to Dickens to have undergone in modern times a mysterious transformation of character, that at first Dickens seems to be telling a story about something very different: until late in the novel it looks as if he is pursuing a thematic consideration of the appropriateness or the prudence of the hero's need to strike out, even violently, against his enemies. But this thematic intention turns out to be a kind of feint of narrative reason, a false perspective. Eventually the thematic perspective comes to a turning point at which the reader can look back and see the novel's earlier phenomena and events fall into a more compelling thematic arrangement and coherence than is supplied by the focus on prudence or aggression. The reader has been on a road the reversal transforms, a road the reader sees clearly and all the more compellingly because of the new vantage point the reversal provides.

The true theme, the essential narrative reasoning, of *Nicholas Nickleby* is an argument that modern marriage is what Dickens calls "a system of annoyance." The turn revealing the theme is found in chapter 45. As he tells Squeers, Ralph Nickleby has decided "to wound" Nicholas "through his own affections and fancies." The novel makes clear that wounding others this way preoccupies a large number of persons and that married men and women can use their marriages especially as a system of such wounding. Ralph himself formulates and names the system; wanting to strike at Nicholas through his affection for Smike, a boy Nicholas has befriended, Ralph concocts a tale whereby Smike will be turned over to a flunky of Squeers, who will claim to be Smike's father and will take him from Nicholas. According to Ralph's lie, the alleged father thinks his son Smike is dead until the alleged father's estranged wife confesses on her deathbed that the boy has not died. "And this confession," Ralph tells the factitious father, instructing him in the plot, "is to the effect that his death was an invention of hers to wound you—was a part of a system of annoyance, in short, which you seem to have adopted towards each other." At this point in the story we recognize that the system of annoyance is not a mere imaginary or singular case but a precise naming of all the cases of marriage appearing in *Nicholas Nickleby*.

In 1838 such cases were not new either in literature or experience. But Dickens presents them with an intensity of concern, of fear even, that is—and remains—new. He wants these marriages to be accepted as representative of an actual contemporary historical condition, not as stock jokes one can laugh at in easy recognition of literary convention. Dickens wants us to feel that our assumptions and expectations about marriage are complacent and blind and that they need the illuminating shock of reversal. The marriages he exhibits embody a will to throttle or manipulate any persons in their sphere in order to defend against the personal emptiness of the spouses and against the social and moral emptiness of the larger community of spouses.

Characteristically marriage in *Nicholas Nickleby* unites two persons by being a constant safeguard against each spouse's knowledge that his self is a nullity. In the marriage of the Mantalinis, the husband demonstrates his intimacy with his wife by speaking of her in the third person when he speaks directly to her. This means that, in order to feel loved by her husband, Madame Mantalini needs to have herself dramatized by him, even if no one else is present. She needs her husband to "put her on"; his impersonal personal treatment of her motivates, manipulates, and controls her entirely—and gives her an ego we feel she would otherwise not have. If Mantalini does not give her a self by "putting her on," she is empty, she wants to commit suicide. And the same is true for him: *he* threatens suicide if she does not stimulate him to play his role. But these ego roles are substitutes for a vacuum; the threat of suicide always draws the spouses back together, for the loss of one partner would expose entirely the emptiness of the other. Nevertheless, as oddly life-preserving as this system is, the Mantalini marriage is always a system of annoyance because for each spouse the means of expressing self and of "making" love is to push the other toward suicide. To those inside it, the system becomes a system of pleasure *and* annoyance, of extreme coercive manipulation, of the will of one partner to harass and throttle the life of the other as a perverse demonstration of love. And it is not only the comic Mantalinis who exhibit this pattern; Dickens shows that society itself—the spousal community—perversely stimulates the self and "lovemaking" by making men and women in effect suicidal.

If this is the truth about modern marriage, Dickens asks, what is to be done in the face of this system of annoyance? He accompanies with a question both his attempted reversal of our assumptions about marriage and the reversal in the plot that makes us see the force and density of the system as the novel's true theme: Can a genuine and decent human success in life and marriage be achieved in a world—a real world whose deep structure the novel's narrative reason represents and discloses—pervaded by systems of annoyance? Nicholas Nickleby and his sister Kate become the symbols of this question, and the emotional effect of the reversal of our sense of the theme of *Nicholas Nickleby* is to draw us more deeply into the search for a way to enact an answer. Our interest in the plot is especially intensified by Nicholas's and Kate's quest (as if it were ours) for conditions and persons who can succeed in making a freely chosen, vital marriage, even in such a world. However, there seems to be very little opportunity in *Nicholas Nickleby* to form life in a way that escapes the system.

The Browdies of Greta Bridge come close to embodying the positive ideal of marriage that Dickens's plot is in search of. They do not marry for the sake of mutual annoyance or for the sake of hiding from and reinforcing personal emptiness. Nor do they seem bent on annoying others systematically, as is the case with the Mantalinis, the Knags, and the Wittitterleys, who try to force the system on other men and women in their spheres. Nevertheless the Browdies are provincial: their marriage would not survive the personally nullifying effects and the stimulation to systems of annoyance exerted by money and sham in London, where Nicholas and Kate must make their way. It is true that one finds an example of a good city marriage in the Kenwigses. But just as the hulking Browdie would never knock down Squeers (as he should), so Kenwigs would be even less likely to knock down his wife's uncle, a variation of Squeers named

Lillyvick. The Kenwigses love and respect each other, their children, and their neighbors; but they worry and nearly destroy their happiness just to please an exponent of the system of annoyance like Lillyvick. Nicholas and Kate thus have virtually no models to inspire their search for a way out of the system. Yet as the story unfolds Dickens demonstrates more and more the desperate need to get out. For the wages of the system of annoyance are not just a threat of suicide but suicide itself, finally carried out by Ralph, the formulator of the system. In another of the novel's most significant reversals, Ralph discovers (on the point of carrying out his plot against his nephew Nicholas) that Smike is his very own son—that his own estranged wife lied, telling Ralph that his son was dead, an invention of hers to wound him. The plot Ralph makes up as a fiction to hurt Nicholas with turns out to be the plot of his real life—a reversal Dickens uses both to make us see the wages of the system and to make us feel how Ralph's own novelistic fiction is the servant of strange but actual truth. Ralph wounds his own affections, not Nicholas's. But Ralph's suicide (in an attic Smike remembers as his boyhood home) does not issue from remorse; it is itself a grimly surprising turn because Dickens presents it as an act of fury and spite. Ralph hangs himself as a way out of coming to grips with the failure of his life, with his own emptiness. He is blindly repeating in his willful death the disabling fatality of the system of annoyance. Nicholas and Kate must escape repeating it in their own lives, or else they will risk both a cultural form of suicide and suicide in fact.

We have seen how reversal in *Nicholas Nickleby* points out the plot's intellectual and moral narrative reasoning. By effecting a turn of our attention to the theme of marriage as a system of annoyance, Dickens's use of peripety gathers the diverse phenomena of his novel into an especially significant and intelligible whole. This wholeness addresses our intellectual response, but the reversal that reveals the intellectual unity of the novel also stresses the urgency of the marriage theme's moral claim on our attention.

We must now consider finally how Dickens uses reversal to point up the hazardous but telling nature of action. Nicholas and Kate do in the end manage to find their appropriate spouses in Madeline Bray and Frank Cheeryble, and although Dickens scarcely describes these latter two characters, we must understand that their personal quality is the same as the hero's and heroine's. We must also understand that escape from the system is a moral venture, a hazard that features its own act because the system provides no models for acts that challenge it. Much more important than the personal objects of Nicholas's and Kate's choice is the brave, risky action of the choosing. "Happiness and misery are realised in action," Aristotle writes, "the goal of life is an action, not a quality." Dickens's sense of plot endorses the *Poetics*—although Dickens always manages to define a quality and imitate an action at the same time. Now the accurate final choosing of spouses by Kate and Nicholas could not have been possible without the insight provided—to both characters and readers—by reversals along the way; and the choice itself is a reversal that checks the power of the system of annoyance.

Let us turn to the widowed Mrs. Nickleby, allegedly "the silliest" character in his story, to show how Dickens combines in her case too the moral hazard or venture whereby a character challenges prevailing convention and enacts a significant reversal in his own life. Mrs. Nickleby does what her children do: she confronts the system of annoyance and makes an escape from it, surprisingly changing her life as well as our expectations about her and making us recognize that she is considerably less silly than she has seemed to be up to the point of reversal. Mrs. Nickleby's decision at this crucial turning point strongly demonstrates how our acts shape us for better or worse and how what we choose not just to think but to do damns us or saves us. Late in the novel, in chapter 49, the widow discovers she has a final chance for marriage. One day while in her garden she finds herself the target of a barrage of phallic-shaped vegetables coming at her from over the garden wall. The assailant shows himself and proposes love, if not exactly a wedding. Unlike Kate Mrs. Nickleby will not shrink in embarrassment from her suitor's erotic aggression; and she refuses to believe he is mad. Dickens wants to instruct, as well as to amuse here. He wants the reader to consider with Mrs. Nickleby that the gentleman is not mad, at least not merely because he is aggressively and directly erotic. The good marriage has to include something of that direct force. Without it marriage might be the kind of beneficent yet rather impersonally sterile and sad alliance it is in that oddly married couple, the Cheeryble brothers. The Cheerybles are not *dei ex machina,* incidentally, as much as they are contributions to the marriage theme, qualifications of the reader's surmise that maybe the only ideal kind of marriage in this world is an unqualified system of benevolence. But Dickens's story insists that the ideal kind of marriage would not depend on unqualified benevolence anymore than it would depend on what the alleged erotomaniac finally represents.

The suitor makes a last assault on Mrs. Nickleby in coming down the chimney of her house and embarrassing the family with a pair of legs in the fireplace. At this point Mrs. Nickleby makes her choice:

"Kate, my dear, . . . you will have the goodness, my love, to explain precisely how this matter stands. I have given him no encouragement— none whatever—not the least in the world. You know that, my dear, perfectly well. He was very respectful, exceedingly respectful, when he declared, as you were a witness to; still at the same time, if I am to be persecuted in this way, if vegetable what's-his-names and all kinds of garden-stuff are to strew my path out of doors, and gentlemen are to come choking up our chimneys at home, I really don't know—upon my word—I do *not* know—what is to become of me. It's a very hard case—harder than anything I was ever exposed to, before I married your poor dear papa, though I suffered a good deal of annoyance then—but that, of course, I expected, and made up my mind for. When I was not nearly so old as you, my dear, there was a young gentleman who sat next us at church, who used, almost every Sunday, to cut my name in large letters in the front of his pew while the sermon was going on. It was gratifying, of course, naturally so, but still it was an annoyance, because the pew was in a very conspicuous place, and he was several times publicly taken out by the beadle for doing it. But that was nothing to this. This is a great deal worse, and a great deal more embarrassing."

She rejects her suitor because he offers her, finally (and "naturally so"?), annoyance entangled with and taking precedence over gratification. Her choice is both very funny and very touching. Had she been thoroughly silly or mad, she would have married him. Indeed from the point of view of the prevailing system of annoyance, she *ought* to marry him. But she still has enough hold on sense to see both his lack of sense and the ultimate if socially unacknowledged destructiveness of the system. This is, in fact, the first time in the novel she confronts a reality that is not a matter of conventional appearances. This is the first time she stops daydreaming: she does not give way to wish fulfillment. The rest of the novel shows her children also keeping closely in touch with a more telling reality than conventional and accepted appearances and systems. "The silliest character in *Nicholas Nickleby* is the hero's mother, a romancer who keeps dreaming impossible happy endings for her children. But the story itself follows her specifications and not those of the sensible people." Is this not simply untrue? In rejecting her suitor Mrs. Nickleby makes sense. This turning point in her life shows how the story itself is a sensible investigation of the pursuit of marriage in the real world. And it is the venturous *act* of making sense, the hazardous choice transformed into a purposive deed that is emphasized by the turning point. This is no mere "twist" in the plot. On the point of choosing her future and her fate, on the point of making a mistake we might well expect her to make, Mrs. Nickleby shortens, sharpens, and resolves her human difficulty by an act that tells its sense in the form of the abrupt change of perspective brought about by a reversal.

DIANNE F. SADOFF

Language Engenders:
David Copperfield
and Great Expectations

An Author feels as if he were dismissing some portion of himself into
the shadowy world, when a crowd of the creatures of his brain are
going from him forever. . . . Of all my books, I like this the best. It
will be easily believed that I am a fond parent to every child of my
fancy, and that no one can ever love that family as dearly as I love
them. But, like many fond parents, I have in my heart of hearts a
favourite child. And his name is DAVID COPPERFIELD.
                                   —CHARLES DICKENS, *David Copperfield*

As this well-known prefatory remark to *David Copperfield* suggests,
Dickens associated writing with figurative fatherhood, with parentage.
Dickens spoke often of his young characters as his progeny—David, Oliver
Twist, Little Nell. About Nell's written death, "Nellicide" as Dickens
called it, he wrote to George Cattermole, the book's illustrator, that he
was "nearly dead with work—and grief for the loss of my child"; to his
friend John Forster, "nobody shall miss her like I shall." The author-as-
father engenders his imagined progeny, his "family," provides them (and
his texts) with legitimacy and himself with authority. For the concept of
"authority," as Edward Said notes, invokes sexual, literary, and theological metaphors associated with masculinity and with the male author's
power to engender. Said quotes the *OED*'s definitions of "authority," all
of which describe power and the obedience it demands. Language creates
and communicates authority: the author originates, begets, begins, fathers,

From *Monsters of Affection: Dickens, Eliot and Bronte on Fatherhood.* © 1982 by
the Johns Hopkins University Press.

and sets forth written statements; he produces, founds, invents, causes, and maintains a right of possession; finally, he maintains the continuity and controls the issue (whether textual or genealogical) of his action. Dickens referred repeatedly to this set of paternal values and attributes in his letters, prefaces, and dedications. He decidedly objected, he grumbled early in his career, to "fathering anybody else's articles"; he refused in rage to "father" a bastard continuation of *Pickwick*. Because his early offspring needed a double legitimacy, Dickens dedicated "The Village Coquettes" to J. P. Hartley, the metaphorical adoptive "father of Dickens's 'bantlings' ''; Hartley would figuratively father "future scions of the same stock, no matter how numerous they may be or how quickly they follow in succession." Dickens's fight for the international copyright itself proved to be a genealogical concern for the inheritance by authors' descendants of a permanent interest in the earnings their fathers' writings accrue.

In Dickens's retroactive structural search for the father as origin and in his thematics of parricide, the son discovers himself in the place of a father. Dickens's metaphor of the author-as-father identifies the writing son's way to become through writing a figurative father, to replace and become his own father. The narrative project serves to originate and engender the son himself. In *David Copperfield, Great Expectations,* and the "autobiographical fragment," Dickens's fictional sons—figures for himself, or parts of himself—attempt to confront or deny, to love and to accuse, their figurative fathers. In each narrative, a son tries to lay to rest "the ghost of a man's own father" by writing his life; in copying the act of fathering by authorship, the writing son fathers himself in language, in narrative. The text creates not only progeny but also the self as one's own progeny. David's, Pip's, and "Dickens's" autobiographical narratives all appear as a fictionalized version of Dickens's own struggle with fatherhood, his attempt through his "sons," his progeny, likewise to engender himself in narrative.

David Copperfield celebrates, Pip Pirrip criticizes, retroactivity and self-engenderment. Both of Dickens's first-person male narrators attempt to account for their origins, recount their experiences, and make themselves subject to themselves in and through narrative. Yet both Pip and David are fatherless, and so their origins become enigmatic. David calls himself a "posthumous child," born after his father's death; Pip never sees his father or mother and has as proof of paternity only his sister's stories and the inscription on his father's gravestone. Metaphorically, then, David and Pip have no identifiable origin, no engendering father, and Pip has no mother as well: these two figures for Dickens owe their creations to no man. David's and Pip's fictions relate these births in which fathers clearly have no engendering function by representing themselves as reborn in narrative.

David's fiction of rebirth imagines a strangely lopsided family scene, whose fatherless structure facilitates and prophesies David's fathering of himself. This scenic structure makes sense only through its own deferral of signification and only in the context of the murdering, punishing father recalled from David's father's grave via David's own oedipal guilt. After feeling himself a "blank space" which "everybody overlooked" while on vacation from school with his new family, David parts from his mother and new baby brother in a mysterious scene of silence, gazing, and subsequent dream. As he rides away from Blunderstone Rookery, his mother calls after him; "I looked out," David tells us, "and she stood at the garden gate alone, holding her baby up in her arms for me to see. It was cold, still weather, and not a hair of her head or a fold of her dress was stirred, as she looked intently at me, holding up her child. So I lost her. So I saw her afterwards, in my sleep at school—a silent presence near my bed—looking at me with the same intent face—holding up her baby in her arms." This triangular intersubjectivity defines Clara as lost to David by virtue of a new infant's arrival, as well as of a new husband's (father's) —who is conspicuously absent from this scene. Yet its uncanny disruption of the narrative, its excessive emotional charge, makes sense only when David's mother too dies, is literally rather than figuratively "lost" to him; this loss effaces his own origin and his last connection to an engendering father, to the Copperfields. After his mother's funeral, David associates himself with the infant who has also died, the child once held up for him to see when leaving home and so figuratively dies himself: "The mother who lay in the grave, was the mother of my infancy; the little creature in her arms, was myself, as I had once been, hushed for ever on her bosom." This narrative moment banishes fathers, enshrines dead mothers, and kills that old young David, leaving him free to create himself.

Yet Murdstone prevents self-origination by putting David to work at Murdstone and Grinby's. To kill off this period of his life, to forget it as part of his self-engendered identity, David must be reborn at Aunt Betsey's cottage. Betsey bathes—purifies—and nourishes him, wraps him in figurative swaddling clothes, and puts him to bed an infant once more. Aunt Betsey changes David's name, the name of his father, and—herself like a father—bestows her own name on him, marking it in his new clothes with "indelible marking-ink" in "her own handwriting." Deprived of his patrimony by Murdstone's hatred and Clara's childishness, David embarks on "another beginning," a "new life, in a new name, and with everything new about [him]," ready again to engender himself.

Pip's fiction of rebirth begins not at the beginning of his narrative but at its end. It represents redemption, a second chance, Pip's desire to transcend his self-deluded "construction[s]" "repeated and thrown back" at him. After eleven years of self-imposed exile and penance as a working-man, Pip returns to Joe and Biddy to find, he says, "sitting on my own little stool . . . I again!" Yet this loving family scene, this reborn self who will redeem the past, must implicitly repeat the struggles of Pip himself. Pip takes little Pip to the churchyard, seats him on a tombstone, and listens to little Pip repeat his own childhood story of "Phillip Pirrip, late of this Parish, and Also Georgiana, Wife of the Above." Pip's equivocal rebirth demands the retelling of the lost link between fatherhood and origin. While the story initiates little Pip into the mysterious metaphysics of identity and self-naming, its status as repetition means rebirth as a figure for self-engendering remains problematic.

The fictions the fatherless David and Pip write about themselves reborn become the books we read. David defines the power of this narrative to define its subject: "Whether I shall turn out to be the hero of my own life, or whether that station will be held by anybody else, these pages must show," he begins. In both novels, an adult man looks back on his life and attempts to give it shape, motivation, and causality by virtue of narrative strategies. As David's comment implies, the recounting of a life, the story told about past experiences, not only retells events but retroactively creates them as well. David cannot be sure at the beginning of his narrative project whether he will prove to be the "hero" of his own life; his narrative will create him as a hero to himself or will demonstrate his lack of heroism or seriousness as subject of the narrative. The writing of the narrative will create his life, not simply retell it; the account of David's past will cause that past, not simply recollect it. In writing the story of his life, David will thus create himself, give birth to himself, engender and so father himself in language.

The narrator who creates himself in the process of writing is the "autobiographer." If language gives birth, language about the self gives birth to the self. The writer of his own life story, his own "biography," makes himself his hero (or nonhero) in a narrative, creates himself in the process of writing his own narrative. Both *David Copperfield* and *Great Expectations* demonstrate the intense self-reflexive and -reflective mode of autobiography: each narrative structures the perceiving writer into the story itself. Pip's narrative circles back on itself through his self-reflection, his continual criticism of and declared distance from his earlier self as origin of his present writing self. His metaphors for his life in that early self figure his new difference: his "mazes," his "poor labyrinth" define that self as self-deceptive and lost. David's narrative, however, nostalgic and immersed in its own self-origination, reflects on itself by virtue of David's occupation: writing. David writes about himself writing. We presumably read the story David writes "out of his experience" while in self-imposed exile in Switzerland after Dora's death. We read David's autobiography, which is also Charles Dickens's fictionalized autobiography. The novel's hero, then, appears to resemble its narrator, who is also its writer, and who resembles its author—as Forster claims he pointed out to the surprised Dickens when he noted David's initials as reversals of Dickens's own. Dickens reflects on David, a part of himself, reflecting on himself; Dickens writes about David, who writes about himself writing. The novel takes as subject its writer in the act of his self-creation.

Yet Dickens's narrative about David, the boy who grows, like the author, into a novelist, surprisingly omits any reference to the process of writing fiction or to the contents of those fictions. David mentions almost as an aside that he writes his first novel; when it gets published, David demurs, "It is not my purpose, in this record, though in all other essentials it is my written memory, to pursue the history of my own fictions. They express themselves, and I leave them to themselves. When I refer to them, incidentally, it is only as a part of my progress." David expunges his writing from his manuscript—which he claims he never intended to publish and which purports to tell only to himself the exact truth—because his writing is important only when it signifies his "progress." This truthful autobiography details not the writing of David's narratives but his career as a writer. Whenever David mentions his novels to, for example, Aunt Betsey, Agnes, Mrs. Steerforth, or Traddles, he or she remarks not on the significance or content of those novels but on their author's growing fame.

David admits his ambitiousness early in the novel, using terminology that unites worldly achievement with a rhetorical strategy for that advancement. Revisiting his old home, David wanders by the graves of his mother and father "by the hour"; his reflections, he confides, "were always associated with the figure I was to make in life, and the distinguished things I was to do. My echoing footsteps went to no other tune, but were as constant to that as if I had come home to build my castles in the air at a living mother's side." Writing will make David a distinguished "figure" or worldly success, a "figure" in his autobiography, in language. The scene in which Dickens sets this admission also identifies David's figurative ambition with his oedipal desires and fears; David's success would please his mother and would demonstrate his ability to become successful without the mention of a father.

Pip, like David, views writing as a vehicle of worldly success. Both figures for Dickens understand that language makes the writer a figure in the world and to himself. David and Pip have in common their aversion to the "common," another terminology that associates language with class, with worldly success or lack of it. David works at Murdstone and Grinby's in a "common way, and with the same common companions, and with the same sense of unmerited degradation as at first"; Pip finds himself defined by Estella as "common and coarse," as a lower-class, unrefined, improper boy who calls the "knave" a "jack." Because they want not to be "common," Pip and David dedicate themselves early to self-education, to autodidaction. Both assume that scholarship—mastering the skills and mysteries of language—will help them "rise" in the class structure. Joe unknowingly defines Pip and David's working-class self-hatred: Mrs. Joe dislikes scholarship, Joe explains, which makes men "rise . . . like a sort of rebel, don't you see?" David desires to rise, as did Dickens, by going to school; with Aunt Betsey's blessing, he studies at Dr. Strong's. Yet David's autobiography mysteriously excludes from its narrative these apparently happy schooldays, just as it elided the process and content of his writing; this time in his life he relates as "A Retrospect"—a whirlwind rehearsal of events without attribution to them of any significance. Pip too decides education and knowing the correct language will cure his coarseness. The "best step" he could take "towards making [himself] uncommon was to get out of Biddy everything she knew"—"all her learning." Pip, in fact, proves so apt and arrogant a pupil he presumes to teach Joe, his figurative father although literal brother-in-law and self-considered equal, the mysteries of language. Joe declares Pip an "oncommon scholar," even when Pip barely prints and totally fails to spell. With Biddy's help, then, Pip learns language; with Miss Havisham's, he supposes, he learns socially appropriate terminology—a "knave" from a "jack"—and so appears to transcend his commonness: he becomes a young gentleman with great expectations, with money in his future.

Each of our autobiographers nevertheless reveals the difficulty of learning to read and write. Pip struggles through the "alphabet as if it had been a bramble-bush; getting considerably worried and scratched by every letter"; he falls "among those thieves, the nine figures" who "disguise themselves and baffle recognition." David, who learned the "easy good-nature of O and Q and S" at his mother's knee, discovers at his punishing father's a "bog of nonsense." Later, when he perseverantly learns stenography, David rediscovers the mysteries of learning to write another language, the changes "rung upon dots," "vagaries . . . played by circles"; when he masters the alphabet, an "Egyptian Temple in itself," David moans, "there then appeared a procession of new horrors, called arbitrary characters; the most despotic characters I have ever known; who insisted, for instance, that a thing like the beginning of a cobweb, meant expectation, and that a pen-and-ink sky-rocket stood for disadvantageous." The mystery of language resides in the arbitrary connections between inscription and significance. Both Pip and David personify the characters of alphabets, portray language and its mastery as figurative. Yet only by mastering this metaphorical language, only by assuming the connection between the "characters" and signification, can Pip and David "rise."

David and Pip value language-learning, then, precisely because it will initiate them into the bourgeois world of successful self-management. After Aunt Betsey's apparent financial ruin, David is once again reborn to a "new life." He leaves the archaic profession of proctoring and becomes a successful parliamentary reporter—as did Dickens and Dickens's father before him. David's journalistic success, like Dickens's, depends on hard work and discipline, on "steady application," "perseverance," "patient and continuous energy," and "the habits of punctuality, order, and diligence." David reports, "Whatever I have tried to do in life, I have tried with all my heart to do well"; "whatever I have devoted myself to, I have devoted myself to completely"; "I have always been thoroughly in earnest, . . . and there is no substitute for thoroughgoing, ardent, and sincere earnestness." The bourgeois and more than slightly anal-retentive virtues that make David successful as a reporter also make him successful as a novelist. "I laboured hard at my book, without allowing it to interfere with the punctual discharge of my newspaper duties; and it came out and was very successful. I was not stunned by the praise which sounded in my ears, notwithstanding that I was keenly alive to it, and thought better of my own performance, I have little doubt, than anybody else did. . . . The more praise I got, the more I tried to deserve." The lessons of learning to write, of writing shorthand or novels, David expounds faithfully: be earnest, work hard but punctually, become self-reliant, and you will be successful, famous, well-paid—in short, a self-made man. David, the autodidact, fails in his autobiography to record the process of his writing because as a figure for his "progress" it signifies not self-knowledge but bourgeois success.

David's, Pip's—and Dickens's—theories of language as a vehicle for worldly success, as a vehicle for engendering the self without the help of fathers, however, is called into question by each autobiography. The subversive figures David chooses to represent language-users, writers, and himself hardly appear bourgeois, successful, or self-reliant. The stories Pip hears about fathers from his own figurative fathers hardly demonstrate that in narrative a son may create himself apart from fathers. David refuses in his autobiography to confront the nostalgia of his paean to bourgeois success and self-creation; Pip criticizes throughout his narrative his earlier desire to originate himself in language. Although Dickens reread *Copperfield* before writing *Expectations* so as not to repeat himself, his second great fictional autobiography repeats with a self-critical perspective the psychoanalytic material about language and fatherhood of the first.

The doubleness, the dark side, of David's drive to become a figure in the world appears in two figures for himself. While David muses about becoming a figure in the world beside the graves of his mother and father, a madman watches David from David's old childhood window as he once watched his father's grave. This figure for David reappears whenever David goes home and demonstrates the lunacy of attempting to become a figure in the world, the figurative nature of bourgeois success. Uriah Heep also appears as a dark figure for David's desire for success and self-creation. Uriah, like David, wants to marry a father's daughter and rise to a higher class. Heep personifies to David greasy-palmed ambition, yet David finds himself curiously attracted to while nervously contemptful of Heep. The narrative in fact surreptitiously identifies their resemblance. Heep sleeps in David's old room at the Wickfields'; Heep sleeps on David's floor in front of the fire. Heep's ambition originates in a father's teaching, as David's originates in the lack or excess of it; Heep's "umbleness" mocks as it imitates David's arrogance. Heep recognizes his resemblance to David, if David does not. "You envy me my rise," he screams at David, who does. "You're quite a dangerous rival," he chuckles to David, who, although refusing to admit it, is. The sexual triangle of David, Uriah, and Agnes finds its ironic biblical metaphor in that of David, Uriah, and Bathsheba—in which David appears as adulterous lover, Uriah as rightful husband.

David's figures for the writer also represent the lunacy of attempting to become a successful hero to oneself in narrative, to engender the self in language. Mr. Dick, Dr. Strong, and Micawber all identify through metaphor the doubleness of language, its insufficiency as a vehicle of the self-made man and the failure of the writer to father himself. Mr. Dick appears in the structural place of a father and represents the autobiographer. Mr. Dick, once "Richard Babley," writes "a Memorial about his own history," as David calls it. This memorial literally petitions the Lord Chancellor for financial relief caused by Mr. Dick's family situation. Like Mr. Dick, Dickens himself wrote a memorial-draft that associated financial relief with family distress and petitioned the Lords of Treasury for redress in his brother Frederick's fight for promotion at the Treasury Office. In *Copperfield,* however, Aunt Betsey explains to David the story the memorial tells of Mr. Dick's love for his favorite sister, his fear of her hateful husband, and his resulting fever. King Charles the First's beheading, which Betsey and Mr. Dick try to keep out of the memorial but cannot, represents "his allegorical way of expressing it"; Betsey says Mr. Dick "connects his illness with great disturbance and agitation," and "that's the figure, or the simile, or whatever it's called, which he chooses to use." Mr. Dick's memorial, then, connects family structures of desire and prohibition with the act of writing, particularly of writing a retrospective narrative about the self. King Charles the First's beheading is a metaphor for the madness of familial desire, for the prohibition that necessarily follows. The Charles head that gets on Mr. Dick's frame, that appears and disappears from Mr. Dick's narrative, that gets cut off over and over, represents the double bind of attempting to write retrospective narrative about triangular and familial structures of desire. Mr. Dick's story is a metaphor for David's story of oedipal desire and the prohibitions visited upon a desiring boy. Mr. Dick with his Charles head beheaded represents Charles Dickens's continual obsession with narrating *his* memorial of family cruelty and desire. King Charles as a figure for the out-of-his-head Mr. Dick also signifies Mr. Dick's attempt to make himself a subject of his narrative, just as David makes himself the hero of his. Yet this writer—a lunatic full of literal common sense—cannot complete his memorial-narrative because he cannot keep that figure for himself, King Charles-Dick, out of the story. Like Mr. Dick, like David, Charles Dickens attempts to become a hero to himself in narrative and so engender himself, attempts to keep the dark and lunatic figures for himself out of narrative only to find them magically reappearing and hindering the completion of his retrospective autobiographical project.

Mr. Dick's failure to keep King Charles out of the memorial spawns a double narrative, just as Dickens's narratives create their double characters, motivations, and plots. Mr. Dick pastes "the old leaves of abortive Memorials"—those in which King Charles appears—on his marvelous kite. Whereas Mr. Dick understands nothing about where the completed memorial would go or what it would achieve, he understands perfectly where the kite will go and what it will achieve. "It flies high," he tells David, and "takes the facts a long way. That's my manner of diffusing 'em. I don't know where they may come down. It's according to circumstances, and the wind, and so forth; but I take my chance of that." While the kite flies, "disseminat[ing] the statements pasted on it," Mr. Dick's mind seems lifted out of its confusion, and his face appears serene; when it comes down, Mr. Dick looks about him "in a lost way." Kite-flying appears to be a metaphor for the process and function of writing, its uses and abuses, its rewards and losses. The kite narrative "diffuses" ("defuses") and "disseminates" the repressed but returned figures for the lunacy of the self in a story of family desire: it spreads about the wordy yet generative tale and provides a pleasant escape from the process of memorializing. Like Dickens's metaphors of his Broadstairs house as "Gammon Lodge" with its "Gammon Aeronautical Balloon association," of the one-volume *Sketches by Boz* as a balloon on which to embark on his writing career, and of those "intrepid astronauts" of the *Curiosity Shop*, Don Zambullo and Asmodée (themselves figures for the narrator and reader who fly hand in hand), Mr. Dick's kite figures the pleasures and powers of narratizing.

Dr. Strong, fast friends with Mr. Dick, also links the powers of language with familial structures of desire. The doctor, figurative father to his young wife Annie, attempts to take language by its tail and get its meanings codified in his dictionary (Dick-tionary?). Annie's mother comments on a dictionary's usefulness, its necessity: "The meaning of words! Without Dr. Johnson, or somebody of that sort, we might have been at this present moment calling an Italian-iron a bedstead." Exactly. Although she does not realize it, the "Old Soldier" identifies the tendency of language to shift, its failure to signify what its speaker intends, its refusal univocally to name its referents. Like Mr. Dick's memorial, Dr. Strong's dictionary demonstrates its failure to codify and complete language: because of his passion for "Greek roots," for retracing linguistic origins, Dr. Strong has gotten only to "D." We know he will get no farther: the head-boy, Adams, mathematically calculates the good doctor will complete the dictionary in 1,649 years! Like Mr. Dick's memorial, then, Dr. Strong's dictionary gets tangled up with the number 1,649 and so metaphorically with the date of King Charles the First's beheading, with desire and prohibition, with the lunacy of fathering the self in language. Dr. Strong's dictionary, like Mr. Dick's memorial, appears as a metaphor for Dickens's obsession in *David Copperfield* with origins and so with fathering, his concentration on "D," his metaphorical association with the 1649 unrest, rebellion, and beheading of a figure for the narrating self.

Micawber as a figure for the writer openly contradicts Dickens's asserted metaphor of the author as father. Micawber, whose improvidence, imprisonment, and love of language Dickens bases on his own father's, announces unknowingly at the end of *Copperfield* the novel's narrative project. "The veil that has long been interposed between Mrs. Micawber and myself, is now withdrawn ... and my children and the Author of their Being can once more come in contact on equal terms." Micawber's confused metaphor of simultaneous paternity and equality merely points out, as do all his actions in the narrative, his irrepressible and irresponsible fatherhood. Yet this improvident father is an "Author," a figure for an engendering God, and, as all readers of the novel remember, a lover of language. He is, above all, a writer of letters. Micawber relishes his epistolary prose, rereads it "under pretence of having lost his place," "smack[s] his lips" over the tasty words, reads as though his letter were an Act of Parliament, or the text of a sermon, or a performance with which he were highly satisfied. Aunt Betsey declares Micawber would "write letters by the ream, if it was a capital offence"—shades of King Charles the First! David, however, understands Micawber's passion for writing letters means he cannot leave any situation without adding a written postscript to real life. Micawber, in fact, enjoys his epistolary powers so fully because language compensates for reality. In his first letter to David, Micawber forecasts his impending imprisonment for debt and likens it to death; David rushes to help but finds Mr. and Mrs. Micawber on the London coach, "the very picture of tranquil enjoyment," as tranquil as they had appeared the evening before the letter's writing and arrival. When Micawber exposes Heep as a fraud, he enjoys reading his document because "describing this unfortunate state of things, really seemed to outweigh any pain or anxiety that the reality could have caused him." Language does not represent reality but instead compensates for its pain. This separation of language from its referent, Micawber's many letters imply, results from the generative power of metaphor, the figurative energy of language. Micawber's faith resides entirely in believing this metaphorical language literal: something will "turn up." Yet Micawber's experience demonstrates the considerable perils of living in the realm of language, of spurning the realities of life as father, provider, and husband. The father as "author" and "Author," the writer as engenderer, the autobiographer as self-engenderer, appear highly suspect.

David, however, fails to interpret Micawber's separation of language and life as associated with himself. Despite his perceptive commentary on Micawber, despite his own educational trials with the figurative energy of language, the separation of inscription and signification, David continues to believe his own theory of language as a form of discipline, earnestness, and self-reliance, as the engendering tools of the self-made, self-written man. Yet the scene in which Micawber exposes David's own dark double, Uriah Heep, as a fraud also causes David to muse on the duplicity of language:

> We talk about the tyranny of words, but we like to tyrannize over them too. We are fond of having a large superfluous establishment of words to wait upon us on great occasions; we think it looks important, and sounds well. As we are not particular about the meaning of our liveries on state occasions if they be but fine and numerous enough, so the meaning or necessity of our words is a secondary consideration, if there be but a great parade of them. And as individuals get into trouble by making too great a show of liveries, or as slaves when they are too numerous rise against their masters, so I think I could mention a nation that has got into many great difficulties, and will get into many greater, from maintaining too large a retinue of words.

David's metaphor of language and writer as servant (or slave) and master proves terribly unstable. Inherent in such metaphorical equivalencies, such ratios, is the slippage of signification brought about by the separation between inscription and signification, language and referent. As David meditates on Micawber's wordiness, on his lack of care about signification itself, David's metaphor undercuts his own linguistic theory of the auto-didact, the writer who fathers himself through language. His meditation transforms his metaphor and radically alters his signification: the writer's control over language becomes language's service to the writer becomes language's rebellion against the writer. Language has a dangerous life of its own, generated by the energy of metaphor. David's insistence on engendering himself in self-referential narrative forces him to repress this dangerous slippage of signification. David goes on to Switzerland and writes his novel, which we read as Dickens's *David Copperfield;* David writes about himself as the hero of his life and ignores the lessons of duplicitous language, ignores the lunatic figures for the writer who call into question self-origination.

The novel's theory of language as a vehicle for making the self without the help of fathers finds its opposite in another of David's doubles, the "small Cain" of the autobiographical fragment. This small Cain, as psychoanalytic literary critics have demonstrated, appears obsessed by oral and anal imagery. He cannot control his urge for stale pastries or puddings with currants, his interest in pineapples and in coffee shops. He cannot manage the economies of his small loaves and cheeses, despite dividing his money into "six little parcels," each containing the "same amount" of money and "labelled with a different day." This concern with the "scantiness of [his] resources," however, seems to me not primarily (although also necessarily) an indication of oral deprivation and the struggle for anal control but a concern with self-dependence and self-reliance which unites yet goes beyond the bodily imagery of Freud's two earliest developmental stages.

This small Cain's fear of self-dependence and self-reliance appears linked to his fears of paternal betrayal and replacement. Dickens, writing out the almost nostalgic grievances of his youth, writes of the small exile's experience at this time of his father's imprisonment and his own lonely working at Warren's Blacking: "I was so young and childish—how could I be otherwise?—to undertake the whole charge of my existence." He supposes his father pays for his lodging, since he pays for everything but that, yet writes with melancholy and repressed anger, "I certainly did not pay it myself; and I certainly had no other assistance whatever . . . from Monday morning until Saturday night. No advice, no counsel, no encouragement, no consolation, no support, from any one that I can call to mind, so help me God." This rhetoric of negation, deprivation, and betrayal finds its way whole into *David Copperfield* and appears, although muted, in the *Pickwick* tale, "The Convict's Return."

The small Cain, however, became David, who became Dickens. Both Cain and David are figures for Dickens's self, and both are fictional. The fatherless exile, the wanderer, gives way to David: Dickens stopped writing the autobiographical fragment when he began *Copperfield*. Although Cain cannot manage his resources and so create himself without his father, David can and does and refuses to confront in his autobiographical narrative the clues that self-origination is at all problematic. Both Cain and David, however, give way to Pip, a later, more fictional, figure for Dickens himself. Pip writes his autobiography to criticize himself for assuming he could engender himself apart from fathers. Pip's story about fatherhood and language demonstrates that the son cannot father himself but must admit, in all his guilt, the father's precedence and origination.

Both Pip's figurative fathers in *Great Expectations* tell him stories about their fathers. Early in the novel, Joe tells Pip about the cruel and irresponsible father who sends him to work at his forge and prevents Joe from going to school. Joe eventually supports his father financially by working at his father's vocation in the forge. In this metaphorical story of father, son, and blacking warehouse, the son does not resent the father's betrayal; Joe's expectations, unlike the small Cain's and unlike Pip's, are not great. He accepts his father and writes a loving epitaph for his father's tombstone: "I made it . . . my own self," Joe tells Pip of the never-carved couplet that details the goodness of his father's heart despite paternal abandonment. Pip, who listens to a version of his own, of Dickens's own, story, doubts Joe's father's goodness of heart. Magwitch's story about his father, unlike Joe's, fails to name the father as betrayer of a son, although Magwitch's language clearly implies paternity: "Summun had run away from me—a man—a tinker—and he'd took the fire with him, and left me wery cold." Magwitch's abandoning father originates and society corroborates his resulting poverty, criminality, and alienation. Magwitch, like Joe, is bitter, yet his story narrates the reality of his existence, of his need to father a young gentleman because he lacked a father, of his making himself in the only way a poor orphan can in a society in which Newgate appears at the center of the city, in which death runs the system—as Dennis the hangman of *Barnaby Rudge* would say.

In both stories of fatherhood and engendering, sonhood appears linked with a "forge." Joe accepts his own place in his father's vocation at the forge, just as Pip apparently should but cannot accept his apprenticeship in the forge. Magwitch gets involved with Compeyson, whose business is swindling and "forging," whose companion, Arthur, is haunted by the ghost of his bridal-robed sister, Miss Havisham. Joe's forge and Magwitch's forgery link the metaphorical blacking warehouse with false writing. These two stories of fatherhood, taken together, represent the lesson Pip feels he must teach himself in writing his own narrative about figurative fatherhood. He must accept Joe as his figurative father and must love his second father as Joe loves *his* father. Although Pip punishes himself in the writing of his autobiography in order to find such love for his originating fathers in his heart, his logical doubt of Joe's clearly sentimentalized sonhood questions his final filial love of both Magwitch and Joe. Pip's love, his writing of himself into that love, springs from guilt. His criticism of self-engendering, of the son creating himself without fathers, appears qualified by that guilt.

Both Pip and David tell their stories about fatherhood and language, and Dickens tells his—the small Cain's—as well as theirs. Pip, David,

Cain, and Dickens, despite the complex attitudes each portrays toward self-engendering, all tell stories in order to survive. All four read the classic novels to which their fathers provide them access. David "reads for his life" when Murdstone appears as his new father. Cain and David make "stories for [themselves] out of the streets" when father and family are imprisoned; David "impersonates" himself as the good characters and Murdstone, his punishing father, as the bad in the narratives he devours. David tells Steerforth stories at school so Steerforth will dispense to him wine and food: storytelling provides nourishment. The young Pip tells Joe—and the adult Pip, us readers—his "inventions," confesses guiltily his "lies," thinking storytelling a "criminal" activity. Despite Pip's—and Dickens's—fears about the falsity of invention, however, despite the lunacy that threatens to disrupt David's glorification of himself as self-made man, Dickens's figures for himself survive on storytelling and narrate that survival. David ultimately realizes that the discipline that enables him to originate himself in narrative grows from that difficult time at Murdstone and Grinby's; Dickens must realize that the discipline that enables him to rewrite the story of fatherhood, language, and self-engendering sprouted in his survival of Warren's Blacking, in its testing and nourishing his imagination.

D. A. MILLER

Discipline in Different Voices: Bureaucracy, Police, Family, *and* Bleak House

Chancery Court in *Bleak House* (1852–53) makes a certain difference in Dickens's representation of social discipline. This representation had hitherto been restricted to places of confinement which, as much as they referred to a disciplinary society committed to the manufacture and diffusion of such enclosures, also carried an even more emphatic allusion to the space between them: a space of freedom or domestic tranquillity that was their "other." The often ferocious architecture that immured the inmates of a carceral institution seemed to immure the operations practiced on them there as well, and if the thick, spiked walls, the multiple gateways, the attendants and the administrators assured the confinement of those within, they seemed equally to provide for the protectedness of those without, including most pertinently the novelist and his readers. Embodied in the prison, the workhouse, the factory, the school, discipline became, quite precisely, a *topic* of Dickensian representation: a site whose redoubtable but all the more easily identified boundaries allowed it to be the target of criticism to the same extent that they isolated it from other, better sites. The topic of the carceral in Dickens—better, the carceral as topic—thus worked to secure the effect of difference between, on the one hand, a confined, institutional space in which power is violently exercised on collectivized subjects, and on the other, a space of "liberal society," generally determined as a free, private, and individual domain and practi-

From *Representations* 1, no. 1 (February 1983). © 1983 by the Regents of the University of California. University of California Press, 1983. Extensive notes, elaborating some aspects of the author's approach, have been omitted here; a reader wishing to consult them may also refer to D. A. Miller, *The Novel and the Police* (Harvard University Press, 1988).

cally specified as the family. Yet clear though the lines of demarcation were, it was alarmingly easy to cross them. After all, what brought carceral institutions into being in the first place were lapses in the proper management of the family: in its failure to constitute itself (the problem of illegitimate or orphaned children and the institutional solution of foundling hospitals and baby farms) or in its failure to sustain itself by means of a self-sufficient domestic economy (the problem of poverty and debt and the institutional responses of workhouses and debtor's prisons). And in the portrayal of its hero in the workhouse, *Oliver Twist* (1837–39) dramatized the shameful facility with which such institutions might mistakenly seize upon what were middle-class subjects to begin with. Still, if to witness the horror of the carceral was always to incur a debt of gratitude for the immunities of middle-class life, then to sense the danger from the carceral was already to learn how this debt had to be acquitted. When Oliver Twist, enchanted by the difference from his previous experience he found in his life at Mr. Brownlow's, begged the latter not to send him back to "the wretched place I came from," Brownlow declared: "You need not be afraid of my deserting you, unless you give me cause." Earlier he had promised Oliver access to the culture represented by the books in his library on similar conditions: "You shall read them, if you behave well." The price of Oliver's deliverance from the carceral (either as the workhouse or as Fagin's gang) would be his absolute submission to the norms, protocols, and regulations of the middle-class family, in which he receives tuition not just from Brownlow but from the Maylies as well. Liberal society and the family were kept free from the carceral institutions that were set up to remedy their failures only by assuming the burden of an immense internal regulation. If discipline was confined to the carceral, then, this was so in order that it might ultimately be extended—in the mode of what was experientially its opposite—to the space outside it.

Chancery Court in *Bleak House* forces upon this representation the necessity of a certain readjustment. In the first place, an essential characteristic of the court is that its operations far exceed the architecture in which it is apparently circumscribed. The distinctive gesture of the carceral—that of locking up—makes little sense here when, at the end of the day, what is locked up is only "the empty court" and not "all the misery it has caused." Though the court is affirmed to be situated "at the very heart of the fog," this literally nebulous information only restates the difficulty of locating it substantially, since there is "fog everywhere." The ultimate unlocalizability of its operations permits them to be in all places at once.

"How many people out of the suit, Jarndyce and Jarndyce has stretched forth its unwholesome hand to spoil and corrupt, would be a very wide question," but it would perhaps also be a moot one, since nearly all the characters we meet in the novel are in the cause, either as parties to it or administrators of it, even those like Esther who seem to have nothing to do with it. And the suit is as long as it is wide, the immense spatial extension of its filiations being matched by the long temporal duration that unfolds under its "eternal heading." Dickens's satire on the inefficiency of the court begins to seem a feeble, even desperate act of whistling in the dark, for the power organized under the name of Chancery is repeatedly demonstrated to be all too effective. Like the fog and dirt that are its first symbols, this power insinuates itself by virtue of its quasi-alchemical subtlety. To violent acts of penetration it prefers the milder modes of permeation, and instead of being densely consolidated into a force prepared to encounter a certain resistance, it is so finely vaporized—sublimated, we should say, thinking of alchemy and psychoanalysis together—that every surface it needs to attack is already porously welcoming it. Unlike, say, the power that keeps order in Dotheboys Hall in *Nicholas Nickleby* (1838–39), this power does not impose itself by physical coercion (though, as the case of Gridley reminds us, it does dispose of carceral sanctions for those who hold it in contempt). Rather, it relies on being voluntarily assumed by its subjects, who, seduced by it, addicted to it, internalize the requirements for maintaining its hold. "Fog everywhere." What Chancery produces, or threatens to do, is an organization of power which, ceasing entirely to be a *topic,* has become topography itself: a system of control which can be all-encompassing because it cannot be compassed in turn. Writing in the nineteenth century, John Forster would not be the last critic of *Bleak House* to notice how "the great Chancery suit, on which the plot hinges, on incidents connected with which, important or trivial, all the passion and suffering turns, is worked into every part of the book." Yet though we see nothing but the effects of Jarndyce and Jarndyce, everywhere present, affecting everyone, everything, we never come close to seeing what the suit is all about, as though this were merely the pretext that allowed for the disposition and deployment of the elaborate channels, targets, and techniques of a state bureaucracy. The interminable process of interpretation to which the original will gives rise, literally maddening to those who bring to it the demand that it issue in final truths and last judgments, is abandoned rather than adjudicated. If Chancery thus names an organization of power that is total but not totalizable, total *because* it is not totalizable, then what is most radically the matter with being "in

Chancery" is not that there may be no way out of it (a dilemma belonging to the problematic of the carceral), but, more seriously, that the binarisms of inside/outside, here/elsewhere become meaningless and the ideological effects they ground impossible.

Furthermore, the nature of Chancery necessarily affects the nature of the resistance to it. Whereas the topic of the carceral, localizing disciplinary practices that thereby seemed to require only local remedies, always implied a feasible politics of reformism, the total social reticulation of Chancery finds its corresponding oppositional practice in the equally total social negation of anarchism. Repeatedly, the court induces in the narration a wish for its wholesale destruction by fire: "If all the injustice it has committed, and all the misery it has caused, could only be locked up with it, and the whole burnt away in a great funeral pyre—why, so much the better for other parties than the parties in Jarndyce and Jarndyce!" Even the elision of agency managed by the passive voice (who, exactly, would burn the court?), stopping short of any subjective assumption of the action, mirrors perfectly the court whose operations are in no one's control. The wish, moreover, may be considered fulfilled (albeit also displaced) when Mr. Krook, who has personified the Chancellor and Chancery from the first, dies of spontaneous combustion. It is as though apocalyptic suddenness were the only conceivable way to put an end to Chancery's meanderings, violent spontaneity the only means to abridge its elaborate procedures, and mere combustion the only response to its accumulation of paperwork. One of the least welcome implications of an all-inclusive system, such as Chancery is implied to be, is that even opposition to it, limited to the specular forms of reflection and inversion, merely intensifies our attachment to the perceptual grid constructed by its practices.

To say so much, of course, is to treat Chancery, if not more radically, then certainly more single-mindedly, than Dickens is ever willing to do. For while a major effort of *Bleak House* is to establish Chancery as an all-pervasive system of domination, another is to refute the fact of this system and recontain the court within a larger spatial organization that would once again permit an elsewhere along with all the ideological effects attaching to it. If Krook's death, for instance, illustrates the apocalyptically anti-social kinds of retribution that are the only adequate responses to Chancery remaining, it can also be seen to reinstate precisely those social and political possibilities that Chancery, as a total order, ought to have made impossible. For insofar as Krook dies, as in certain modern etiologies of cancer, of his own internal repressions, then Chancery can be safely trusted to collapse from its own refusal to release what is unhealthily accumulating in its system. Alternatively, insofar as Krook's violent end is meant to foreshadow what is in store for the institution he figures, then his death carries a warning to the court to amend its ways or else. In either case, we are reinstalled within the reformist perspectives that Chancery had, we thought, in principle annulled.

Even the omnipresence of the Chancery suit that Forster rightly noted is frequently neutralized by a certain inconsequentiality. John Jarndyce, Ada Clare, and Esther Summerson are all in the suit without being spoiled or corrupted by it—indeed, they constitute the domestic retreat to which the institutional, social space of the court can then be contrasted. Richard Carstone, whose aimlessness internalizes the procedural protractions of the court, makes a better example of Chancery's power to spoil and corrupt. Yet it is also possible to argue, as did an early critic of the novel, under the impression that he was exposing its deficiency, that Richard "is not made reckless and unsteady by his interest in the great suit, but simply expends his recklessness and unsteadiness on it, as he would on something else if it were nonexistent." It is, of course, Dickens's own text that opens up the possibility of this moral explanation in its reluctance to commit itself to social determination:

> "How much of this indecision of character," Mr. Jarndyce said to me, "is chargeable on that incomprehensible heap of uncertainty and procrastination on which he has been thrown from his birth, I don't pretend to say; but that Chancery, among its other sins, is responsible for some of it, I can plainly see. It has engendered or confirmed in him a habit of putting off—and trusting to this, that, and the other chance, without knowing what chance—and dismissing everything as unsettled, uncertain, and confused. The character of much older and steadier people may be even changed by the circumstances surrounding them. It would be too much to expect that a boy's, in its formation, should be the subject of such influences, and escape them."

Jarndyce kind-heartedly proposes the sociological key to Richard's character in the same breath as he admits its insufficiency. And what is at stake in his hesitation between "engendered" and "confirmed," between the court as cause and the court as occasion, goes beyond the double view of Richard. Ultimately, the text oscillates between two seemingly incompatible sets of assumptions about the nature of Chancery's power—one deriving from the perception of total domination, the other still attached to the topic of the carceral. Thus, just as the satire on the inefficiency of the court contradicts the demonstrated power of such inefficiency, so too the anachronism of Chancery, upheld as "a slow, expensive, British, constitutional sort of thing" by such fossils as Sir Leicester, counters the newness of the phenomenon that Dickens is describing under that name: the expanded development of the Victorian state bureaucracy that is at least as current as the novel's official exhibit of modernity in the Detective Police.

All the evidence of Chancery's totalizing effects—of its productivity as an all-englobing system of power—is equivocal in such ways, as the text at once claims that this system is and isn't efficient, is and isn't everywhere, can and cannot be reformed. In the literal sense of giving utterance to a double discourse, *Bleak House* is a contradictory text. Yet as we continue to consider the operation of such "contradiction" in the text, we should be wary of prejudging it, in a certain Marxist manner, as the "symptom" of an ideological bind, obligingly betrayed to our notice in the text's taken-for-granted "distanciation" from its own program. We need rather to be prepared to find in the source of "incoherence," the very resource on which the text draws for its consistency; in the ideological "conflict," a precise means of addressing and solving it; in the "failure" of intention on the part of the text, a positively advantageous *strategy*.

II

Of all the mysteries that will crop up in *Bleak House,* not the least instructive concerns the curious formal torsion whereby a novel dealing with a civil suit becomes a murder mystery, and whereby the themes of power and social control are passed accordingly from the abyssal filiations of the law into the capable hands of the detective police. By what kinds of logic or necessity is the law thus turned over to the police, and the civil suit turned into the criminal case? For if Jarndyce and Jarndyce provides the ground from which mysteries and the consequent detections originate, it is certainly not because the suit is itself a mystery. In one sense, it is so illegible that we don't even have a sense, as we should with a mystery, of what needs to be explained or, more importantly, of what might constitute either the clues or the cruxes of such an explanation. In another, the suit may be read fully and at leisure: in the reams of dusty warrants, in the tens of thousands of Chancery-folio pages, in the battery of blue bags with their heavy charges of paper—in all the archival litter that has accumulated over the dead letter of the original will. Dickens's presentation offers either too little or else too much to amount to mystery. Besides, nothing about the suit is secret or hidden, unless we count the second will found late in the novel, and this hardly brings us closer to a judgment. All that is even unavailable are the dead legator's intentions.

It would be seriously misleading, however, on the basis of this exception, to deconstruct the suit into an allegory of interpretation as that which, confronting the absence of an immediate meaning effected by the very nature of the sign or text, must unfold as an interminable proliferation of readings. For one thing, if the suit can be thought to give expression to such difficulties of interpretation, this is because, more than merely finding them acceptable, it goes out of its way to manufacture them; and no response would serve Chancery or the logic of its law better than to see this manufacture as inhering in the nature of "textuality" rather than belonging to an institutional practice that seeks to implant and sanction its own technical procedures. For another, it seems willful to see the work of interpretation occurring in what is far more obviously and actually the profitable business of deferring it indefinitely. With its endless referrals, relays, remands, its ecologically terrifying production of papers, minutes, memoranda, Dickens's bureaucracy works positively to elude the project of interpretation that nominally guides it. (And by the time that the Circumlocution Office in *Little Dorrit* [1855–57] avows the principle "HOW NOT TO DO IT," even the nominal commitment seems abandoned.) Esther properly recognizes how "ridiculous" it is to speak of a Chancery suit as "in progress," since the term implies a linear directedness which, while fully suitable to the project that subtends Esther's own narration (indicatively begun under the title of "A Progress"), must be wholly absent from a case which, typically, "seemed to die out of its own vapidity, without coming, or being by anybody expected to come, to any result." Moreover, to see that, in Chancery, the process of decision and interpretation is diverted is also to see that it is diverted *into* Chancery, as an apparatus. It is diverted, in other words, into the work of establishing the very channels for its diversion: channels by means of which a legal establishment is ramified, its points of contact multiplied, and routes of circulation organized for the subjects who are thus recruited under its power.

Yet Chancery can never dispense with the judgments that it also never dispenses. Though the project of interpretation is virtually annulled in the workings of its formalism ("the lantern that has no light in it"), the *promise* of interpretation, as that which initiates and facilitates this formalism, remains absolutely necessary. At the theoretical level of ideology, the promise functions to confer legitimacy on Chancery proceedings: as even poor crazed Miss Flyte, in her confusion of the Last Judgment with the long-delayed judgment in her own case, is capable of revealing, the legal system must appeal for its authority to transcendent concepts of truth, justice, meaning, and ending, even when its actual work will be to hold these concepts in profitable abeyance or to redefine and contain them as functions of its own operations. And at the practical and technical level of such operations, the promise of judgment becomes the lure of advertising, extended by venalities such as Vholes to promote the purchase and exercise of their services.

Perhaps the most interesting effect of all produced by the promise, however, considerably exceeds these theoretical and practical functions. If Chancery exploits the logic of a promise by perpetually maintaining it as *no more than such,* then the suit must obviously produce as much frustration as hopefulness. Accordingly, one consequence of a system that, as it engenders an interpretative project, simultaneously deprives it of all the requirements for its accomplishment is the desire for an interpretative project that would *not* be so balked. This desire is called into being from within the ground of a system that, it bears repeating, resists interpretation on two counts: because it cannot be localized as an object of interpretation, and because it is never willing to become the agency or subject of interpretation. What such a desire effectively seeks, therefore, is a reduced model of the untotalizable system and a legible version of the undecidable suit. What such a desire calls for, in short, both as a concept and as a fact, is the detective story.

The detective story gives obscurity a name and a local habitation: in that highly specific "mystery" whose ultimate uncovering motivates an equally specific program of detection. If the Chancery system includes everything but settles nothing, then one way in which it differs from the detective story is that the latter is, precisely, a *story:* sufficiently selective to allow for the emergence of a narrative and properly committed, once one has emerged, to bringing it to completion. In relation to an organization so complex that it often tempts its subjects to misunderstand it as chaos, the detective story realizes the possibility of an easily comprehensible version of order. And in the face—or facelessness—of a system where it is generally impossible to assign responsibility for its workings to any single person or group of persons, where even the process of victimization seems capricious, the detective story performs a drastic simplification of power as well. For unlike Chancery, the detective story is fully prepared to affirm the efficacy and priority of personal agency, be it that of the criminal figures who do the work of concealment or that of the detective figures who undo it. It is not at all surprising, therefore, that the desire for the detective story first emerges from within the legal community itself, in Tulkinghorn and Guppy, since lawyers, having charge of the system, are most likely to be aware of the extent to which they merely convey a power which is theirs only to hold and not to have. It is entirely suitable that those who continually *exercise* this power—in the root sense, that is, of driving it on—should be the first to dream of *possessing* it, so that the calling of Mr. Tulkinghorn, for instance, "eke solicitor of the High Court of Chancery," becomes "the acquisition of secrets and the holding possession of such power as they give him, with no sharer or opponent in it." At the other end of the legal hierarchy (though not, one may be sure, for long), Mr. Guppy prepares for a similar vocation:

> Mr. Guppy suspects everybody who enters on the occupation of a stool in Kenge and Carboy's office, of entertaining, as a matter of course, sinister designs upon him. He is clear that every such person wants to depose him. If he be ever asked how, why, when, or wherefore, he shuts up one eye and shakes his head. On the strength of these profound views, he in the most ingenious manner takes infinite pains to counter-plot, when there is no plot; and plays the deepest games of chess without any adversary.

Guppy's counter-plotting "when there is no plot" may be seen as the usefully paranoid attempt of an ambitious clerk to grasp the power of the legal system over him by turning everybody in it into his personal enemy. It may also be seen as the desperately fanciful effort of an otherwise bored office worker to overwrite the impersonal and inconsequential tedium of his tasks with lively dramas centered on himself. In either case, it suggests precisely the sense in which the non-narrative system of Chancery generates narratives both to grasp its evasiveness and equally to evade its grasp.

Yet within this perspective, one must register the general failure of the amateur detectives in *Bleak House* to impose a will to truth and power. Anecdotally, their stories all reach a final point of checkmate. Guppy's chance to lay his hands on the decisive evidence goes up in smoke with Krook; Tulkinghorn is murdered before he has quite decided how to make use of his discovery; and even Mrs. Snagsby is still "on the great high road that is to terminate in Mr. Snagsby's full exposure" when Mr. Bucket is obliged to set her straight. These abortive endings, which effectively place the stories under the paradigm of the interminable Chancery suit, also carry "political" rebukes, as the detectives are denied the power to which their knowledge seemed to entitle them. Tulkinghorn's violent death at the hands of a woman over whom he had flaunted his control is the most dramatic example of such chastisement; but another is Guppy's rejection by Esther, the woman who initially inspired his detective work and who he hoped might reward it with her hand; and still another is the gentle but public reprimand that Mrs. Snagsby receives from Mr. Bucket. The profound reason for the anecdotal failure of these stories is that they are undertaken as individual projects. That individuality not only must debilitate the power of the will-to-power, but also qualifies the general validity of the production of truth. Even when the stories have more to go on than Mrs. Snagsby's—exemplary in its forced, false, but flawless coherence—, they are marred by an egocentricity that confers on them the epistemologically suspect tautology of wish-fulfillments. Just as Guppy's detection is part and parcel of his *arrivisme,* an ambitious attempt to ennoble the woman of his choice and to win her gratitude for doing so, similarly, Tulkinghorn, who holds that women "are at the bottom of all that goes wrong in [the world]," finds his sexual resentment justified in a story of female error and deceit. Even Mrs. Snagsby's fantasy that Jo has been illegitimately sired by her husband likewise satisfies her need to see herself as wronged, and so consolidates the basis of her domestic tyranny. It is not enough to say that, if the detective story is meant to be an individual rendition of an order and a power that are social and institutional in nature, then a great deal must be lost in the translation. For that loss to be registered as *its* loss, in its formal incompletion, its cognitive inadequacy, and its political failure, what must also be asserted is the priority assumed by social and institutional categories over the individual projects that they will ultimately reabsorb.

Even as a failure, however, the project of detection enjoys a certain dangerous efficacy. For it fails in every respect except that of catching on. Its weakness as an individual enterprise becomes a demonstrable strength as the number of individuals undertaking it increases and it thereby acquires a certain social distribution and consistency. As a *common* individual project, detection poses a threat to the social and institutional orders that continue to doom it to failure as a single undertaking. From beginning to end, the project sanctions the unwholesomely deviate erotic desire that inspires it and that it releases into action. The unsavory sexual secrets in which this desire, having been liberated, is ultimately gratified, are themselves subversive of socially given arrangements. Regularly involving a double transgression, of class as well as conjugal boundaries, they give scandal to the twin unities that Dickens puts at the basis of a decent social order, family and station. To disclose these secrets, moreover, exacerbates their scandalous effects, as when what Mrs. Snagsby thinks she knows leads her to seek a marital separation, and what Tulkinghorn tells Lady Dedlock prompts her public flight. In a context where home and family are the chief bulwarks against drifting into the interminable circulations of Chancery Court, the kind of individuality implied and exfoliating in the project of detection must seem ultimately anarchic. Born, as Tulkinghorn's case makes particularly clear, when the law is taken into one's own hands, it gives birth to the familiar rivalrous, *sauve-quipeut* world of which the tension between Tulkinghorn and Guppy is an early symptom, and in which the murderous personal arrogations of Mademoiselle Hortense are, though shocking, perfectly proper.

We begin to see why the detective narratives require to come under the management of a master-agency charged with the task both of suppressing their successes (in fostering extreme threats to social order) and also of supplying their failures (to provide a widely available, consoling simplification of this order). We begin to understand, in other words, the profound necessity of the police in *Bleak House*. Though Chancery Court, to make itself tolerable, produces a desire for the detective story, as for that which will confer on it the legibility of a traditionally patterned meaning, this desire, far from issuing in an order that can be comfortingly proffered and consumed as the essence of the chaos that is Chancery's appearance, threatens to reduplicate such chaos in the yet more explicit form of social disaggregation. What keeps the production of this desire from being dangerously excessive—what in fact turns the dangerous excess back into profit—is that the detective story, following the same logic whereby it was produced among the effects of Chancery, produces among *its* effects the desire for its own authoritative version and regulatory agency. Out of control to the point that, at Tulkinghorn's murder, the very principle of sense-making appears to have gone "stark mad," the detective story eventually asks to be arrested by the Detective Police.

Such regulation should not be seen purely as a repressive practice, involving, for instance, the capture of a murderer like Mademoiselle Hortense or a runaway like Lady Dedlock. The police not only repress but also, profoundly, satisfy the desire to which Chancery gives rise. For in addition to doing the negative work of correcting for the socially undesirable consequences of amateur projects of detection, it performs the positive work of discharging for society as a whole the function that these amateur projects had assumed unsuccessfully: that of providing, within the elusive organization of Chancery, a simplified representation of order and power.

The novel's shift in focus from Chancery Court to the Detective Police encompasses a number of concomitant shifts, which all operate in the direction of this simplification: from civil law and questions of liability to criminal law and less merely legal questions of guilt; from trivial legal hair-splitting to the urgency of the fact, beyond such disputing, of murder; from a cause with countless parties represented by countless attorneys in an anonymous system, to a case essentially reduced to two personal duels, between the criminal and his victim and between the criminal and the detective; from long, slow, to all appearances utterly inefficient procedures to swift and productive ones; and finally, from an institution which cannot justify its power to one which, for all the above reasons, quite persuasively can. It is as though every complaint that could be made about the one institution had been redressed in the organization of the other, so that one might even argue, on the basis of Dickens's notorious willingness to serve as a propagandist for the New Police, that the excruciating *longueurs* of Chancery existed mainly to create the market for Mr. Bucket's expeditious *coups*. Along these lines, one might even want to read, in the police activity that develops over the dead body of the law ("or Mr. Tulkinghorn, one of its trustiest representatives"), Dickens's exhilarated announcement of the agencies and practices of social discipline that, claiming to be merely supplementing the law, will come in large part to supplant it. Yet to the extent that we stress, in the evident archaism of Chancery, the emergence of a new kind of bureaucratic organization, and in the blatantly modern Detective Police (instituted only ten years before the novel began to appear), a harkening back to a traditional and familiar model of power, then we need to retain the possibility that Dickens's New Police still polices, substantively as well as nominally, *for* the law, for the Chancery system, and that, as a representation, it serves a particular ideological function within this system, and not against it. Made so desirable as a sort of institutional "alternative" to Chancery, the police derive their ideological efficacy from providing, within a total system of power, *a representation of the containment of power*. The shift from Chancery to the police dramatically localizes the field, exercise, and agents of power, as well as, of course, justifies such power, which, confined to a case of murder and contained in a Mr. Bucket, occupies what we can now think of as the right side. And when the novel passes from adulatory wonder at the efficiency of the police to sad, resigned acknowledgment of its limits (such as emerges in Hortense's last exchange with Bucket), the circumscription of power, reaching the end to which it always tended, has merely come full circle.

III

The police thus allow for the existence of a field outside the dynamic of power and free from its effects. Once installed in this realmless realm, one could cease to internalize—as the desperate, hopeful psychology of compulsion—the lures of the Chancery system; from within it, one could bear witness to the possibility of a genuine criticism of that system, one that would no longer be merely the sign of the impossibility of withdrawing from it. Shifting focus from Chancery Court to the Detective Police, the novel works toward the recovery of this place elsewhere, in a two-pronged strategy whose other line of attack lies in Esther's absolute refusal to be touched by the suit and in the constitution of Bleak House that her refusal enables. For in point of fact the "outside" of power is specified as a domestic space, occupied by an ideal of the family. Not the least evil of the Chancery system in this respect was that, in it, police and family blurred into one another. As an apparatus of power concerned to impose, protect, and extend itself, Chancery naturally included a policing function, but it had the aspect of a family as well, not only because the suits that came before it arose from family disputes, but also because (as when it put its wards Ada and Richard under the guardianship of John Jarndyce) it sanctioned families of its own. In effect, the emergence of Bleak House on the one hand and Mr. Bucket (who, though Mrs. Bucket is as fond of children as himself, has none) on the other achieves the extrication of the family from the police, a disarticulation into separate domains of what it was a trick of Chancery's domination to have knitted seamlessly together.

We mustn't be surprised, however, if there is a trick to this new arrangement too—and perhaps a far better one. When Mr. Bucket escorts Mr. Snagsby through Tom-all-Alone's (much as Inspector Field took Dickens with him on his tours of duty), the detective's thoroughgoing knowledge of the place as well as the extreme deference shown to him by its inhabitants (who call him "master") indicate the degree to which the police have saturated the delinquent milieu. If the saturation doesn't appear to have much curtailed delinquency, or even, strangely, to have prevented Tom-all-Alone's from continuing to serve as a refuge for those wanted by the police, these perhaps were never the ends of police penetration. What such penetration indubitably does secure is an apparent containment of crime and power together, which both become visible mainly in a peripheral place, "avoided by all decent people." The raison d'etre of Tom-all-Alone's is that it *be* all alone, as the text is prepared to admit when it speculates "whether the traditional title is a comprehensive name for a

retreat cut off from honest company." Yet the marginal localization of the
police thus achieved is subjected to a dramatic ambiguity as soon as,
beyond ensuring the circulation of vagrants like Jo or the apprehension of
murderers who, doubly exotic, come from foreign parts and the servant
class both, the police pass into the fashionable upper-class world of Chesney
Wold or even the just barely respectable shooting gallery of Mr. George.
Though disturbed by Bucket's nighttime visit, heralded only by the glare of
his bull's-eye, the denizens of Tom-all-Alone's are neither surprised nor
shamed by what is evidently a very familiar occurrence. Compare their
dull acceptance to Sir Leicester's appalled imagination:

> Heaven knows what he sees. The green, green woods of Chesney
> Wold, the noble house, the pictures of his forefathers, strangers
> defacing them, officers of police coarsely handling his most
> precious heirlooms, thousands of fingers pointing at him, thou-
> sands of faces sneering at him.

Compare it even to Mr. George's sharp mortification:

> "You see . . . I have been handcuffed and taken into custody,
> and brought here. I am a marked and disgraced man, and here I
> am. My shooting-gallery is rummaged, high and low, by Bucket;
> such property as I have—'tis small—is turned this way and
> that, till it don't know itself."

The sense of scandal that informs both passages, even as it acknowledges
that the police can break out of their limits to become a total, all-pervasive
institution like Chancery, reinforces our perception of the boundaries that
ordinarily keep them in their place. It qualifies the police intervention in
either case as an exceptional state of affairs, warranted only by the
exceptional circumstances that call it into being.

The representation of the police, then, is not just organized by a
comforting principle of localization; it is also organized within the fear-
inspiring prospect of *the possible suspension of this principle.* One may
read the resulting ambiguity in the very character of Mr. Bucket. The fact
that the representation of the police is virtually entirely confined to the
portrayal of this one character is already revealing of the strategy of
containment whereby the topic of the police is constituted. Chancery
Court required dozens of lawyers in the attempt to represent it, and even
then the attempt had always to remain unequal to a system whose essential
anonymity resisted being seized as character. The police, however, can be
adequately rendered in the character of a single one of its agents, and this

fact, among others, makes it a superior institution. Whereas the law is impersonal and anonymous, the law enforcement is capable of showing a human face—if that is the word for the mechanically recurring tics and character-traits that caused Inspector Bucket to be received at the time of the novel's publication as one of Dickens's most "delightful" creations. Yet if police power is contained in Bucket, Bucket himself is *not* contained in the way that characters ordinarily are. A master of disguise, who makes himself appear in as "ghostly" a manner as, with a touch of his stick, he makes others "instantly evaporate," Bucket seems superhuman and his powers magical. To Mr. Snagsby, confused and impressed, he appears "to possess an unlimited number of eyes"; and Jo, in his ignorance and delirium, believes him "to be everywhere, and cognizant of everything." With ironic reservations that only refine the ambiguity, the narration even offers its own language in support of these baffled perceptions: "Time and place cannot bind Mr. Bucket," it tells us, and "nothing escapes him."

Another way to bring out the ambiguity that invests the established limits of the police is to ask: on behalf of whom or what does the Detective Police do its policing? Answers in the text, accurately reflecting an historical ambiguity, are various. Bucket works now in the capacity of a private detective employed by individuals such as Tulkinghorn; now as the public official of a state apparatus that enjoins him, for instance, to secure Gridley for contempt of court; and now in some obscure combination of the two functions, as when, at the end, he seems to police simultaneously on behalf of society at large and at the behest of Sir Leicester Dedlock. In a sense, the progress toward the legitimacy of power that we read in the focal shift from Chancery to the Detective Police occurs within the representation of the police itself, which, at the beginning acting as the agent of an arbitrary system or an equally arbitrary individual will, acquires in the end—via murder and a missing person—the means of legitimizing the exercise of its power, even though this is still nominally in the hire of Sir Leicester. Yet this effort of the narrative sequence to legitimize the power of the police leaves looking all the more unresolved the question of their whereabouts, which are established in so many places, as so many indistinct, overlapping, competing jurisdictions, that they cease to seem established at all.

All the ambiguities about the police, of course, serve to establish a radical uncertainty in the nature of private, familial space. "As [Mr. Bucket] says himself, what is public life without private ties? He is in his humble way a public man, but it is not in that sphere that he finds happiness. No, it must be sought within the confines of domestic bliss."

But as we know, Bucket here maintains the difference between public (institutional) and private (domestic) spheres as part of a successful attempt to neutralize it. The difference on which he affably insists allows him to be welcomed into the Bagnet household, where at the proper moment—no longer as a new friend of the family, but now a public official—he can arrest their friend and guest Mr. George. Is the private sphere autonomous or not? The representation of the police in *Bleak House* permits us to answer the question either way: to insist, when this is necessary, on the elsewhere opened up by the localization of the police (who considerately police, among other things, their own limits); or to suggest, when this is desirable, the extent to which this elsewhere is constantly liable to being transgressed by the police. The police simultaneously produce and permeate (produce as permeable) the space they leave to be "free."

If, therefore, we need to say that, in its representation of bureaucracy and the police, *Bleak House* regularly produces a difference between these institutions and the domestic space outside them, we must also recognize that it no less regularly produces this difference *as a question,* in the mode of the "problematic." The bar of separation and even opposition that it draws between the two terms is now buttressed, now breached, firm and fragile by turns. On one hand, Chancery is a total system of domination, engendering resistances whose mere inversions or duplications of its injunctions only entrench its power more deeply. On the other hand, Chancery's domination seems to cease precisely at the points where one elects to erect bulwarks against it such as Esther's Bleak House. Or again: if the police represent a reduction of the domination of Chancery, and thus permit a domestic autonomy, it is also suggested that the police, as all-encompassing as Chancery, can at any moment abolish that autonomy. Or still again: the police are other, better than Chancery, but they are also the organ that polices on its behalf and thus works to preserve it. We cannot too strongly insist that these "paradoxes" are not merely confusions or historical contradictions that tug and pull at a text helpless to regulate them, but rather productive ambiguities that facilitate the disposition, functioning, and promotion of certain ideological effects, some of which we have already suggested. Neither, however, should "*Bleak House,* by Charles Dickens" be denounced—or congratulated—as the ultimate strategist of these effects, as though one could allow such effects their broad cultural resonance without also recognizing their broad cultural production and distribution. Yet if the novel no more "manipulates" the equivocations we have traced than "succumbs" to them, perhaps the most pertinent reason is that it lacks the distance from them required to do either. We shall see how, in the first place, these equivocations *are its own*, always already borne in the novel as a form; and also how, in the last instance, these equivocations *come to be its own*, as the novel reproduces in the relationship between form and content the dialectic that occurs within each of its terms.

IV

It would certainly appear as though the existence of that sheltered space which the novelistic representation labors to produce—but with, we have seen, such dubious results—is unconditionally taken for granted in the novel form, whose unfolding or consumption has never ceased to occur in such a space all along. Since the novel counts among the conditions for this consumption the consumer's leisured withdrawal to the private, domestic sphere, then every novel-reading subject is constituted—willy-nilly and almost before he has read a word—within the categories of the individual, the inward, the domestic. There is no doubt that the shift in the dominant literary form from the drama to the novel at the end of the seventeenth century had to do with the latter's superior efficacy in producing and providing for privatized subjects. The only significant attempt to transcend the individualism projected by the novel took place precisely in Victorian England as the practice of the *family reading,* which may be understood as an effort to mitigate the possible excesses of the novel written for individuals by changing the locus of reading from the study—or worse, the boudoir—to the hearth, enlivened but also consolidated as a *foyer d'intrigue.* A Victorian novel such as *Bleak House* speaks not merely for the hearth, in its prudent care to avoid materials or levels of explicitness about them unsuitable for family entertainment, but from the hearth as well, implicity grounding its critical perspective on the world within a domesticity that is more or less protected against mundane contamination.

Yet if only by virtue of the characteristic length that prevents it from being read in a single sitting, the novel inevitably enjoins not one, but several withdrawals to the private sphere. Poe, who first raised the issue of the effects of this length, considered the discontinuousness of novel-reading one of the liabilities of the form, which thereby had to forego "the immense benefit of *totality.*" In the novel state, Poe thought, the autonomy of "literary concerns" was always being frustrated by the foreign intervention of "worldly interests." If, however, novel-reading presupposes so many disparate withdrawals to the private sphere, by the same token it equally presupposes so many matching returns to the public, institutional one. An important dimension of what reading a novel entails, then, would lie—outside the moment and situation of actual perusal—in the times and places that interrupt this perusal and render it in the plural, as a series. Just as we read the novel in the awareness that we must put it down before finishing it, so even when we are not reading it, we continue to "live" the form in the mode of *having to get back to it*. Phenomenologically, the novel form includes the interruptions that fracture the process of reading it. And the technical equivalent of this phenomenological interpenetration of literary and worldly interests would be the practice of various realisms, which, despite their manifold differences, all ensure that the novel is always centrally about the world one has left behind to read it and that the world to which one will be recalled has been reduced to attesting the truth (or falsehood) of the novel. It is not quite true, therefore, that the novel is simply concerned to attach us to individuality and domesticity, to privacy and leisure. What the form really secures is a close *imbrication* of individ- ual and social, domestic and institutional, private and public, leisure and work. A drill in the rhythms of bourgeois industrial culture, the novel generates a nostalgic desire to get home (where the novel can be resumed) in the same degree as it inures its readers to the necessity of periodically renouncing home (for the world where the novel finds its justification and its truth). In reading the novel, one is made to rehearse how to live a problematic—always surrendered, but then again always recovered—privacy.

V

The same opposition—or at least the question of one—between private- domestic and social-institutional domains that is produced in the represen- tation and consumed as the form occurs again in the relationship between the representation and the form. For though the form projects itself as a kind of home, what is housed in this home, as its contents, are not merely or even mainly comfortable domestic quarters, but also the social-institutional world at large. If the novel is substantially to allege its otherness in relation to this world, and thus to vouch for its competence to survey, judge, and understand it, then far from seeking to be adequate or isomorphic to its contents (when these are carceral, disciplinary, institutional), it is instead obliged to defend itself against them by differentiating the practices of the world from the practices of representing it. The current critical fondness for assimilating form and content (via homologies, thematizations, *mises- en-abyme*) becomes no more than a facile sleight-of-hand if it does not face the complication it in fact encounters in the question of the difference between the two that the novel regularly raises. Specifically, as I hope to show in a moment, *Bleak House* is involved in an effort to distinguish its own enormous length from the protractedness of the Chancery suit, and also its own closure from the closed case of the Detective Police. But even remaining at a general and fundamental level, we can see the difference imposing itself in the fact that, for instance, while the world of *Bleak House* is dreary enough, yet were the novel itself ever to become as dreary, were it ever to cease *making itself desirable,* it would also by the same token cease to be read. Pleasurably, at our leisure and in our homes, we read the novel of suffering, the serious business of life, and the world out-of-doors. Moreover, the critical and often indignant attitude that *Bleak House,* by no means untypically, takes toward its social world reinforces this "erotic" difference with a cognitive one: the novel views the world in better, more clear-sighted and disinterested ways than the world views itself.

The suit in *Bleak House* has only to be mentioned for its monstrous length to be observed and censured. "Jarndyce and Jarndyce·still drags its dreary length before the Court, perenially hopeless." The suit is not merely long, but—here lies the affront—excessively so, longer than it is felt it ought to be. Yet what Dickens calls the "protracted misery" of the suit—by which he means the misery of its protractedness as well as vice versa— cannot be explained merely as the consequence of gratuitous *additions* to a necessary and proper length, left intact, which they simply inordinately "pad." One of the ill effects of the length of the suit has been precisely to render unavailable the reality of a proper measure, of which the suit could be seen as an unwarranted expansion and to which it would be theoretically possible to restore it by some judicious abridgment. The further the length of the suit is elaborated, the more it abandons any responsibility to the *telos* or finality that originally called it forth, nominally continues to guide it even now, and would ultimately reabsorb it as the pathway leading to its own achievement. And along with the *formality* of an ending—the juridical act of decision—, what would constitute the *substance* of one is concomitantly put in jeopardy: namely, the establishment of the meaning of the original will. So nearly intertwined are ending and meaning that to adjourn the one seems to be to abjure the other: "This scarecrow of a suit has, in course of time, become so complicated that no man alive knows what it means."

The suit's effective suspension of teleology is, of course, scandalously exemplary of a whole social sphere that seems to run on the principle of a purposiveness without purpose. The principle is enunciated and enforced not only by the bureaucratic officials who, when Jo is sick, "must have been appointed for their skill in evading their duties, instead of performing them," but even by the various policemen in the novel who enjoin Jo to "move on" in his perpetually maintained, displaced itinerary to nowhere. Internalized, it emerges as character defects: the long-windedness of Chadband, the aestheticism of Skimpole (who begins sketches "he never finished"), the flightiness of Richard. Such instances, however, in which the sense of an ending seems entirely given up are no more symptomatic of the general social suspension of finality than the abstract impatience and hopeful voluntarism with which the sense of an ending is merely imposed on a state of affairs which must thereby be misunderstood. Miss Flyte is mad to expect a judgment "shortly," and Richard is certainly on the way to madness when, choplogically, he argues that "the longer [the suit] goes on, . . . the nearer it must be to a settlement one way or other." In the progress of Hegelian Spirit, "the length of this path has to be endured because, for one thing, each moment is necessary" to the emergence of the result; whereas, in the mere ongoingness of the un-Hegelian suit, any attempt to make sense of this length as a necessity, or in terms of the end-orientation which it formally retains but from which it has substantially removed itself, brings those who make it to madness. Finally, however, to recognize that the length of the suit is devoid of necessity is true only in terms of an eventual judgment. Just as the inefficiency of power in Chancery showed up from another standpoint as the power of inefficiency, so too what are on one perspective the superfluous, self-subversive elongations of procedure become on another the necessary developments of a power that—call it the English law—has for its one great principle "to make business for itself." Accordingly, the delays and remands that amount to an effective suspension of its declared end should not be seen to debilitate Chancery, but rather to allow one to take it seriously as—in Dickens's facetious phrase from *The Old Curiosity Shop* (1840–41)—"the long and strong arm of the law."

In light of the fact that the novel about this long arm itself exercises a considerable reach—that the representation *of* length goes on *at* length too—, we are invited to consider the extent to which the novel runs the risk of resembling the Chancery suit that it holds in despite. Certainly, the unfolding of the novel could be thought to parallel the elaboration of the suit insofar as it threatens an analogous failure to bring its ever more abundant materials to a proper or conceivably adequate summation. We already noted how the long novel foregoes "the immense benefit of *total-*

ity" because it cannot be read at a single sitting; but even if we were to export to the nineteenth century the anachronism of a "speed-reader," Victorian practices of distributing the novel-product would still render the interruptedness of reading all but inevitable. Serial publication necessarily barred the reader from ever having full physical possession of the text he was reading until he was almost done with it; and even once the novel was published in volume form as a "three-decker," the ordinary subscription to the circulating libraries (which provided the majority of readers with their access to it) allowed to a borrower only one volume at a time. These determinations are of course merely external, but they are fully matched by the compositional principles of discontinuity and delay that organize the form from within its own structure: not only in the formal breaks of chapters, installments, volumes, but also in the substantive shifts from this plot-line to that, or from one point of view or narration to another; and generally in the shrewd administration of suspense that keeps the novel always tending toward a denouement that is continually being withheld. In Dickens, of course, the fissured and diffused character of novel form is far more marked than in the work of any of his contemporaries, extending from the extraordinary multitude of memorably disjunct characters, each psychologically sealed off from understanding another, to the series of equally disparate and isolated spaces across which they collide. And, like the larger structure of suspense, even individual sentences will frequently derive their effects from the lengths to which they will go in withholding predication. No doubt, both as a system of distribution and as a text, the Victorian novel establishes a little bureaucracy of its own, generating an immense amount of paperwork and both physically and mentally sending its readers here, there, backward and forward, like the circumlocutory agencies that Dickens satirizes. On this basis, it could be argued that, despite or by means of its superficially hostile attitude toward bureaucracy, a novel like *Bleak House* is profoundly concerned to train us—as, at least since the eighteenth century, play usually trains us for work—in the sensibility for inhabiting the new bureaucratic, administrative structures.

This of course would be to neglect what Roland Barthes has identified as the "readerly" orientation of the traditional novel: the tendency of its organization to knit its discontinuities together by means of codes such as those ordering our perception of plot and suspense. If *Bleak House* baffles us in the first few hundred pages by featuring a profusion of characters who seem to have nothing to do with one another, a miscellany of events whose bearing on a possible plot is undecidable, and even two separate systems of narration that are unequal and unrelated, it simultaneously encourages us to anticipate the end of bafflement and the acquisition of various structures of coherence: in the revelation or development of relationships among characters; in the emergence of a plot whereby the mysteries of the text will be enlightened and its meanings fully named; and in the tendency of the two narrations to converge, as Esther's account comes to include characters and information that at first appeared exclusively in the anonymous one. In other words, the novel dramatizes the liabilities of fragmentation and postponement within the hopeful prospect that they will eventually be overcome. We consume the enormous length of a novel like *Bleak House* in the belief that it is eminently digestible—capable, that is, of being ultimately rendered in a readerly *digest:* a final abridgment of plot and character which stands for—and so dispenses with—all that came before it. From the standpoint of this promised end, the massive bulk of the novel will always have concealed the perfectly manageable and unmonstrous proportions of a much shorter, tauter form.

Yet however sustained, the mere promise of an ending, far from being sufficient to differentiate the novel from Chancery, would positively enlarge on the analogy between the novel's practices and those of the Court, which also entices its subjects by means of promises, promises. We read the novel under the same assumption as Richard makes about the suit, that "the longer it goes on, . . . the nearer it must be to a settlement"; and if the assumption is to be validated in the one case as it is discredited in the other, the novel is under obligation to make good its promise by issuing in judgments and resolutions. For even if we always know about the novel (as we do not about the suit) that its length is finite, involving only so many pages or installments, the vulgar evidence of an endpoint can never amount to the assurance of an *ending:* that is, the presence of a complex of narrative summations that would match or motivate the external termination of discourse with its internal closure. The suit, which attains an endpoint but no ending, embodies the distinction that the novel, to be different, will have to obliterate. Though the suit reaches a point at which it is correctly declared "over for good," this point is determined extrinsically by the lack of funds that prevents the protracted, complex cause from being pursued to a proper conclusion of its own. "Thus the suit lapses and melts away," instead of coming to the judgment that would have constituted a proper internal resolution. It is never known, for instance, whether the new will is a genuine document, and the project of finding out has been "checked—brought up suddenly" upon what Conversation Kenge retains sufficient professional finesse to term the "threshold."

In a pointed and self-serving contrast, the novel brings its characters to judgment, its mysteries to solution and its plots to issues that would make further narrative superfluous. Immediately following the end of the suit, as a sort of consequence and reversal of it, Richard's death illustrates the contrast. Insofar as this death is premature, of course, it may look as though Richard will merely reenact the abrupt check of the suit. Juridical discourse has ceased not because it has said what it wanted to say, but only for lack of funds to say it; and similarly, Richard's utterance is simply "stopped by his mouth being full of blood." But what is staged on the scene of Richard's deathbed is in fact his full recovery. In the paradoxical logic of nineteenth-century novelistic closure, whereby one sums up by subtracting, Richard is purged of unsteadiness and suspicion and so made whole. Whereas the suit ends as up in the air as ever it was, Richard's end achieves a fundamental clarification: "the clouds have cleared away, and it is bright now." His tearful recognition that John Jarndyce, whom he mistrusted, is "a good man" renders him once more a good man himself. And his desire to be removed to the new Bleak House ("I feel as if I should get well there, sooner than anywhere") announces the redemptive turn from public institutional involvements to the domestic haven. As a result, even his death—no longer premature, but occurring only *after* the resolution of his character has been attained—bears witness to the seriousness of his conversion by making it permanent, the last word possible about him.

Unlike Chancery, then, the novel is willing to reward the patience that, like Chancery, it has required. The destiny of the long-suffering Esther is only the most obvious figure for the link the novel everywhere secures between the practice of patience and its pay-off. In the reader's case, the link is affirmed each time he gets an answer to one of the questions or riddles he has endured; each time he enjoys the jubilation of recognizing a character who has appeared earlier; each time a new installment comes out to reward his month-long wait for it. It isn't Esther alone in *Bleak House* who is extraordinarily self-deprecating and diffident in the face of authority, be it the heavenly Father in whom "it was so gracious ... to have made my orphan way so smooth and easy," or simply John Jarndyce, to whom she declares: "I am quite sure that if there were anything I ought to know, or had any need to know, I should not have to ask you to tell it to me. If my whole reliance and confidence were not placed in you, I must have a hard heart indeed." The novel puts every reader in an equally subservient position of reliance upon the author, who, if one waits long enough (as, given the nature of the readerly text, one cannot but do), will delight us with the full revelation of his design, offering the supreme example of those happy surprises that Dickens's benevolent father-figures are fond of providing for those they patronize. Still less obviously, the novel develops our trust in the machinery of distribution itself, which can, for instance, be counted upon to provide the next installment at exactly the interval promised. In short, the novel encourages a series of deferential cathexes—all the more fundamental for being unconscious—onto various instances of authority. What is promoted in the process is a paternalism that, despite the dim view the novel takes of the power-structures of the British state, can only be useful in maintaining such structures. To submit to the novel's duration is already to be installed within an upbeat ethic of endurance. If, as we speculated above, the novel trains us to abide in Chancery-like structures—by getting us to wait, as it were, in its very long lines—, it does this only insofar as it is organized as a *reformed* Chancery, a Chancery that can moralize its procrastinations in a practice of delayed gratification. Recklessly, the Court demanded an attendance so futile that it inspired dangerously anarchistic fantasies of destruction. More prudently, the novel, urging us to wait, also promises (to use the very formula of prudence) that we shall wait *and see*.

VI

Though it goes to great lengths, *Bleak House* also goes to extremities to save these lengths from lapsing into the mere unproductive extensions of the Chancery suit. Or rather, it saves them from such a fate *at* the extremities, or end-parts, in the production of a closure. Even so the novel cannot yet be considered to have won free of public, institutional attachments. For the very closure that secures a formal narrative difference between the novel and bureaucracy simultaneously implicates the novel in a formal narrative resemblance to the institution that has played a sort of rival to the bureaucracy, the police. It is clear that the difference that obtains between Chancery and the novel applies equally in the relationship between Chancery and the police. In determining its own closure as revelation and fixed repose, the novel appears to have rejected the conception of termination proper to bureaucracy only to espouse that proper to the police. The closural specimen that takes place, for example, at Richard's death-bed, even if it begins as though it will merely reflect the bureaucratic logic of lapse, achieves a permanent clarification of his character that rather subsumes the scene under the police model of closure as a double (cognitive and practical) apprehension. It can be further argued that, as it arouses a desire for expeditious, conclusive solutions, but only represents a single agency capable of providing them, the novel subtly identifies the reader's demand for closure with a general social need for the police, thus continuing (with only a considerable increase of cunning) the apologetics for the new forces of order that Dickens began as an essayist in *Household Words*.

The novel, however, is just as little anxious to appear an agency of the police as it was to resemble a relay of the Chancery system. The relatively friendly treatment that *Bleak House* accords to the Detective Police is qualified by a number of reservations about the nature and effects of its power. Most of these, like the other aspects of the police, are carried in the characterization of Inspector Bucket. His black clothes, linking him sartorially with Tulkinghorn and Vholes, darken his character as well with an association to the Court; and like the undertaker to whose costume this dress also makes allusion, Bucket induces an ambivalence even in those he works for. Depending on the regularity of corruption, his profession has the doubly offensive aspect of a speculation on human weakness that happens also to be invariably justified. Yet the grief betokened by "the great mourning ring on his little finger" might as well take Bucket himself for its object as any of his clients. His nature subdued to what it works in, Bucket too may be counted among the victims of crime. "Pour bien faire de la police," Napoleon is supposed to have said, "il faut être sans passion." The moral horror of crime, which Dickens preserves (among other things) in his sensationalistic treatment of it, must be irrelevant— might even be counterproductive—to the professional dispassion required for the task of apprehending the criminal. This task may no doubt be considered itself a moral one. But the game function of detection thoroughly dominates whatever ethical ends it presumably serves; and, as Bucket himself can assure Sir Leicester, his profession has placed him utterly beyond the possibility of being scandalized:

> "I know so much about so many characters, high and low, that a piece of information more or less, don't signify a straw. I don't suppose there's a move on the board that would surprise *me;* and as to this or that move having taken place, why my knowing it is no odds at all; any possible move whatever (provided it's in a wrong direction) being a probable move according to my experience."

The ethical perspective survives only in the faint melancholy with which Bucket, truly the "modern prince" in this respect, appears to regret the necessity of his own pessimism; or in the personal askesis that, when every consequence of desire proves criminal, is perhaps the only humane response remaining. Nonetheless, the melancholy is hardly sufficient to prevent him from eliciting the very weaknesses that are the object of its contemplation. The momentary collaboration between Skimpole and Bucket revealed at the end of the novel, an alliance of two species of moral indifference, throws no more discredit on the aesthete who delivers a dangerously ill child over to the police for no better reason than a bribe, than on the officer who extends the bribe for no better reason than to cover his client's prying. Even the askesis surrenders its moral truth to the extent that it is the very evidence of Bucket's amoral professionalization. As Tulkinghorn's fate exemplifies, amateur detectives run amok because they are motivated by personal desires for possession. Renunciation is thus for the professional detective a positive qualification, much as what Bucket appears to lament as his barren marriage shows a clear profit as an amicable and highly efficient business partnership.

These reservations are most tellingly inscribed in the novel as a narrative difference, once again centering on the question of ending, between the novel and the detective story that it includes. According to what will later be codified as the "classical" model, the detective story in *Bleak House* reaches its proper end when Bucket, having provided a complete and provable account of her guilt, arrests Mademoiselle Hortense for Tulkinghorn's murder. In the classical model, one may observe, though the security of its preferred decor, the locked room, is regularly breached, it is also invariably recovered in the detective's unassailable *reconstruction* of the crime. And similarly, in this not yet quite classical example, Bucket's ironclad case against Hortense may be understood as the reparation of Tulkinghorn's tragically vulnerable chambers. Yet if one tradition, the detective story, violates its closed rooms only to produce better defended versions of them in the detective's closed cases, another tradition, let us call it the Novel, violates even these cases. In this latter tradition, to which *Bleak House* ultimately bears allegiance, there is no police case so flawless that a loophole cannot be found through which its claims to closure may be challenged. Here our vision of the loophole is supplied by Mlle. Hortense:

> "Listen then, my angel," says she, after several sarcastic nods.
> "You are very spiritual. But can you restore him back to life?"
> Mr Bucket answers, "Not exactly."
> "That is droll. Listen yet one time. You are very spiritual.
> Can you make an honourable lady of Her?"

"Don't be so malicious," says Mr Bucket.

"Or a haughty gentleman of *Him?*" cries Mademoiselle, re-ferring to Sir Leicester with ineffable disdain. "Eh! O then regard him! The poor infant! Ha! ha! ha!"

"Come, come, why this is worse Parlaying than the other," says Mr Bucket. "Come along."

"You cannot do these things? Then you can do as you please with me. It is but the death, it is all the same. Let us go, my angel. Adieu you old man, grey. I pity you, and I des-pise you!"

Hortense enumerates the various existential problems that, outlasting Bucket's solution, make it seem trivial and all but inconsequential. Her purely verbal qualification is soon worked into the actual plot when Bucket sets out in search of Lady Dedlock and finds her dead body instead. However skillfully prosecuted, the work of detection appears capable only of attaining to a shell from which the vital principal has departed. Other closural moments in *Bleak House* similarly end by pro-ducing a corpse, as though the novel wanted to attest, not just the finality, but also the failure of a closure that, even as it was achieved, missed the essence of what it aspired to grasp. In its ostentatious awareness of this failure, the novel defines its relationship to the materials of police fiction that it has adopted. On one side of this relationship there would be a detective story whose shallow solution naively gratifies our appetite for closure; on the other, there would be a novel which, insisting at the very moment of solution on the insoluble, abiding mysteriousness of human and literary experience, provides superior nourishment by keeping us hungry. Not to be identified with Chancery, the novel contrasts the aimless suspension of the suit with the achievement of its own ending; but not to be confused with the police either, it counters the tidy conclusion of the case with a conspicuous recognition of all that must elude any such achievement. If in the first instance, the novel must affirm the possibility of closure, in the second it is driven to admit the *inadequacy* of this closure.

In the end, then,—precisely there—the novel's attempt to differentiate its own narrative procedures from those of the institutions it portrays falters, and the effort to disentangle itself from one institution only impli-cates it once again in another. So the seemingly perverse pattern continues wherein the novel is eager to produce a sheltered space whose integrity it is equally willing to endanger. We have seen how the novel establishes the opposition between the private-domestic and the social-institutional (1) within the representation, as the contrast between Esther's Bleak House and Chancery, and between the former and the police; (2) as a formal practice of consumption, in which the novel-reading subject shuttles to and fro between the home in which the novel is read and the world in which it is verified; and (3) at the intersection of the novel's own representational practice with the represented practice of institutions that it includes in its content. We have also seen how, in every instance, the opposition is accompanied by the possibility that it may be, or have been, nullified. At the same time as the existence of an "outside" to institutional power is affirmed, that very affirmation is undercut with doubt.

Yet to describe the novel's rhetorical operation in this way, as the work of destructuration and subversion, is to identify it wholly with what is in fact only its negative moment. We need to envision the positivity of this operation too, for what is put in question has also by the same token been put in place, and can be put to use as well. The ideological dividends paid in the difference between the "inside" and the "outside" of power are clear. The "outside" gives the assurance of liberty that makes tolerable the increasingly total administration of the "inside" and helps avoid a politicization of society as a whole. It also provides an authentically critical space from which amendments and reforms useful to this administration can be effectively broached and imposed. As we began by observing, however, *Bleak House* troubles the straightforwardness of this difference, which it transforms into the question of a difference. What, then, are the ideological dividends paid in *bringing the difference in question?* A full answer would have to inquire into a whole range of practices whereby our culture has become increasingly adept in taking benefit of doubt. But we can provide the synecdoche of an answer by turning in conclusion to the specific practice that, though we have seen it continually emerge both as an effect of various institutions and as the term of sundry oppositions, we have stopped short of considering in itself. Yet it is the practice that *Bleak House* is most concerned to promote: the practice of the family.

VII

Even in what otherwise would be her triumph, when the recognition of her merit has assumed public proportions, Esther Summerson retains her modest blindfold: "The people even praise Me as the doctor's wife. The people even like Me as I go about, and make so much of me that I am quite abashed. I owe it all to him, my love, my pride! They like me for his sake, as I do everything I do in life for his sake." And to Allan's affirmation that she is prettier than ever she was, she can only respond:

> I did not know that; I am not certain that I know it now. But I
> know that my dearest little pets are very pretty, and that my
> darling is very beautiful, and that my husband is very hand-
> some, and that my guardian has the brightest and most benevo-
> lent face that ever was seen; and that they can very well do
> without much beauty in me—even supposing—.

Just as earlier Esther could barely speak of Allan, or her desire for him, so
now, at the moment this desire is returned, she can only stammer. With
her unfinished sentence, *Bleak House* "ends." Though one easily supplies
what Esther keeps from saying ("even supposing I have my beauty back"),
the modesty that consigns this assertion to silence is, to the last, radically
inconclusive. Like woman's work, which is the external means to Esther's
social recognition, the labors of modesty, its inner correlative, are never
done.

What might be a matter for grief or grievance, however, as Esther's
"neurotic" inability to relinquish her self-doubt in the hour of success, also
means that the energy that has gone into consolidating and sustaining one
Bleak House after another will not be dissipated in the complacency of
enjoyment or relaxation. The text has posed the origin of Esther's self-
doubt in the question of her proper place in a family structure (her
illegitimacy), and this origin has shaped her tacit ambition to install herself
securely within such a structure. Given a twist, however, by the psychology of modesty through which it is obliged to pass, the ambition attains to
a frustration that is exactly proportionate to its achievements. Esther never
ceases to earn her place, as though, were she to do so, she might even at
the end be displaced from it. Yet there is a twist to the frustration too, as
Esther's endless modesty finds its non-neurotic social validation in the
family that, no less precarious than her own sense of identity, requires
precisely such anxious and unremitting devotion for its survival. Or, as
these relations might be generally summarized: the insecurity of the family
subject is indispensable to counter the instability of the family structure, of
which it is an effect.

The instability of the family, therefore, is constitutive of its very
maintenance. As Jacques Donzelot has shown, the nineteenth-century family develops within two registers, which he calls *contract* and *tutelage*.
Contract indicates the free and easy family autonomy ensured through
"the observance of norms that guarantee the social usefulness of [its]
members"; whereas tutelage designates the system of "external penetration" of the family, transformed into an object of surveillance and disci-

pline. The two registers are positive and negative dimensions of a single policy of incentive: if the family satisfactorily performs its social tasks, then it is granted the liberty and autonomy of contract; but should it fail to pay back the privileges thereby conferred upon it in the proper accomplishment of responsibilities, then it must fall back into the register of tutelage.

With these two registers, one can correlate the two causes that Dickens's novels regularly ascribe to the faultiness of the family: on one hand, the external interference of institutions that (like the workhouse in *Oliver Twist*) dislocate and disjoin the family; and on the other, the internal dynamic that (as exemplified in *Oliver Twist* by Monks's oedipal and sibling rivalry) determines its own divisions and displacements. If the first cause amounts to a demand for contract, the second is a concession to the necessity of tutelage. The theme of outside interference bears a message to society at large to reform its institutions in the interest of preserving the only natural and naturally free space within it. (The argument is never free from the utilitarianism that Dickens's sentimentality about the family rationalizes rather than resists. The novels continually imply the family's advantages over other agencies in producing acceptable citizens of the liberal state both in quantitative terms—as its greater economy—and in qualitative ones—as the superiority of the bonds between its members.) The theme of internal disruption, on the other hand, addresses its message to the family itself, which had better do its utmost to stay together or else face the misery of being dispersed or colonized by remedial institutions. In the first instance, Dickens advises society to police for the family, which would thereby be safeguarded as the home of freedom; in the second, he counsels the family to police itself, that it might remain free by becoming its own house of correction. The two apparently incompatible themes, informing the representation of the family throughout Dickens's work, are in fact complementary. Likewise, the "practical" recommendations attached to each find their mutual coherence precisely in the way that they cancel one another out. For if society reformed itself so that state institutions would, if not wither away, become minimal and humane, then there would no longer exist an outside threat to consolidate the family in the face of its internal dangers; and to the extent that the family could successfully repress these dangers itself, it would only reproduce such institutions in their worst aspects. With the disappearance of social discipline, the emancipated family would prove in greater need of it than ever; and in the enjoyment of its unobstructed independence, it would restore the discipline from which it was meant as an asylum, either in its own practice or in that of the institutions that would inevitably make their reappearance upon its breakdown.

Neither the social nor the familial "policing of the family," therefore, can be carried very far without giving rise to the very regimentation it was supposed to curtail. In this respect at least, Dickens's vigorous reformism makes better sense as an undeclared defense of the status quo: the social recommendations would merely be the weights (like most weights, not meant to be carried very far) to preserve the family in its present delicate balance. For the family's freedom is founded in the possibility of its discipline, and thus to enjoy the former means to have consented to the latter. Esther's insecurity, we said, works to oppose the instability of the family structure from which it results. It supplies the constant vigilance wanted to keep the contractual family from lapsing into the subjection of tutelage. It is equally true, however, that Esther's insecurity *confirms* the family in its faultiness. In the same degree as it propagates the worry and anxiety needed to maintain the family, it keeps alive the ever-present danger of its fall. The novel everywhere publishes the same fear of falling and implies the same urgency about holding one's place. The "outside" of power regularly incurs the risk that it may be annexed—or worse, may already have been annexed—by the "inside." So, for instance, the family will sometimes be shown for only a slight modulation of Chancery bureaucracy (comfortably domesticated with the Jellybys), or of the police (one of whose different voices can be heard in Mrs. Pardiggle, the "moral Policeman" who regiments her own family in the same spirit she takes others "into custody." And the risk touches us more nearly than do these unadmirable characters, for even the excellent Bagnets rely on an explicitly military order, and Esther herself may be only better directed than Mrs. Jellyby when she sits at her desk "full of business, examining tradesmen's books, adding up columns, paying money, filing receipts, and . . . making a great bustle about it." Envisioning the family now as a firm counterweight to social institutions, now as a docile function of them, here as the insuperable refuge from the carceral, there as the insufferable replica of it, the novel poses the question of the family, which it thereby designates as the object of struggle. Rather as Esther takes up this question as the necessity of founding and keeping Bleak House, so the novel extends the question to its readers, both as a principle of hope and an exhortation, as it were, to work at home. Mr. Bagnet's famous catchword formulates what is no less the objective than the condition of the family in Dickens's representation of it: "Discipline"—within the domestic circle as well as outside it—"must be maintained."

VIII

Queen Victoria confided to her diaries: "I never feel quite at ease or at home when reading a Novel." *Bleak House* makes itself as anxiogenic and incomplete as the home with which it identifies. For in an age in which productivity is valued at least as much as the product, the novel must claim no less the inadequacy than the necessity of closure. This inadequacy can now be understood—not in the old-fashioned way, as a failure of organic form, nor even in the new-fashioned way, as the success of a failure of organic form—but, in the broader context of institutional requirements and cultural needs, as the novel's own "work ethic," its imposing refusal of rest and enjoyment. Certainly, reading this novel, though in the reasons of the hearth it finds its own reason for being, one never feels quite at home; perhaps, having finished it, one knows why one never *can* feel at home. For what now is home—not securely possessed in perpetuity, but only leased from day to day on payment of continual exertions—but a House? And what is this House—neither wholly blackened by the institutions that make use of its cover, nor wholly bleached of their stain—but (in the full etymological ambiguity of the word) irresolvably Bleak? "Bleak House has an exposed sound."

STEPHEN J. SPECTOR

Monsters of Metonymy: Hard Times and Knowing the Working Class

Every house put out a sign of the kind of people who might be expected to be born in it.
 —DICKENS, *Hard Times*

What sort of outside is the certain sign that there is or is not such an inhabitant within?
 —LOCKE, *An Essay Concerning Human Understanding*

Dickens bestows hardly a single spark of his vitalizing genius upon Stephen Blackpool and Rachael, *Hard Times*'s thwarted working-class lovers. Like Victor Frankenstein's creation, a monstrous assemblage with limbs and features ironically chosen for their beauty, Stephen and Rachael are automatons compounded of such Victorian middle-class virtues as industry, honesty, self-denial, chastity, and deference. Where Frankenstein's unattractive child entertains, Dickens's beau ideal of the industrial worker bores. Silhouetted against a vivid environment, the new industrial landscape of Coketown, the textile workers' lifelessness stands out in bold relief. Coketown continues to serve as a model of the grimy factory town and as a demonstration of the power of Dickens's realism, which, as his contemporaries were fond of repeating, rivalled the photograph. Therefore, it is hardly surprising that as early as 1856 the incommensurability of the stereotyped industrial workers to their finely drawn environment should have been noticed. In the *Westminster Review* George Eliot, in one sentence, brought forth the classic indictment of Dickens: "We have one great

From *ELH* 51, no. 2 (Summer 1984). © 1984 by the Johns Hopkins University Press.

novelist who is gifted with the utmost power of rendering the external traits of our town population; and if he could give us their psychological character—their conception of life, and their emotions—with the same truth as their idiom and manners, his books would be the greatest contributions."

At least as regards Dickens's portrayal of industrial workers, Eliot is right. The great question is why Dickens failed. George Bernard Shaw, in the course of criticizing Slackbridge, the trade union organizer, provides the obvious answer: "All this is pure middle-class ignorance. It is much as if a tramp were to write a description of millionaires smoking large cigars in church, with their wives in low-necked dresses and diamonds. We cannot say that Dickens did not know the working classes, because he knew humanity too well to be ignorant of any class. . . . But of the segregated factory populations of our purely industrial towns he knew no more than an observant professional man can pick up on a flying visit to Manchester."

Shaw's amusing answer captures part of the truth, but it fails to ask why Dickens, certainly aware of his "middle-class ignorance," had the confidence even to attempt to write about the industrial worker. Moreover, Dickens's failure joins a long, undistinguished line of unconvincing industrial workers who burden not just novels but serious nonfiction as well. In this essay I will argue that Dickens's confidence, and ultimately his failure, rests upon his implicit faith in the power of language, and more specifically upon epistemological assumptions embedded in the rhetoric of realism.

Because a double-barreled phrase like "the rhetoric of realism" is daunting, it will be best to make a few prefatory remarks about each term separately and then let them combine, following the procedure of Pott, editor of the Eatanswill Gazette, when writing on what Mr. Pickwick accurately called the "abstruse subject" of Chinese metaphysics: "he read for metaphysics under the letter M, and for China under the letter C, and combined his information" (*Pickwick Papers,* chap. 51).

Realism seems safely immune from definition, but one can say with some confidence that realistic texts, like realistic paintings and photographs, intend to tell the truth: what they report they intend to be verifiable. The realistic text, of which the newspaper report accompanied by a photograph is probably the archetype, assumes that it is simply telling the truth by presenting a scene. When *Hard Times* presents industrial workers it embraces that assumption. Dickens, at times a working reporter, solicits readers to use the standards of journalism; and, as the critical record shows, readers have done just that. The reader of realism naturally focuses on content, not style. When a realistic text is discussed or questioned, the issue is its mimetic truth. As David Lodge points out, to comment upon realistic writing usually means to ignore style and instead discuss "truthfulness, or representativeness, its contribution to, and consistency with, the sum of human wisdom." In fact, from the point of view of reader-response criticism, a text can be called realistic if the discussion it generates is predominantly about its verisimilitude. In this light, attacks on the accuracy of *Hard Times* attest to its status as a realistic text just as much as does praise for its accuracy.

Rhetorical figures informing realism tend to be invisible because they belong to a mode of discourse in which, by convention, tropes are overlooked. Not until Roman Jakobson's famous formulation, in which metonymy, in contrast to metaphor, was identified as the basic trope of realism, did rhetorical analysis decisively enter the interpretation of realism. As Jakobson's model would predict, when Dickens strives to produce the effect of realism, as he does when he describes the industrial workers, he relies heavily on metonymy. Broadly speaking, metonymy is a figure in which one entity is identified by another with which it is contiguous; to cite the standard example, a king is called the crown because he wears one. In *Hard Times,* as in realism generally, a person's character is "read" by contiguous exteriors such as his actions, his environment, his clothing, and—in the novelist's formula—his face and figure. To identify an invisible quality—character—by a visible exterior is realism's fundamental metonymy. And in a wider perspective metonymy is more than a rhetorical figure used to express knowledge about a person; it is also the process through which such knowledge is obtained. Because Dickens, like writers before and after him, shared the assumption that what he could observe about the industrial workers would be a reliable index of their subjectivity, he set out on his project confidently.

Yet *Hard Times* is extraordinary because it casts doubt on its own premises. With at times disarming candor it asks whether metonymy generates truth, especially in regard to industrial workers. The limitations of metonymy become most apparent in *Hard Times* when Dickens, the virtuoso observer of character, must admit that no amount of observation will permit him to penetrate the "mystery" of the workers' subjectivity. Indeed, after Louisa Gradgrind realizes she is totally ignorant of the Coketown Hands as individuals (about midway in the novel) Dickens drops the workers except for Stephen Blackpool's brief, pathetic death scene.

But when Dickens first broaches the industrial theme, he is at his self-assured best:

> It was a town of red brick, or of brick that would have been red if the smoke and ashes had allowed it; but as matters stood, it was a town of unnatural red and black like the painted face of a savage. It was a town of machinery and tall chimneys, out of which interminable serpents of smoke trailed themselves for ever and ever, and never got uncoiled. It had a black canal in it, and a river that ran purple with ill-smelling dye, and vast piles of buildings full of windows where there was a rattling and a trembling all day long, and where the piston of the steam-engine worked monotonously up and down like the head of an elephant in a state of melancholy madness. It contained several large streets all very like one another, and many small streets still more like one another, inhabited by people equally like one another, who all went in and out at the same hours, with the same sound upon the same pavements, to do the same work, and to whom every day was the same as yesterday and tomorrow, and every year the counterpart of the last and the next.

Dickens's description of Coketown, the "keynote" of *Hard Times,* is justifiably famous. In it, the new industrial landscape—what David Craig recognizes as the verisimilitude of realism when he calls it a "specific real location" in a "specific society"—finds embodiment in language that seems adequate to its task. To describe a scene that left many observers speechless, as Steven Marcus has pointed out in connection with Engels, was no easy achievement. The passage triumphs because Dickens imaginatively transforms the scene through the use of figurative language: the town becomes the "painted face of a savage"; the smoke becomes "interminable serpents"; the piston the "head of an elephant in a state of melancholy madness." Such metaphorical transformations are habitual with Dickens, whose figures of speech often involve an exchange of the attributes of the human and non-human, the animate and the inanimate. But in this context the transformations take on a special sense of correctness because Dickens makes it clear that the city is a system of economic exchange and prior to that a transformation of the natural landscape: clay is turned into brick whose natural earthy color is further transformed into an "unnatural red and black"; the river has been similarly discolored, and it is yoked with the artificial river, the "black canal." When the already denaturalized scene metamorphoses again—into the savage, the snake, and the elephant—Dickens has in effect forced a thematization of the process of change (or exchange) itself.

The reader is left with a disorienting and defamiliarizing picture. Human beings, in such a setting, are especially and ironically—since human labor must be the agent of the metamorphosis—out of place. Only at the *end* of the passage are human beings mentioned, and properly so, since they are subsumed by the savage, unnatural city as interchangeable parts in a machine they have created but which seems to run without them. Each person has been reduced to a small, repetitive "behavior." Instead of being human creators (producers), they become the same as the objects they produce; "equally like one another," as Dickens says.

Dickens's keynote is a standard "reading" of the new industrial scene. This reading, which imagines industrialization as a cataclysm for the workers, promises to be a disaster for the novelist subscribing to Victorian ideas about character; without differentiation and individuation the Dickensian novel cannot exist. Thus *Hard Times* must ultimately repudiate its keynote; and in fact, the people of Coketown—Rachael, Stephen Blackpool, Slackbridge, and the factory operatives—are not "equally like one another," though as Peter Keating has argued, their uniform seriousness makes them less idiosyncratic than Dickens's urban poor. The failure of the keynote's assertion informs almost every aspect of the novel, not just the description of the operatives themselves.

The same theme, the difference between what the industrial workers are really like and what outsiders assume them to be, animates the subtly ironic narrative of "On Strike," Dickens's article about his visit in January 1854 to witness the textile workers' strike in Preston. Published in *Household Words* on February 11, 1854, about three weeks after Dickens began writing *Hard Times* and about six weeks before the first installment of the novel appeared (also in *Household Words*), "On Strike" reveals, with the clarity afforded by small compass, the contradictions that disturb the novel.

"On Strike" begins with a description of Dickens's train ride north, seated next to a man whom he transforms into Mr. Snapper, a typical Dickens character. Snapper's view of the strike is that the workers "want to be ground." While Dickens has some fun with this cousin to Gradgrind and Bounderby, the straw man does force Dickens, who has been confidently expounding his views on the necessity of "feeling and sentiment" between "employers and employed," to face a serious problem. Snapper's challenge, which betrays his stereotypical and classbound view of the workers, is unexpectedly pointed: "You *know* very little of the improvi-

dent and unreasoning habits of the common people" (emphasis added).
Dickens's response is so characteristic that it is worth examining at some
length:

> "Yet I *know* something of those people, too," was my reply. "In
> fact, Mr.———," I had so nearly called him Snapper! "in fact,
> sir, I doubt the existence at this present time of many faults that
> are merely class faults. In the main, I am disposed to think that
> whatever faults you may find to exist, in your own neighbour-
> hood for instance, among the hands, you will find tolerably
> equal in amount among the masters also, and even among the
> classes above the masters. They will be modified by circum-
> stances . . . but they will be pretty fairly distributed. I have a
> strong expectation that we shall live to see the conventional
> adjectives now apparently inseparable from the phrases work-
> ing people and lower orders, gradually fall into complete dis-
> use for this reason" [emphasis added].

Nowhere does this response give any evidence that Dickens does *know* the
"common people," despite the anxiety-covering modesty of his initial
claim to "know something" of them. Not only are all specifics about
"those people" omitted—Dickens's level of generality is the same as Mr.
Snapper's—but whatever knowledge he possesses is cast as a theory whose
validity awaits the test of time. This qualified knowledge is further weakened by a series of mitigating phrases. The repeated "in fact" is followed
by "I doubt"; the generalizing "in the main" is qualified by "I am disposed
to think"; and the concluding sentence begins with the anticlimactic "I
have a strong expectation." While the persuasive rhetoric of the character
of "Dickens"—and Dickens has created a persona here—is meant to
indicate that the speaker is a model of reason as opposed to the snap-
judgmental Mr. Snapper, that same rhetoric, in all its calculated *class*iness,
inaugurates a distance between Dickens and the workers that will not be
easily overcome.

The Dickens persona in "On Strike" is a reporter, a role he was long
accustomed to and in which he found his vocation. His purpose is the
quintessence of journalism: "*to look* at the strike" (emphasis added).
While Dickens's response to Mr. Snapper casts his knowledge of the
working man in the form of an "expectation," the report of the observant
journalist on the "scene" consists largely of expectations that are proved
false. Of course, the text needs to be read as propagandist persuasion in
which Dickens's expectations are calculated to coincide with those of his

readers. For example, he underscores repeatedly his difference from the workers, as when at a strike meeting he describes himself and his "companion" as "the only persons present, not of their [the workers'] own order." However, there is little reason to suspect that the persona and the historical Dickens differ in any fundamental way in their attitudes toward the working man.

As he begins his description of Preston, Dickens sounds two disturbingly familiar themes found in middle-class writings about the industrial workers; first, the fearful expectation that the workers will be an angry, hostile mob; and second, in a slightly submerged form, the feeling that the workers are like foreigners, just as the new industrial city is a foreign country uncannily growing up in the homeland—

> When I got to Preston, it was four o'clock in the afternoon. The day being Saturday and market-day, a foreigner might have *expected,* from among so many idle and not over-fed people as the town contained, to find a turbulent, ill-conditioned crowd in the streets. But, except for the cold smokeless factory chimneys, the placards at the street corners, and the groups of working people attentively reading them, nor foreigner nor Englishman could have had the least suspicion that there existed any interruption to the usual labours of the place [emphasis added].

No doubt Dickens is sounding a note of patriotic pride here: the expectation of an angry mob is attributed to a "foreigner," but it is Dickens's expectation too. Indeed, as Keating has shown, Dickens is performing a function that was familiar to his readers: as a member of the middle class he is visiting the new nation of workers growing up in the north and reporting on the sights. Significantly, Dickens does not plunge into the scene and evoke it in sensuous detail or figural language. Instead, he adapts himself to this new world by self-consciously "reading" the scene— quite literally reading the handwriting on the wall—by quoting texts he finds in the town: a letter to the operatives from the strike committee, workers' songs, the balance sheet of "receipts and expenditures," and doggerel written on contribution lists. Dickens scrutinizes the texts, expecting violent demagoguery, and makes gratuitously negative pronouncements, but he concludes on a note of surprise: "The Masters' placards were not torn down or disfigured, but were being read quite as attentively as those on the opposite side." Implicit once more is the expectation that the workers would be violent and disrespectful. In fact, one of the most curious notes in "On Strike" is Dickens's repeatedly expressed feeling of relief that his person was treated with respect. At a Delegates' meeting, he assures himself and his readers that he is different from the workers, but that, surprisingly, his fears of active hostility are without foundation:

> the unexpected appearance of a stranger differently dressed from themselves, and with his own individual peculiarities of course, might, without offence, have had something droll in it even to more polite assemblies. But I stood there, looking on, as free from remark as if I had come to be paid with the rest.

While Dickens's fearful and condescending middle-class expectations are striking because they keep returning despite repeatedly being thwarted, his most severe reversal of expectation is this: "Perhaps *the world could not afford a more remarkable contrast* than between the deliberate collected manner of these men proceeding with their business, and the clash and hurry of the engines among which their lives are passed" (emphasis added). This sentence comes close to revealing the crux of the problem by showing how the truth about the workers would normally come to Dickens. What he knows comes from a "reading" of the new industrial scene that is based on the familiar assumption of realism, that men must be like their environment: the workers should be like the most striking and visible aspect of their lives, the machines. Thus the expectation that the workers will be a violent, unthinking mob is based explicitly on their contiguity with the violent, unthinking machines. That the workers are peaceful and reflective astonishes Dickens the observer. The note of astonishment, of firm expectations defeated, gains much of its strength because it results from a failure of the fundamental assumption of reporting: Dickens has discovered that there is no way to know what the workers are like from "looking" at the scene.

The keynote statement of *Hard Times* that the workers are "equally like one another" is generated by the same reportorial assumption. Within the dense web of metaphor that describes Coketown, Dickens says that "it contained several large streets all very like one another, inhabited by people equally like one another." The people, Dickens assumes, must be alike because they live in streets that are alike. Here metonymy functions with almost primitive simplicity, generating a reading of character so common that it approaches the linguistic invisibility of dead metaphor; in fact, it might be called dead metonymy. For Dickens metonymy is habitual; it is the trope upon which he relied to create characters in his fictional world. From the very beginning of his career, when in *Sketches by Boz* he created characters out of secondhand clothes hanging in store windows, through his late novels in which urban environments become dominating symbols of modern life, Dickens relied upon the truth of metonymy. Yet in *Hard Times* the link between environment and character breaks. One of the central metonymic figures, the synecdochic correspondence between container and contents, outside and inside, fails. The premise that "to look" or "to see" is "to know" does not stand up, and as a consequence the figure loses its reliability.

Hard Times cannot be read, however, as a thorough and continuous rupture of metonymy, just as it would be absurd to imagine that it is a novel without characters—which for Dickens would be one consequence of such a permanent break. It is important to recall that there is a legible correspondence between the outside and the inside for most of the characters in the novel. The circus people, Mrs. Sparsit, Harthouse, Bounderby, Slackbridge, Bitzer, M'Choakumchild, and the Gradgrinds can be known by observing their appearance and environment. Metonymic character creation begins the novel in the figure of Mr. Gradgrind, who exhorts the students about "Facts" in "a plain, bare, monotonous vault of a schoolroom," which is echoed in "the speaker's square forefinger" and "square wall of a forehead, which had his eyebrows for its base." The progression from the container to its contents and the equation of one with the other are paradigmatically Dickensian. When Dickens describes Gradgrind's house, the easily understood figure of speech is extended so that the home of the man hoping to become "an arithmetical figure in Parliament" is itself once more that simplest geometrical figure: "A great square house, with a heavy portico darkening the principal windows, as its master's heavy brows overshadowed his eyes." While Dickens's procedure here is transparent and self-conscious (it does not seem stretching things to guess that Dickens intends "figure" to read as a pun that includes the meaning "trope"), the "realism" of the presentation is not seriously compromised by that reflexive clarity. Certainly no hint of irony is present when Dickens contrasts the evil Slackbridge with the essentially good workers by simply contrasting appearances: "An ill-made, high-shouldered man, with lowering brows, and his features crushed into an habitually sour expression, he contrasted most unfavourably, even in his mongrel dress, with the great body of his hearers in their plain working clothes." Similarly, moral quality and outward appearance are equated in the figure of Stephen's wife: "A creature so foul to look at, in her tatters, stains and splashes, but so much fouler than that in her moral infamy, that it was a shameful thing even to see her."

Such metonymies function throughout the novel, but they exist alongside an awareness that there is no basis for believing such metonymic readings to be true. Indeed, when in chapter 11 Dickens repeats the keynote, he thematizes the fact that contiguity of environment and person fails to provide a reliable reading of character. The opening paragraph, using the same imagery as the original keynote, paints the industrial scene as one of sameness and repetition. Nature (the diurnal cycle), the machines, and human beings (reduced to the sound of footsteps) are presented as a monotonous routine:

> The Fairy palaces burst into illumination, before pale morning showed the monstrous serpents of smoke trailing themselves over Coketown. A clattering of clogs upon the pavement; a rapid ringing of bells; and all the melancholy mad elephants, polished and oiled up for the day's monotony, were at their heavy exercise again.

The next two paragraphs, however, end with a recognition that such metonymy is misreading. First Stephen and his fellow workers are described in words that sound the note of defeated expectations of "On Strike": "Stephen bent over his loom, quiet, watchful, and steady. *A special contrast,* as every man was in the forest of looms where Stephen worked, to the crashing, smashing, tearing piece of mechanism at which he laboured" (emphasis added). Revealingly, the next sentence states the difference between the machines and the men, not in the form of the narrator's astonishment or surprise, as in "On Strike," but projected onto the reader: "Never fear, good people of an anxious turn of mind, that Art will consign Nature to oblivion. Set anywhere, side by side, the work of GOD and the work of man; and the former; even though it be a troop of Hands of very small account, will gain in dignity from the comparison." But the next paragraph concludes with a statement that has disquieting implications not only for a distanced reader but for Dickens himself. He postulates the presence of something unknowable within the workers: "there is an unfathomable mystery in the meanest of them, for ever."

Dickens's recognition that the workers' selves can never be known completely is, in context, directed at the purveyors of "fact"—compilers of Blue Books, utilitarians, laissez faire economists, etc.—but his own method of knowing (observing, reporting) is implicated also, since he bases his knowledge on that which is the bedrock of "fact"—the visible. Dickens's intention in *Hard Times* is to move beyond a surface reading of the workers and to reveal them in their particular, complex reality. That he fails to create a convincingly "real" working-class character makes his effort more poignant, but it does not detract from his awareness of the gap between himself and his subject. His position is more or less Louisa Gradgrind's as she enters Stephen Blackpool's lodging:

> For the first time in her life Louisa had come into one of the dwellings of the Coketown hands; for the first time in her life she was face to face with anything like individuality in connexion with them. . . . She knew them in crowds passing to and from their nests, like ants or beetles. But she knew from her reading infinitely more of the ways of toiling insects than of these toiling men and women.

Louisa faces directly the dilemma that Dickens's persona in "On Strike" faces only obliquely. In *Hard Times,* ironically, Dickens most convincingly illustrates the seemingly insurmountable problems faced by the middle-class observer who would like to know the mysterious character of the working class. Stephen Blackpool speaks for Dickens and the middle class when he proclaims over and over, " ' 'Deed we are in a muddle.' "

The presence of "mystery" and "muddle"—figures of illegibility—continually undercuts the authority of the presentation of the working class. No matter how carefully Dickens reports the workers' conditions, he recognizes the severe limits of his knowledge. His modesty is apparent when he describes Stephen Blackpool's knowledge of the workers: "he knew them, far below their surface weaknesses and misconceptions, as no one but their fellow-labourer could." Even this statement is questionable, since the narrator cannot know what a worker knows or does not know. To "mystery" and "muddle" must be added the recurring figure of the labyrinth. There is no need to document what is so well known—that the labyrinth appears throughout Dickens's works—but its significance becomes clear when it is juxtaposed with the figure of the city as a machine. Basically, the city as machine is a figure of legibility. The machine, however demonic, is rational; and through metonymy its inhabitants partake of that rationality and are made knowable. The labyrinth, while familiar, is a figure of illegibility. If the city is an endless maze whose pattern cannot be mapped, then its inhabitants, by the synecdochic equation of the contained and the container, are similarly mysterious. Dickens does not, then, completely abandon metonymy—perhaps an impossible task—when he offers the labyrinth as a figure to compete with the machine, but instead invokes a metonymy that signals its own limitations.

II

Dickens's honest admission of his own limitations stands out clearly if it is juxtaposed with another attempt to "know" the industrial worker, Engels's *The Condition of the Working Class.* Like *Hard Times,* it has become an established classic in literature about the working class, despite challenges to its factual accuracy. And recently, in the light of Steven Marcus's much acclaimed analysis, Engels's ability to penetrate to the reality of the industrial worker has been given high marks. In sharp contrast to Dickens, Engels faced the labyrinth of the new industrial landscape and turned it into a knowable pattern. As he proclaimed in his Dedication addressed to the "Working Classes of Great Britain," Engels's claim to knowledge, like Dickens's, came not from theory or reading but from seeing: "I have not been satisfied with this [reading documents] . . . I wanted *to see* you in your own homes, *to observe* you in your every-day life, to chat with you on your condition and grievances, to *witness* your struggles against the social and political power of your oppressors" (emphasis added). And despite the chaos that assaults his sight when he makes his expedition into the interior of Manchester, Engels manages, to use Marcus's apt phrase, to read the illegible. In fact, Engels produces not just a discursive reading but a virtual schematization of the city—complete with maps. These maps are both product and process: Engels masters the labyrinth by turning it into a geometrical figure. In his geometry, Manchester has a center (the commercial quarter) surrounded by concentric circles of residential housing. The concentric circles are intersected by main thoroughfares lined with shops hiding the housing behind them, so the upper classes can travel through the city oblivious to the workers' existence. As Marcus observes, Engels's reading of the city is a triumph of observation and analysis.

Engels falters, however, whenever he attempts to identify the intention of the builders—a sure sign that the truth of metonymy is getting shaky. The vexed question of intention leads to sentences that seek to clarify but only obfuscate. Even propagandistic invective cannot paper over Engels's uncertainty: "When the middle classes zealously proclaim that all is well with the working classes, I cannot help feeling that the politically 'progressive' industrialists, the Manchester 'Bigwigs,' are not quite so innocent of this shameful piece of town planning as they pretend."

On the other hand, Engels hardly wavers when he reads the minds of the workers. In this connection it is worth recalling that Dickens's assertion that the people of Coketown are "equally like one another," while embedded in the metonymy that equates a city and its inhabitants, is part of his larger association of machine and labor that reinforces the definition of the workers' character. The paragraph that follows the famous keynote passage states: "These attributes of Coketown were in the main inseparable from the work by which it was sustained." To assume that work or activity defines a person—another metonymic figure—is deeply etched in many Victorian elevations of work, and it is present in Dickens.

For Engels the connection between work and character is clear—dull work signifies a dull character:

> In den meisten Arbeitszweigen ist die Tätigkeit des Arbeiters auf eine kleinliche, rein mechanische Manipulation beschränkt, die sich Minute für Minute wiederholt und jahraus, jahrein dieselbe bleibt. Wer von Kindesbeinen an jeden Tag zwölf Stunden und drüber Nadelknöpfe gemacht oder Kammräder abgefeilt und äusserdem in den Verhältnissen eines englischen Proletariers gelebt hat, wieviel menschliche Gefühle und Fähigkeiten mag der in sein dreissigstes Jahr hinüberretten?

> [In most branches of industry,] the activity of the worker is limited to some insignificant and purely mechanical [repetitive] manipulation, repeated minute after minute, remaining year in and year out the same. How much human feeling or capacities can a man of thirty expect to retain if since childhood he has spent twelve hours or more every day making pin heads or filing cogwheels, and has in addition lived amid [all the other] circumstances of the English proletariat.

Engels's premise, following the law of metonymy, is that a worker who performs repetitive, mechanical tasks must be reduced to a subhuman entity, usually an animal or a machine.

Engels usually imagines only one alternative to that metamorphosis: a refusal to be transformed, generated by the workers' own anger and hatred. For Engels the workers are finally of two kinds: those who submit and those who rebel. Those actions are perfect mirrors of the two interior states he allows the workers: animal stupidity or aggressive anger. The stark simplicity of this psychology is an ineluctable conclusion because of the rhetorical premises by which Engels operates. Ironically, Engels's characterization of the workers therefore sounds like the absurd rhetoric of Josiah Bounderby. If workers are not filled with violent class hatred, Engels imagines that the "physical and mental powers" of those workers are "atrophied" ("seine körperlichen und geistigen Kräfte gänzlich in dieser Langeweile verkommen zu lassen"). Because of the "torture" of factory work, the workers' minds, which must correspond to their disfigured bodies, are "stunted" ("Sie wirkt aber auch im höchsten Grade abstumfend, wie auf den Körper so auch auf den Geist des Arbeiters"). Submission to factory work means one is a "mere animal" ("und dann vertiert er ganz gewiss"), and children especially are turned into beasts by the boredom of their labor. In a polarity that Bounderby will reproduce in his tirade against Stephen Blackpool, Engels writes: "if they are workers who are not inspired to a fury of indignation against their oppressors, then they sink into drunkenness and all other forms of demoralising vice" ("Und wenn diese Indignation gegen die Bourgeoisie nicht zum vorherrschenden Gefühl beim Arbeiter wird, so ist die notwendige Folge der Trunk und überhaupt alles das, was man gewöhnlich Demoralisation nennt"). Such violent, degrading rhetoric, because of its obvious distortion of reality, exerts a centripetal force that calls into question the author's control over his language. Engels, swept up by his rhetoric, does not seem to recognize that he is disfiguring the men he seeks to praise.

The opportunities for the "fury" of the workers to manifest itself were frequent in England in 1844, and never more so than in the mining strike in Durham and Northumberland of that year. What Engels has to say about that strike dramatically reveals what he "knows" about the workers, much as Dickens's "knowledge" of the working class is displayed in his report about the Preston strike of 1853–54. The colliers' strike, like that at Preston, resulted in extreme privation and hardship. The strike was a prolonged one that finally collapsed, but the strikers committed no acts of violence. The keynote of Engels's description of the workers' behavior during the strike is their "self-control" ("Selbstbeherrschung"), precisely the attribute that would strike Dickens so forcibly at Preston a decade later. Moderation, rationality, and self-control—those middle-class traits Engels witnessed in the workers—are attributes that his figural system could not predict. What Engels expected is evident from his enumeration of what did *not* occur:

> trotz alledem blieben die Grubenleute fest und, was noch mehr sagen will, bei allen Feindseligkeiten und Herausforderungen der Grubenbesitzer und ihrer getreuen Diener ruhig und friedlich. Kein Akt der Rache wurde geübt, kein einzelner Abtrünniger misshandelt, kein einziger Diebstahl verübt.

> And to their credit let it be said that they remained quiet and peaceful in the face of every provocation that the coal-

owners and their faithful lackeys could devise. No act of vengeance occurred: no blackleg was molested: no theft was committed.

Engels is led to attribute an incredible heroism of character to the strikers. His rhetoric demands that the workers had to be in the grip of "burning hatred against their oppressors" because they were not acting like "mere machines" or "stupid animals." The strike, therefore, must represent a triumph of collective self-repression: the acquisition of "self-control." Engels, like Dickens, is amazed that the workers were able to display that preeminent middle-class virtue: "And what a struggle it was—not a fight against visible enemies who could be struck down, but a fight against hunger and want, destitute misery and hopelessness—against their own passions which had been provoked almost to madness by the brutality of wealth" ("Und welch einen Kampf—nicht gegen sichtbare, tödliche Feinde, sondern gegen Hunger und Not, Elend und Obdachlosigkeit, gegen die eignen, durch die Brutalität des Reichtums bis zum Wahnsinn herausgeforderten Leidenschaften").

What such rhetoric reveals about Engels, as it does about Dickens, is the gap between the character of the workers generated by his rhetoric and their character as revealed in their actions. Or, put another way, the gap demonstrates that between character and action no meaningful linkage necessarily exists. Character and action are simply two terms of a metonymic relationship, like character and work, character and clothes, and character and environment. It seems naive to assume that the two terms of these metonymic pairs are identical, but that assumption occurs repeatedly and without notice. The readings of the industrial workers' character constituted by those metonymic operations in *The Condition of the Working Class* are not subtle; instead, they are crude and distasteful. To find such monstrous characters drawn by a perceptive, sympathetic writer testifies to the power and pervasiveness of the rhetoric of metonymy.

III

After *Hard Times* and *The Condition of the Working Class*, relatively early attempts to represent industrial workers, equating the worker and his environment became almost automatic. *Germinal* (1885), the most influential literary representation of the industrial worker, in the Engels-Dickens tradition based on direct observation (Zola's trip in 1884 to the mining region during the Anzin strike), carries the metonymic characterization of workers as machines and animals to the limits of intelligibility—and for many readers beyond the bounds of realism. Miners become a brutal, mechanical herd, indistinguishable from the pits and machinery that devour them. Zola's personal and nightmarish vision is unmistakable, but he creates his miners by following the impersonal convention of realistic metonymy: he indentifies them with their horrific surroundings. Zola would have had no trouble accepting Disraeli's formulaic description of the people of the factory town of Wodgate in *Sybil, or The Two Nations*, published in the same year as *The Condition of the Working Class*, forty years before *Germinal*: "they are animals; unconscious; their minds a blank; and their worst actions only the impulse of a gross or savage instinct."

The lifelessness of Dickens's industrial workers in *Hard Times*, when seen in this tradition, paradoxically may be taken as a sign of his humaneness. Instead of allowing them to develop into savages or grotesque robots, he lets them fade into the colorless anonymity of moral personifications while quietly relinquishing the project of presenting the truth about them. He permits his initial expectation that the new industrial world would be peopled by a mob of interchangeable, mass-produced characters to be shown a delusion, revealing in the process that he had been mistaken in assuming a necessary connection between Coketown and its inhabitants. Because it dramatizes its own futility, *Hard Times* displays an unusual intellectual and moral honesty. After all, in the equivalence of work and character in the dogma of social prophets like Carlyle, Ruskin, and Marx; in the insistence upon the determining effects of environment on character in realist and naturalist fiction and painting; in the belief in the photographic image as a means of knowledge—in these and countless other macroscopic ways, the microscopic truth of metonymy dominated the nineteenth century. For Dickens to resist both his own and his culture's inner laws was an act, if not of what Morse Peckham has called "cultural transcendence," at least of unusual humility.

EVE KOSOFSKY SEDGWICK

Homophobia, Misogyny, and Capital: *The Example of* Our Mutual Friend

O*ur Mutual Friend* has had an emboldening effect on at any rate the
thematic project of *Between Men,* because it is so thick with themes
associated with male homophobia and homosexuality. After all, *Our Mu-*
tual Friend is *the* English novel that everyone knows is about anality. The
inheritance at the center of the plot is immensely valuable real estate that
contains a cluster of what Dickens calls "dust heaps." Layers of scholarly
controversy have been devoted to the contents of Victorian dust heaps;
and, led by Humphry House's *The Dickens World,* many critics have
agreed that human excrement was an important (and financially valuable)
component of the mounds. Such critics as Earle Davis, Monroe Engel, J.
Hillis Miller, and Sylvia Bank Manning have given this thematic element
a good deal of play, often, as F. S. Schwarzbach says, "with the intention of establishing whether Dickens did or did not understand Freud's
later formulation of the psychic relation between human waste and
money." But although many of those who write about Dickens's conjunction of excrement and money refer to Freud, sometimes by way
of Norman O. Brown, most of the substance of Freud's (and Brown's)
argument is missing from their accounts. Their point is most often
far simpler and essentially moralistic: that money and excrement are
alike because (more or less) they are worthless, *bad.* Thus Earle Davis
writes,

Economically speaking, [Dickens's] world could see no difference between unearned increment and diffused excrement. . . .
[I]n every part of London he saw mankind straining and struggling over a dung heap. . . . His pen became an excretory organ
spouting out a sizzling cover for all the organic corruption
which lay festering in the values that money set, the awful offal
of Victorian standards.

Davis concludes his "post-Freudian" reading with the ancient favorite text
of Chaucer's Pardoner:

At the bottom of all is money, the love of money at the cost of
everything else. It is the overweening desire for money which
lands most people in the filth of Hell.

Perhaps it would be more precise, then, to say that *Our Mutual
Friend* is the only English novel that everyone *says* is about excrement in
order that they may *forget* that it is about anality. For the Freudian
insights, elided in the critics' moralistic yoking of filth and lucre, are erotic
ones. They are insights into the pleasures, desires, bonds, and forms of
eros that have to do with the anus. And it is precisely the repression of
these pleasures and desires that, in Freud, turns feces into filth and filth
into gold. A novel about the whole issue of anal eroticism, and not merely
a sanitized invective against money or "filthy lucre" or what critics have
come to call "the dust-money equation," would have to concern itself with
other elements in the chain Freud describes: love between man and man,
for instance; the sphincter, its control, and the relation of these to sadism;
the relations among bodily images, material accumulation, and economic
status. It would also offer some intimations, at least, of adult genital
desire, and repression, in relation to the anus. Furthermore a novel that
treated these issues would necessarily cast them in the mold of a particular, historical vision of society, class, power, money, and gender.

One curious thematic marker in *Our Mutual Friend* that has gone
critically unnoticed, and that the novel itself tends to muffle, is a name. An
important character in the novel chooses to call herself Jenny Wren, but
we are told—just once—that that is not the name she was born with. Her
real name is Fanny Cleaver. Unlike the later, funny, almost childishly
deflationary name, Fanny Assingham, in *The Golden Bowl*, Fanny Cleaver
is a name that hints at aggression—specifically, at rape, and perhaps at
homosexual rape. The pun would seem a trivial accident, were it not a
small pointer to something much more striking: that there are two scenes

in *Our Mutual Friend* whose language does indeed strongly suggest male rape. These are Bradley Headstone's attack on Rogue Riderhood (discussed below), and the attack on John Harmon in chapter 13 (discussed [elsewhere]). Another thematic "clue" functions at a different level to solicit the twentieth-century reader's attention to the male homosocial components in the book. One of the male protagonists lives in domestic happiness with another man, and at moments of particular intensity he says things like, "I love you, Mortimer."

In some simple sense, therefore, this must be a novel that delineates something close to the whole extent of the male homosocial spectrum, including elements of homosexual genitality. Just what version of male homosociality most concerns it, however? The sweet avowal, "I love you, Mortimer," almost promises the sunny, Pickwickian innocence of encompassing homosocial love rendered in the absence of homophobia. At the same time, to give a *woman* a name like Fanny Cleaver may suggest something almost opposite: homophobia, in the absence of homosexuality. And those golden dust heaps are the emblem of a wholly abstracted anality: they do not refer us to any individual or sentient anus. To understand the very excess, the supervisibility of the homosocial/homophobic/homosexual thematics in this novel requires us to see that for Dickens the erotic fate of every female or male is also cast in the terms and propelled by the forces of class and economic accumulation.

Let me begin by tracing a chain of Girardian triangles within one of the novel's plots, a chain reaching from the lowest class up to the professional class. It begins with the three members of the Hexam family: Gaffer Hexam, the father, an illiterate scavenger who makes his living by fishing corpses from the Thames and robbing them; Lizzie Hexam, his beautiful, good, and loyal daughter; and Charley Hexam, his son, whom Lizzie protects from their father's violent resentment until Charley is old enough to run away and go to school. These three comprise the first triangle.

Charley is determined and industrious enough to go from a Ragged School to a National School, where he becomes a pupil-teacher under the sponsorship of a young schoolmaster, Bradley Headstone. Bradley, like Charley, began as a pauper, and Dickens says, "regarding that origin of his, he was proud, moody, and sullen, desiring it to be forgotten." Yet an intense bond soon develops between the schoolmaster and young Charley. After the father's death, Bradley advises Charley to have no more to do with his impoverished, illiterate sister. Charley begs Bradley to come meet Lizzie first, however, and Bradley finds himself, as if by compulsion, violently in love with her.

The triangles of the Hexam family and of Charley, Lizzie, and Bradley are complicated by another triangle. Eugene Wrayburn, a young barrister and one of the heroes of the novel, also falls in love with Lizzie. He, like Bradley, has an intense encounter with Charley before meeting Lizzie, although in this case the intensity takes the form of instant, almost allergic dislike on both sides. And Eugene has another, apparently non-triangular, love relationship—it is he who says, "I love you, Mortimer." Mortimer Lightwood is an old friend and protégé of Eugene's from public school, and the two, while making languid efforts to succeed in the law, make a household together.

Already contrasts of class are appearing under the guise of contrasts of personality and sexuality. One great evidence of class and control divides this little world in two as absolutely as gender does, though less permanently: the division of the literate from the illiterate. And after Gaffer's early death, only one of these people—Lizzie, the desired woman—remains illiterate. The quarrel between the schoolmaster and Eugene is over who will teach her to read. But even within the masculine world of literacy, the gradations of class are unforgiving. Charley's and Bradley's relation to knowledge is always marked by the anxious, compulsive circumstances of its acquisition. Dickens says of the schoolmaster,

> From his early childhood up, his mind had been a place of mechanical stowage. . . . There was a kind of settled trouble in the face. It was the face belonging to a normally slow or inattentive intellect that had toiled hard to get what it had won, and that had to hold it now that it was gotten.
>
> (bk. 2, chap. 1)

Bradley seems always to be in pain, "like . . . one who was being physically hurt, and was unwilling to cry out"; his infliction of pain on others seems to come from even greater spasms of it within himself; talking to Lizzie about his desire to teach her to read, for example, he seems to be hemorrhaging internally:

> He looked at Lizzie again, and held the look. And his face turned from burning red to white, and from white back to burning red, and so for the time to lasting deadly white.
>
> (bk. 2, chap. 11)

In fact, to borrow an image from a patient of Freud's, the schoolmaster behaves socially like a man with a hungry rat in his bowels. And for him, the rat represents not money but more specifically his small private capital of knowledge. Or rather it represents the alienation from himself of the profit of his knowledge. For the knowledge never makes *him* wiser; it is quite worthless outside the schoolroom; it merely places him, more decisively even than illiteracy would, in a particular, low position in the line of production of labor for a capitalism whose needs now included a literate, rather than merely a massive, workforce. Bradley's one effort to invest his nest egg for his own profit—to teach Lizzie to read, as part of that triangular transaction with Charley—is imperiously overruled by Eugene, who wants to pay for his own person to do the teaching. "Are you her schoolmaster as well as her brother's?" asks Eugene scornfully, and instead of using his name, will only call him, "Schoolmaster." Bradley, as usual, loses control of his composure and complexion—for he is merely "used to the little audience of a school, and unused to the larger ways of men" (bk. 2, chap. 6).

Eugene, on the other hand, though not wealthy, is a gentleman and a public-school boy. His relation to his own store of knowledge is the confident one of inconspicuous consumption: he can afford to be funny and silly. He likes to say things like "But then I mean so much that I—that I don't mean." Or

> "You know that when I became enough of a man to find myself an embodied conundrum, I bored myself to the last degree by trying to find out what I meant. You know that at length I gave it up, and declined to guess any more."
>
> (bk. 2, chap. 6)

Mortimer sees him affectionately as "this utterly careless Eugene." He has no consciousness of knowledge, or even of power, as something to be struggled for, although his unconscious wielding of them makes him not only more loveable and relaxed than Bradley but also much more destructive. The moral ugliness of Eugene's taunts against the schoolmaster is always less striking, in the novel's presentation, than the unloveliness of the schoolmaster's anxiety and frustration. Bradley the pauper, thinking to make himself independent by his learning, finds that he has struggled himself into a powerless, alienating position in an impervious hierarchical economy. Eugene Wrayburn, like Yorick imagining himself as marginal, passive, and unempowered in his relation to the economy, nevertheless speaks with the full-throated authority of a man near its very center.

Bradley's relation with Charley and Eugene's with Mortimer differ on the basis of class, and the position of Lizzie in each relationship is accordingly different. Charley's offer of Lizzie to his schoolmaster represents the purest form of the male traffic in women. Charley explains it to Lizzie this way:

> "Then *I* come in. Mr. Headstone has always got me on, and he has a good deal in his power, and of course if he was my brother-in-law he wouldn't get me on less, but would get me on more. Mr. Headstone comes and confides in me, in a very delicate way, and says, 'I hope my marrying your sister would be agreeable to you, Hexam, and useful to you?' I say, 'There's nothing in the world, Mr. Headstone, that I could be better pleased with.' Mr. Headstone says, 'Then I may rely upon your intimate knowledge of me for your good word with your sister, Hexam?' And I say, 'Certainly, Mr. Headstone, and naturally I have a good deal of influence with her.' So I have; haven't I, Liz?"
>
> "Yes, Charley."
>
> "Well said! Now you see, we begin to get on, the moment we begin to be really talking it over, like brother and sister."
>
> (bk. 2, chap. 15)

To Bradley, his triangle with Charley and Lizzie represents not access to power within the society but a dire sliding away from it; and this is true whether one takes his desire for Lizzie or for Charley to represent the main erotic bond. No wonder he says to Lizzie, in an example of his resentful style of courtship:

> "You are the ruin—the ruin—the ruin—of me. . . . I have never been quit of you since I first saw you. Oh, that was a wretched day for me! That was a wretched, miserable day!"
>
> (bk. 2, chap. 15)

No; the closest relation to patriarchal power for Bradley in this tangle comes in the link of rivalry between himself and Eugene Wrayburn. And it soon emerges that this is, indeed, for him, the focus of the whole affair. In the painful scene with Lizzie I have been quoting, Bradley makes a threat against Eugene, and when she responds, indignantly, "He is nothing to you, I think," he insists, "Oh yes he is. There you mistake. He is much to me." What? she asks.

> "He can be a rival to me *among other things.* . . . I knew all this about Mr. Eugene Wrayburn, all the while you were drawing me to you. . . . With Mr. Eugene Wrayburn in my mind, I

went on. With Mr. Eugene Wrayburn in my mind, I spoke to
you just now. With Mr. Eugene Wrayburn in my mind, I have
been set aside and I have been cast out."

(bk. 2, chap. 15; emphasis added)

After Lizzie has refused Bradley and left London, the desiring relation
between Bradley and Eugene, far from dissipating, becomes hotter and
more reciprocal. The schoolmaster decides—wrongly—that he can find
Lizzie by following Eugene everywhere he goes, and, Eugene says,

> "I goad the schoolmaster to madness. . . . I tempt him on, all
> over London. . . . Sometimes, I walk; sometimes, I proceed in
> cabs, draining the pocket of the schoolmaster, who then fol-
> lows in cabs. I study and get up abstruse No Thoroughfares in
> the course of the day [while Bradley is teaching]. With Venetian
> mystery I seek those No Thoroughfares at night, glide into
> them by means of dark courts, tempt the schoolmaster to
> follow, turn suddenly, and catch him before he can retreat.
> Then we face one another, and I pass him as unaware of his
> existence, and he undergoes grinding torments. . . . Thus I en-
> joy the pleasures of the chase. . . . just now I am a little excited
> by the glorious fact that a southerly wind and a cloudy sky
> proclaim a hunting evening."

(bk. 3, chap. 10)

In Surtees's *Handley Cross*, Mr. Jorrocks declaims that " 'Unting" is
"the image of war without its guilt, and only five-and-twenty per cent. of
its danger," but it is less lucky than that for the men who are caught up in
this chase. One day on a towpath Bradley attacks Eugene from behind; the
two men struggle in an embrace, and Eugene, both arms broken, nearly
drowns. Soon after that, another man, a lockkeeper with the sinister and
important name Rogue Riderhood, who has been dogging and blackmail-
ing Bradley Headstone, finds himself, too, attacked from behind. This is
one of the scenes whose language is that of male rape:

> Bradley had caught him round the body. He seemed to be
> girdled with an iron ring. . . . Bradley got him round, with his
> back to the Lock, and still worked him backward. . . . "I'll
> hold you living, and I'll hold you dead! Come down!"
>   Riderhood went over into the smooth pit, backward, and
> Bradley Headstone upon him. When the two were found, lying
> under the ooze and scum behind one of the rotting gates,

> Riderhood's hold had relaxed, probably in falling, and his eyes
> were staring upward. But, he was girdled still with Bradley's
> iron ring, and the rivets of the iron ring held tight.
>
> (bk. 4, chap. 15)

Sphincter domination is Bradley Headstone's only mode of grappling for
the power that is continually flowing away from him. Unfortunately for
him, sphincter control can't give him any leverage at all with women—
with Lizzie, who simply never engages with him, who eludes him from the
start. It only succeeds in grappling more closely to him men who have
already been drawn into a fascinated mirroring relation to him—Eugene,
with whom he has been engaged in that reversible hunt, and Rogue
Riderhood, in whose clothing he had disguised himself for the assault on
Eugene. His initial, hating terror of Lizzie was a terror of, as he kept
putting it, being "drawn" from himself, having his accumulated value
sucked from him down the great void of her illiteracy and powerlessness.
But, classically, he is the Pinchwife-like man who, fearing to entrust his
relations with patriarchy to a powerless counter, a woman, can himself
only be used as a woman, and valued as a woman, by the men with whom
he comes into narcissistic relation.

In the novel's social mapping of the body, Bradley, like some other
figures at the lower end of the respectable classes, powerfully represents
the repressive divorce of the private thematics of the anus from the social
forces of desire and pleasure. Dickens does precede Freud, Ferenczi, Norman O. Brown, and Deleuze/Guattari, among others, in seeing digestion
and the control of the anus as the crucial images for the illusion of
economic individualism: cross-culturally, Brown remarks, "the category of
'possession,' and power based on possession, is apparently indigenous to
the magic-dirt complex." One thematic portrayal of this exclusion is a
splitting of the body between twin images of a distended gut and a
distended disembodied head. Bradley Headstone (and note his name), the
most wrackingly anal of the characters, also appears repeatedly as a
floating "haggard head in the air" (bk. 3, chaps. 10, 11); Mr. Venus, a
taxidermist and articulator of skeletons, with his shop full of hydroce-
phalic babies in jars, is himself given to "floating his powerful mind
in tea" (bk. 3, chap. 7); illiterate "Noddy" Boffin dandles the head
of his walking stick at his ear like the head of a floating "familiar
spirit" or baby, and himself seems to turn into a great heavyheaded
puppet at the end of the novel (bk. 4, chaps. 3, 13); and so on. The
unanxious version of *homo digestivus* is the "hideous solidity" that the

firmly bourgeois Podsnaps and their circle share with their "corpulent straddling" tableware:

> Everything said boastfully, "Here you have as much of me in my ugliness as if I were only lead; but I am so many ounces of precious metal worth so much an ounce; wouldn't you like to melt me down?" . . . All the big silver spoons and forks widened the mouths of the company expressly for the purpose of thrusting the sentiment down their throats with every morsel they ate. The majority of the guests were like the plate.
>
> (bk. 1, chap. 11)

This strain of imagery, of course, culminates in the monstrous dust-heaps themselves. In short, one thing that goes on when the human body is taken as a capitalist emblem is that the relation of parts to wholes becomes problematic; there is no intelligible form of circulation; the parts swell up with accumulated value, they take on an autonomous life of their own, and eventually power comes to be expressed as power over reified doubles fashioned in one's own image from the waste of one's own body. Power is over dolls, puppets, and articulated skeletons, over the narcissistic, singular, nondesiring phantoms of individuality.

For Bradley Headstone, dissociation, anxiety, toil, and a crippling somatic self-consciousness mark the transition into respectability, and make heavy and humiliating work of his heterosexual involvement. How differently they manage these things in the upper classes. While Bradley's intentions toward Lizzie, however uneasy, had been strictly honorable, Eugene Wrayburn has no intentions toward her at all. Mortimer asks him,

> "Eugene, do you design to capture and desert this girl?"
> "My dear fellow, no."
> "Do you design to marry her?"
> "My dear fellow, no."
> "Do you design to pursue her?"
> "My dear fellow, I don't design anything. I have no design whatsoever. I am incapable of designs. If I conceived a design, I should speedily abandon it, exhausted by the operation."
>
> (bk. 2, chap. 6)

This is the opposite of Bradley's compulsive, grasping relation to power. Eugene sees himself as a little leaf borne upon a stream; and an image that is often associated with him is the pretty river that supplies power to the papermill where Lizzie finally gets work. But Eugene's lack of will is enormously more potent than Bradley's clenched, entrapping will, simply because the powerful, "natural" trajectory of this stream is eternally toward swelling the exploitive power of ruling-class men over working-class women. Resolute and independent as Lizzie is, weak and passive as *he* is, Eugene barely has to make a decision, much less form a design, in order to ruin her.

> The rippling of the river seemed to cause a correspondent stir in his uneasy reflections. He would have laid them asleep if he could, but they were in movement, like the stream, and all tending one way with a strong current. . . . "Out of the question to marry her," said Eugene, "and out of the question to leave her."
>
> (bk. 4, chap. 6)

It is traditional, in criticism of *Our Mutual Friend*, to distinguish two groups of thematic imagery, that surrounding the river and that surrounding the dust-heaps. If, as I have suggested, the dust-heaps can be said to represent an anthropomorphization of capital that is most closely responsive to the anxieties of the petit-bourgeoisie, then the river, in a sense, offers a critique of that in terms of a more collectively scaled capitalism, organized around alienation and the flow of currency. Its gender implications are pointed and odd: all the men in this waterside novel are strikingly incompetent about the water; there are seven drownings or near-drownings, all of males; men are always dragging each other into the river; and only one person, Lizzie, has the skill to navigate a rescue. At the same time, women are in control only in correctly understanding the current of power as always flowing away from themselves. Gazing into the river, both Lizzie and Eugene read in it the image of Lizzie's inability to resist ruin.

Just as Eugene's higher status enables his heterosexual relationship to be at once more exploitive and less guilty than Bradley's, so his desiring relationship with a man can be at once much more open and much less embroiled in repressive conflict than any of Bradley's. Interestingly, though it is more open, it also seems much less tinged with the sexual. Imagery of the sphincter, the girdle, the embrace, the "iron ring" of the male grasp, was salient in those murderous attacks on men by Bradley Headstone. By contrast it is utterly absent from the tenderer love between Eugene and Mortimer. They live together like Bert and Ernie on Sesame Street—and who ever wonders what Muppets do in bed? This thematic reticence, if it is reticence, in contrast to the hypersaturation with anal thematics of

Bradley's part of the story, can perhaps best be accounted for not by some vague invocation of "Victorian prudery," but by thinking about how the libidinal careers of Victorian gentlemen were distinguished, in fiction and in ideology at any rate, from those of males of higher and lower class.

The obstacles to mapping this territory have been suggested before. The historical research on primary sources that would add texture and specificity to generalizations is only beginning to be done, or at any rate published; at the same time, the paradigms available for understanding the history of sexuality are in rapid and productive flux. The best that I can attempt here is perhaps to lay out in a useful codified form what the "common sense" or "common knowledge" of the (essentially middle-class) Victorian reader of novels might be likely to have been, buttressed by some evidence from biographies. I wish to make clear how tentative and how thoroughly filtered through the ideological lens of middle-class literature these generalizations are, but still to make them available *for* revision by other scholars.

With respect to homosocial/homosexual style, it seems to be possible to divide Victorian men among three rough categories according to class. The first includes aristocratic men and small groups of their friends and dependents, including bohemians and prostitutes; for these people, by 1865, a distinct homosexual role and culture seem already to have been in existence in England for several centuries. This seems to have been a milieu, at once courtly and in touch with the criminal, related to those in which the usages of the term "gay" recorded by John Boswell occurred. It seems to have constituted a genuine subculture, facilitated in the face of an ideologically hostile dominant culture by money, privilege, internationalism, and, for the most part, the ability to command secrecy. Pope's lines on Sporus in "Epistle to Dr. Arbuthnot" do, however, presuppose his audience's knowledge that such a role and culture exist. This role is closely related to—is in fact, through Oscar Wilde, the antecedent of—the particular stereotype that at least until recently has characterized American middle-class gay homosexuality; its strongest associations, as we have noted [earlier], are with effeminacy, transvestitism, promiscuity, prostitution, continental European culture, and the arts.

For classes below the nobility, however, there seems in the nineteenth century not to have been an association of a particular personal style with the genital activities now thought of as "homosexual." The class of men about which we know most—the educated middle class, the men who produced the novels and journalism and are the subjects of the biographies—operated sexually in what seems to have been startlingly close to a cognitive vacuum. A gentleman (I will use the word "gentleman" to distinguish the educated bourgeois from the aristocrat as well as from the working-class man—a usage that accords, not with Victorian ideology, but with Victorian practice) had a good deal of objective sexual freedom, especially if he were single, having managed to evade the great cult of the family and, with it, much of the enforcing machinery of his class and time. At the same time, he seems not to have had easy access to the alternative subculture, the stylized discourse, or the sense of immunity of the aristocratic/bohemian sexual minority. So perhaps it is not surprising that the sexual histories of English gentlemen, unlike those of men above and below them socially, are so marked by a resourceful, makeshift, *sui generis* quality, in their denials, their rationalizations, their fears and guilts, their sublimations, and their quite various genital outlets alike. Biographies of English gentlemen of the nineteenth and early twentieth centuries are full of oddities, surprises, and apparent false starts; they seem to have no predetermined sexual trajectory. Good examples include Lewis Carroll, Charles Kingsley, John Ruskin, and a little later, T. E. Lawrence, James M. Barrie, T. H. White, Havelock Ellis, and J. R. Ackerley, who describes in an autobiography how he moved from a furtive promiscuous homosexuality to a fifteen-year-long affair of the heart with a female dog. The sexuality of a single gentleman was silent, tentative, protean, and relatively divorced from expectations of genre, though not of gender.

In fiction, a thematically tamer but structurally interesting and emotionally—very often—turbid and preoccupying relationship was common between single gentlemen: Pendennis and Warrington, Clive Newcome and J. J. Ridley, the two Armadales of Collins's *Armadale*, the gentlemen of the Pickwick Club, resemble Eugene and Mortimer in the lack of remark surrounding their union and in the shadowy presence of a mysterious imperative (physical debility, hereditary curse, secret unhappy prior marriage, or simply extreme disinclination) that bars at least one of the partners in each union forever from marriage.

Of the sexuality of English people below the middle class, reliable accounts are difficult to assemble. Both aristocratic and (early twentieth-century) middle-class English male homosexuality seem to have been organized to a striking degree around the objectification of proletarian men, as we read in accounts by or of Forster, Isherwood, Ackerley, Edward Carpenter, Tom Driberg, and others; at the same time, there is no evidence (from these middle-class-oriented accounts) of a homosexual role or subculture indigenous to men of the working class, apart from their sexual value to more privileged men. It is possible that for the great balance of the non-public-school-educated classes, overt homosexual acts may have been recognized mainly as instances of violence: English law before the Labouchère amendment of 1885 did not codify or criminalize most of the spectrum of male bodily contacts, so that homosexual acts would more often have become *legally* visible for the violence that may have accompanied them than for their distinctively sexual content. In middle-class accounts of the working class, at any rate, and possibly within the working class itself, there seems to have been an association between male homosexual genitality and violence, as in Dickens's treatment of Bradley Headstone's anal eroticism in terms exclusively of murder and mutilation.

Since most Victorians neither named nor recognized a syndrome of male homosexuality as our society thinks of it, the various classes probably grouped this range of sexual activities under various moral and psychological headings. I have suggested that the working class may have grouped it with violence. In aristocrats—or, again, in aristocrats as perceived by the middle class—it came under the heading of dissolution, at the very time when dissolution was itself becoming the (wishful?) bourgeois-ideological name for aristocracy itself. Profligate young lords in Victorian novels almost *all* share the traits of the Sporus-like aristocratic homosexual "type," and it is impossible to predict from their feckless, "effeminate" behavior whether their final ruin will be the work of male favorites, female favorites, the racecourse, or the bottle; waste and wastage is the presiding category of scandal. Fictional examples of this ambiguous style include Lord Frederick Verisopht (with his more "masculine," less aristocratic sidekick, Sir Mulberry Hawk), in *Nicholas Nickleby;* Count Fosco, (with his more "masculine," less aristocratic sidekick, Sir Percival Glyde) in *The Woman in White;* Lord Porlock, in *The Small House at Allington* and *Doctor Thorne;* in a more admiring version, Patrick, Earl of Desmond (with his more "masculine," less aristocratic sidekick, Owen Fitzgerald) in Trollope's *Castle Richmond;* and Lord Nidderdale (with Dolly Longstaffe) in *The Way We Live Now*. In each case there is explicit mention of only female erotic objects, if any; but in each case the allegedly vicious or dissolute drive seems more visibly to be directed at a man in more immediate proximity. Perhaps the most overtly sympathetic—at any rate the least grotesque, the closest to "normal"-seeming—of the men in this category is also one who is without a title, although within the context of the novel he represents the vitiated line of a rural aristocracy. That is Harold Transome, in *Felix Holt*. To his sexual history we receive three clues, each tantalizing in its own way: we hear—mentioned once, without elaboration—that the woman he had married in his Eastern travels was one whom he had bought as a slave; we hear—mentioned once, without elaboration—that he has brought a (different) woman back with him from the East; but the person of whom we hear incessantly in connection with Harold is his plangent, ubiquitous manservant-companion:

> "I don't know whether he's most of a Jew, a Greek, an Italian, or a Spaniard. He speaks five or six languages, one as well as another. He's cook, valet, major-domo, and secretary all in one; and what's more, he's an affectionate fellow. . . . That's a sort of human specimen that doesn't grow here in England, I fancy. I should have been badly off if I could not have brought Dominic."

Throughout a plot elaboration that depends heavily on the tergiversations of a slippery group of servants-who-are-not-quite-servants, who have un-explained bonds from the past with Dominic, one waits for the omniscient, serviceable, ingratiating character of Dominic to emerge into its full sinis-terness or glamor or sexual insistence—in vain, since the exploitive "orien-tal" luxuries of his master can be perceived only in a sexually irresolute blur of "decadence." Perhaps similarly, the lurid dissipations of the char-acters in *The Picture of Dorian Gray* are presented in heterosexual terms when detailed at all, even though (biographical hindsight aside) the trian-gular relationship of Basil, Dorian, and Lord Henry makes sense only in homosexual terms.

Between the extremes of upper-class male homosocial desire, grouped with dissipation, and working-class male homosocial desire, grouped per-haps with violence, the view of the gentleman, the public-school product, was different again. School itself was, of course, a crucial link in ruling-class male homosocial formation. Disraeli (who was not himself an Etonian) offers the flattering ideological version of Eton friendships in *Coningsby:*

> At school, friendship is a passion. It entrances the being; it tears the soul. All loves of after life can never bring its rapture, or its wretchedness; no bliss so absorbing, no pangs of jealousy or despair so crushing and so keen! What tenderness and what devotion; what illimitable confidence; what infinite revelations of inmost thoughts; what ecstatic present and romantic future; what bitter estrangements and what melting reconciliations; what scenes of wild recrimination, agitating explanations, pas-sionate correspondence; what insane sensitiveness, and what frantic sensibility; what earthquakes of the heart, and whirl-

winds of the soul, are confined in that simple phrase—a school-boy's friendship!

Candid accounts agree that in most of the public schools, the whirlwinds of the soul were often acted out in the flesh. Like the young aristocrat, the young gentleman at those same public schools would have seen or engaged in a variety of sexual activities among males; but unlike the aristocrat, most gentlemen found neither a community nor a shared, distinctive sexual identity ready for adults who wanted more of the same. A twentieth-century writer, Michael Nelson, reports asking a school friend, "Have you ever had any homosexual inclinations since leaving Eton?" "I say, steady on," his friend replied. "It's all right for fellows to mess one another about a bit at school. But when we grow up we put aside childish things, don't we?"

David Copperfield, among other books, makes the same point. David's infatuation with his friend Steerforth, who calls him "Daisy" and treats him like a girl, is simply part of David's education—though another, later part is the painful learning of how to triangulate from Steerforth onto women, and finally, although incompletely, to hate Steerforth and grow at the expense of his death. In short, a gentleman will associate the erotic end of the homosocial spectrum, not with dissipation, not with viciousness or violence, but with childishness, as an infantile need, a mark of powerlessness, which, while it may be viewed with shame or scorn or denial, is unlikely to provoke the virulent, accusatory projection that characterizes twentieth-century homophobia.

This slow, distinctive two-stage progression from schoolboy desire to adult homophobia seems to take its structure from the distinctive anxieties that came with being educated for the relatively new class of middle-class "gentlemen." Unlike title, wealth, or land, the terms that defined the gentleman were not clearly and simply hereditary but had somehow to be earned by being a particular kind of person who spent time and money in particular ways. But the early prerequisites for membership in this powerful but nebulous class—to speak with a certain accent, to spend years translating Latin and Greek, to leave family and the society of women—all made one unfit for any other form of work, long before they entitled one to chance one's fortune actively in the ruling class.

The action of *Our Mutual Friend* brings to a close that long abeyance in Eugene's life between, so to speak, being *called* and being *chosen* for the professional work of empire. (For instance, he has been called to the Bar, but no one has yet chosen to employ him.) His position is awash with patriarchal authority, the authority of the law itself, but none of it belongs to him yet. In just the same way, having been removed from his family as a child, he will soon be required to return—and in the enforcing position of *paterfamilias,* a position that will lend a retroactive meaning and hetero-sexual trajectory to his improvised, provisional relationship with Mortimer and his apparently aimless courtship of Lizzie. In the violence at the end of the novel, we see the implacability with which this heterosexual, homo-phobic meaning is impressed on Eugene's narrative: Bradley, his rival, nearly kills him by drowning; Lizzie saves him; while he seems to be dying, Mortimer interprets his last wishes as being that he might marry Lizzie; and when he comes back to life, he is already a married man. "But would you believe," Lizzie asks afterwards, "that on our wedding day he told me he almost thought the best thing he could do, was to die?" (bk. 4, chap. 16).

There is one character to whom this homophobic reinscription of the bourgeois family is even more crippling than it is to Eugene, who already, by the end of the novel, looks almost "as though he had never been mutilated" (bk. 4, chap. 16). That person is, of course, Lizzie. The formal, ideological requirements for a fairy-tale "happy ending" for her are satis-fied by the fact that she is not "ruined" by Eugene, not cast into the urban underclass of prostitution, but raised up into whatever class the wife of a Victorian barrister belongs to. Eugene is determined to fight for his right to have her regarded as a lady. But with all that good news, Dickens makes no attempt to disguise the terrible diminution in her personal stature as she moves from being the resentful, veiled, muscular, illiterate figure rowing a scavenger boat on the Thames, to being a factory worker in love, to being Mrs. Eugene Wrayburn *tout court.* Admittedly, Lizzie has been a reaction-ary all along. But she has been a blazing, courageous reactionary: she has defended and defied her violent father; she has sacrificed everything for her beastly brother; she gave up a chance to form an alliance with an older woman, a tavern-keeper, just because the woman would not accept her father; she took off for the countryside to save her honor from the man she loved; and she unhesitatingly risked her life to save his life. But all her reactionary courage meets with a stiflingly reactionary reward. Lizzie stops being Lizzie, once she is Mrs. Eugene Wrayburn.

As we see how unrelentingly Lizzie is diminished by her increasingly distinct gender assignment, it becomes clearer why "childishness," rather than femininity, should at that moment have been the ideological way the ruling class categorized its own male homosexuality. As Jean Baker Miller points out in *Toward a New Psychology of Women,* an attribution of gender difference marks a structure of *permanent* inequality, while the relation between adult and child is the prototype of the *temporary* inequality that in principle—or in ideology—exists only in order to be overcome: children are supposed to grow up into parents, but wives are not supposed to grow up into husbands. Now, the newly significant class of "gentlemen," the flagship class of English high capitalism, was to include a very wide range of status and economic position, from plutocrats down to impoverished functionaries. In order to maintain the illusion of equality, or at any rate of meritocratic pseudoequality, *within* the class of gentlemen, and at the same time justify the magnification of distinctions within the class, it clearly made sense to envision a long, complicated period of individual psychic testing and preparation, full of fallings-away, redefinitions, and crossings and recrossings of lines of identification. This protracted, baffling narrative of the self, a direct forerunner of the twentieth-century oedipal narrative, enabled the process of social and vocational sorting to occur under the less invidious shape of different rates of individual maturation.

Not until this psychologistic, "developmental" way of thinking had been firmly established was the *aristocratic* link between male homosexuality and *femininity* allowed to become an article of wide public consumption—a change that was crystallized in the Wilde affair and that coincided (in the 1890s) with the beginnings of a dissemination across classes of language about male homosexuality (e.g., the word "homosexual"), and with the medicalization of homosexuality through an array of scientific "third sex" and "intersex" theories.

But during all this time, for women, the immutability of gender inequality was being inscribed more and more firmly, moralistically, and descriptively in the structure of bourgeois institutions. As the contrasting bodily images in *Our Mutual Friend* suggest, woman's deepening understanding, as she saw the current flowing away under her own image, came for the most part at the cost of renouncing individual ownership and accumulation. The division of cognitive labor that emerged with the bourgeois family was not a means of power for women, but another part of the edifice of master-slave subordination to men. Sentient middle-class women of this time perceive the triangular path of circulation that enforces patriarchal power as being routed through them, but never ending in them—while capitalist man, with his prehensile, precapitalist image of the body, is always deluded about what it is that he pursues, and in whose service. His delusion is, however, often indistinguishable from real empowerment; and indeed it is blindest, and closest to real empowerment, in his triangular transactions through women with other men.

SHULI BARZILAI

Dickens's Great Expectations:
The Motive for Moral Masochism

It is a critical commonplace that the crux of *Great Expectations* is guilt. The plot unfolds, the settings change, the characters develop, but the sense of guilt is constant. J. Hillis Miller observes that in *Great Expectations* "the Dickensian hero becomes aware of himself as guilty. His very existence is a matter of reproach and a shameful thing." Similarly, Robert Barnard: "The all-pervasive theme of *Great Expectations* is not money, but guilt—guilt imposed, guilt assumed, guilt transcended. . . . young Pip soaks up guilt like a sponge." The hero's assumption of guilt is apparent after his first fight with Herbert Pocket in Miss Havisham's courtyard:

> I felt that the pale young gentleman's blood was on my head, and that the law would avenge it. . . . For some days, I even kept close at home . . . lest the officers of the county jail should pounce upon me. The pale young gentleman's nose had stained my trousers, and I tried to wash out that evidence of my guilt in the dead of night.

Pip's concern with cleansing stains and spots of blood "in the dead of night" echoes Lady Macbeth's nocturnal efforts to rid herself of proof of her criminality. But the "evidence" notwithstanding, Herbert was knocked down, not murdered by Pip. Moreover, it was Herbert, not Pip, who started the fight—a moral distinction children usually make. The disparity

---

From *American Imago* 42, no. 1 (Spring 1985). © 1985 by the Association for Applied Psychoanalysis, Inc.

between young Pip's actual deed and his acute sense of remorse has no doubt a comic function. But this comedy of conscience does not cancel the gravity of his suffering. It would seem that Pip is placed in a no-win situation by his guilt.

The guilt Pip feels always seems in excess of the immediate occasion that provokes it. Thus, the signing of his apprenticeship papers at the Town Hall turns into a scene of trial and punishment:

> I was pushed over by Pumblechook, exactly as if I had that moment picked a pocket or fired a rick; indeed, it was the general impression in court that I had been taken red-handed; for, as Pumblechook shoved me before him through the crowd, I heard some people say, "What's he done?" and others, "He's a young 'un, too, but looks bad, don't he?" One person . . . even gave me a tract ornamented with a woodcut of a malevolent young man fitted up with a perfect sausage-shop of fetters, and entitled, TO BE READ IN MY CELL.
>
> Here, in a corner, my indentures were duly signed and attested, and I was "bound;" Mr. Pumblechook holding me all the while as if we had looked in on our way to the scaffold to have these little preliminaries disposed of.
>
> (chap. 13)

Throughout *Great Expectations*, Pip tells a story in which another, younger version of himself participated. This creates a complication of the first-person retrospective narrative situation which can be seen in the passage just quoted. It is difficult at times to determine whether the passage records what actually happened at the Town Hall, or the child's experience of these events, or the adult narrator's perceptions in which a belated sense of guilt has been projected on to the scene. The child may be serving here as an instrument through which the adult feels his guilt. The comparative clauses, at the beginning and end of this passage, seem to mark a distinction between what actually happened and what Pip experienced. "As if" connects two separate statements: this is what Pumblechook did; this is how I felt about it. But this division leaves the identity of the perceiver and the mimetic status of the section between the two clauses in doubt. Which Pip, the child or the adult, focalizes the scene? To which half of the comparative statement does the description of the crowd belong? Was it a fact that "it was the general impression in court that [he] had been taken red-handed"; or does Pip's sense of guilt color what he sees? And why, in any case, should Pip—which Pip?—feel like a criminal?

Some of these questions must remain in abeyance, although the immediate cause of Pip's guilt in this scene can be compacted into one word: Bound. He is legally bound to Joe Gargery as an apprentice; he is also bound to Joe through ties of gratitude which it would be a "crime" to break. But Pip has already met the proud and beautiful Estella at Miss Havisham's manor, and the blacksmith's trade now seems to bar the way before his expectations. The forge is indeed a prison, if thinking makes it so. All of which still does not provide an adequate explanation for the image of the scaffold that looms so largely before him.

A similar distortion or disproportion of guilt is evident in the scene of Wopsle's reading from the "affecting tragedy of George Barnwell." The passage moves from pronominal distinctness, with Pip saying "I thought he never would go to the scaffold," to an identification so strong that Pip cannot seem to separate himself from Barnwell or his fate:

> When Barnwell began to go wrong, I declare I felt positively apologetic, Pumblechook's indignant stare so taxed me with it. Wopsle, too, took pains to present me in the worst light. At once ferocious and maudlin, I was made to murder my uncle with no extenuating circumstances whatever ... and all I can say for my gasping and procrastinating conduct on the fatal morning is that it was worthy of the general feebleness of my character. Even after I was happily hanged and Wopsle had closed the book, Pumblechook sat staring at me, and shaking his head, and saying, "Take warning, boy, take warning!" as if it were a well-known fact that I contemplated murdering a near relation, provided I could only induce one to have the weakness to become my benefactor.
>
> (chap. 15)

Again it is difficult to determine to what extent this state of mind is informed by external circumstance, by Wopsle's and Pumblechook's actual attitude, and to what extent it is induced by the pressures of Pip's guilt. Again it is "as if": the comparative clause subverts the "well-known fact" that Pip contemplates murdering a near relation-cum-benefactor. For though he has good cause to wish that composite figure ill, he has not in fact harmed either Mrs. Joe or Miss Havisham.

The excessive burden of guilt borne by Pip puzzles critics of *Great Expectations.* His one actual "crime" in the novel, his snobbish neglect of

Joe and biddy, is a sin of omission rather than commission. This excess of emotion in respect of cause has frequently led critics to postulate the presence of an objective correlative in the text. Dorothy Van Ghent finds it in the figure of Magwitch: "Pip carries Magwitch (his 'father') within him, and the apparition of the criminal is the apparition of Pip's own guilt." Implicit in Van Ghent's reading is the assumption of a Judeo-Christian ethos: the sins of the fathers shall be visited upon the sons. Julian Moynahan explains the connection between Pip and guilt through the intermediacy of Orlick and Bentley Drummle. They act as Pip's alter egos and punitive agents. By punishing the women who injured Pip, they fulfill his secret wishes and commit the crimes he harbors in his heart. According to Moynahan: "In *Great Expectations* criminality is displaced from the hero on to a melodramatic villain." Karl Wentersdorf establishes an even more elaborate pattern of objective correlatives. Using the image of Faustus with a good and an evil angel at each shoulder to describe Pip's moral situation, Wentersdorf finds Pip mirrored in a triadic set of alter egos: Orlick and Herbert Pocket; Drummle and Startop; Pepper and Trabb's boy.

It seems to me that the neglected alter ego in *Great Expectations,* the secret sharer of Pip's guilt, is Estella Provis. Perhaps the sexual difference makes the equivalence less than obvious to critics accustomed to assigning literary identifications along lines of sexual bias. Or, perhaps, the analogy is indeed a latent and elusive one. For Estella most overtly seems what Pip is not: a child cherished by a loving parent and surrounded by every material comfort and security. The narrative quickly moves to establish the otherness of Estella. Even her name is the sign of a distance. Estella is a star, an unreachable object, an illusory expectation upon which life's happiness founders.

However, Estella and Pip are linked through ties of identification as well as opposition. In this sense Estella is the mirror-image of Pip: "if we observe the role of the mirror apparatus in the appearances of the *double,* in which psychical realities, however heterogeneous, are manifested." The inverted symmetry of Lacan's mirror stage, which "symbolizes the mental permanence of the I, at the same time as it prefigures its alienating destination," is itself perhaps derived from Freud's discussion of the means of representation used in dreams. Freud proposes: "One class of cases which can be comprised under the heading of 'contraries' are . . . simply represented by identification—cases, that is, in which the idea of an exchange or substitution can be brought into connection with the contrast." Freud attributes his understanding of this mechanism of the unconscious to his readings of philological studies which showed him that, in some of the oldest languages known to man, "there was a large number of words that denoted at once a thing and its opposite," and therefore these words had double meanings which were antithetical. The dream-work, Freud observes, is often carried out through condensation of this type; for in comparison with the interpretation of dreams, which requires laborious analysis, the dream itself is a laconic compression of content. Compression is, of course, also a characteristic which distinguishes the literary work from other modes of discourse. This common characteristic seems to me one of the grounds for what Kenneth Burke calls the "margin of overlap" between the analytic methods developed for the interpretation of two different kinds of text: the text of the mind and the text of the poem. It is from within that margin of overlap that I shall now labor to examine the condensed mirror-image represented by Estella: first as a figure of opposition and then as a figure of identification.

In *Dickens and the Art of Analogy,* H. M. Daleski demonstrates that the analogical patterns of the Dickensian plot are often indices of the protagonists' hidden relationships. At the level of plot or evident analogy, the tie that brings Estella and Pip together is a spurious mother-benefactor: Miss Havisham. Her name enounces what she offers. Neither Estella's real mother nor Pip's real benefactor, Miss Havisham is false to them both in other less literal ways. Concealed behind this ghostly or "ghastly" (chap. 11) mother, draped in yellowing bridal white, is an authentic father-benefactor: Abel Magwitch. The mystery (or marsh-mist) surrounding his identity is dispelled during the slow denouement of the plot. Estella is the real daughter of Magwitch the criminal, who conceived Pip the gentleman, his no less real though adopted son. This is the hidden tie that binds. Pip's passion for Estella is overtly forbidden and frustrated because she is above his social station and because of the manner of her upbringing by Miss Havisham. But the passion is truly illicit, out of bounds, because of their secret sibling relationship, because a consummation cannot be convened without incest.

This is the source of Estella's lure for Pip, that is to say, for Dickens. In "Creative Writers and Day-Dreaming" Freud speculates about the connection between the life of the writer and his literary productions: "A strong experience in the present awakens in the creative writer a memory of an earlier experience (usually belonging to his childhood) from which there now proceeds a wish which finds its fulfilment in the creative work. The work itself exhibits elements of the recent provoking occasion as well as of the old memory." The life of the writer is then a text, apart from and, yet, a part of his other works. Although Freud's theory need not provide an explanation for the origin of every work of art, what I would suggest is that the riddle of *Great Expectations* may be resolved, the cause of Pip's excessive, seemingly unmotivated guilt may be named, with the help of this borrowed insight. For in the case of Dickens and *Great Expectations* all three factors are present: a childhood experience, an actual experience, and a wish that finds expression, if not fulfilment, in a literary work.

The story is old and often told; it is, in brief, a family romance. Charles Dickens was two years old when he was abandoned, as he saw it, for a younger sibling. He then turned to his sister Fanny, who was only a year older than he, for the succoring love which was suddenly withheld by his real but false mother. For eight years Charles and Fanny seem to have been a separate, self-contained unit within the large Dickens household. Their special closeness lasted until the family moved to London in 1822. Then, at the age of ten, he was abruptly separated from the little sister who was a mother to him. Fanny was accepted as a student at the Royal Academy of Music, and Charles was sent to work in a blacking ware-house. The loss for the child was compounded by the humiliation. Fanny was now to her brother what Estella with the starry jewels in her hair was to the forge-bound Pip: far more than a class apart and still too close by far.

In "A Special Type of Choice of Object Made by Men," Freud ob-serves that "the notion of something irreplaceable, when it is active in the unconscious, frequently appears as broken up into an endless series: endless for the very reason that every surrogate nevertheless fails to pro-vide the desired satisfaction." For Dickens, substitution and loss, love and abandonment gradually locked into a pattern. To the list of mother, sister and Maria Beadnell—the sweetheart who soured and rejected him—other names were added. To recapitulate some of the facts: Mary Hogarth came to live with Charles and Catherine Dickens during the first year of their ill-fated marriage. It was a strange but thoroughly conventional Victorian arrangement, for Mary was Catherine's younger sister. She was also beau-tiful and good, and as Edgar Johnson records in his biography, "[she] made her way more deeply and intimately into Dickens's heart even than either of his sisters." Mary Hogarth died of a sudden illness in Dickens's arms when she was only seventeen. Five years later, Dickens invited his wife's fifteen-year-old sister, Georgina Hogarth, to live with them, and she remained a member of his household even after his wife was no longer welcome there.

The Latin word "textum" denotes web, and in this sense, Dickens's life may indeed be read as a text. He repeatedly spun out of his past the complex of circumstances which both ensnared him in the present and prompted his literary production. The actual experience which closed the circuit between his childhood experience and the writing of *Great Expectations* was Dickens's illicit relationship with Ellen Ternan. She was young enough to have been his older sister or even his mother—had Dickens been a child. In fact he was forty-five and famous, she an aspiring eighteen-year-old actress, when they met. Edgar Johnson writes: "It is inevitable that we should associate Pip's helpless enslavement to Estella with Dickens's passion for Ellen Ternan. Never before had he portrayed a man's love for a woman with such depth or revealed its desperation of compulsive suffering."

Thus, for Dickens, as for Pip, the yearning for the forbidden playmate does not cease with childhood. Its affects are a predominance of seemingly unmotivated guilt and a concomitant masochism. "A sense of guilt," writes Freud, "is invariably the factor that transforms sadism into masochism." Both tendencies are evident as Dickens not only has Estella punished by putting her through the ordeal by marriage to Bentley Drummle, but Pip himself is made to suffer greatly for the folly of loving her. Lure becomes punishment. Again, it is Freud who illuminates this chain of psychic causality: "None of these incestuous loves can avoid the fate of repression. They may succumb to it on the occasion of . . . the unwelcome birth of a new brother or sister (which is felt as faithlessness). . . . At the same time as this process of repression takes place, a sense of guilt appears. . . . it is justified by the persistence of those [incestuous] wishes in the unconscious." Elsewhere, Freud describes the relation between repression and repetition: "the patient does not *remember* anything of what he has forgotten and repressed, but *acts* it out. He reproduces it not as a memory but as an action; he *repeats* it, without, of course, knowing that he is repeating it." On this view, the writing of *Great Expectations* is itself the repetition of a memory that underwent repression. The beautiful Estella is a reproduction or artifact, which may be stretched to say, art-after-the-fact-of-life.

It is in this context that I suggest the following scene be understood. Pip is again in a transport of guilt, while waiting in a coach-office for Estella's arrival in London:

> I consumed the whole time in thinking how strange it was that
> I should be encompassed by all this taint of prison and crime. . . .
> I wished that Wemmick had not met me, or that I had not

yielded to him and gone with him, so that . . . on this day I
might not have had Newgate in my breath and on my clothes. I
beat the prison dust off my feet as I sauntered to and fro, and
I shook it out of my dress, and I exhaled its air from my lungs.
So contaminated did I feel, remembering who was coming that
the coach came quickly after all.

(chap. 32)

The manifest cause of Pip's criminal contamination is his recent tour of
Newgate prison with Wemmick. However, an abrupt relocation or realloca-
tion of guilt occurs in the last sentence, as Pip's sense of contamination becomes diverted and associated with Estella. "So contaminated did I feel,
remembering who was coming" tells all, without knowing what it tells.

In summary: Estella is the incestuous love choice and the cause of
guilt; she is the other who torments the self.

But Estella is also the self-same as Pip. As Richard is a lion and as love
is a red-red rose, so Estella is Pip. What are the grounds for my metaphor?
for this assertion of identity between two distinct characters? That it is so,
Pip himself confirms; although why it should be so, he cannot explain.
Meeting with Estella after a long absence, Pip says that in effect they have
never parted: "it was impossible for me to separate her, in the past or in
the present from the innermost life of my life" (chap. 29). During the
dramatic scene in which Estella announces her decision to marry Bentley
Drummle, she tells Pip that he will get her out of his thoughts "in a week."
In Pip's passionate protests there is a reaffirmation of their consubstantiality:

"Out of my thoughts! You are part of my existence, part of
myself. You have been in every line I have ever read. . . . You
have been the embodiment of every graceful fancy that my
mind has ever become acquainted with. . . . Estella, to the last
hour of my life, you cannot choose but remain part of my
character, part of the little good in me, part of the evil."

(chap. 44)

The question remains: How can Estella be both Pip and not Pip? Here is
Kenneth Burke's description of the pressure that collapses this distinction:
"symbolic incest is often but a roundabout mode of self-engrossment, a
narcissistic independence, quite likely at the decadent end of individualism,
where the poet is but expressing in sexual imagery a pattern of thought
that we might call simply 'communion with the self,' and is giving this
state of mind concrete material body in the imagery of sexual cohabitation

with someone 'of the same substance' as the self." An alternative version of the myth of Narcissus quickly explains: "Narcissus had a twin sister whom he loved, and when she died he used to console himself by looking at his own reflection in the spring as a sort of picture of her."

That Estella is "of the same substance" as Pip may be shown again through the analogical movements of the plot. The proof goes back, as all things tend in *Great Expectations,* to the trials of childhood. Orphaned in infancy, Estella and Pip are raised by "bad" adoptive mothers. Although the abuse of Estella by Miss Havisham is less obvious, its results are as crippling as the mental and physical abuse suffered by Pip at the forge of his undoing, Mrs. Joe Gargery. For Miss Havisham, Estella is a plaything, a toy to be decked in finery and jewels, wound up and set out into the world (from which Miss Havisham has excluded herself) in order to wreak vengeance on men. For Mrs. Joe, Pip is also an object, a means to satisfy the drive for self-aggrandizement and aggression. In image after image, she is described handling Pip as any varied number of things, as almost anything but himself, a child: "She concluded by throwing me—I often served as a connubial missile—at Joe" (chap. 2); "a pint of this mixture [tar-water] . . . was poured down my throat . . . while Mrs. Joe held my head under her arm, as a boot would be held in a bootjack" (chap. 2); "I went upstairs in the dark, with my head tingling—from Mrs. Joe's thimble having played the tambourine upon it, to accompany her last words—" (chap. 2); and "she pounced on me, like an eagle on a lamb, and my face was squeezed into wooden bowls in sinks" (chap. 7).

Etymologically, victim means "beast for sacrifice." Both Estella and Pip are victimized—dehumanized by their false mothers and made over into objects—after their true mothers have disappeared or died. This is, of course, a strategy of fairy tales in which the ambivalence toward the mother is resolved by splitting her into two characters: the good but defunct mother and the wicked active stepmother. But children learn well the lessons of their use, and as they begin to master their worlds, they try to abuse others as they have been abused themselves. The victim turns into a victimizer. The measure of Pip's moral transformation is his treatment of Joe Gargery: the simple blacksmith, who loves and cares for Pip, becomes the object of Pip's shame. Pip learns to be a snob at Satis House, the Havisham family residence, and this is perhaps why snobbery becomes the locus of so much guilt in *Great Expectations.* It is transferred from its cause (Estella) to one of its effects (Joe). Snobbery is an easier crime to acknowledge than the wish to cohabit with someone of the same substance as the self.

The dehumanization that takes place within the central protagonists of *Great Expectations* is exteriorized most strangely in insect form. Franz Kafka's great metamorphosis of Gregor Samsa into a beetle, an allegorical extension of the underlying metaphor, "Gregor Samsa is a dung beetle," is comparable to Dickens's less explicit but no less fantastic metaphor for the spiritual condition of his characters: the spider. Here is the description of the home, sweet home for many spiders in *Great Expectations*, Miss Havisham's wedding cake:

> it was so heavily overhung with cobwebs that its form was quite undistinguishable; and, as I looked along the yellow expanse out of which I remember its seeming to grow, like a black fungus, I saw speckled-legged spiders with blotchy bodies running home to it, and running out from it, as if some circumstance of the greatest public importance had just transpired in the spider community. . . .
>
> "What do you think that is?" she asked me, again pointing with her stick; "that, where those cobwebs are?"
>
> "I can't guess what it is, ma'am."
>
> "It's a great cake. A bride-cake. Mine!"
>
> (chap. 11)

The identification is as clear as the cake in possession. Festooned with cobwebs and crawling with spiders, the cake belongs to and denotes Miss Havisham. According to Van Ghent's formulation of the "law of conversion of spirit into matter" in the Dickens world: "the decayed wedding cake offers a supplementary image of the necrosis that is taking place in the human agent," and "there is a great deal of 'inner life,' transposed to other forms than that of character; . . . for instance, to the symbolic activity of the speckled-legged spiders."

This interpretation avoids rather than explains the significance of the spider. Why spiders and not, for instance, swarms of ants? What aspects of the "inner life" does the spider represent? Karl Abraham already noted long ago that the spider is the symbol of the mother, the bad mother whose embrace inflicts injury and death. Erich Neumann found the spider related to "the Great Mother in her function of fixation and not releasing what aspires toward independence and freedom," and therefore net, noose and spider with its ensnaring arms are typical symbols of "the Feminine's terrible power to bind and fetter." To the noose it will be necessary to return, but for the moment, let us view the family seat of the spider-woman in *Great Expectations*, the ironically named Satis House, as it is described by Pip:

> Within a quarter of an hour we came to Miss Havisham's house, which was of old brick, and dismal, and had a great many iron bars to it. Some of the windows had been walled up; of those that remained, all the lower were rustily barred. There was a court-yard in front and that was barred; so, we had to wait.
>
> (chap. 8)

And while Pip "waits," I would like to take a detour through other contexts in which the varied mother functions of the spider are explicitly enacted.

An elaborate instance of the negative capacity of the feminine is to be found in Jeremias Gotthelf's novella *The Black Spider*. The story of this spider, a medieval plague legend, is placed within a realistic setting. An old grandfather tells a circle of rapt listeners about the origins of a hideous black spider, an intimate of the devil, who centuries earlier had roamed and ravaged the countryside, bringing black plague and death everywhere. The spider was born of a kiss which sealed a pact between the devil and a bold, proud woman named Christine, who agreed to deliver an unbaptized child to the devil. Here is the moment of conception:

> Then the sharp mouth touched her face, and it seemed to her as if the heat from a red-hot spit were pouring through her veins, and yellow lightning flashed between them, showing Christine the Green Man's face in a devilish grin, and thunder rolled over her as if Heaven had burst. . . . there was a roaring in her head as if a mighty river were plunging overtowering black rocks into a black gulf beneath.

Jeremias Gotthelf is the pseudonym of Albert Bitzius, who was a pastor in the Swiss country parish of Lützelflüh. And there is a strange admixture of God's unholy fires, of hell and passion, in the heat which pours through Christine's veins at the touch of the devil. At that moment Christine loses her immortal soul and later her body, too, as the spot on her cheek which bore the devil's kiss begins to grow: "the black spot spread and spread, dark stripes crawled out of it, and near her mouth a little swelling seemed to be rising on the spot." At a later stage: "Distinct legs ran out of it, short hairs grew on it, gleaming spots and stripes came out on its back, and the little swelling turned into a head which glittered venomously as if from two eyes." The more the spider grows, the less woman there is. Finally, Christine disintegrates completely and turns into a spider: "Christine shrank together in a rain of sparks with a horrible hiss like wool in fire, like chalk in water, shrank down to the black, huge, swollen, hideous Spider in her face." Christine denies her essential humanity by consigning a child to the devil and so loses all human form. In keeping with the tradition of realism within which Dickens writes, the content-form relation is less direct in *Great Expectations* than in *The Black Spider*. Nevertheless, the course of Miss Havisham's action is remarkably analogous to Christine's, for she sells a child to the devils within herself and is radically altered in the process.

To go back yet further, the prototype for the conversion of a once proud and beautiful woman into a spider is Arachne. In "Muiopotomos: or the Fate of the Butterflie" (1590), Edmund Spenser describes the fate of the "presumptuous damzel" who rashly challenged the goddess Minerva to a contest of weaving skill. Although Spenser's Arachne weaves a "goodly work, full fit for kingly bowres," she is defeated by the greater art of the goddess. Arachne's pride and self-love then changes into spleen and hate. Content becomes form, within is turned out, as Arachne is transformed into a spider:

> Yet did she inly fret, and felly burne,
> And all her blood to poysonous rancor turne:
> . . . .
> She grew to hideous shape of dryrihed
> Pined with griefe of follie late repented:
> Eftsoones her white streight legs were altered
> To crooked crawling shankes of marrowe empted,
> And her faire face to fowle and loathsome hewe,
> And her fine corpes to a bag of venim grewe.
>   ("Muiopotomos," 11. 344–52)

An analogous process seems to take place within Miss Havisham after her jilting, an event which is anterior to Pip's story and motivates her desire for vengeance on men. In the narrative present the metamorphosis of Miss Havisham is represented by the many spiders running in and out of the wedding cake which is an image of her thwarted expectations of nourishment. This conspicuous failure of consumption—the cake that was not eaten, the marriage that was not consummated—brings out the "ravenous intensity" (chap. 29), the oral aggression or spider hunger in Miss Havisham.

In Spenser's poem, the spirit of spite which transforms the mother also infests Aragnoll, her spider son, a "cursed creature, mindfull of that olde / Enfested grudge, the which his mother felt." Aragnoll becomes the instrument of Arachne's revenge, the male extension and expression of her malice. This corresponds with what Karl Abraham found in his analytic work on spider phobias and fantasies: the spider may represent, on the one hand, the masculine mother who possesses a destructive male organ and, on the other, the sexually desirable but dangerous mother, contact with whom signifies incest and death. In the final lines of "Muiopotomos" both hands appear to work as the hungry spider deftly falls upon the hapless butterfly:

> he seized greedelie
> On the resistless pray, and with fell spight,
> Under the left wing stroke his weapon slie
> Into his heart, that his deepe groning spright
> In bloodie streames forth fled into the aire,
> His bodie left the spectacle of care.

Some further special effects of the dangerous masculine component within the destructive mother are dramatized in Heinrich Mann's *Professor Unrat* (1905). The central character of Mann's novel is Professor Rath, nicknamed Unrat or filth by his pupils. The professor, "Old Mud" in the English translation, is explicitly compared to a spider only twice, briefly in the novel: "Old Mud tiptoes about among the undergarments lying on the floor and furniture like a great black spider, waiting to snatch with his crooked limbs"; and later "How ghastly the man looked! Something between a spider and a cat." However, the resemblance is sustained throughout, most frequently by references to the professor's "poisonous [giftig] glances," and also to his "crooked fingers," and the "streets he crept about."

Humiliated for years by his pupils, by his status among the townspeople, Professor Rath decides to trap or "catch" them all. The rod of his wrath is Rosa. Rath fashions Rosa, the dissolute young cabaret singer whom he marries, like a honeyed trap: "her admirers would be kept waiting while Old Mud helped her to dress and make up." He moulds her mind and educates her manners, always with one obsessive end in view: "He began to dream of the boys whom she should have brought to ruin," and "[Rosa] drove the crowd of her admirers day and night in any direction she pleased, as if throwing a stick for dogs to fetch. And Old Mud watched it all with his ironical smile, rubbing his hands with delight."

Similarly, Miss Havisham fashions Estella in the spirit of her own defor-
mity, "taking an impressionable child to mould into the form that her wild
resentment, spurned affection, and wounded pride found vengeance in"
(chap. 49). But Estella is initially innocent, drawn into Miss Havisham's
web as a child without choice; Rosa is already corrupted, in the full bloom
of her sensuality, when Rath meets her and directs her natural inclinations
towards his own end.

Through its double meaning the phrase "towards his own end" points
to an involution which is central to both novels. The nexus of events,
which the professor spins to catch others, finally folds in upon itself and
entangles the victimizers: "His obsession was always too concerned with
the ruin of others to take heed for his own interests, and from the evil they
[Rath and Rosa] wrought sprang their own undoing." Miss Havisham,
too, is caught in her own trap, hoist by the petard she helped to make. In
both novels the practice of malice proves that entrapment and self-entrapment
are interdependent. The spider is in some deep and ineluctable sense a fly,
caught in the dialectic of the web, the circular route of the victim—who
would be victimizer—who becomes victim again.

That Arachne breeds an Aragnoll is within the nature of things. That
Estella gradually acquires a family resemblance to her adoptive mother
impresses itself upon Pip in a moment of remarkable perspicacity:

> In some of her looks and gestures there was that tinge of
> resemblance to Miss Havisham, which may often be noticed to
> have been acquired by children from grown persons with whom
> they have been much associated and secluded.
>
> (chap. 29)

The occasion for Pip's observation is a reunion with Estella at Satis House
many years after the day of their first meeting when he saw her walking on
the casks in the brewery yard. In that scene, Dorothy Van Ghent observes,
Dickens superimposes onto the image of a young girl engaged in "an
enchanting ritual dance of childhood" another image, namely, the suicidal
figure of Miss Havisham, hanging by the neck from the brewery beam.
Van Ghent cites this example of Dickens's use of montage effects as
evidence that "one implies the other," that Miss Havisham and Estella are
"not two characters but a single one, a continuum." This argument taken
a step further would suggest that the same insect which represents Miss
Havisham is, by association and contamination, the emblem of Estella's
condition. In brief, if Miss Havisham is a spider, then Estella is a spider,
too. There is a convergence of identities here as in metaphor: Estella is

Miss Havisham. But, I have already said, Estella is Pip. It must follow, then, that Pip is Miss Havisham.

The equation between Miss Havisham and Pip is confirmed by hanging. Scaffolds and spiders connect, or at least I believe they do, in *Great Expectations.* For in addition to his hallucinatory visions of Miss Havisham hanging from her neck, Pip repeatedly sentences himself to death by hanging. Moreover, the noose (like the web or net) is an arachnocentric symbol. Not only the notion of entrapment, the "function of ensnaring," as Neumann has suggested, links these elements; the literal image of a spider suspended by a thread also provides strong visual grounds for this connection.

Pip sees Miss Havisham hanging on two separate occasions: the first, already mentioned, occurs after his initial humiliating visit to Satis House as a young boy; the second, at the end of his last visit as a young man, when he already knows how cruelly Miss Havisham has used and deceived him. On both occasions, the visions are clearly derivative forms of Pip's rage and desire for vengeance. Thus the passions Miss Havisham provokes are a reflection of the fires that both energize and enervate her and that ultimately destroy her. She makes of Pip a mirror; or, as she puts it to him, with belated regrets for what she has done: "I saw in you a looking-glass that showed me what I once felt myself" (chap. 49).

The two scenes in which scaffolds present themselves and beckon personally to Pip, at the Town Hall trial and during Wopsle's representation of George Barnwell ("I was happily hanged"), have already been cited as examples of Pip's sense of guilt and need for punishment, a need actuated by means of Estella. Yet even before these scenes take place, Pip envisions himself as sentenced to hang. The night of his fateful first encounter with Magwitch, after he has agreed to steal food and a file for the convict, Pip dreams of drifting down river to the prison ships across the marshes: "a ghostly pirate [called] out to me through a speaking-trumpet, as I passed the gibbet-station, that I had better come ashore and be hanged there at once, and not put it off" (chap. 2). But then, it may be argued, the call for punishment can only be attributed to Pip's contact and identification with Magwitch. At this early stage he has not even met Estella or Miss Havisham, and so there can be no connection between Pip's feelings of guilt and his oedipal longings. Against this contention it must be remembered that the one who gives us this account of events as the child saw and felt them is the adult narrator and that the second Pip casts a shadow which cannot be detached from the substance of the first.

An exterior referent is helpful at this point. In an essay "On Spiders,

Hanging and Oral Sadism," Richard Sterba reports the case history of a young man who made several attempts to commit suicide by hanging. Although it became apparent that these attempts were manifestations of an identification with his mother who was seriously ill, the patient's preference for the noose seemed inexplicable. This in itself might not be so interesting, were it not that the young man also had bad dreams. The following dream occurred shortly after he became aware of his hostility to his father who died several years before the analysis began: "great spidery monsters," orally threatening creatures, appeared in the sky and then came down to earth, causing much death. Sterba suggests that behind the spiders in the sky is hidden the figure of the father who is in heaven. To this constellation I would add another, the mother who is behind the spiders here on earth.

What I would like now to extend is a series of equations in which seemingly opposed characters become interchangeable. In this sense it will not matter of which character I speak: Miss Havisham, Estella or Pip. They are all one and the same. But in order to complete the assertion of these identities, one more character remains to be drawn into the web: Bentley Drummle, nicknamed the Spider. Critics, such as Moynahan and Wentersdorf, have suggested that Drummle is bound to Pip as his double. Wentersdorf stresses their orientation towards what I would call the self-same object: "Above all, Drummle's dogged pursuit of Estella . . . is a sinister parody of Pip's despairing attempts to win Estella's love." Drummle's type is immediately cast by Mr. Jaggers, Pip's acute London lawyer and an expert criminologist. "Who's the spider?" Jaggers asks Pip when Drummle comes to dinner, "The blotchy, sprawly, sulky fellow" (chap. 26). The description reinforces the family resemblance between Drummle and the "speckled-legged spiders with blotchy bodies" crawling around Miss Havisham's wedding cake. Relatedly, the metaphoric reference to the "Newgate cobwebs" which surround Pip (chap. 37) links him in the equational chain with Bentley the Spider and Miss Havisham.

On what grounds, however, other than the arachnoid connection can one equate Estella with Bentley Drummle? The answer, again provided by Freud, is on the grounds of moral masochism, "a need which is satisfied by punishment and suffering." Why does this craving arise? Because of an "unconscious sense of guilt" which Freud further defines as "a need for punishment at the hands of a parental power." But why should the self seek such punishment? Because in Freud's view: "Conscience and morality have arisen through the overcoming, the desexualization, of the Oedipus complex; but through moral masochism morality becomes sexualized once more, the Oedipus complex is revived." The gratification of this sense of guilt requires that a constant level of suffering be maintained. "The true masochist," writes Freud in a finely subversive allusion, "always turns his cheek whenever he has a chance of receiving a blow."

In marrying Bentley Drummle, Estella makes a deliberate, morally masochistic choice. "It is my own act," she tells Pip. For Estella, Drummle is not an alter ego, but rather an exteriorization of the function of the super-ego: the punishing, parental authority of conscience within the self. What Estella seeks and finds in marriage is a spider surrogate, not a displacement but a replacement for the deformative influence on her childhood. Drummle's physical brutality is an extension of the abuses practiced by Miss Havisham. Thus Estella repeats her past. Ironically, in choosing Drummle, she seems to fulfil the role assigned to her by Miss Havisham: she breaks Pip's heart. But by punishing Pip, Estella is actually punishing herself, which means to say, she is punishing them all. The true smiter is indeed none other than the self.

According to the published version of *Great Expectations,* Pip and Estella survive the dangerous situation in which they have placed themselves. Bentley Drummle dies by accident: "consequent on his ill-treatment of a horse." Miss Havisham dies by fire: the flames leap out of her hearth, or is it perhaps her heart? But Pip and Estella emerge, purged and transformed by their suffering. Reconstituted as one, they leave Satis House forever behind them: "we went out of the ruined place." There is a neatness to this conclusion which seems a kind of wish-fulfilment. First one sins, then one is punished, then one is born again pure and whole.

According to Dickens's earlier, darker conclusion (which he altered at the request of Bulwer-Lytton), Estella and Pip meet, recognize each other as fellow victims and sufferers, and separate again forever. The implication seems that no amount of punishment is ever enough to expurgate the sense of guilt which is man's, or some men's, fate. Interestingly, most critics have preferred the original version to the final happy ending. Julian Moynahan exemplifies this tendency when he writes: "the cruelly beautiful original ending of the novel remains the only possible 'true' ending. Estella and Pip face each other across the insurmountable barrier of lost innocence." This preference derives perhaps from the sense that the unhappy ending denotes most truly the inner reality of Dickens's own experience, the burden of guilt which he bore within himself and brought to what he wrote, and perhaps, if one may so presume, the first ending also corresponds most closely to the truth of an experience which the readers know without knowing in themselves.

NED LUKACHER

The Dickensian "No Thoroughfare"

[Dickens] knew all about the back streets behind Holborn, the courts and alleys of the Borough, the shabby sidling streets of the remoter suburbs, the crooked little alleys of the City, the dark and oozy whays of the waterside.
　　　　　　　—GEORGE AUGUSTUS SALA, *Charles Dickens: An Essay*

Le vrai Paris est naturellement une cité noire, boueuse, maleolens, étriquée dans ses rues étroites . . . fourmillant d'impasses, de culs-de-sac, d'allées mystérieuses, de labyrinthes qui vous mènent chez le diable.
　　　　　　　—PAUL-ERNST DE RATTIER, *Paris n'existe pas*

Walking for walking's sake may be as highly laudable and exemplary a thing as it is held to be by those who practise it. My objection is that it stops the brain.
　　　　　　　—MAX BEERBOHM, "Going Out for a Walk"

If I couldn't walk fast and far, I should explode and perish.
　　　　　　　—CHARLES DICKENS, to John Forster

Walter Benjamin's interest in Dickens seems to have extended no further than a reading of G. K. Chesterton's classic study, *Charles Dickens* (1906). He cites it in both "The Paris of the Second Empire in Baudelaire" and in the *Passage Work*. He is particularly interested in what Chesterton calls Dickens's "realistic principle—the principle that the most fantastic thing of all is often the precise fact." Dickens's power to endow inanimate objects with life creates what Chesterton calls an "elvish kind of realism," "the unbearable realism of a dream." Chesterton's next sentence must have

From *Primal Scenes: Literature, Philosophy, Psychoanalysis.* © 1986 by Cornell University. Cornell University Press, 1986.

281

particularly struck Benjamin: "And this kind of realism can only be gained by walking dreamily in a place; it cannot be gained by walking observantly."

Benjamin is not interested in Chesterton's larger thesis regarding Dickens's experience in the streets, but it is important for us to turn to that thesis, for it contains in outline the essential features of my reading of Dickens. The difficult years of Dickens's childhood, writes Chesterton, "may have given him many moral and mental wounds, from which he never recovered. But they gave him the key of the street."

Dickens's childhood suffering has, of course, become legendary in the annals of literary biography. The victim of a demanding mother and a weak, spendthrift father, Dickens found himself at the age of twelve ignominiously employed at Warren's Blacking Warehouse, where, much to the amusement of passersby and much to his own everlasting shame, he was forced to use blacking to waterproof buckets in the warehouse window, a task at which he eventually became quite proficient. Left to his own devices at so early an age, the young Dickens took to the streets. The origin of what Chesterton calls his "eerie realism," the power to "vitalize some dark or dull corner of London," is surely to be found here in the uncanny alienation he must have felt as a young boy wandering to and from the infernal warehouse, alienated to the point where the streets became a kind of home—a frightful place, to be sure, but a reprieve from both the agony of work and the despair of life with his family. Early on he came to know very well what his disciple, George Sala, calls "the crooked little alleys of the City, the dark and oozy whays of the waterside." This was indeed the neighborhood through which he had to pass to and from the site of his shame. It was in this underworld, Chesterton suggests (in a passage cited by Benjamin), that Dickens discovered a kind of utopia: "The street at night is a great house locked up. But Dickens had, if ever man had, the key of the street. . . . He could open the inmost door of his house—the door that leads onto the secret passage which is lined with houses and roofed with stars."

It is curious that since the phrase "the key of the street" is Chesterton's leitmotif, he does not acknowledge that it is also the title of the first article George Sala published in Dickens's magazine, *Household Words*, in 1851. It was Sala's keen observation of the streets that first attracted Dickens to him; Dickens must have recognized how well Sala understood his own work to that point. From "The Key of the Street" to *Charles Dickens: An Essay* (1870), Sala was doubtless the first to intuit the key to the master's world, and this insight makes him perhaps the most interesting of the "Dickens men." Like Sala, Chesterton recognized the streets as the "key" that opens the "secret passage" into the Dickens world. Like the arcades of the Palais-Royal, which were demolished in 1828 but which announced the phantasmagoric life-style of the Second Empire, the streets of London that Dickens experienced during the 1820s (he was born in 1812) announced the phantasmagoric London that he would construct throughout his novelistic career.

The primary sources of our understanding of Dickens's childhood experiences are *David Copperfield* (1850) and the autobiographical fragment that the author gave to John Forster in 1847 and that Forster published in the first chapter of his *Life of Dickens* (1872–74): "That I suffered in secret, and that I suffered exquisitely, no one ever knew but I. How much I suffered, it is, as I have said already, utterly beyond my power to tell. No man's imagination can overstep the reality." At the age of thirty-five, twenty-three years after the fact, Dickens makes an extraordinary admission: "I often forget in my dreams that I have a dear wife and children; even that I am a man; and wander desolately back to that time of my life." He confesses that until his first child could speak, he could not bring himself to return to the neighborhood around Warren's. Since that child, Charlie, was born in January 1837, it was not until perhaps 1839 or 1840 that Dickens was able to return to the back streets along the Strand near Hungerford Market. And then, in a statement Benjamin enables us to understand fully, Dickens writes that it was not until "the very nature of the ground had changed" that he "had the courage to go back to the place where my servitude began." Only after the neighborhood itself had been renovated could Dickens bring himself to tread such haunted ground. Roughly, then, it must have been during the period between the completion of *Nicholas Nickleby* and the beginning of the abortive *Master Humphrey's Clock* that Dickens began to wander the back streets at night. Interestingly, the renovation of the dilapidated wharfside neighborhood coincides not only with Dickens's return to the streets but also with a new maturity and complexity in his writing. The 1847 fragment continues: "In my walks at night I have walked there often, since then, and by degrees I have come to write this. It does not seem a tithe of what I might have written, or of what I meant to write."

It is once again Benjamin who helps us grasp the relation between these compulsive walks and the problem of artistic creativity. It is precisely in conjunction with the problem of "the overtaxing of the productive person in the name of a principle, the principle of 'creativity,' " that Benjamin links Baudelaire and Dickens: "This overtaxing is all the more dangerous because as it fetters the self-esteem of the productive person, it

effectively guards the interests of the social order that is hostile to him."
Benjamin regards Dickens's "steady peregrinations" and Baudelaire's effort "to capture the streets" as inhibiting or repressive activities, compulsions that over-burden the artist, at once deflect and deplete his energies,
and thus prevent him from directing those energies toward a concentrated
probing of the social order. It is as though the artist is exiled into the
streets by a demand for creativity that paradoxically, but very effectively,
succeeds only in thwarting his true creative potential.

Benjamin's point seems to ring particularly true with regard to Dickens. Coerced as a child into an anxiety-producing cycle of overproduction,
Dickens the adult, once again compelled to please the crowd, once again
returns to the streets that he has always identified with such feelings of
crisis. He is certain of only two things, that he must write and that he
must walk. Dickens's primal scene was thus perhaps reinforced by his
artistic dilemma. The demand for something new becomes so overwhelming that his only recourse is to flee the study and rush into the street. But
for Dickens the experience of the street is not simply an escape from
creativity but rather the scene of his most difficult memories. For Dickens
it seems that there was little occasion to escape either the burden of
overproduction or the anxiety of his own childhood. He was indeed
caught in a vicious circle, consumed by the obsessive pattern that indissol-
ubly joined his nightwalks and his artistic production. In the public readings, which became his obsession in the 1860s and which finally killed
him, one can see a kind of synthesis of these two deadly activities: he not
only creates directly before his audience but must also run frantically from
one lecture hall to another. It is as though in deciding against all advice
and common sense to throw himself madly into his public readings,
Dickens was simply trying to bring to an end as speedily as possible an
insidious process that had begun as early as 1824 and that had been fully
articulated by 1839–40. The streets are, therefore, the site both of Dickens's mystification as the place where his energies are at once generated
and contained, and of his destruction as the place where he is consumed,
devoured, eaten alive.

Benjamin links Baudelaire to Poe as well as to Dickens in his compulsion to walk the streets all night long. Benjamin does not suspect, however,
that in this respect Poe is more closely linked to Dickens than to Baudelaire.
Of Poe's "The Man of the Crowd" (1840), Benjamin writes that "the
crowd is not only the newest asylum of outlaws; it is also the latest
narcotic for those abandoned." In Poe's story we follow a mysterious old
man, whom Poe calls "the type and genius of deep crime," as he rushes

madly through the city. After having followed him throughout the night, the narrator abandons his effort to understand the mystery that the old man seems to incarnate: the narrator's epigraph for the old man is: *"Er lasst sich nicht lesen"* (He does not permit himself to be read). Benjamin does not consider the possibility that Poe's confrontation with the mysterious unreadability of the night-walker may itself be a figure of Poe's confrontation with the text of Dickens. As Poe was writing this story, he was reading installments of *Master Humphrey's Clock* and *The Old Curiosity Shop;* he published reviews of these works as he had of Dickens's earlier *Sketches by Boz.* The old man in "The Man of the Crowd" combines elements from each of these texts: the sordidness of "The Drunkard's Tale" in *Boz* and the obsessive nocturnal peregrinations of both Master Humphrey and Little Nell's grandfather. Poe was also doubtlessly influenced by the madman's tale in *Pickwick Papers.*

The Poe-Dickens relationship has yet to be fully analyzed. When it is, we may discover that Poe, like Sala and Chesterton but before either of them, saw into the very essence of the Dickens world. Dickens met Poe in Philadelphia in 1842 and tried, unsuccessfully, to find an English publisher for his two-volume *Tales of the Grotesque and Arabesque.* Poe's untimely death in 1849 may have seemed to Dickens in retrospect a more horribly compressed version of his own fate as an overburdened artist. Poe was, in any case, in Dickens's thoughts in 1868 when, in the course of the American reading tour that contributed decisively to his death two years later, he paid a visit to Poe's aunt, Mrs. Clemm, in Richmond and gave her a hundred dollars. Dickens must have known that "The Man of the Crowd" had proved strangely prophetic of his own fate throughout the 1850s and 1860s, and that he too would never "pass from out of the turmoil of that street."

Benjamin describes the arcades of the Palais-Royal, whose most famous literary representation is in Balzac's *Illusions perdues* (1837), as being at once arcadia and inferno, utopia and the underworld, a fairyland for those who could enjoy the goods sold there, a nightmare for those who could not. Those wooden arcades were the forerunners of the glass and iron arcades or *passages* that sprang up all over Paris in the mid- and later nineteenth century. Inspired by Louis Aragon's surrealist meditation, *Le Paysan de Paris* (1926), in which Aragon discusses how his experience of the *Passage de l'Opéra* was heightened when he learned that this landmark would soon be demolished, Benjamin saw in the image of the *passage* the crystallization of all his thinking. "For it is only now that the pickaxe threatens them," writes Aragon, "that they have become the sanctuaries of a cult of the ephemeral, the ghostly landscape of forbidden pleasures and professions, incomprehensible yesterday and gone tomorrow." In these glass-covered palaces of consumerism, these "human aquariums," as Aragon calls them, Benjamin saw a surreptitious return to the subterranean, submarine Paris, the ancient, chthonian Paris that was still lodged in the swamp of the Seine valley. What Aragon regarded as the "abysmal, unfathomable" effect of the greenish hue created by the tinted glass, which he suggestively compares to the "glimmer of a leg beneath a suddenly raised skirt," becomes in Benjamin the abyss of prehistory itself, the repository of all the experiences that conventional history invariably omits. For Benjamin the *passages* become the place where modernity disappears in the abyss of prehistory. The *Passage de l'Opéra* was also, as Aragon notes, [Auguste] Blanqui's Paris address.

Dickens recalls in the 1847 fragment that Warren's Blacking was not far from the Lowther Arcade in the Strand. Inspired by Benjamin's *Passage Work,* Johann Geist has catalogued all the nineteenth-century arcades. He cites a history of London toy shops that describes the Lowther Arcade, which was demolished in 1902, as "an Aladdin fairy palace crowded with all the glories and wonders a child's fancy can conceive." Between Warren's Blacking and the Lowther Arcade, the twelve-year-old Dickens must have suffered exquisitely indeed. The "secret passage" of Dickens's primal scene runs from the workhouse to a child's fairyland. The task of reading Dickens is the task of locating that "secret passage" in each of his texts, and of rewriting the history that history always forgets.

Baudelaire's term for the artist's resistance to remembrance, and for the negativity that remembrance entails, is *spleen*. Of Baudelaire's opposition, *spleen et idéal,* Benjamin writes: "The *idéal* supplies the power of remembrance; the *spleen* musters the multitude of the seconds against it." In blocking the restorative work of remembrance, spleen locks one into the repetition compulsion. Baudelaire cannot continue the work of remembrance within the context of his own experience of history and must therefore seek redemption in an otherworldly version of prehistory. Proust, however, fares better: "The fact that Proust's restorative will remains within the limits of earthly existence, whereas Baudelaire's transcends it, may be regarded as symptomatic of the incomparably more elemental and powerful counterforces that Baudelaire faced." For Benjamin, Baudelaire's experience of spleen registers the burden of historical alienation, a burden so onerous that Baudelaire is finally driven out of history altogether, though not without leaving behind some "scattered fragments of genuine historical experience." In Baudelaire's experience the work of remembrance is inseparable from the cutting edge of Time, *le Temps,* whose devouring energies, in the form of spleen, consume every effort by the poet to remain in history, to seek a literal truth. The poet is finally devoured by Time, cut off from history, swallowed by the allegorical figurations that sweep away all his efforts to remember and to constitute a moment of "genuine historical experience." Of the Baudelairean image, Barbara Johnson writes: "In order to work, the figure must forget, kill, erase, the literal meaning it is supposed to derive from." Following a logic very similar to Benjamin's, Johnson's deconstructive reading of Baudelaire retraces the path of Baudelaire's flight from history into allegory. It is ultimately Time itself that figures the consuming, irresistible power of allegory. It is, paradoxically, the figure of Time that negates the possibility of historical experience or literal meaning. And it is to the figure of devouring Time, set loose on the dark streets of mid-nineteenth-century London, that we turn now in our reading of Dickens.

Dickens announces at the beginning of *Master Humphrey's Clock* that he hopes "to beguile time from the heart of time itself." While Humphrey appears to be making only a clever allusion to his habit of offering up a new tale every week from "the piles of dusty papers" that he keeps in the case of his grandfather clock, the 1847 fragment suggests how much more was at stake in Dickens's relation to time in 1839–40. Dickens originally planned to have Humphrey narrate the so-called *Giant Chronicles.* "Nothing," writes Chesterton, "could have been nearer the heart of Dickens than his great Gargantuan conception of Gog and Magog telling London legends to each other all through the night." The two fourteen-foot statues of the giants in the Guildhall were to come to life at night and tell stories of events they had witnessed in centuries past. Though this plan was soon abandoned, Dickens's account of his novelistic objectives is revealing: he wants "to cheat [the hours] of their heaviness," "to scatter a few slight flowers in the Old Mower's path," and to slow "the tread of Time." This passage, read against the horizon of the 1847 fragment, shows that it is clearly Time itself that Dickens hopes somehow to mediate, avoid, or deflect. *Master Humphrey's Clock* is Dickens's first, and understandably abortive, effort to master the memory of what he calls "the slow agony" of his youth. It is no wonder that he had to abandon the project. The wonder is that he had the courage to confront it so directly in the first place. In the future he would be more cautious.

Dickens met Carlyle in 1840. The question of this relationship is a complex one that has not been reduced by the numerous studies on the subject. My impression, however, is that Dickens's fascination with Carlyle is responsible for much of what Marx would call Dickens's political "mystery-mongering." The formative influence of Carlyle's reactionary politics upon a generation of British liberals is one of the most intriguing subjects in the history of Victorian ideology. Dickens's radical political posturing during the early 1840s is unquestionably the upshot of his misreading of Carlyle. Carlyle's coolness to Dickens, which Dickens never understood, is itself a good indication of his suspicion of the younger man's effort to translate his right-wing revolution into a watered-down blend of utopian socialism and paternalistic liberalism.

I will return to some of these questions in the context of Carlyle's response to *Dombey and Son*. Here, however, my interest in Dickens's relationship with Carlyle is limited to a solitary passage from the latter's masterpiece *Sartor Resartus* (1833), for it is from this passage that Dickens, who claimed to know Carlyle's work better than anyone else, probably derived the figure of Saturn-Chronos, or Time, a figure that would play such a prominent role in many of his novels. "It continues ever true," proclaims Carlyle's Teufelsdröckh, "that Saturn, or Chronos, or what we call *Time,* devours all his children. . . . Me, however, as a son of Time, unhappier than some others, was Time threatening to eat quite prematurely." In the devouring jaws of Saturn, Dickens found the perfect figure for his post-1839 experience of remembrance. For from then on, he too felt that he was about to be devoured by his past. Moreover, as we will soon see, he uses the figure of Saturn to describe his experience of the streets, to endow the inanimate streets with an uncanny, monstrous life. For Dickens, the "Agenbite of Inwit," the gnawing memories of his shameful victimage as a child are figured in this most archaic of images. In his novels Saturn becomes a dialectical image in which the crisis of alienation in the modern city is mixed with elements of prehistory. The melancholy image of Saturn, which had fascinated Benjamin in his *Trauerspiel* book, becomes in Dickens an image of the prehistory of the nineteenth century.

Let us take a step back to *Nicholas Nickleby* (1839). The prime mover of the plot is the moneylender, Ralph Nickleby, whose Carlylean motto is "Time *is* money." How literally Dickens means this is most obvious in the vision that Ralph's secretary has of his master swallowing "one of every English coin." It is Ralph's rapacity that drives his nephew Nicholas and his impoverished family into the streets. As a kind of latter-day Saturn, Ralph's throat is of the utmost interest to Dickens. When Ralph hesitates as he hypocritically blesses the niece whom he is at the same time trying to prostitute to one of his debauched clients, Dickens writes: "The blessing seemed to stick in the throat, as if it were not used to the thoroughfare, and didn't know the way out." Not knowing one's way out is indeed the basic problem of *Nicholas Nickleby,* and one that applies as much to Dickens's plot construction as to his imagery. Having carefully constructed a labyrinth from which Nicholas and his sister have absolutely no possibility of escaping, Dickens introduces the utopian *deus ex machina* of the Cheeryble brothers, which gives the novel's conclusion an entirely supplementary and fortuitous character. The dark center of the labyrinth and the true conclusion to the novel are reached when, following the villainous Sir Mulberry Hawk's murder (in a duel) of his newly reformed protégé, thus ending any hope that the Nicklebys might escape Hawk's grasp, Nicholas wends his way through London's sorriest neighborhoods. We should note that this occurs in chapter 53, which was published in the seventeenth installment in August 1839—that is, on the cusp of the author's *crise de conscience* of 1839–40. With Hawk still a menace, and with all hope apparently gone of ever possessing his beloved Madeline, Nicholas, after a sleepless night, "paced the streets and listlessly looked round on the gradually increasing bustle and preparation for the day." It is then that he sees those who "died in soul, and had no chance of life," those who are led toward terrible ends "by circumstances darkly curtaining their very cradles' heads." It is here amidst the byways of the poor and the wretched that we can glimpse the primal scene of *Nicholas Nickleby.* "But youth is not prone to contemplate the darkest side of a picture it can shift at will." Soon all obstacles to the family's happiness are overcome.

There is another moment in the text that serves as a counterblast to the utopian conclusion. The dialectical image in *Nicholas Nickleby* is to be found in the description of Manchester Buildings, the apartment house where Nicholas goes for an unsuccessful job interview with a Member of Parliament. Dickens transforms this building into the phantasmagorical figure of an insatiable Saturn. The remarkable edifice lies in "the ancient city of Westminster," in "a narrow and dirty region." The most curious feature of this lodging house for parliamentarians is that its architecture strangely causes every sound to reverberate as it makes its way to the solitary entrance of the building. Whenever there is "a gust of wind sweeping across the water which washes the Buildings' feet," it blows every sound, be it the continual "rattling of latch-keys" or an MP "practising the morrow's speech," toward the structure's "awkward mouth." One might imagine that as a parliamentary reporter Dickens himself had had occasion to call upon an MP in such a building. Nothing that goes into the Manchester Buildings can get out by advancing but only be retreating. The edifice constitutes a figure of the ontological impasse that characterizes the novel in general. The Manchester Buildings, like *Nicholas Nickleby*, is a "no thoroughfare" that "leads to nothing beyond itself." Like all of Dickens's saturnine imagery, the Manchester Buildings is a figure for the infinite figurality of the Dickens world:

> All the livelong day there is a grinding of organs and clashing and clanging of little boxes of music, for Manchester Buildings is an eelpot, which has no outlet but its awkward mouth—a case-bottle which has no thoroughfare, and a short and narrow neck—and in this respect it may be typical of the fate of some few among its more adventurous residents, who, after wriggling themselves into Parliament by violent efforts and contortions, find that it too is a no thoroughfare for them; that, like Manchester Buildings, it leads to nothing beyond itself; and that they are fain at last to back out, no wiser, no richer, not one whit more famous, than they went in.

It is interesting that this first fully articulated image of Saturn as a topographical site should be concerned primarily with the fate of politicians. It is they who are being devoured by Manchester Buildings. Given such a dolorous state of affairs, there can be no hope of ever addressing one's grievances to the House of Commons. Dickens's refusal to run as the Liberal candidate for Reading, when he was asked to do so two years later, was already a foregone conclusion for readers of this page of *Nicholas Nickleby*. Politics would always be for Dickens synonymous with the most grievous corruption and depravity. Here he depicts the MPs as being trapped in the belly of the beast. Politics like every other potential avenue of escape is a "no thoroughfare." The "no thoroughfare" structure is "typical of the fate" of all true denizens of the Dickens world.

The last installment of *Nicholas Nickleby* was published in October 1839. *The Old Curiosity Shop* began to appear in late April 1840. In the interim Dickens had begun to walk in earnest. "Night is generally my time for walking"—so begins *The Old Curiosity Shop*. The narrator goes on to tell us of his fascination with "that never-ending restlessness, that incessant tread of feet wearing the rough stones smooth and glossy." Poe saw that beneath the calm veneer of this narrator's speech lay the mad obsession of the old man in "The Man of the Crowd." When Dickens realized that the tale he had begun as one of Master Humphrey's stories would soon outgrow the first-person narrative, he shifted to third person, but not without incurring certain problems. At the end of the novel he reveals that the first-person narrator was actually the younger brother of Nell's grandfather. This is contradicted, however, by the younger brother himself, whose remarks elsewhere make it clear that he was not in London at the time he claims to have met Nell and her grandfather in the course of one of his night walks. A remark by one of the puppeteers whom Nell meets in the countryside could well serve as the novel's epigraph: "Can't you think of anything more suitable to present circumstances than saying things and then contradicting 'em?" This contradiction is important insofar as it seems to be related to the novel's larger concern with the themes of mystery and impenetrability. The problem is that of determining just who is walking so late at night and why. Is it Humphrey, or the younger brother, or Dickens himself? It would appear, therefore, that Dickens feels a certain uneasiness about identifying with these troubled night walkers. When the mysterious first-person narrator remarks that Nell's grandfather's nocturnal wandering "only became the more impenetrable, in proportion as I sought to solve it," he is defining the fundamental concealment of the novel as a whole. Here we seem to hear Dickens's own reflection on the mysterious compulsion that sends him into the streets. The revelation that the old man is actually en route to the gambling tables does nothing to clear up the abiding mystery. For the fact is that the narrator himself, whoever he is, is similarly compelled to walk, and his unnamed obsession has nothing to do with gambling, nor can we believe that it is due simply to his love of the sound of footsteps.

It is well known that in depicting the death of Little Nell, Dickens experienced a repetition of the traumatic grief he felt at the death of his sister-in-law, Mary Hogarth, in May of 1837. "The old wounds" that, as he told Forster, "bleed afresh" as he writes the death scene cannot be separated from those "many and mortal wounds" of which Chesterton spoke in connection with Dickens's childhood. The writing of Nell's death scene simply underlines the already obvious point that for Dickens the work of remembrance was not restorative; quite to the contrary, it was traumatic. Every effort to master the compulsive memories of loss and abandonment seems only to have increased the intensity of the compulsion. Nell, says the first-person narrator, "seemed to exist in a kind of allegory," which he would have missed entirely had it not been "for the heaps of fantastic things I had seen huddled together in the curiosity-dealer's warehouse. These, crowding upon my mind, in connection with the child, and gathering round her, as it were, brought her condition palpably before me." The allegory is of course that of the Christ-Child in the manger at the Adoration, and Little Nell's pilgrimage, suffering, and death present a transparent version of a secular Calvary. Dickens's most interesting twist in the presentation of Little Nell lies in her very name, for her fate is already inscribed in the pun Little *Knell*. Like the curiosities that surround her, Nell herself has a clearly defined destiny. Dickens was doing much more than simply playing on the Christian piety of his audience; he was also defining his vocation as an artist as the commemoration of the dead. Like an analyst ministering to himself, Dickens in *The Old Curiosity Shop* reconstructs the primal scene of his own deepest anguish. In the act of sounding the knell that only he could hear, he confronted the most impenetrable mystery in his existence.

The figure of Time makes its appearance late in the novel, in the scene where the old sexton leads Nell to a subterranean well in the church crypt, "in a dim and murky spot" that stands at the mysterious center of the novel. The well is a veritable abyss that both Nell and the sexton agree "looks like a grave itself." "I have often had the fancy" observes the sexton, "that it might have been dug at first to make the old place more gloomy, and the monks more religious. It's to be closed up, and built over." Like a "no thoroughfare" in a London back street, this fanciful *memento mori* is about to be covered over, concealed, renovated, rebuilt. Like Nell's, its knell is about to be rung. The allegory is plain enough: Nell is looking into the abyss of death under the watchful eye of Old Time himself. Here it is the grave rather than Chronos that will do the swallowing. Daniel Maclise's well-known illustration of the scene helps to make even more apparent the connection between the sexton's dangerous abyss, into which he is fearful Nell might fall ("lest you should stumble and fall in"), and the figure of Saturn-Chronos. Alexander Welsh remarks of the drawing, "The sexton . . . suggests, with his crutch, the figure of Time." And Jane Cohen reminds us in her excellent study of Dickens's illustrators that Maclise's drawing appears in the first edition of the novel immediately after the words, "The child complied and gazed down into the pit" and is followed on the page by the words, "It looks a grave itself"; thus Dickens's text literally becomes a legend to the emblem of Old Time. Cohen also notes that Dickens suggested including an hourglass in the drawing, but Maclise protested that that would be overdoing it, and Dickens pressed him no further.

Dickens himself is quite explicit about the pun on Nell's name, and as might be expected, he allows the novel's trickster, Dick Swiveller, to make the point for him. Twice, in connection with Swiveller, Dickens cites a line from *The Merchant of Venice:* "Let us all ring fancy's knell" (3.2.70). The first occasion is early in the novel when Swiveller visits the shop hoping to woo Nell, who he believes will be a rich heiress. But Nell and her grandfather have already left on their fateful pilgrimage, and Swiveller disappointedly quips, "Let us go ring fancy's knell." The second occasion is right after the funeral scene in the church crypt. We are once again back in London. Dickens writes that the ringing of a doorbell sounded peculiar just then in Swiveller's ears; it sounded like, "if we may adopt the sound to his then humour, a knell." It would seem that like Oscar Wilde, Dickens himself could not read *The Old Curiosity Shop* without laughing. Despite his genuine melancholy, he could nevertheless laugh at the curiously morbid turn of his fancy. He clearly recognized how crucial these feelings of remorse and the uncanny were to his creativity. His linguistic exuberance with regard to Nell's name plainly reveals the delight he also takes in elaborating the impenetrable mystery that the work of remembrance had become for him. What Dickens says of the old bachelor who comes to Nell's aid late in the novel is true of himself: "He was not one of those rough spirits who would strip fair Truth of every little shadowy vestment in which time and teeming fancies love to array her." The truth of one's relation to the otherness of one's incorporated memories can only ever appear through the figure of concealment. In *The Old Curiosity Shop*, Dickens recognized the disfiguration that is inherent in every figure, and the concealment that characterizes every revelation.

In *Barnaby Rudge* (1841), part of which was composed contemporaneously with *The Old Curiosity Shop*, Dickens rings not fancy's but "the murderer's knell." The "remorseless toll" on the village bell for Little Nell becomes in *Barnaby Rudge* the tocsin or alarm bell rung in London during the Gordon Riots of 1780. The death knell becomes the tocsin. Dickens believed that *Barnaby Rudge* signaled the emergence of his radical politics. "By Jove how radical I am getting," he wrote to Forster in August 1841. "I wax stronger and stronger in the true principles every day." But if Dickens believed he was demonstrating his solidarity with the Chartists, whose agitations dominated the political scene in 1841, he certainly had an odd way of showing it, for he depicts the Gordon Riots and the Bastille-like raid on Newgate Prison as the work of a collective and motiveless madness. More precisely, Dickens links Rudge's private madness and guilt at the murder of his master, years before, to the public madness of the rioters. Though Dickens may have thought he was furthering radical principles, his text is an unabashedly reactionary tract. As Gordon Spence remarks in the introduction to his edition of the novel, Dickens's "imaginative sympathy, necessary for artistic creation, is combined with a recoil in horror from 'the rabble's unappeasable and maniac rage,' and this combination of opposing emotions gives a peculiar tension to Dickens's description of the riots."

What is radical in *Barnaby Rudge* is not its politics but the way it reduces the logic of revolution to the etiology of an individual neurosis. It is through the tolling of the tocsin that Dickens stages this reduction. The primal scene of the novel is Rudge's murder of his master, Reuben Haredale, who is slain just as he grasps the bell rope and has begun to sound the alarm. The significance of this primal scene becomes particularly evident when we recall that it takes place in Haredale's estate, which is called the *Warren*. Dickens's covert allusion here to his primal scene at Warren's Blacking underlines the structural role that the murder will play in the novel as the principle of repetition. The murder at the Warren haunts Rudge just as Warren's haunts Dickens. The return of the repressed occurs when Rudge hears the tocsin during the riots and falls into a "visionary" state. To him the bell speaks "the language of the dead"; "the Bell tolled on and on and seemed to follow him." Rushing madly through the riot-torn streets, through byways and thoroughfares, Rudge finds that for him there is no escape from the memories of his tortured conscience: "What hunt of spectres could surpass that dread pursuit and flight! Had there been a legion of them on his track, he would have better borne it. There would have been a beginning and an end, but here all space was full. The one pursuing voice was everywhere." Dickens has discovered the creative uses to which his own agonizing experience of remembrance could be put. The "remorseless toll" of *The Old Curiosity Shop* has become "the remorseless crying of that awful voice" of the tocsin in *Barnaby Rudge,* and Dickens could doubtless hear in both the remorseless voice of his own memories. Rudge continues to hear the toll even after it has ceased because "the knell was at his heart." Dickens's ambivalence in *The Old Curiosity Shop* about identifying with the nerve-racked night walkers has here become a full-scale identification: though Dickens is a victim and Rudge a criminal, *Barnaby Rudge* signals Dickens's recognition that in their suffering they are alike. This recognition will be one of the most important leitmotifs in his subsequent novels. It is this profound identification with the conscience of the criminal that constitutes the true radicality of *Barnaby Rudge*.

In *Martin Chuzzlewit* (1844), Dickens intensifies his focus on the tortures of conscience. Jonas Chuzzlewit's crime is not simply murder but parricide. Instead of the tocsin or death knell, Dickens here pursues the figure of the "veil" in order to describe the way memories enclose and wrap around the recollecting self. The schizophrenic Sairey Gamp is the

vehicle of Dickens's verbal wit in *Chuzzlewit*. Through her inimitable
discourse Dickens transforms London itself into a kind of monstrous Levia-
than; the streets become part of the digestive apparatus of a gigantic
saturnine figure that is very much like a whale. In Sairey's imaginary alter
ego, whom she calls Mrs. Harris, Dickens takes the notion of an incorporated other to its obvious extreme. The resulting doubleness of Sairey's
discourse is expressed above all in her penchant for the phrase "What a
blessed thing is this vale of a life," which in her Cockney accent becomes
this "wale of a life." This mispronunciation in turn causes her to have an
understandable fondness for the parable of Jonah and the whale. In
Sairey's speech the words "vale," "veil," "wale," and "whale" become not
only homonyms but synonyms. Dickens uses the slippage of the signifier in
Sairey's speech to link conscience or recollection casting a deadly *veil* over
consciousness with the parable of Jonah being swallowed by the *whale*.
The work of remembrance has here become both an enclosing veil and a
devouring whale.

As she watches the evil Jonas board a vessel in an effort to flee
England and a host of troubles, Sairey says that she hopes the ship ends up
in "Jonadge's belly," obviously confounding, as Dickens notes, "the prophet
with the whale in this miraculous aspiration." Though Jonas's flight is
thwarted, Sairey's wish is fulfilled on the figurative level of the devouring
conscience. Describing Jonas as he is about to commit yet another murder,
this time to silence a blackmailer, Dickens writes: "It may be (as it *has*
been) that a shadowy veil was dropping round him, closing out all his
thoughts but the presentiment and vague fore-knowledge of impending
doom." The veil/whale has been closing around him since the novel's
beginning. And of course the setting for the final moment of irreversible
enclosure is (how could it be otherwise?) the streets. Making his way to his
murderous rendezvous by way of "a narrow covered passage or blind alley
. . . not much in use as a thoroughfare at any hour," and passing through
"great crowds . . . rushing down an interminable perspective," Jonas is
simultaneously devoured by conscience and the streets. Having murdered
the blackmailer, Jonas "became in a manner his own ghost and phantom,
and was at once the haunting spirit and the haunted man." Dickens has
learned to make the night walker's phantasies the central focus of his
fiction.

As Manchester Buildings was the consummate image of *Nicholas
Nickleby*, Todgers's lodging house stands at the center of the labyrinth
that is *Martin Chuzzlewit*: "Todgers's was in a labyrinth, whereof the
mystery was known but to a chosen few." Near the river and not far from

Monument Yard, one enters, in the neighborhood around Todgers's, a mysterious archaic world. To walk near Todgers's is to experience the "no thoroughfare" structure in its purest form. Here one is devoured not by conscience but by its most phantasmagoric expression, the city itself; "A kind of resigned distraction came over the stranger as he trod these devious mazes, and, giving himself up for lost, went in and out and round about and quietly turned back again when he came to a dead wall or was stopped by an iron railing, and felt that the means of escape might possibly present themselves in their own good time, but that to anticipate them was hopeless." In the following passage, which brings the preceding remarks to their conclusion, Dickens transforms the inanimate back streets of London into a living, breathing prehistoric monster:

> Among the narrow thoroughfares at hand, there lingered, here and there, an ancient doorway of carved oak, from which, of old, the sounds of revelry and feasting often came; but now these mansions, only used for storehouses, were dark and dull, and being filled with wool, and cotton, and the like—such heavy merchandise as stifles sound and stops the throat of echo—had an air of palpable deadness about them which, added to their silence and desertion, made them very grim. . . . In the throats and maws of dark no-thoroughfares near Todgers's, individual wine-merchants and wholesale dealers in grocery-ware had perfect little towns of their own; and, deep among the foundations of these buildings, the ground was undermined and burrowed out into stables, where cart-horses, troubled by rats, might be heard on a quiet Sunday rattling their halters, as disturbed spirits in tales of haunted houses are said to clank their chains.

Just as Manchester Buildings was concerned with politics, Todgers's is concerned with the London commodity trade. It is the transformation of the old neighborhood into warehouses for the storage of various commodities that has turned the ground around Todgers's into a beast that stifles sound and seems to have devoured life itself. Here is Dickens's bitterest indictment to date of the warehouses in the neighborhood of Warren's Blacking. It is a far more radical political gesture than he may have realized, for what Dickens does here is link the "no thoroughfare" structure to the power of capital itself. The killing, devouring force of Saturn and Old Time is here identified with the accumulation and distribution of commodities. Dickens is attacking the very principle of a capitalist economy. The "throats and maws of the dark no-thoroughfares near Todgers's" constitute one of the most striking dialectical images in the entire Dickens canon because here the very principle of capital formation is figured in terms of the most barbaric prehistoric force.

Between *Martin Chuzzlewit* and *Dombey and Son* (1848), Dickens's experience of the streets seems to have become increasingly more obsessive and anxiety-producing. It was during these years that he began to turn to mesmerism, doubtless in an effort to understand and perhaps rid himself of the memories that oppressed him. Vacationing in Italy after the completion of *Chuzzlewit,* he performed mesmeric cures on his sister-in-law Georgina Hogarth and on Madame de la Rue. One can imagine that Dickens had a special insight into the uncanny dominance that the hypnotist is able to wield over his subject. His experience of his own incorporated other enabled him to appeal with a particular efficacy to the unconscious desires of his "patients." In the hypnotic session he was able to exert over them the same sort of power to which he himself submitted with regard to his own agonizing memories. Knowing the susceptibilities of the conscious self, he knew how to circumvent its watchfulness and place it under his spell. In his mesmeric experiments, as in his writing, he was able to work upon others the same suggestive art of persuasion and domination that had been practiced on him by that "remorseless voice" within. In the difficult years following the crisis of 1839–40, he had come to realize that every effort to flee the voice led to yet another "no thoroughfare."

In *Pictures from Italy* (1847), which collects the essays he wrote on his European sojourn, Dickens remarks that the byways of Lyons in summer were a veritable inferno: "All the little side streets whose name is Legion, were scorching, blistering, and sweltering." In Rome he was struck by a "narrow little throat of street . . . dressed out with flaring lamps." The newly installed gaslamps of Rome remind him of nothing so much as the pathway to hell. This transposition of modernity into prehistory, of modern Rome into the ancient underworld, is of a piece with Dickens's overall effort during the mid 1840s to exorcize the demons of modernity. He wanted to drive out the demons from himself, from his "patients," and from the modern world at large. His frequent use during this period of the phrase "whose name is Legion" is telling in this regard. Its source is the story of a man possessed by devils (Mark 5:9) who, when Christ asks him his name, responds, "My name is Legion, for there are so many of us." No biblical image speaks more directly to Dickens's dilemma. Like Christ, Dickens wanted to cast out the demons. During the mid 1840s his inability to do so made him increasingly desperate.

Since the word "dickens" is a euphemism for the "devil," one might say that Dickens was trying to escape from the truly proper name that was ready-made within his signature. Writing to Forster from Lausanne in 1846, in a letter that Benjamin cites in "The Paris of the Second Empire in Baudelaire," Dickens complains that he, like his fictional characters, needs the crowd if he is not to become stagnate and unproductive. "I cannot express," he wrote of the streets of London, "how much I want these."

Forster relates another incident that reveals in much starker terms the extent of Dickens's desperation. In Paris on the night of February 12, 1847, Forster writes, "he seemed troubled with a phantasmagorical belief that all Paris had gathered around us that night on the Rue St. Honoré, and urged him on with frantic shouts." At the time of this incident, Dickens had published only four installments of *Dombey and Son*. It was in 1847, we should recall, that Dickens wrote and gave to Forster the autobiographical fragment. In *Dombey and Son* we will see both the persistence of that "remorseless voice" and Dickens's first effort to translate his mesmeric experiments into fictional form.

In *Dombey and Son* the oral sadism that characterized the saturnine streets of the earlier novels is extended across the entire social spectrum. Dickens here appropriates the image of Saturn-Chronos to depict what Raymond Williams calls "an unprecedented—crowding and rushing—human and social organization." Dickens's response to the capitalist expansion of the late 1840s, which laid the foundation for the prosperity of the 1850s, was to project the image of Time the devourer into the new sign of the times. *Dombey and Son* was written in the period of the overproduction crisis that culminated in the recession of 1847, which was followed by an extraordinary economic recovery. In his saturnine imagery Dickens registers the complex transformation that England experienced during this period.

The novel opens with a personification of the "remorseless twins," "Time and his brother Care." These two are at work preparing the sorry fate of Dombey's newborn son Paul, whose infant creases are already being smoothed out "with the flat part of [Time's] scythe, as a preparation of the surface for his deeper operations." Swallowing and consuming are the prerogatives of both the father and his trading firm, Dombey and Son. He himself is a kind of Chronos sporting a "very loud ticking" pocket watch. As a result of the expansion in trade and shipbuilding, "all other trades were swallowed up." The expanding railway system is likewise a kind of Saturn that has "swallowed up" the landmarks of a former age. London itself, the hub of this unprecedented technological and economic revolution, is figured as a monster who has "swallowed up" countless lives.

The devouring zeal that characterizes the collective experience of the age is no less true of personal relationships. Here it will suffice to deal with only the most egregious example of the predatory capitalist. The figuration of *Dombey and Son* reaches its apotheosis in the character of Carker, Dombey's business manager, who not only runs off with Dombey's wife but is responsible for bringing the firm to bankruptcy. Dickens himself reminds us that the name Carker comes from the Middle English "cark" —which means "to worry" or "to care"—when he alludes to the "carking anxieties" that afflict the denizens of the Dombey world. Dickens told Forster that he wrote *Dombey* in a time "full of disquietude and anxiety." In the character of Carker this "disquietude" is translated into a nightmarish distortion of humanity. More precisely, it is through the figure of Carker's mouth and teeth that the menacing anxieties of the age come most sharply into focus. They are figures for the hypnotic and destructive power of capital over individuals and over society at large. The consummate image of *Dombey and Son* is that of Carker as he rushes, "with his gleaming teeth, through the dark rooms like a mouth." When Carker parts his lips, which are as elastic as "India rubber," what he reveals are "two unbroken rows of glistening teeth, whose regularity and whiteness were quite distressing." They are the fetish object par excellence. They embody the secret mystery of both his sexual and his economic power. More interestingly still, they literally have a hypnotic effect upon the others. They are the key to his apparent managerial skill, and they enable him to weave a spell over certain susceptible individuals such as Rob the Grinder, who, in a kind of magnetic stupor, does Carker's bidding.

But it is their effect upon Dombey's wife, Edith, that is most interesting of all. Edith is strangely the one most alert and most vulnerable to the mesmeric power of Carker's orality: "She raised her eyes no higher than his mouth, but she saw the means of mischief vaunted in every tooth it contained." Her everlastingly heaving "milk white" bosom seems from the novel's beginning to be the inevitable destination of Carker's "worrying" teeth. Though Dickens teases us into anticipating that Carker's oral sadism will eventually regress to its most primordial object, he never lets Carker go all the way. We are finally less interested in whether or not Edith will go to bed with him, which she does not, than whether or not he will bite her always conveniently available breasts. In his essay on the "Oral Dickens," Ian Watt also notes the sublimated violence of this aspect of the text. Moreover, he points out that "it was only because of Lord Jeffrey's objection that Dickens did not . . . allow Carker to sink his ever-bared teeth into Edith's white breasts." One wishes Lord Jeffrey had stayed out of it. Like Poe and his Egaeus, who is obsessed with Berenice's "excessively white [teeth], with the pale lips writhing about them, as in the very moment of their first terrible development," Dickens, with more than a little humor and spite, projects his anxieties upon Carker's phantasmagoric mouth.

Dickens stages the overcoming of these anxieties in the scene where Carker is annihilated by a speeding locomotive, "whirled away upon a jagged mill, that spun him round and round, and struck him limb from limb, and licked his stream of life up with its fiery heat, and cast his mutilated fragments in the air." Such a histrionic fate belies the gravity of Carker's menace. Dickens is here rewriting Teufelsdröckh's dystopian vision of the universe as "one huge, dead, immeasurable steam-engine, rolling on, in its dead indifference, to grind me limb from limb. O, the vast, gloomy, solitary Golgotha and Mill of Death." Carlyle's "Mill of Death," with its possibly ungenerous allusion to J. S. Mill's utilitarianism, becomes Dickens's "jagged mill," which, like the blade Jupiter used to castrate his devouring father Saturn, here cuts down the oppressive force of capital. Or so Dickens would have us believe, for the question is whether it is the economic system that must be changed or merely the villains into whose hands that system has unfortunately fallen. On reading the recently published *Dombey and Son* and *Vanity Fair,* Carlyle was disappointed: "Not *reapers* they, either of them. In fact, the business of rope-dancing goes to a great height." Carlyle must have recognized that *Dombey*'s conclusion is only a sentimental evasion of the problems the text presents. The dismantling and reconstruction of the Dombey family, which is the fundamental task of the narrative, simply enables a new group of capitalists to enter the field after the larger-than-life figures of an earlier epoch have been disposed of. The economic and political system is left untouched, and this despite all of Dickens's rumblings about the rapacity of unrestrained capitalist expansion. Completed in April 1848, while the Continent was rocked by revolution, *Dombey and Son* clearly reveals why the forces of counterrevolution were able to win in England without a fight, for the radicals themselves, like Dickens, did not focus upon concrete economic and political changes. In *Dombey and Son,* Dickens managed both to rail against social injustice and to defend the status quo. Here too perhaps lies part of the secret of his great success with his audience.

Raymond Williams notes that it is not until "after 1850, when most of the society became more settled, more confident, more optimistic of reasonable change, [that] Dickens became harsher, more disturbed and questioning, more uncertain of any foreseeable outcome." As we have seen, however, the "no thoroughfare" structure was already there; it had been hidden at the dark center of the Dickens world since 1839. It is more precisely the case that it is not until after 1848–50 that the impasse, which had been so effectively concealed, is finally brought to the surface. What Dickens reveals then is the fundamental concealment that has been the motive force of his work for a decade.

Dickens's post-1848 dilemma is well described by Monroe Engel: "This is the dejection of a man who sees life bound in the rigor mortis of an old dead system, yet cannot reconcile himself to any violent breaking free." Though he was antagonistic to the political structure, to the class structure and the economic oppression on which it depended, Dickens was unwilling to commit himself to any program of reform. Unlike Marx, who bided his time during the 1850s and waited for the right time to act—which came in 1864 with the founding of the International Workingmen's Association—Dickens had from the beginning placed himself not on the margins of politics, but completely above politics. The dust heaps in *Our Mutual Friend* (1865) are Dickens's figure for the Houses of Parliament and the refuse they produce. In a letter of July 3, 1850, on the subject of the death of Sir Robert Peel, Dickens wrote: "He was a man of merit who could ill be spared from the Great Dust Heap down at Westminster." For Dickens all politics were tainted. He approved of Peel's laissez-faire policies because they at least approximated his own apolitical thinking. In seeking, like Carlyle, not political or economic remedies but personal conversions, revolutions of the head and heart rather than of the marketplace or the assembly hall, Dickens became vulnerable to all sorts of idealizing political mystagogues. As a bridge to my reading of *David Copperfield* (1850) and the later Dickens, I am going to turn to an exemplary incident that demonstrates the price Dickens paid for his political naiveté. This incident has the additional advantage of enabling us to link Dickens directly to the Marx of the 1850s.

In November 1850, just as the last installment of *David Copperfield* appeared, Dickens wrote an article for *Household Words* about a certain Dr. Gottfried Kinkel, who in 1848 had been a professor of theology at the University of Bonn but who now languished in a Prussian prison under a life sentence for his participation in the uprising of the spring of 1848. Dickens's purpose is to win sympathy for the much-maligned Professor Kinkel, who was clearly the victim of the hysterical atmosphere of the Prussian reaction to the events of 1848. Dickens hopes that his article will persuade men of good conscience to intervene on Kinkel's behalf and petition the Prussian government to allow Kinkel "permission to emigrate to England or America."

There is certainly nothing objectionable about Dickens's humanitarian concern in the case; as he observes, the Prussian government had plainly decided to make Kinkel an example to other middle-class intellectuals. What is objectionable is Dickens's uncritical celebration of Kinkel as the very spirit of the liberal conscience. He was not alone in falling under the professor's spell; many radicals regarded Kinkel as the incarnation of the spirit of the revolution. It was in order to dispel such delusions that Marx and Engels wrote a book entitled *The Great Men of the Exile,* the first third of which is given over to a scathing indictment of Kinkel and everything he represents. This work was written in 1852 but was not published until the twentieth century. What Marx found most objectionable about the widespread sympathy for Kinkel was that it created a romantic and highly sentimental misconception of the revolution. It is in this respect that Dickens's article is particularly culpable. He presents us with a vision of Kinkel "in sackcloth, with shaven head, and attenuated frame . . . spinning his last threads." Dickens seems to have seen in Kinkel an image of the selfless patriot he himself would like to have been:

> He sides with the Left, or democratic party; he advocates the cause of the oppressed people and the poor; he argues manfully and perseveringly the real interests of all governments, in grant-ing a rational amount of liberty, showing that in the present stage of the moral world, it is the only thing to prevent vio-lence, and to secure good order. His speeches breathe a pro-phetic spirit.

One would never guess from Dickens's account that Kinkel was a sup-posed revolutionary. Dickens makes him out to be something very close to a conservative Englishman, rather like himself beneath all his radical prattle. I do not know whether Dickens read Kinkel's speeches, but Marx did, and he quotes from them extensively. Far from the "prophetic spirit" Dickens appears to have heard there, Marx reveals a ridiculous poseur whose writing was filled with theological bombast and political nonsense. Dickens goes on to assure his readers that Kinkel had nothing to do with "red republicanism" and that he had joined the revolution only in order to secure for Prussia "a constitutional monarchy, like ours in England," add-ing enigmatically, "with such improvements as ours manifestly needs."

A few weeks after the appearance of Dickens's article, Kinkel escaped from prison and fled to England, where he visited Dickens. His escape sent a shock wave through the Prussian government. In his introduction to Marx's *Cologne Communist Trial,* Rodney Livingstone demonstrates that the escape of the celebrated Kinkel was a key factor in the government's decision to launch its conspiracy against the Communist League. The Prussians needed another scapegoat, and with Kinkel safe in England, the Communists would have to do. Livingstone cites a letter from King Frederick Wilhelm IV to his prime minister, expressing his fears for the survival of the government now that Kinkel was once again on the loose. It is indeed preposterous that the harmless professor should have sent fear and trembling into the hearts of the Prussian ruling class. It was in order to demystify the similarly hysterical atmosphere that Kinkel inspired among many of the revolutionaries themselves that Marx satirized him in *The Great Men of the Exile.*

In Marx's close stylistic analysis of his speeches, Kinkel emerges as a politico-theological pundit whose rhetorical technique is that of the blustering *"rodomontade."* Marx writes that Kinkel's method was to inspire his students to righteousness by endowing "every little occurrence in his theologico-lyrical past" with prophetic significance. Marx points to passages where Kinkel alternately imagines that he is Noah, Elijah, even Christ. Marx on Kinkel resembles nothing so much as Swift's *Tale of a Tub,* where the rhetoric of enthusiasm is unmasked as the hideously self-indulgent farce it is. Kinkel's pietistic posturing helped to send the revolution in the wrong direction, and it is a sign of Dickens's political naiveté that he was so easily fooled. More alarming still, Kinkel's fundamentally apolitical brand of messianic Christianity was perhaps the alternative Dickens seriously preferred to politics of any sort, radical or otherwise. Like Kinkel, Dickens was more concerned with professions of Christian sympathy for the poor than he was with concrete strategies. That Dickens should have turned to Gottfried Kinkel indicates that he was in search not of a political strategy but of a messianic revelation. In his later works Dickens depicts a world so depraved, so fallen, so far beyond the pale of political remedies that only a redeemer could save it. He constructs a muddle so dark and unreadable, a labyrinth so inescapable and defeating that it could be illuminated only by the sudden flashes of what Benjamin calls "chips of Messianic time." Dickens's admiration of Kinkel's "prophetic spirit" is finally an indication of the depth of his own political despair. In the later Dickens the personal experience of the "no thoroughfare" has become the structure of historical experience in the modern world.

Mr. Micawber anticipates the task of the *Passage Work* when he offers to assist young Copperfield in "penetrating the arcana of the modern Babylon" that was London in the 1820s. Copperfield's penetration into the dark heart of the city culminates late in the novel when, in an effort to find Emily, David and Peggotty follow her friend, the prostitute Martha Endell, into a neighborhood that was "as oppressive, sad, and solitary by night, as any about London." David calls this chapter his "night-picture," and it is indeed a Dantean vision: amidst the corruption of "strange objects, accumulated by some speculator," the riverside has been transformed into a "melancholy waste," where everything has "gradually decomposed into that nightmare condition, out of the overflowings of the polluted stream." This is where Martha has come to end her life. Like Benjamin, David is led by the prostitute into a virtually undiscovered part of the city. It is only after having reached this dark center of urban indifference that the novel's work of reparation can begin. Martha is saved, and Emily is recovered soon afterward. Here in the ebb tide where the Thames has become the River Styx, David learns that despair is the inability to forget. In the blighted stream that "creeps through the dismal streets, defiled and miserable," Martha sees an image of herself: "I know it's like me." "I have never," writes David, "known what despair was, except in the tone of those words." What Martha says of the river, "I can't forget it. It haunts me day and night," is what David feels about his ignominious past at Murdstone and Grinby's, and it is what Dickens had written of Warren's in the 1847 fragment.

The inability to forget is the great theme of *David Copperfield*. It is what compelled Dickens to restage what I am calling his primal scene in each of his novels after 1839. It is what compelled him to write the 1847 fragment, which in turn he elaborated into *David Copperfield*. We have already considered Martha Endell; besides David himself, I will also want to look closely at the character of Rosa Dartle. In each of them Dickens examines a different response to the pain of memory.

David's experience of the work of remembrance can be best presented in an early scene where he visits Micawber, who has been imprisoned for debt. Micawber is trying to be something of a politician in this scene, for he has organized the debtors to sign a petition "for an alteration in the law of imprisonment for debt." The futility of the gesture is what David finds most affecting. As he describes the prisoners filing past to sign the petition, David stops to wonder whether in the act of recollecting and writing the scene he has not sentimentalized the strange and sordid pathos it actually represents:

> I set down this remembrance here, because it is an instance to myself of the manner in which I fitted my old books to my altered life, and made stories for myself out of the streets, and out of men and women; and how some main points in the character I shall unconsciously develop, I suppose, in writing my life, were gradually forming all this while.... When my thoughts go back now to the slow agony of my youth, I wonder how much of the histories I invented for such people hangs like a mist of fancy over well-remembered facts! When I tread the old ground, I do not wonder that I seem to see and pity, going on before me, an innocent romantic boy, making his imaginative world out of such strange experiences and sordid things.

Dickens discovers in this extraordinary passage what Freud discovered in the 1890s when he noticed that the patient's ability to see him- or herself in the recollected scene called into question the legitimacy of the scene and offered an opportunity for the analyst to uncover other displacements and repressions. Dickens discovers further that no recollection can proceed beyond the "mist of fancy" that hangs over the ostensibly "well-remembered facts." For David, the work of remembrance is never pure; it is always derivative, already woven into the fabric of the books he has read, in this case the prison scenes in the novels of Defoe, Fielding, and Smollett. In recognizing that in the very act of writing, something is always developing "unconsciously," David recognizes and reveals the fundamental concealment, the insurmountable unreadability, at work in the act of writing and remembering.

There is another element in this passage that we have not touched on before. It is related to the growing suspicion in the later Dickens that writing itself is tainted, that a life of writing, like a political life, is a charade, a ghastly pretense without meaning or truth. David's recognition here that his memories are unreliable, and that something is always at work that makes the determination of the literal truth difficult if not impossible, is the first step in a process that will continue to intensify throughout the last twenty years of Dickens's life and will culminate in Boffin's preposterous charade as a miser in *Our Mutual Friend* and in the enigmas of *The Mystery of Edwin Drood*. David's recognition here marks an inevitably reflexive extension of the "no thoroughfare" structure to the act of composition itself. Dickens, who had long identified with the criminal, will soon see his own work as essentially criminal, for like the criminal the writer steals, misrepresents, and hoards; even worse, like an insane criminal he often perpetrates these crimes unconsciously, without even knowing what he is doing. Like those of the prisoners filing by to sign Micawber's petition, the writer's signature no longer has any legitimacy whatsoever.

Rosa Dartle is another who cannot forget the "slow agony" of her shame, the shame of having been manipulated and betrayed by Steerforth. Rosa is Dickens's most brilliant sketch of a woman scorned. The scar on her upper lip is the external mark of what David calls "some wasting fire within her." She is disfigured in a way that David finds troubling and impossible to interpret. "She brings everything to a grindstone," Steerforth says of her, "and sharpens it, as she has sharpened her own face and figure these years past. She is all edge." Her pride and her inability to accept disappointment have worn her down. She has in effect put herself to the grindstone of her own conscience. For Rosa, remembrance is destructive and disfiguring. It is through the imagery of the grindstone that we will be able to link Rosa's agonizing experience of recollection to David's.

David's stepfather is named Murdstone, and the firm he owns in London is called Mur*dstone* and *Grin*by's, which contains an anagram of Grindstone. Thinking back to the experience at Warren's Blacking is for Dickens like putting himself to the grindstone. Even Murdstone's eye, like that of several Dickensian villains, is "disfigured . . . by a cast," which is to say that he possesses the hypnotic power of the evil eye. His effect on David is to disfigure the boy's experience of memory for ever. He takes it upon himself to dull the edge of David's character. Bantering with a friend about his plan to marry David's mother, Murdstone warns his friend to be careful lest David, who is with them, should catch their drift:

> "Quinion," said Mr. Murdstone, "take care, if you please. Somebody's sharp."
> "Who is?" asked the gentleman, laughing.
> "Only Brooks of Sheffield." said Mr. Murdstone.

Sheffield is the center of the English cutlery industry. Unlike Rosa, however, David does not allow the disfiguring experiences of his past to gnaw away at his very being. The truth for Dickens was somewhere between the two. There is a great deal of Charles Dickens in Rosa Dartle. He would have preferred, no doubt, to have more David Copperfield in him than there actually was.

Chesterton, who understands so well the role of wounding in Dickens, cites a description by Mrs. Carlyle that helps me to make this link between

Rosa and her creator. Mrs. Carlyle remarked that Dickens "has a face made of steel":

> This was probably felt in a flash when she saw, in some social crowd, the clear, eager face of Dickens cutting through those near him like a knife. Any people who had met him from year to year would each year have found a man weakly troubled about his worldly decline; and each year they would have found him higher up in the world. His was a character very hard for any man of slow and placable temperament to understand; he was the character whom anybody can hurt and nobody can kill.

Like Rosa, it seems that Dickens himself was "all edge."

The leitmotif of David's relationship with his stepfather is disfiguration. David's first traumatic experience occurs even before his arrival in London, when, on the occasion of being beaten by Murdstone for no reason whatsoever, David in desperation bites his torturer's hand. Murdstone is temporarily disfigured by the experience, but David is permanently so: "It was only a moment that I stopped him, for he cut me heavily an instant afterwards, and in the same instant I caught the hand with which he held me in my mouth, between my teeth, and bit it through. It sets my teeth on edge to think of it." We examine the relation between this passage and a very similar scene in Freud's case history of the Rat-Man [elsewhere]. Here, however, it is important to note that this scene is David's primal or originary trauma. The content is certainly consistent with Dickens's interest in oral aggression, but more important than the scene itself is David's response to it. What Dickens is describing here, I believe, is the catastrophic effect of painful memories upon the mind of the child. "The fathers have eaten sour grapes, and the children's teeth are set on edge" (Ezek. 18:2). This is the line that Dickens and his readers would have heard in reading David's account. What Dickens is saying is that the disfiguring effect of painful memories is an experience no less catastrophic than hereditary sin would be. The linkage of these two ideas is itself important, and we will pursue it momentarily in connection with *Little Dorrit*. In *David Copperfield*, the biting scene is the primal scene because it is this incident that disfigures David's experience of memory and his relation to his own past.

The effect of the experience on David is so disruptive that henceforth he cannot "recall how I had felt, and what sort of boy I used to be, before I bit Mr. Murdstone: which I couldn't satisfy myself about by any means, I seemed to have bitten him in such a remote antiquity." David remembers the scene; [Freud's] Rat-Man cannot. But for both of them the biting scene marks the limits of remembrance and the threshold of prehistory. It is the thought of this humiliating incident that David finds so unbearable that it sends him out of the house: "What walks I took alone, down muddy lanes, in the bad wintry weather, carrying that parlour, and Mr. and Miss Murdstone in it, everywhere: a monstrous load that I was obliged to bear, a daymare that there was no possibility of breaking in, a weight that brooded on my wits, and blunted them." "There's something in his soul," as Claudius says of Hamlet, "O'er which his melancholy sits on brood" (3.1.166–67). The pain of David's memories has "blunted" his purpose. He will never be able to escape his "daymare." But by writing, he will at least be able to sharpen his blunted wits. Like Mr. Dick—whose way of dealing with the memory of a "great disturbance and agitation," "his allegorical way of expressing it," is to write what he calls his King Charles Memorial—David also turns to writing as a way of managing or containing the destructive work of remembrance. Mr. Dick writes about a certain Charles who lost his head; Dickens must write repeatedly about the primal scene in which his experience of life was inalterably disfigured.

George Gissing called *Bleak House* (1853) "a brilliant, admirable, and most righteous satire upon the monstrous iniquity of old Father Antic the Law." Gissing's point is well taken; old Father Antic the Law is the latest guise in which Dickens presents Old Father Time. Dickens told Forster that the motto of the novel should be *Tempus edax rerum*, "Time, devourer of things," because both Chancery and Krook's shop consume everyone and everything they come in contact with:

> *Edax rerum*, the motto of both, but with a difference. Out of the lumber of the shop emerges slowly some fragments of evidence by which the chief actors in the story are sensibly affected, and to which Chancery itself might have succumbed if its devouring capacities had been less complete. But by the time there is found among the lumber the will which puts all to rights in the Jarndyce suit, it is found to be too late to put anything to rights. The costs have swallowed up the estate, and there is an end to the matter.

From Chancery and Krook's to the vampiric lawyer Vholes, who in effect "had swallowed the last morsel of his client," Richard Carstone, *Bleak House* unveils a world in the process of cannibalizing itself.

Bleak House continues *Copperfield*'s examination of the notion of disfigurement. Here in fact it becomes the organizing principle linking the novel's two narratives, for both Esther Summerson's first-person narrative and the Jeremiad-like third-person narrative are concerned with, respectively, private and public disfigurement. While Esther is literally disfigured after a bout of smallpox, the omniscient narrator focuses our attention relentlessly on the disfigurements of the London landscape. What Esther calls "my disfigurement, and my inheritance of shame" refers simply to her bastardy and the ravages that the disease has wrought on her face—ravages that render literal the figurative scars of her illegitimacy. She had caught the contagion from Jo, who brought it from out of the unspeakable world of Tom-all-Alone's, where her ill-fated father had spent his last ignominious days. The omniscient narrator surveys the disfigurements of London as he poetically traces a "stream" of moonlight through the "wilderness" of the city. Like David in his "night-picture," he follows the "stream" by houses and bridges "where wharves and shipping make it black and awful, where it winds from those disfigurements through marshes whose grim beacons stand like skeletons washed ashore." Even the moonlight is disfigured in *Bleak House*. The two narratives, despite their radical difference in tone, are finally like the city crowd that rushes by the pathetic Jo "in two streams—everything moving on to some purpose and to one end." And that "one end" is to be consumed in the deadly cycle of voracious possession. Jo's fate is emblematic of that of the *Bleak House* world in general: "At last the fugitive, hard-pressed, takes to a narrow passage, and a court which has no thoroughfare." Like the court in which Jo perishes, Chancery Court is a "no thoroughfare."

During the early and mid 1850s Dickens's experience took on an increasingly somber and morbid cast. These were the years of his father's death and of his divorce. But the forces at work upon Dickens cannot be contained by the notion of the family. During this period his night walks took on a more frantic character than ever before, and he became dangerously obsessed with death and corpses, as evidenced by his regular pilgrimages to the Paris Morgue. The culmination of Dickens's most melancholy, most insomniac years to that date was of course *Little Dorrit* (1857). "There is no denying," writes Chesterton, "that this is Dickens's dark moment. . . . He did what all really happy men have done: he descended into Hell." *Little Dorrit*, argues Chesterton, is about the terrible similarity between "ancient Calvinism and modern Evolutionism," for both deny the possibility of human freedom. It is to this awful thought that Chesterton believes Dickens succumbed in *Little Dorrit*, and he is right. In Arthur Clennam, Dickens pursued once more a narrative of a man who suffers for the fault of another. In the shadow that Mrs. Clennam casts on her husband's illegitimate son, Dickens projected yet one more version of the destructive work of remembrance. Mrs. Clennam is Rosa Dartle grown old and sadistic. So injured is she by her husband's infidelity that she makes his bastard feel as though his life is under an incomprehensible shadow. In Mrs. Clennam the work of remembrance has become destructive as never before in Dickens. The past is twisted into unrecognizability. She misreads and distorts the past so radically that there is no longer any way to retrace origins or even approximate the legitimacy of memory. Moreover, in Arthur she has raised an individual who is so perfectly conditioned by her Calvinist teaching that he never questions the impenetrable mysteries that surround him but accepts them as being quite natural, no matter how painful. Arthur's misreading of his dilemma, like Mrs. Clennam's misreading of her husband's reminder to share his estate with his mistress's family, is finally of a piece with the infinite deferrals and delays of the Circumlocution Office. In *Little Dorrit,* absolutely everything has become an allegory; there is no way out of the destructive figures of twisted memory into the literal truth of history. Dickens's lesson in *Little Dorrit* is that when memory has been undermined utterly and irreversibly, there is no longer any freedom.

After *David Copperfield,* Dickens began to lose hope of ever overcoming the destructive effects of remembrance and even of the ability of writing to contain those effects. He began, in other words, to lose faith in the legitimacy of the constructions he had made of the world and of his experience. In *Bleak House* and *Little Dorrit* the process of deterioration became rampant. By the time of *Little Dorrit,* Dickens felt as though he had completely slipped out of history into allegory. His feeling was precisely what Benjamin describes with regard to Baudelaire's experience of urban *spleen,* the experience of losing the capacity for experience:

> The big-city dweller knows this feeling on Sundays; Baudelaire
> has it *avant la lettre* in one of his *Spleen* poems:
>> Suddenly bells leap forth with fury,
>> Hurling a hideous howling to the sky,
>> Like wandering and homeless spirits
>> Who break into stubborn wailing.
> The bells, which once were part of holidays, have been dropped
> from the calendar, like human beings. They are like the poor
> souls that wander restlessly, but outside of history.

Baudelaire's experience of a Parisian Sunday in 1857 is echoed by Dickens's account of Arthur's experience of a contemporaneous London Sunday: "In every thoroughfare, up almost every alley, and down almost every turning, some doleful bell was throbbing, jerking, tolling, as if the Plague were in the city and the dead-carts were going round." As always in Dickens, the resulting anxiety is registered in a vista of the streets: "Nothing to see but streets, streets, streets. Nothing to breathe but streets, streets, streets." Into the city dweller's experience of the tolling of bells on a Sunday, Dickens projects the experience of his night walks, the experience he has projected at least since *Barnaby Rudge:* "There was a Legion of Sundays, all days of unserviceable bitterness and mortification, slowly passing before him." In *Little Dorrit* the experience of the modern city gives way to the archaic sensation of the "eternal return."

Little Dorrit is full of "no thoroughfares," both literal and figurative, from Mrs. Gowan's parlour at Hampton Court to Casby's London residence. In this novel the clanking machinery of the plot is louder than ever, which is the clearest indication of the lengths to which Dickens must go in order to stage the denouement. Through his reliance on the preposterous codicil to Gilbert Clennam's will, Dickens makes appallingly apparent just how desperate he is in the "no thoroughfare" that is *Little Dorrit.* His terrible recognition here is that the novel has become an extension of the world it vilifies, that like the bureaucrats of the Circumlocution Office, he too has become accustomed to a life lived in the "howling labyrinths of sentences."

The "clicking" sound of a clock or of a trap closing is the key to Dickens's analysis of the work of remembrance in *Great Expectations* (1861). "Something clicked in his throat," writes Pip of Magwitch, "as if he had works in him like a clock, and was going to strike." The "click" is Saturn's signature in *Great Expectations.* When Magwitch comes to visit him in London years later, Pip writes, "The click came in his throat which I well remembered." The "click" registers the shock effect one feels at finding oneself caught in the trap of repetition. Wemm*ick*, whose name and "post-office of a mouth" are implicated here, describes Jagger's courtroom technique: "Always seems to me as if he had set a mantrap and was watching it. Suddenly—click—you're caught." In the "click" one hears the sound of involuntary memory, of compulsive and traumatic remembrance. As an admirer of Browning, Dickens may well be citing from "Childe Roland to the Dark Tower Came" (1855):

> When, in the very nick
> Of giving up, one time more, came a click
> As when a trap shuts—you're inside the den.

Dickens's rewriting helps us to see that Browning's man-eating giant is a figure of the destructive work of memory. When Miss Havisham tells Pip that though the mice have gnawed her wedding feast, "even sharper teeth than teeth of mice have gnawed at me," we recognize that both of them are caught in the trap of memory.

The "man of *ressentiment*," writes Nietzsche, is a devious man who never forgets and who loves "hiding places, secret paths and back doors." Dickens's experience of memory gave him an extraordinary insight into the kind of fawning, obsequious villain he most despised. The resulting identification with such figures is responsible for some of the most ambivalent and disturbing moments in his work. Dickens's horrified recognition in *Our Mutual Friend* is that the future of England is in the hands of such men and very little can be done to change it. No well-meaning alliance between the déclassé aristocrats and the proletariat can alter the historical inevitability toward which the whole novel tends. The only alternative Dickens is able to imagine at this point is the otherworldly utopian one expressed in Jenny Wren's haunting refrain, "Come back and be dead." "Only those who are Lazarus back from the dead," writes Hillis Miller of *Our Mutual Friend*, "can be reconciled to their inescapable enclosure in society." In the world of *Our Mutual Friend*, only those who have died can live; only those who have undergone a mythic rebirth can tolerate the labyrinthine corruption of modern life. Dickens's flight from politics and memory has led him to a phantasmagoric myth of redemption on the rooftops above "the people who are alive, crying, and working and calling to one another in the close dark streets." Such a myth indicates how desperate Dickens was to forget, to say, along with Riah, Jenny, and Eugene Wrayburn, that one's "life down in the dark was over."

Eugene's sadistic torture of Bradley Headstone provides a more accurate gauge of Dickens's dilemma in *Our Mutual Friend*. Eugene's construction of what he calls "abstruse No Thoroughfares" provides an insight into Dickens's estimation of his own art as a novelist. Eugene's relation to his victim becomes a figure, in the following passage, of Dickens's relation to his reader. The most egregious example of his manipulation of the reader in *Our Mutual Friend* is of course the good-hearted Boffin's charade as a miser. But the problem is larger than that. In the gratuitous complications of John Harmon's disappearance and in his reliance once again on a ridiculous search for a missing will, Dickens openly abuses his readers, as Henry James was perhaps the first to realize in his scathing review of the novel. We would be wrong, however, to regard these faults as the result of Dickens's dotage. No, quite to the contrary, they are instrumental to his effort to stage the autodestruction of art, to reveal, like Mr. Venus, all the normally concealed "articulations" of the novel's bone structure. In *Our Mutual Friend,* Dickens sought nothing less than to sound the death knell of the novel as a vehicle of truth and meaning. In Eugene's description of taunting Bradley, Dickens gives us an allegorical account of his assault on novel reading and writing:

> I study and get up abstruse No Thoroughfares in the course of the day. With Venetian mystery I seek those No Thoroughfares at night, glide into them by means of dark courts, tempt the schoolmaster [Bradley] to follow, turn suddenly, and catch him before he can retreat. Then we face one another, and I pass him as unaware of his existence, and he undergoes grinding torments. Similarly, I walk at a great pace down a short street, rapidly turn the corner, and, getting out of his view, as rapidly turn back. I catch him coming on post, again pass him as unaware of his existence, and again he undergoes grinding torments. Night after night his disappointment is acute, but hope springs eternal in the scholastic breast, and he follows me again to-morrow. Thus I enjoy the pleasures of the chase, and derive great benefit from the healthful exercise.

"Reading in its critical use," to borrow Eugene's own phrase, must be alert to the artist's clandestine allegories and to his love of concealment, mystery, and ruses of all sorts. Dickens can undo the mimetic expectations of his readers only by acknowledging, with horror, his complicity as an artist with the "man of *ressentiment.*"

At the time of the Staplehurst railway accident on June 9, 1865, Dickens was nearly finished with *Our Mutual Friend* and in fact had the next installment on board with him. As is well known, the effect of the accident on his already weakened condition was catastrophic. It reopened, one might say, all the deep psychological scars of the past. For the next five years he suffered a traumatic fear of any sort of swift movement, and died on the fifth anniversary of the accident, June 9, 1870. "I have sudden vague rushes of terror," he wrote to a friend more than three years after the crash, "even while riding in a hansom cab, which are perfectly unreasonable but quite insurmountable." The accident placed an unbearable strain upon Dickens's predisposition to involuntary reactions and compulsive memories. In conjunction with these difficulties, he also suffered from a circulatory disorder as a result of the gout and, after 1865, a number of apoplectic symptoms, including occasional paralysis of the left side. Like Baudelaire's poet in *Le Soleil,* Dickens now walked with a "jerky gait" (*pas saccadé*), and like Freud at the close of *Beyond the Pleasure Principle,* he could hope it was no sin to limp. It was under these dolorous conditions that he wrote *No Thoroughfare* (1867) and the unfinished *Mystery of Edwin Drood* (1870).

Like Dickens himself during this period, the supercilious Obenreizer in *No Thoroughfare* and the demonic Jasper in *Drood* experience uncontrollable traumatic seizures. The two texts are closely related; in many respects *No Thoroughfare* is a dress rehearsal for *Drood.* In the character of John Jasper, Dickens's exploration of the problems of memory and forgetfulness reaches the logical end toward which it had been tending. Dickens had always been concerned with the inability to forget, and now in Jasper he constructs a criminally insane split personality whose normal self cannot recollect the acts committed by its psychotic double. Jasper kills his nephew Edwin Drood in an insane and, as it happens, unnecessary rage of sexual jealousy. In the completed portion of the novel, there is no doubt that he is the guilty one. The problems begin when we try to figure out how Dickens planned to bring him to justice, and how and whether Jasper would become aware of his crime. In the most well-reasoned and convincing account of the *Drood* problem to date, Charles Forsyte maintains that Dickens planned to have Jasper hang himself in prison when he suddenly breaks through the barrier separating his divided personality and remembers what he has done. This means that in his very last work Dickens finally discovered a situation in which remembrance seemed to have been blocked formally and finally, in which forgetfulness was possible— but no, even in the depths of Jasper's psychotic mind, memory slowly and inexorably makes its way to the surface. Here at the very end of his career, Dickens reminds himself and his readers that there is "no thoroughfare," no way to escape from the insidious work of remembrance.

In Cloisterham, where *Drood* is set, almost all the streets and by-ways are "no thoroughfare." This is a place where there are all sorts of obstacles to communication and where one makes one's way only with difficulty. As Mr. Grewgious, through whose eyes we first recognize Jasper's villainy, looks into the Cloisterham cathedral where Jasper is leading the choir, he exclaims, " 'Dear me . . . it's like looking down the throat of Old Time.' Old Time heaved a mouldy sigh from tomb and arch and vault; and gloomy shadows began to deepen in corners." Old Time's uncanny sigh passes almost unnoticeably into the "one feeble voice" of the choirmaster.

In *No Thoroughfare*'s opening paragraph, we are presented with a phantasmagoric image in which the sonorous tolling of the "heavy bell" of St. Paul's sweeps over the sound of all the other London church bells just "as if the winged father who devours his children, had made a sounding sweep with his gigantic scythe in flying over the city." As Dickens's experience of memory literally became crippling, and as he felt more than ever haunted by "the pen-and-ink-ubus of writing"—which was one of his very favorite expressions—it was the image of the devouring Saturn that seemed to tighten its grip over his imagination. "Always seems to me as if he had a mantrap and was watching it. Suddenly—click—you're caught."

JEFF NUNOKAWA

Getting and Having:
Some Versions of Possession
in Little Dorrit

The first person who, having fenced off a plot of ground, took
it into his head to say *this is mine* and found people simple
enough to believe him, was the true founder of civil society.
What crimes, wars, murders, what miseries and horrors would
the human race have been spared by someone who, uprooting
the stakes or filling in the ditch, had shouted to his fellow men:
Beware of listening to this imposter; you are lost if you forget
that the fruits belong to all and the earth to no one.

Rousseau's famous account of the origin of ownership posits two genealo-
gies. If the formation of property brings about the maladies mentioned in
this passage, property is in turn invented by an act of acquisition: the
founder of civil society must enclose and claim a plot of land in order to
make it his. While Rousseau asserts that the founder of civil society engages
in an act of theft when he appropriates something that didn't previously
belong to him, since "the fruits belong to all and the earth to no one," the
conception of property that R. H. Tawney, in *The Acquisitive Society,*
describes as "the Traditional Doctrine" regards possession as legitimate to
the extent that it results from such appropriation:

Whatever may have been the historical process by which [it
has] been established and recognized, the *rationale* of private
property traditional in England is that which sees in it either

the results of the personal labour of its owner, or—what is in effect the same thing—the security that each man will reap what he has sown. Locke argued that a man necessarily and legitimately becomes the owner of "whatsoever he removes out of the state that nature hath provided."

The acquisition that invents property is a crime, according to Rousseau, while a similar act justifies the property which is its fruit for "the Traditional Doctrine," but in either case, ownership is inaugurated by an act of appropriation. Both the founder of civil society as well as Locke's laborer own what they own by taking something that wasn't theirs before. The influence of the claim expressed in these passages may be reflected in our conception of acquisition and ownership as the terms of a tautology: to possess is to take possession.

In the figure of inheritance, *Little Dorrit* constructs a conception of a kind of unacquired property which might dispute our sense of an inevitable intimacy between ownership and appropriation. Arthur Clennam illustrates the novel's idealized version of inheritance in his proleptic announcement to Amy Dorrit of her father's fortune: "He will be a rich man. He is a rich man. A great sum of money is waiting to be paid over to him as his inheritance; you are all henceforth very wealthy." Clennam's confusion of William Dorrit's future enfranchisement ("He will be a rich man") with his present condition ("He is a rich man") cancels the work of *taking* possession: Dorrit's inheritance is already his, property that waits to be discovered rather than appropriated.

This conception of inheritance as a form of immanent enfranchisement may be regarded as an effort to secure possession against the destabilizing demands of equivalent exchange: in *Little Dorrit*, anything that can be taken can be taken away. But if the figure of inheritance furnishes a paradigm for the novel's effort to construct forms of possession that are removed from the destabilizing terms of circulation, inheritance itself fails from the start to maintain this distance; inheritance itself is exposed in the novel as a form of "portable property."

Clennam's account of the Dorrit's legacy casts inheritance as the form for the "rare but not extinct surprise" of unacquired allotment, but everywhere else in the novel, it is baffled or haunted by the prospect or memory of its acquisition. The vague sense of guilt which inhabits all of Arthur Clennam's thoughts about his family fortune registers again the failure of inheritance to transcend the terms of gain and loss. "[T]he shadow of a supposed act of injustice" that darkens Clennam's inheritance throughout the novel is his suspicion that "in grasping at money . . . someone may have been greviously deceived, injured, ruined." While the revelation that his stepmother stole Little Dorrit's annuity confirms Clennam's fear that his fortune includes money taken from someone else, it fails to account for the pervasiveness of his sense of guilt. It is not sufficient to explain why his apprehension "so vague and formless it might be the result of a reality widely remote from his idea of it," is enough to render him "ready at any moment to lay down all he had, and begin the world anew," since the amount withheld from Little Dorrit wouldn't have required Clennam to relinquish "all he had" in order to restore it to her.

I want to suggest that Clennam's "vague sense of guilt" registers not merely his suspicion that the accumulation of the fortune of his family generated some pain or crime, but his recognition that it was accumulated at all. The specter that haunts Clennam's inheritance is not simply the rumor that it is constituted in part by a specific appropriation, that in "grasping at money, someone may have been greviously deceived, injured, ruined," but instead a more general apprehension which is expressed but not comprehended by his suspicion of a particular theft. That his fortune was "grasp[ed]" is all Clennam knows when he states his willingness to "lay down all he has": the acquired character of Clennam's fortune is sufficient in itself to render him ready to relinquish it. His stepmother accurately accuses Clennam of identifying "the goods of this world, which [his parents] have painfully got together" as "so much plunder" that must be "given up, as reparation and restitution." Unlike the Dorrits' legacy, Clennam's own fortune is acquired property which resides as a term within a system of equivalent exchange. His willingness to "lay down all he ha[s]" may be regarded as his apprehension of the fact that when inheritance is acquired, it must also be relinquished.

The final defeat of William Dorrit's vexed efforts in the second part of the narrative to pretend that he always possessed fortune furnishes a general image for the failure of inheritance to maintain distance from the work of acquisition:

> When he had been sinking . . . for two or three days, she observed him to be troubled by the ticking of his watch . . . At length he roused himself to explain that he wanted money to be raised on this watch. He was quite pleased when she pretended to take it away for the purpose, and afterwards had a relish for his little tastes of wine and jelly, that he had not had before.

As Little Dorrit's errands to the pawnshop suggest, inheritance is dissolved in the novel not simply because it is exposed as acquired property, but also because it is defined and enlisted as acquisitive capacity; not only because it is an acquired object but also because it is an acquisitive subject. Both the Clennam and Dorrit fortunes are cast as forms of getting: the Dorrits' inheritance is figured by Clennam as exchange value ("the means to possess and enjoy"); his own inheritance consists of a share in a family firm, a share which he in turn invests in the venture that he undertakes with Doyce. Such property has a split character. If acquisitive capacity is one dimension of commodified property, its other aspect appears when it is lost in the catastrophe that occurs under the sign of Merdle, the merchant emperor, cursed with the touch of Midas.

Little Dorrit's conviction that a rule of equivalent exchange governs economic activity shapes its conception of capitalist possession as a self-cancelling term. While the property of the heir in the novel is ideally always already possessed, the property of the capitalist is always already lost. Merdle's fortune consists of a capacity for acquisition which can be measured or exercised only by its loss in exchange for what it gets: "nobody knew with the least precision what Mr. Merdle's business was, except that it was to coin money."

Thus the novel regards the disaster that divests Merdle of his property as immanent in the circulating character of capitalist possession. What is said about Merdle after the collapse of his empire describes the general paradox that pertains to capitalized property in *Little Dorrit*: "As the whispers became louder, which they did from that time every minute, they became more threatening. He had sprung from nothing, by no natural growth or process that anyone could account for . . . he had never any money of his own." Merdle's ruin is an apocalypse of absence, a revelation of the loss inherent in the fortune of the capitalist when he is bound, as the novel conceives him to be, to the requirement of equivalent exchange. Property that is acquired must be relinquished; property that acquires is already relinquished. In *Little Dorrit*, the estate of the capitalist is a form of loss.

II

"[I]n the very self-same course of time" that *Little Dorrit* identifies the heir and his property as subjects of acquisition and thus dissolves the stabilizing distance between inherited property and the terms of exchange, various strategies of segregation may be discerned in the novel to produce forms of ownership that appear independent of acquisitive activity by suppressing the actual connection between these things. The separation between the work of acquisition and the provenance of possession is sometimes constituted in *Little Dorrit* as a conspiracy between characters in which one of the terms of the relation contains the work of getting while the other appears to inhabit a domain of ownership that seems disengaged from the activity of the first.

In each of these cases, the distinction between ownership and acquisition is a conspiracy or conceit that falters or fails when the repressed connection between these things is revealed. Pancks, Christopher Casby's truculent debt collector, exposes his employer as the real subject of acquisition ("Pancks is only the Works; but here's the Winder!"); William Dorrit's ignominity leaks out in the various ways that he admits that he knows what everyone else knows about his dependence on the labor of his daughter; Mrs. Clennam's Calvinist convictions about the legitimacy of her possession ("it was appointed to me") is cast by the novel as a thinly disguised projection. But while *Little Dorrit* narrates the collapse of various individual schemes to produce a space of ownership that is disengaged from the activity of acquisition, the topography of the novel works to produce such a space in different terms. The disengagement of the heir and his property from the work of getting is replaced by a difference between this work and various forms of nonmimetic representation.

Paradoxically, the novel reestablishes a realm of ownership removed from the work of getting while exposing the falsity of the "Proprieter's" claim of distance from this activity:

> Christopher Casby was a mere Inn signpost without any Inn—an invitation to rest and be thankful, when there was no place to put up at, and nothing whatever to be thankful for . . . a crafty imposter . . . It was said . . . that . . . he now got more money out of his own wretched lettings, unquestioned than anybody with a less knobby and less shining crown could possibly have done. In a word, it was represented . . . that many people select their models, much as the painters . . . select theirs; and that, whereas in the Royal Academy some evil old Ruffian of a Dogstealer will annually be found embodying all the cardinal virtues, on account of his eyelashes, or his chin, or his legs . . . so, in the great social Exhibition, accessories are often accepted in lieu of the internal character.

While it reveals the distance between Casby's ownership of "the property" and the grasp of acquisition to be an optical illusion, this text works on another level to produce a different version of this distance. Casby is a proprietor uninvolved with acquisition to the extent that he is a subject for painters, a purely fictive entity, "a mere Inn signpost without any Inn." By calling the "Proprietor" a fiction, the novel reenacts the removal that it refuses Casby by casting the subject of referentless representation in his place: it is the mirage of the "Proprietor" rather than Christopher Casby who reproduces the character of the heir. The fictional character of the claim of disengagement from the work of getting designates fiction itself as the site removed from this work. An illusion *of* distinction casts illusion *as* distinction.

The provenance of the heir is preserved as the realm of the fictive and it is to this site that Little Dorrit accedes in the second part of the novel, when, at the urging of her father, she joins an aristocracy of painterly surfaces. While the Dorrits rely on the wage labor of its youngest member in "Poverty," this activity becomes embarrassing in "Riches": "There is a topic . . . which I wish—ha—altogether to obliterate . . . You, Amy . . . you alone and only you—constantly revive the topic." The topic that only Amy revives is wage labor: " 'Fanny' . . . [said] Mrs. General, 'has force of character and self-reliance. Amy none.' None? O Mrs. General . . . ask the milliner who taught her to work, and the dancing master who taught her sister to dance. O Mrs. General, Mrs. General ask . . . [her father] what . . . [he] owe[s] her." Her father's effort to remove the traces of acquisitive activity that mark Little Dorrit may be characterized as an attempt to situate her with the mirage of Christopher Casby. The translation of the wage laborer into the aristocrat's daughter is her "formation" as "a surface . . . the graceful equanimity of surface which is so expressive of good breeding." Like the portraits of "noble Venetians" to whom Frederick Dorrit "paid his court with great exactness," the "surface" produced by Mrs. General's "smoothing hand" is the site of "good breeding." The "departed glory" of aristocracy is landed again in the painterly surfaces admired by the uncle and produced by the governess.

Like the "Inn signpost without any Inn," this surface aristocracy is defined by its disconnection from the real. The portraits of Venetian gentry attract Frederick Dorrit "merely as pictures" or because "he confusedly identified them with a glory that was departed, like the strength of his own mind." Both conceptions of the portraits furnished here assert a distance between them and an external referent: They are either "mere pictures," or images of "*departed* glory." And if the "unrealities" that surround the

Dorrits in Venice are affiliated with the aristocratic, the real consists of images of the work of getting. "[P]illared galleries" and "painted chambers" make way for "beggars of all sorts everywhere: pitiful, picturesque, hungry, merry: children beggars and aged beggars. Often at posting houses, and other halting places, these miserable creatures would appear to her the only realities of the day." A division proposed by the narrative succeeds where the conspiracies of its characters fail: the boundary between getting and owning which defines the realm of the heir is reproduced by the novel as the difference between the fiction of breeding and the fact of beggars; between a "merely pict[orial]" court of nobility and a reality of acquisitive activity.

III

Little Dorrit reconstitutes the compromised realm of inheritance not only by reproducing versions of ownership that are defined by their distance from the work of acquisition, but also by constructing a realm of domestic relations which furnishes versions of property untainted by traces of their acquisition or prophecies of their loss: inherited estate is recapitulated in the form of the daughter and approximated in the form of the wife. Like the immanent possession of the heir, the patriarch's property is fashioned in *Little Dorrit* as the content of an original allotment. Alternately, a feminine appropriation which takes place outside the figure of the father's estate is removed from the destabilizing requirements of exchange through its status as a kind of nonmimetic representation. The woman "[l]ocked" in her lover's arms is safe from the demands of circulation through her character as a form of substitution for an earlier term of exchange. In a novel about the anxiety of portable property, what Paul de Man calls the rhetoric of temporality functions to soften the sting of this portability by removing the fortunes of romance from a destabilizing involvement in the terms of one kind of circulation (the economy of equivalent exchange), while inscribing it another (the play of allegorical substitution).

The novel's denomination of both William Dorrit and Christopher Casby as fathers signals through parody the character of the patriarch's provenance. If, in *Little Dorrit*, the patriarch is affiliated with the position of the heir, his daughters are cast by the novel as property that resembles inherited estate. This identification inhabits the common expression that Clennam employs to ask "Papa" Meagles about his girls: "May I ask you, if I have not gathered from your good wife that you have had other children?" The appearance of his daughters in "Papa" Meagles's provenance is the announcement of possession rather than the enactment of acquisition: the daughter is always already part of the father's estate.

Clennam's possession of Little Dorrit takes place outside the patriarch's provenance and does not so easily transcend the terms of exchange: she must be *made* his and the work that makes her so must be hidden. Just as Clennam and Little Dorrit prepare to wed by destroying the "folded paper" which documents the fact that his fortune includes property taken from her, the act of appropriation which makes her body his fortune is obscured by the narrative. Clennam's possession of Little Dorrit takes place through an act of acquisition that we can construe only in retrospect. Like the property that is already fenced off when the founder of Civil Society ("the first person who, having fenced off a plot of ground took it into his head to say 'this is mine'") declared his possession of it in Rousseau's account, Clennam's embrace of Little Dorrit has already occurred when it is seen for the first time. She is "[l]ocked in his arms, held to his heart," but the clasp that made her so is elided. All that is manifest is the announcement of possession: "I am rich in being taken by you."

This announcement is made after Little Dorrit declares that her fortune, like Clennam's own, has been swept away in the flow of circulation figured by the rise and fall of Merdle: "I have nothing in the world. I am as poor as when I lived here . . . papa . . . confided everything he had to [Merdle's] hands, and it is all swept away." Divested of all property that is subject to gain or loss, the lovers are left with inalienable treasure. For Clennam, this possession is the woman he loves: "Never to part, my dearest Arthur; never any more until the last! . . . I am rich in being taken by you . . . I am yours anywhere, everywhere! I love you dearly!" Little Dorrit's inalienable wealth, in turn, is to be possessed: stripped of her fortune, she is "rich" in "being taken" by the man she adores. If Clennam is the subject who already possesses, Little Dorrit is the object already "possessed," the "being" already "taken."

The anteriority of the lovers' embrace in this passage may be interpreted as the emblem and outcome of the temporal segregation which separates getting from having in the sphere of Clennam's erotic economy. His possession of the woman now "locked in his arms" is predicated on an earlier exchange in which he acquired a different woman. It is after he has discharged the debt generated by this prior acquisition that Clennam appears to discover rather than appropriate the final fortune of his desire:

To review his life, was like descending a green tree in fruit and flower, and seeing all the branches wither and drop off one by one, as he came down towards them.

"From the unhappy suppression of my youngest days . . . down to the afternoon of this day with poor Flora," said Arthur Clennam, "what have I found!"

His door was softly opened, and these spoken words startled him, and came as if they were an answer:

"Little Dorrit."

At the end of his term in debtor's prison, William Dorrit declares his intention to repay all that he owes: "Everybody . . . shall be remembered. I will not go away from here in anybody's debt." Although Clennam's ruining review dismembers a green past rather than restores borrowed money, it is a similar settling of accounts: the destruction of his old love, the withering of "poor Flora" is Clennam's way of repaying the debt that he incurred by acquiring her in the first place:

> In his youth he had ardently loved this woman, and had heaped upon her all the locked-up wealth of his affection and imagination. That wealth had been, in his desert home, like Robinson Crusoe's money; exchangeable with no one, lying idle in the dark to rust, until he poured it out for her.

For Clennam, the activity of first love is the activation of the work of exchange, the conversion of "locked-up wealth" into the currency of trade. And if Flora Finching is the recipient of Clennam's amorous capital, which "like Robinson Crusoe's money" had previously been "exchangeable with no one," she is also the property acquired through the expenditure of this currency: "exchangeable with no one . . . until he poured it out *for* her." Clennam's expenditure in exchange *for* his childhood love is not exhausted by the "locked-up wealth" that he pours out in the first place. His acquisition of Flora incurs a debt that exceeds this initial outlay, a debt which cannot be fully satisfied until he "lay[s] down *all* he ha[s]" (my emphasis). Clennam begins this restitution immediately after his primal acquisition: "Ever since that memorable time . . . he had . . . completely dismissed her."

My claim that the dismissal of Flora is the labor of repayment depends on the assertion of temporal distinction which links the form of this relinquishing with the form of Clennam's vow to repair the secret theft that he supposes to be a part of his family fortune. Clennam casts away the original object of his desire by characterizing it as an irretrievable anterior: "Ever since that memorable time . . . he had as completely dismissed her from any association with his Present or Future as if she had been dead," much as he promises to sacrifice his fortune in order to restore what was taken by "lay[ing] down all he had and begin[ning] anew." For Clennam, to lay down all he has *is* to begin anew; the difference between present and past is the discharge of debt.

Conversely, to shirk the duty of restitution is to make past and present the same:

> If his apprehensions ["of a supposed act of injustice"] should prove to be well founded, he was ready at any moment to lay down all he had, and begin the world anew. . . . Duty on earth, restitution on earth, action on earth . . . Strait was the gate and narrow was the way; far straiter and narrower than the broad high road paved with vain professions and vain repetitions . . . all cheap materials costing nothing.

These words refer to the changeless character of Clennam's stepmother, whose "vain repetitions" are arguments against relinquishing the money she stole. The adamantine debtor is described by images of temporal stasis and circularity: both the woman and the watch that she clutches throughout the novel are figures of the temporal sameness identified by *Little Dorrit* with the refusal to repay:

> She laid her wrathful hand upon the watch on the table . . . More than forty years had passed over the grey head of the determined woman . . . More than forty years of strife and struggle . . . nothing through all eternity could change [her] nature.

Clennam's dismissal of the first girl he loved is a figure of repayment, like the construction of the new which inhabits his idea of what it would mean to relinquish his fortune. In both cases, the demands of exchange are satisfied through the production of temporal difference. What Clennam relinquishes by his dismissal of Flora Finching is something like a failed version of what Marx calls surplus value, something covertly acquired through an exchange of apparent equivalents. Clennam's "locked-up wealth" is "poured out for Flora Finching," but this isn't sufficient to pay for everything he gets for this expenditure. The wealth that he exchanges for her manages to procure a secret surplus which, like the "cloud of a supposed act of injustice" that darkens his fortune, can only be repaid by laying down *all* he has.

Moreover, if relinquishing the past is the way that Clennam discharges his erotic debts, he completes his restitution by destroying a second form of surplus that persists after he has cast out Flora Finching. This second surplus consists of the memories that he keeps of her in "an old sacred place": "the object of his old passion," "an old fancy of the Past":

> Clennam's eyes no sooner fell upon the object of his old passion, than it shivered and broke to pieces.
>
> Most men will be found sufficiently true to themselves to be true to an old idea. . . . When the idea will not bear close comparison with the reality . . . the contrast is a fatal shock to it. . . . Though he had . . . as completely dismissed her from any association with his Present or Future as if she had been dead . . . he had kept the old fancy of the Past unchanged, in its old sacred place. And now, after all, the last of the Patriarchs coolly walked into the parlor, saying in effect, "Be good enough to throw it down and dance upon it. This is Flora."

But the final finding of Clennam's desire swerves from the demands of exchange. Something is ultimately left over in the economy of love: here it isn't necessary for the guilt-ridden heir to lay down *all* he has. The pervasive rule of equivalent exchange that compels Clennam to divest himself of what he has gotten is finally evaded by the woman whose appearance while he "review[s]" his life casts her as a part of his primitive erotic acquisition: "Dear Mr. Clennam, don't let me see you weep! Unless you weep with pleasure to see me . . . Your own poor child come back."

Little Dorrit, however, only looks like a child, as a streetwalker who mistakes her for one discovers to her dismay: " 'My God,' she said, recoiling, 'you're a woman!' " The streetwalker's error measures Little Dorrit's capacity as erotic capital: Clennam can possess the woman "[l]ocked in his arms" because she substitutes for rather than restores the child love that he must relinquish in order to satisfy the requirements of equivalent exchange: "His door was softly opened, and these spoken words startled him, and came *as if* they were an answer: 'Little Dorrit' " (my emphasis). The substitution which startles Clennam is an alibi for an irrevocable anterior and thus occupies what de Man calls "the world of allegory":

> The meaning constituted by the allegorical sign can . . . consist
> only in the *repetition* . . . of a previous sign with which it can
> never coincide, since it is of the essence of this previous sign to
> be pure anteriority. . . . Whereas the symbol postulates the
> possibility of an identity or identification, allegory designates
> primarily a distance in relation to its own origin, and, renounc-
> ing the nostalgia and the desire to coincide, it establishes its
> language in the void of its temporal difference.

Here a form of nonmimetic representation constitutes the object of apparently unacquired property just as, elsewhere in the novel, other versions of
nonmimetic representation constitute the subject of unacquisitive ownership. Little Dorrit can only signify rather than symbolize Clennam's prior
acquisition, because what he actually acquired is lost to the demands of
exchange. Nevertheless, while Clennam doesn't take hold of her, his possession of her is predicated on his acquisition of a prior term. This allegorical figure succeeds as a kind of surplus value because, unlike the versions
of surplus that Clennam must eventually sacrifice or destroy, it appears by
means of but not in the enactment of exchange, it is something possessed
through a trade of equivalents rather than something secretly taken or
withheld from such a trade ("Flora" and "an old fancy of the Past"),
which must be repaid eventually in order to satisfy the requirements of
reciprocity.

Despite George Bernard Shaw's famous assertion that *Little Dorrit* is
"more seditious than *Das Kapital*," the walled worth of domestic devotion
which, in the novel, provides sanctuary from the risks and corruptions of
capital furnishes a far closer approximation of Marx's conception of the
character of capitalist possession than the unstable versions of such property that the novel deplores. The crisis of ownership that occurs in *Little
Dorrit* when property appears to be acquired, comes to an end when a
lover embraces a bodily fortune that he didn't appear to get and which he
therefore holds securely: "Locked in his arms, held to his heart . . . 'Never
to part, my dearest Arthur; never any more until the last!' " *Little Dorrit*'s
figuration of the property of Merdle and the House of Clennam as terms
of exchange which require an equivalent repayment and are therefore only
forms of debt or loss relies on what Marx regarded as an ideologically
characteristic misrecognition of capitalist activity as the exchange of equivalents rather than the extraction of surplus value. The possessions of
Clennam and Merdle inhabit a "sphere of circulation or commodity exchange . . . in which equivalent [appears to be exchanged] for equivalent"

(Karl Marx, *Capital*, volume 1, translated by Ben Fowkes). Thus Merdle never really owns anything; thus Clennam must relinquish all he has when what he has is recognized as acquired. But in the novel's erotic economy, Clennam's property is produced by an apparent exchange of equivalents, just as, in Marx's account of the formation of capital, the capitalist has value in surplus of the terms of the exchange that takes place between himself and the laborer. Clennam's erotic bildungsroman is a narrative in which he eventually discovers something like the capitalist principle of exploitation. The feminine fortune that the lover possesses is at first the material of the discrepancy between what he gets and what he returns. This is unstable wealth, because the rule of equivalent exchange eventually requires its sacrifice. The final fortune of Clennam's desire exists in an allegorical relation to the value gained and lost in exchange which may be said to correspond to the relation between the exchange value and the use value of labor according to Marx's account:

> One consequence of the peculiar nature of labour-power as a commodity is this, that it does not in reality pass straight away into the hands of the buyer on the conclusion of the contract between buyer and seller. Its [exchange] value, like that of every other commodity, is already determined before it enters into circulation, for a definite quantity of social labour has been spent in the production of the labour power. But its use-value consists in the subsequent exercise of that power. The alienation [*Versusserung*] of labour-power and its real manifestation [*Ausserung*]; i.e. the period of its existence as a use-value, do not coincide in time.

In "the subsequent exercise of that power" labor produces value which exceeds its exchange value, the cost of reproducing its needs. Thus, the surplus value that capital gains, like Clennam's embrace of Little Dorrit, is distinguished temporally from the value that it exchanges, but, like Clennam's allegorical possession, this apparently unappropriated surplus is nevertheless contingent upon the value previously exchanged. (In Clennam's case the temporal disjunction which separates these things is itself the term of repayment.) The domestic estate in the novel represents the formation of, rather than a flight from something like capital. Its security depends on the same separation that enables the accumulation of capital, the temporal disjunction which separates it from the terms of exchange. This similarity between the provenance of the capitalist in Marx's account and the lover's fortune in *Little Dorrit* becomes dramatic when Little Dorrit reveals her love to be labor-power: "I am yours anywhere, everywhere! I love you dearly! I would rather pass my life here with you, and go out daily, working for our bread, than I would have the greatest fortune that ever was told."

I want to compare Clennam's allegorical wealth to "the Shadow of Someone" that a "tiny woman" keeps as her "great, great treasure" in Little Dorrit's fairy tale in order to consider a way in which the novel assesses a difference in gender or class, or gender as class. At first, Little Dorrit's story appears to indicate that the possibility of allegorical possession is entirely reversible, that a woman can possess without appearing to acquire a temporally displaced version of a man in the erotic economy of *Little Dorrit*, just as a man possesses a displaced version of a woman. But the novel draws a distinction between masculine and feminine versions of this estate of substitution: while Clennam's erotic fortune is a form of surplus value, the tiny woman's shadow hoard is a fantasy of possession.

In Little Dorrit's narrative, the "tiny woman" who harbors "the shadow of Someone who had gone by long before" is confronted by a Princess:

> The Princess was such a wonderful Princess that she had the power of knowing secrets, and she said to the tiny woman, "Why do you keep it there?" This showed her directly that the Princess knew why she lived all alone by herself . . . It was the shadow of Someone who had gone by long before: of Someone who had gone on far away quite out of reach, never, never, to come back. It was brighter to look at; and when the tiny woman showed it to the Princess, she was proud of it with all her heart, as a great, great, treasure. When the Princess had considered it a little while, she said to the tiny woman, "And you keep watch over this every day?" And she cast down her eyes, and whispered, "Yes." The Princess said, "Remind me why." To which the other replied, that no one so good and kind had ever passed that way, and that was why in the beginning. She said too, that nobody missed it, that nobody was the worse for it, that Someone had gone on to those who were expecting him . . . and that this remembrance was stolen, or kept back from nobody.

The tiny woman's shadow treasure is removed from the movement of circulation described by the path of "Someone who had gone on far away quite out of reach." Unable to acquire Someone when he is within "reach," the humble cottager doesn't mourn his loss when he is gone. Instead, she harbors Someone's shadow, a belated representation which appears uninvolved in the movement of gain and loss. Her proud proprietorship resembles the condition of her interlocutor: like the Princess, who possesses cognitive property without appearing to get it, the tiny woman has the shadow of Someone without appearing to engage in the work of acquiring it: "nobody missed it, nobody was the worse for it . . . this remembrance was stolen or kept back from nobody."

The shadow property offers the appearance of a possession that is not taken and it is this appearance which constitutes its inalienability for the cottager:

> [T]his remembrance was stolen or kept back from nobody. The Princess made answer, "Ah! But when the cottager died it would be discovered there." The tiny woman told her No; when that time came, it would sink quietly into her own grave, and would never be found . . . [When the cottager died] [t]he Princess . . . went . . . to search for the treasured shadow. But there was no sign of it to be found anywhere; and then she knew that the tiny woman had told her the truth, and that it . . . had sunk quietly into her own grave, and that she and it were at rest together.

While Someone has "gone on far away quite out of reach," his shadow appertains to the tiny woman as apparently unacquired and thus inalienable property which disappears with her death. Here again, belated representation rather than real estate is the form of property secure from the destabilizing force of commodification; here again, the stability of inheritance is replaced by the stability of a shadow.

But unlike the allegorical term that constitutes Clennam's secure estate, the consolation of the humble cottager is an object of representation ("the shadow of Someone") which substitutes for an original object that *wasn't* gotten ("Someone . . . who has gone on far away quite out of reach"), rather than an object that was gotten and then released. Here, the allegorical term doesn't appear as the shadow of a previously acquired and relinquished primary object; rather, it furnishes a kind of property that stands in for an original object that wasn't gained in the first place.

Little Dorrit's cottage inhabits a spatial and temporal margin outside and after a system of circulation inscribed by the movement of "Someone who had gone by long before: of Someone who had gone on far away quite out of reach . . . Someone had gone on to those who were expecting him." Like the wandering destitute who inhabit sidewalks and shopping malls, gathering about them the mirage of property as their symbolic citizenship in a polis of purchasers, the humble cottager proudly possesses a shadow treasure instead of what she would have had if she were able to make a place for herself on a path of circulation which excludes her.

If Clennam's possession of allegorical surplus value is predicated on earlier acquisition and loss of primary property, the cottager's shadow hoard is predicated on the absence of this prior involvement in the work of exchange. Clennam's erotic estate appears after the discharging of this work; the cottager's shadow treasure signals her exclusion from it. In *Little Dorrit*, property removed from the flow of circulation by its secondary character furnishes in a form of surplus value the security of the heir to the anxious capitalist. But for a woman who resides on the margins of a system of allotment, the allegorical supplies consolation for an unchosen distance from this flow. Property distanced from circulation may be the material of a shelter or a ghetto, depending on the economic character of its occupant.

IV

Among the "traces of the migratory habits of the family" housed in the Meagles domicile is a collection of "pictorial acquisitions" that Mr. Meagles procured during their tours abroad.

> Of articles collected on his various expeditions, there was such
> a vast miscellany that it was like the dwelling of an amiable
> Corsair . . . There were views, like and unlike, of a multitude of
> places; and there was one little picture-room devoted to a few
> of the regular sticky old Saints . . . Of these pictorial acquisi-
> tions Mr. Meagles spoke in the usual manner. He was no judge,
> he had picked them up, dirt-cheap, and people *had* considered
> them rather fine. One man, who at any rate ought to know
> something of the subject, had declared that "Sage, Reading"
> . . . to be a fine Guercino.

In the novel's description of these paintings, the corsair's acquisition of spectacle gives way to the spectacle of acquisition:

> a few of the regular sticky old Saints, with . . . hair like Nep-
> tune's, wrinkles like tattooing, and coats of varnish . . . [which]
> served for a fly-trap, and became what is now called in the

> vulgar tongue a Catch-em-alive O ... a specially oily old
> gentleman, with a swan's-down tippet for a beard, and a web
> of cracks all over him like rich pie crust.

If these are figures of acquisitive activity, they are also allusions to Dickens's conception of the various parts of the female. The images and agents of getting which occupy the surfaces of Meagles's paintings cover the range of Dickens's usual construction of the feminine; "rich pie crust" serves as a metonymy for homey virtues; "varnish" describes the consorts of social corruption. But in league with the work of getting, these allusions undergo nightmare distortions. As acquisitive capacity, the feminine ceases to be good, or merely false, and becomes instead a form of genitalia which scars and "stick[s]."

Acquisitiveness is a "*view*" when it appears in the shape of a vagina that wounds and ensnares: I want to suggest that the web of cracks and the fly trap signal the panic caused in the novel by a "perverse" and explicitly acquisitive woman. They suggest the figure of Miss Wade, a "myster[ious]" female who describes the relation between men and women in terms that recall Clennam's primal desire for spending and getting, instead of a later passion which seems disengaged from the demands of exchange. Her account of her own betrothal characterizes it as a transaction that the spectacle of Clennam's possession of Little Dorrit appears to transcend:

> [My suitor] caused me to feel among the rich people as if he
> had bought me for my looks, and made a show of his purchase
> to justify himself ... [His aunt] seemed to think that her
> distinguished nephew had gone into a slave-market and pur-
> chased a wife.

Wade's alliance with Tattycoram "is founded in a common cause. What your broken plaything is at birth, I am." According to Wade, her fellow orphan woman, like Wade herself, is acquired rather than natural property. Like the "spoils" that Meagles shows his guests before he leads them to his "own snug room," Tattycoram "stops outside the door" of both the father's filial estate and the lover's erotic museum. In contrast to the natural property of a father or the souvenir of a lover, the orphan laborer is explicitly acquired by her "master" and is thus "portable property," located within a system of circulation which appears again when "Miss Wade ... put her arm around her waist as if she took possession of her for evermore."

By discerning and recapitulating the acquisition of women, Wade makes the work of exchange visible in a sphere that the novel and its characters seek to remove from its destabilizing demands. The ominous form of her femininity is affiliated with a transgression that briefly disturbs the security of phallic estate:

> "I am alone here, gentlemen," observed Miss Wade . . . "Say anything you will."
> "Politeness must yield to this misguided girl, ma'am," said Mr. Meagles, "at her present pass . . . If it should happen that you are a woman, who, from whatever cause, has a perverted delight in making a sister-woman as wretched as she is (I am old enough to have heard of such) I warn her against you, and I warn you against yourself."

Part of the charge of "perversity" which Meagles levels against the same sex urge of Miss Wade (and which the narrative levels again when it brands Wade's account of Tattycoram's domestic "enslavement" by Meagles a "perver[sion]" of "his motives and actions" is the accusation that it works to subvert a boundary that separates acquisitive activity from what normally falls outside it. The term denominates this subversion elsewhere in the novel: according to Little Dorrit, her family "pervert[s]" Maggy when they send her to get money from Clennam, since this compromises the dutiful daughter's efforts to contain it: "If we should want it so very, very badly that we cannot do without it, let *me* ask . . . for it." Wade's "delight" in "making a sister-woman as wretched as she is" perversely transgresses the boundary which appears elsewhere in the novel to construct the feminine as a form of apparently unacquired property.

In *Little Dorrit*, the delight of perversity is the sign of poverty. Like the heroine of the fairy tale who apprehends a previous arrangement which prohibits her from having the object of her desire, ("Someone had gone on to those who were expecting him"), Wade recognizes an impoverishing predetermined circumstance which prevents her from "securing" what she wants in either explicitly economic or domestic spheres. Having inherited insufficient property to sustain herself, Wade is compelled to work as a governess. Her account of this labor culminates in her recognition that she can't "secure" the affection of her charges because of "a rosy-faced woman . . . who had nursed them both, and who had secured their affections before I saw them." Unlike Clennam, whose loss of capital is his access to secure domestic fortune, Wade is ineligible for either form of allotment.

The act of taking a woman is visible only in and to a woman who has felt a desire to do so defeated. While the origin of Clennam's successful acquisition of Little Dorrit is effaced, the desire of a woman for a woman is made conscious by its failure: "When we were left alone in our bedroom at night, I would reproach her . . . loving her as much as ever, and often feeling as if, rather than suffer so, I could hold her in my arms and plunge to the bottom of a river—where I could still hold her, after we were both dead."

Perversity's explicit embrace triumphs for a moment when "Miss Wade . . . put[s] her arm around [Tattycoram's] waist as if she took possession of her for evermore," but it is finally defeated when Tattycoram goes back to the Meagles. It may be, as Wade believes, that the servant's return to her "master" measures again the difference that appears between the capitalized admiration of Wade's suitor ("as if he had bought me") and her own forlorn and impoverished desire to hold another woman ("I . . . often fel[t] as if, rather than suffer so, I could hold her in my arms and plunge to the bottom of the river"); it may be, as Wade believes, that the servant's return charts the greater acquisitive power of capital over other ways of getting: "You prefer their plenty to your less fat living here . . . My poverty will not bear competition with their money." But the voice of Miss Wade is lost in a reunion where all traces of the servant's appropriation are absent. No longer a foreign acquisition, the "handsome girl with lustrous dark hair and eyes" is now the prodigal daughter, restored to the embrace of the parents: "Father and Mother Meagles never deserved their names better, than when they took the headstrong foundling girl into their protection again."

And here the spectacle of apparently unacquired property works twice to make appropriation covert. The returning servant girl brings with her the now secure secret of a troubling acquisition:

> Another opening of the door, and Tattycoram subsided, and Little Dorrit came in, and Mr. Meagles with pride and joy produced the box, and her gentle face was lighted up with grateful happiness and joy. The secret was safe now! She could keep her own part of it from him; he should never know of her loss; in time to come, he should know all that was of import to himself; but he should never know what concerned her, only.

The figure of restoration has for its freight the secret of acquisition, private knowledge of a theft available only to its victim.

Chronology

1812   Charles John Huffam Dickens, the second of eight children, is born February 7 to John and Elizabeth Dickens.

1814   John Dickens, a clerk in the Navy Pay Office, is transferred from Portsea to London. During these early years, from 1814 to 1821, Dickens is taught his letters by his mother, and he immerses himself in the fiction classics of his father's library.

1817   John Dickens moves family to Chatham.

1821   Dickens begins school with the son of a Baptist minister; he remains at this school for a time even after his family is transferred again to London in 1822.

1824   John Dickens is arrested for debt and sent to Marshalsea Prison, accompanied by his wife and younger children. Charles soon finds lodging in a poor neighborhood and begins work at Warren's Blacking Factory. His father is released three months later and Charles returns to school.

1824–26 Dickens attends Wellington House Academy, London.

1827   Works as a law clerk and spends time reading in the British Museum.

1830   Meets Maria Beadnell; he eventually falls in love with her, but she jilts him upon return from a trip to Paris in 1833.

1831   Becomes a reporter for the *Mirror of Parliament*.

1832   Becomes a staff writer for the *True Sun*.

1833   Dickens's first published piece, "A Dinner at Poplar Walk," appears in a December issue of the *Monthly Magazine* under the pen name "Boz."

1834   Dickens becomes a staff writer on the *Morning Chronicle*. His "street sketches" begin to appear in the *Evening Chronicle*. Dickens meets his future wife, Catherine Hogarth. Also, John Dickens is arrested again for debt.

1836   *Sketches by Boz*, illustrated by George Cruikshank, published. Dickens marries Catherine Hogarth in April. Also in this year, his first play, *The Strange Gentleman*, runs for two months at the St. James's Theatre. A second play, *The Village Coquettes*, is produced at the same theatre. Dickens meets John Forster, who becomes a life-long friend and his biographer.

1836–37   *Pickwick Papers* published in monthly installments from April through the following November.

1837   *Pickwick Papers* appears in book form. *Oliver Twist* begins to appear in *Bentley's Miscellany*. *Is She His Wife?* produced at the St. James's. Dickens's first child born, and the family moves to Doughty Street. Catherine's sister Mary, deeply loved by Dickens, dies suddenly.

1838   *Nicholas Nickleby* appears in installments; completed in October of 1839. Dickens's first daughter born.

1839   The Dickenses move to Devonshire Terrace. A second daughter born. *Nickleby* appears in book form.

1840   Dickens edits *Master Humphrey's Clock*, a weekly periodical, in which *The Old Curiosity Shop* appears.

1841   *Barnaby Rudge* appears in *Master Humphrey's Clock*. Another son born.

1842   Dickens and his wife tour America from January to June; Dickens publishes *American Notes* and begins *Martin Chuzzlewit*.

1843   *Martin Chuzzlewit* appears in monthly installments (January 1843–July 1844). *A Christmas Carol* published.

1844   Dickens tours Italy and Switzerland. Another Christmas book, *The Chimes*, completed. A third son born.

1845   Dickens produces *Every Man in His Humour* in England. *The Cricket on the Hearth* is written by Christmas, and Dickens begins *Pictures from Italy*. A fourth son born.

1846   Dickens creates and edits the *Daily News*, but resigns as editor after seventeen days. Begins *Dombey and Son* while in Lausanne; the novel appears in twenty monthly installments (October 1846–April 1848). *The Battle of Life: A Love Story* appears for Christmas.

1847   Dickens begins to manage a theatrical company and arranges a benefit tour of *Every Man in His Humour*. Fifth son born.

1848   Daughter Fanny dies. Dickens's theatrical company performs for Queen Victoria. It also performs *The Merry Wives of Windsor* to raise money for the preservation of Shakespeare's birthplace. Dickens's last Christmas book, *The Haunted Man*, published.

1849   Dickens begins *David Copperfield* (published May 1849–November 1850). A sixth son born.

1850   *Household Words*, a weekly periodical, established with Dickens as editor. A third daughter born, who dies within a year.

1851   Dickens and his company participate in theatrical fund-raising. Dickens's father dies.

1852   *Bleak House* appears in monthly installments (March 1852–September 1853). The first bound volume of *A Child's History of England* appears. The Dickens's last child, their seventh son, born.

1853   Dickens gives first public readings, from the Christmas books. Travels to France and Italy.

1854   *Hard Times* published in *Household Words* (April 1–August 12) and appears in book form.

1855   *Little Dorrit* appears in monthly installments (December 1855–June 1857). Dickens and family travel at year's end to Paris, where the novelist meets other leading literary and theatrical persons.

1856   Dickens purchases Gad's Hill Place, and the family returns to London.

1857   Dickens is involved primarily with theatrical productions.

1858   Dickens announces his separation from his wife, about which he writes a personal statement in *Household Words*. Begins to give his immensely popular public readings.

1859   Dickens concludes *Household Words* and establishes a new weekly, *All the Year Round*. *A Tale of Two Cities* appears there from April 20 to November 26, and is published in book form in December.

1860   *Great Expectations* underway in weekly installments (December 1860–August 1861).

1861   *The Uncommercial Traveller*, a collection of pieces from *All the Year Round*, published.

1862   Dickens gives many public readings and travels to Paris.

1863   Dickens continues his readings in Paris and London. Daughter Elizabeth dies.

1864   *Our Mutual Friend* appears in monthly installments for publisher Chapman and Hall (May 1864–November 1865).

1865   Dickens suffers a stroke that leaves him lame. Involved in train accident, which causes him to change the ending of *Our Mutual Friend*. *Our Mutual Friend* appears in book form. The second collection of *The Uncommercial Traveller* published.

1866   Dickens gives thirty public readings in the English provinces.

1867   Continues the provincial readings, then travels to America in November, where he reads in Boston and New York. This tour permanently breaks the novelist's health.

1868   In April, Dickens returns to England, where he continues to tour.

1869   The first public reading of the murder of Nancy (from *Oliver Twist*) performed, but his doctors recommend he discontinue the tour. *The Mystery of Edwin Drood* begun.

1870   Dickens gives twelve readings in London. Six parts of *Edwin Drood* appear from April to September. On June 9, Charles Dickens dies, aged 58. He is buried in the Poets' Corner, Westminster Abbey.

Contributors

HAROLD BLOOM, Sterling Professor of the Humanities at Yale University, is the author of *The Anxiety of Influence, Poetry and Repression*, and many other volumes of literary criticism. His forthcoming study, *Freud: Transference and Authority*, attempts a full-scale reading of all of Freud's major writings. A MacArthur Prize Fellow, he is general editor of five series of literary criticism published by Chelsea House.

J. HILLIS MILLER is Professor of English at the University of California, Irvine. His books of criticism include *Poetry of Reality: Six Twentieth-Century Writers, Fiction and Repetition: Seven English Novels*, and *The Linguistic Moment: From Wordsworth to Stevens*.

NORTHROP FRYE, University Professor Emeritus at the University of Toronto, is one of the major literary critics in the Western tradition. His major works are *Fearful Symmetry, Anatomy of Criticism*, and *The Great Code*.

ROBERT ALTER is the author of numerous books of criticism on novel theory, modern Hebrew literature, and biblical narrative and poetry. He teaches at the University of California, Berkeley.

RAYMOND WILLIAMS, Judith F. Wilson Professor of Drama at Cambridge University, is the most influential of British Marxist critics of literature. His books include *Culture and Society, The Long Revolution*, and *The Country and the City*.

STEVEN MARCUS, a member of the Department of Humanities at Columbia, is author of *Dickens: From Pickwick to Dombey, The Other Victorians*, and studies of aspects of Victorian culture and society.

HARRY STONE is Professor of English at California State University, Northridge.

ROBERT L. CASERIO teaches English at the University of Utah. He is author of *Plot, Story, and the Novel* and a forthcoming study of Rudyard Kipling.

DIANNE F. SADOFF is an Associate Professor at Colby College. In addition to her book *Monsters of Affection: Dickens, Eliot, and Brontë on Fatherhood*, she has written articles on Victorian poetry.

D. A. MILLER is Professor of English and Comparative Literature at the University of California, Berkeley. He is author of *Narrative and Its Discontents: Problems of Closure in the Traditional Novel*.

STEPHEN J. SPECTOR is Professor of English at the University of Bridgeport.

EVE KOSOFSKY SEDGWICK is Associate Professor of English at Amherst College. She is author of *The Coherence of Gothic Conventions* and *Between Men: English Literature and Male Homosocial Desire.*

SHULI BARZILAI teaches at the Hebrew University, Jerusalem.

NED LUKACHER is Assistant Professor of English at the University of Illinois, Chicago. He is author of *Primal Scenes: Literature, Philosophy, Psychoanalysis* and has translated two French books on Freud and psychoanalysis.

JEFF NUNOKAWA teaches in the English Department at Cornell University.

Bibliography

Amalric, Jean-Claude, ed. *Studies in the Later Dickens*. Montpellier: Université Paul Valéry, 1973.

Arac, Jonathan. *Commissioned Spirits: The Shaping of Social Motion in Dickens, Carlyle, Melville, and Hawthorne*. New Brunswick, N.J.: Rutgers University Press, 1979.

Axton, William F. *Circle of Fire: Dickens' Vision and Style and the Popular Victorian Theatre*. Lexington: University of Kentucky Press, 1966.

————. "Dickens Now." In *The Victorian Experience: The Novelists*, edited by Richard A. Levine, 19–48. Athens: Ohio University Press, 1976.

————. "The Trouble with Esther." *Modern Language Quarterly* 26 (1965): 545–57.

Baker, Robert S. "Imagination and Literacy in Dickens' *Our Mutual Friend*." *Criticism* 18 (1976): 57–72.

Barnard, Robert. *Imagery and Theme in the Novels of Dickens*. Oslo: Universitetsforlaget, 1974.

Barrett, Edward B. "*Little Dorrit* and the Disease of Modern Life." *Nineteenth-Century Fiction* 25 (1970): 199–215.

Bayley, John. "Dickens and His Critics." In *The Uses of Division: Unity and Disharmony in Literature*. New York: Viking, 1976.

Blain, Virginia. "Double Vision and the Double Standard in *Bleak House*: A Feminist Perspective." *Literature and History* 11, no. 1 (1985): 31–46.

Boege, Fred W. "Point of View in Dickens." *PMLA* 65 (1950): 90–105.

Bornstein, George. "Miscultivated Field and Corrupted Garden: Imagery in *Hard Times*." *Nineteenth-Century Fiction* 26 (1971): 158–70.

Brantlinger, Patrick. *The Spirit of Reform: British Literature and Politics, 1832–1867*. Cambridge: Harvard University Press, 1977.

Brook, George L. *The Language of Dickens*. London: Andre Deutsch, 1970.

Brown, Arthur Washburn. *Sexual Analysis of Dickens' Props*. New York: Emerson, 1971.

Buckley, Jerome Hamilton. "Dickens, David and Pip." In *Season of Youth: The Bildungsroman from Dickens to Golding*. Cambridge: Harvard University Press, 1974.

————, ed. *The Worlds of Victorian Fiction*. Harvard English Studies 6. Cambridge: Harvard University Press, 1975.

Burke, Alan R. "The Strategy and Theme of Urban Observation in *Bleak House*." *Studies in English Literature* 9 (1969): 659–76.

Butt, John, and Kathleen Tillotson. *Dickens at Work*. Fairlawn, N.J.: Essential Books, 1958.

Byrd, Max. " 'Reading' in *Great Expectations*." *PMLA* 91 (1976): 259–65.

Carey, John. *The Violent Effigy: A Study of Dickens' Imagination*. London: Faber & Faber, 1973.

Carlisle, Janice. *The Sense of an Audience: Dickens, Thackeray & George Eliot at Mid-Century*. Athens: University of Georgia Press, 1981.

Chesterton, G. K. *Charles Dickens*. London: Methuen, 1906.

Churchill, R. C., comp. and ed. *Bibliography of Dickensian Criticism 1836–1975*. New York: Garland, 1975.

Clark, Robert. "Riddling the Family Firm: The Sexual Economy in *Dombey and Son*." *ELH* 51 (1984): 69–84.

Clayborough, Arthur. *The Grotesque in English Literature*. Oxford: Clarendon, 1965.

Cockshut, A. O. J. *The Imagination of Charles Dickens*. New York: New York University Press, 1962.

Cohan, Steven. " 'They Are All Secret': The Fantasy Content of *Bleak House*." *Literature and Psychology* 26 (1976): 79–91.

Collins, Philip. "*Carol* Philosophy, Cheerful Views." *Etudes Anglaises* 23 (1970): 158–67.

———. "*David Copperfield*: 'A Very Complicated Interweaving of Truth and Fiction.' " In *Essays and Studies 1970*, edited by A. R. Humphreys. London: John Murray, 1970.

———. *Dickens and Crime*. London: Macmillan, 1962.

———. "Dickens and Industrialism." *Studies in English Literature* 20 (1980): 261–73.

———. "Queen Mab's Chariot among the Steam Engines: Dickens and 'Fancy.' " *English Studies* 42 (1961): 78–90.

———, ed. *Dickens: The Critical Heritage*. London: Routledge & Kegan Paul, 1971.

Connor, Steven. *Charles Dickens*. London: Basil Blackwell, 1985.

Coolidge, Archibald C., Jr. *Charles Dickens as Serial Novelist*. Ames: Iowa State University Press, 1967.

Coveney, Peter. *Poor Monkey: The Child in Literature*. London: Rockliff, 1957.

Curran, Stuart. "The Lost Paradises of *Martin Chuzzlewit*." *Nineteenth-Century Fiction* 25 (1970): 51–67.

Dabney, Ross. *Love and Property in the Novels of Dickens*. Berkeley: University of California Press, 1967.

Daleski, H. M. *Dickens and the Art of Analogy*. London: Faber & Faber, 1970.

Dessner, Lawrence Jay. "*Great Expectations*: 'The Ghost of a Man's Own Father.' " *PMLA* 91 (1976): 436–49.

Dickens Studies Annual: Essays in Victorian Fiction. Vols. 1–7 (1970–78), Carbondale: Southern Illinois University Press. Vols. 8–13 (1980–85), New York: AMS.

Dickens Studies Newsletter (1970–83). Changed to *Dickens Quarterly*, 1984–.

Dickensian, The, 1905–.

Dobie, Ann B. "Early Stream-of-Consciousness Writing: *Great Expectations.*" *Nineteenth-Century Fiction* 25 (1971): 405–16.

Donoghue, Denis. "The English Dickens and *Dombey and Son.*" *Nineteenth-Century Fiction* 24 (1970): 383–403.

Duckworth, Alistair M. "*Little Dorrit* and the Question of Closure." *Nineteenth-Century Fiction* 33 (1978): 110–32.

Duncan, Robert W. "Types of Subjective Narration in the Novels of Dickens." *English Language Notes* 18 (1980): 36–46.

Dunn, Albert A. "Time and Design in *David Copperfield.*" *English Studies* 59 (1978): 225–36.

Dyson, A. E. *The Inimitable Dickens: A Reading of the Novels.* London: Macmillan, 1970.

Eagleton, Terry. *Criticism and Ideology.* London: New Left Books, 1976.

Easson, Angus. "The Mythic Sorrows of Charles Dickens." *Literature and History* 1 (March 1975): 49–61.

Eldredge, Patricia R. "The Lost Self of Esther Summerson." *Literary Review* 24, no. 2 (1981): 252–78.

Engel, Monroe. "A Kind of Allegory: *The Old Curiosity Shop.*" In *The Interpretation of Narrative: Theory and Practice,* edited by Morton W. Bloomfield. Cambridge: Harvard University Press, 1970.

———. *The Maturity of Dickens.* Cambridge: Harvard University Press, 1959.

Fanger, Donald. *Dostoevsky and Romantic Realism: A Study of Dostoevsky in Relation to Balzac, Dickens, and Gogol.* Chicago: University of Chicago Press, 1968.

Fenstermaker, John J. *Charles Dickens, 1940–1975: An Analytical Subject Index to Periodical Criticism of the Novels and Christmas Books.* Boston: G. K. Hall, 1979.

Fielding, K. J. *Charles Dickens: A Critical Introduction.* London: Longmans, Green, 1958.

———. "*Hard Times* and Common Things." In *Imagined Worlds: Essays on Some English Novels and Novelists in Honour of John Butt,* edited by Maynard Mack and Ian Gregor, 183–203. London: Methuen, 1968.

Fleishman, Avrom. "The Fictions of Autobiographical Fiction." *Genre* 9 (1976): 73–86.

———. "Master and Servant in *Little Dorrit.*" In *Nineteenth-Century Literary Perspectives: Essays in Honor of Lionel Stevenson,* edited by Clyde deL. Ryals, 219–36. Durham, N.C.: Duke University Press, 1974.

Ford, George H. *Dickens and His Readers: Aspects of Novel Criticism since 1836.* Princeton: Princeton University Press, 1955.

Ford, George H., and Lauriat Lane, Jr., eds. *The Dickens Critics.* Ithaca: Cornell University Press, 1961.

Forster, E. M. *Aspects of the Novel.* New York: Harcourt, Brace, 1927.

Forster, John. *The Life of Charles Dickens.* Edited by A. J. Hoppé. 2 vols. London: Dent, 1966.

Frank, Lawrence. "Dickens's *A Tale of Two Cities*: The Poetics of Impasse." *American Imago* 36 (1979): 125–44.

Friedman, Stanley. "The Motif of Reading in *Our Mutual Friend.*" *Nineteenth-Century Fiction* 28 (1973): 38–61.

Ganz, Margaret. "*Nicholas Nickleby*: The Victories of Humor." *Mosaic* 9, no. 4 (1976): 107–29.

Garis, Robert E. *The Dickens Theatre: A Reassessment of the Novels*. Oxford: Clarendon, 1965.

Garrett, Peter. *The Victorian Multiplot: Studies in Dialogical Form*. New Haven: Yale University Press, 1980.

Giddings, Robert, ed. *The Changing World of Charles Dickens*. London: Vision, 1983.

Gilbert, Elliot L. "The Ceremony of Innocence: Charles Dickens's *A Christmas Carol*." *PMLA* 90 (1975): 22–31.

Gissing, George. *Charles Dickens: A Critical Study*. London: Gresham, 1904.

Gold, Joseph. *Charles Dickens: Radical Moralist*. Minneapolis: University of Minnesota Press, 1972.

Goldberg, Michael. *Carlyle and Dickens*. Athens: University of Georgia Press, 1972.

Gray, Paul Edward, ed. *Twentieth-Century Interpretations of Hard Times: A Collection of Critical Essays*. Englewood Cliffs, N.J.: Prentice-Hall, 1969.

Greene, Graham. "The Young Dickens." In *The Lost Childhood and Other Essays*. London: Eyre & Spottiswoode, 1951.

Gribble, Jennifer. "Depth and Surface in *Our Mutual Friend*." *Essays in Criticism* 25 (1975): 197–214.

Gross, John, and Gabriel Pearson, eds. *Dickens and the Twentieth Century*. London: Routledge & Kegan Paul, 1962.

Guerard, Albert J. *The Triumph of the Novel: Dickens, Dostoevsky, Faulkner*. New York: Oxford University Press, 1976.

Hardy, Barbara. *Charles Dickens: The Writer and His Work*. Windsor, Berkshire: Profile Books, 1983.

———. *Dickens: The Later Novels*. London: Longmans, Green, 1968.

———. *Forms of Feeling in Victorian Fiction*. London: Peter Owen, 1985.

———. *The Moral Art of Dickens*. New York: Oxford University Press, 1970.

Hayward, Arthur Lawrence. *The Dickens Encyclopaedia*. Hamden, Conn.: Archon, 1969.

Herbert, Christopher. "Converging Worlds in *Pickwick Papers*." *Nineteenth-Century Fiction* 27 (1972): 1–20.

———. "The Occult in *Bleak House*." *Novel* 17, no. 2 (1984): 101–15.

Holderness, Graham. "Imagination in *A Christmas Carol*." *Etudes Anglaises* 32 (1979): 28–45.

Hollington, Michael. *Dickens and the Grotesque*. Totowa, N.J.: Barnes & Noble, 1984.

Holloway, John. "*Hard Times*, A History and a Criticism." In *Dickens and the Twentieth Century*, edited by John Gross and Gabriel Pearson. Toronto: University of Toronto Press, 1962.

Hornback, Bert G. "*Noah's Arkitecture*": A Study of Dickens's Mythology. Athens: Ohio University Press, 1972.

House, Humphrey. *The Dickens World*. 2d ed. London: Oxford University Press, 1961.

Hughes, Felicity. "Narrative Complexity in *David Copperfield.*" *ELH* 41 (1974): 89–105.

Hutter, Albert D. "Crime and Fantasy in *Great Expectations.*" In *Psychoanalysis and Literary Process*, edited by Frederick Crews. Cambridge, Mass.: Winthrop, 1970.

———. "Nation and Generation in *A Tale of Two Cities.*" *PMLA* 93 (1978): 448–62.

Ingham, Patricia. "Speech and Non-Communication in *Dombey and Son.*" *The Review of English Studies* 30 (1979): 144–53.

Jefferson, D. W. "The Artistry of *Bleak House.*" In *Essays and Studies 1974*, edited by Kenneth Muir, 37–51. London: John Murray, 1974.

Johnson, Edgar H. *Charles Dickens: His Tragedy and Triumph.* Rev. ed. London: Allen Lane, 1977.

Kaplan, Fred. *Dickens and Mesmerism: The Hidden Springs of Fiction.* Princeton: Princeton University Press, 1975.

Kennedy, G. W. "Dickens's Endings." *Studies in the Novel* 6 (1974): 280–87.

———. "Naming and Language in *Our Mutual Friend.*" *Nineteenth-Century Fiction* 28 (1973): 165–78.

Kettle, Arnold. "Balzac and Dickens." In *The Modern World, II: Realities*, edited by David Daiches and Anthony Thorlby, 239–66. London: Aldus Books, 1972.

Keyser, Lester J. "A Scrooge for All Seasons." In *The English Novel and the Movies*, edited by Michael Klein, 121–31. New York: Frederick Ungar, 1981.

Kincaid, James R. *Dickens and the Rhetoric of Laughter.* Oxford: Clarendon, 1971.

Kincaid, James R., and Albert J. Kuhn, eds. *Victorian Literature and Society: Essays Presented to Richard D. Altick.* Columbus: Ohio State University Press, 1984.

Knoepflmacher, U. C., and G. B. Tennyson. *Nature and the Victorian Imagination.* Berkeley: University of California Press, 1977.

Kotzin, Michael C. *Dickens and the Fairy Tale.* Bowling Green, Ohio: Bowling Green University Popular Press, 1972.

Kucich, John. "Action in the Dickens Ending: *Bleak House* and *Great Expectations.*" *Nineteenth-Century Fiction* 33 (1978): 88–109.

———. *Excess and Restraint in the Novels of Charles Dickens.* Athens: University of Georgia Press, 1981.

Kurrik, Maire Jaanus. "Dickens." In *Literature and Negation*, 162–83. New York: Columbia University Press, 1979.

LaCapra, Dominick. "Ideology and Critique in Dickens's *Bleak House.*" *Representations* 6 (Spring 1984): 116–23.

Langbauer, Laurie. "Dickens's Streetwalkers: Women and the Form of Romance." *ELH* 53 (1986): 411–31.

Lanham, Richard A. "*Our Mutual Friend*: The Birds of Prey." *Victorian Newsletter* 24 (Fall 1963): 6–12.

Lankford, William T. " 'The Deep of Time': Narrative Order in *David Copperfield.*" *ELH* 46 (1979): 452–67.

——. " 'The Parish Boy's Progress': The Evolving Form of *Oliver Twist*." *PMLA* 93 (1978): 20–32.

Leavis, F. R. *The Great Tradition*. London: Chatto & Windus, 1973.

Leavis, F. R., and Q. D. Leavis. *Dickens the Novelist*. London: Chatto & Windus, 1970.

Lerner, Laurence. *Love and Marriage: Literature and Its Social Context*. London: Edward Arnold, 1979.

Lucas, John. *The Melancholy Man: A Study of Dickens's Novels*. Totowa, N.J.: Barnes & Noble, 1980.

Manheim, Leonard F. "The Law as Father: An Aspect of the Dickens Pattern." *American Imago* 12 (1955): 17–23.

——. "*The Personal History of David Copperfield*: A Study in Psychoanalytic Criticism." *American Imago* 9 (1952): 21–43.

Manning, John. *Dickens on Education*. Toronto: University of Toronto Press, 1959.

Manning, Sylvia Bank. *Dickens as Satirist*. New Haven: Yale University Press, 1971.

Marcus, David D. "The Carlylean Vision of *A Tale of Two Cities*." *Studies in the Novel* 8 (1976): 56–88.

——. "*Martin Chuzzlewit*: The Art of the Critical Imagination." *Victorian Newsletter* 54 (1978): 10–16.

Marlow, James E. "Memory, Romance, and the Expressive Symbol in Dickens." *Nineteenth-Century Fiction* 30 (1975): 20–32.

——. "Pickwick's Writing: Propriety and Language." *ELH* 52 (1985): 939–63.

McGowan, John P. "*David Copperfield*: The Trial of Realism." *Nineteenth-Century Fiction* 34 (1979): 1–19.

McMaster, Juliet. "Visual Design in *Pickwick Papers*." *Studies in English Literature* 23, no. 4 (1983): 595–614.

Miller, J. Hillis. *The Form of Victorian Fiction: Thackeray, Dickens, Trollope, George Eliot, Meredith, and Hardy*. Notre Dame, Ind.: University of Notre Dame Press, 1970.

——. "The Source of Dickens's Comic Art." *Nineteenth-Century Fiction* 24 (1970): 467–76.

Miller, J. Hillis, and David Borowitz. *Charles Dickens and George Cruikshank*. Los Angeles: Williams Andrews Memorial Library, University of California, 1971.

Monod, Sylvère. *Dickens the Novelist*. Norman: University of Oklahoma Press, 1968.

Moynahan, Julian. "The Hero's Guilt: The Case of *Great Expectations*." *Essays in Criticism* 10 (1960): 60–79.

Muir, Kenneth. "Image and Structure in *Our Mutual Friend*." In *Essays and Studies 1966*, edited by R. M. Wilson, 92–105. London: John Murray, 1966.

Myers, William. "The Radicalism of *Little Dorrit*." In *Literature and Politics in the Nineteenth Century*, edited by John Lucas. London: Methuen, 1971.

Nadel, Ira Bruce. " 'Wonderful Deception': Art and the Artist in *Little Dorrit*." *Criticism* 19 (1977): 17–33.

Needham, Gwendolyn. "The Undisciplined Heart of David Copperfield." *Nineteenth-Century Fiction* 9 (1954): 81–107.

Newman, S. J. *Dickens at Play*. London: Macmillan, 1981.

Newsom, Robert. *Dickens on the Romantic Side of Familiar Things:* Bleak House *and the Novel Tradition*. New York: Columbia University Press, 1977.

Nineteenth-Century Fiction 24, no. 4 (March 1970). Charles Dickens centennial issue.

Nisbet, Ada, and Blake Nevius. *Dickens Centennial Essays*. Berkeley: University of California Press, 1971.

Oddie, William. *Dickens and Carlyle: The Question of Influence*. London: Centenary, 1972.

Orwell, George. "Charles Dickens." In *Dickens, Dali, and Others: Studies in Popular Culture*. New York: Reynal & Hitchcock, 1946.

Ousby, Ian. "The Broken Glass: Vision and Comprehension in *Bleak House*." *Nineteenth-Century Fiction* 29 (1975): 381–92.

Page, Norman. *A Dickens Companion*. London: Macmillan, 1984.

Palmer, William J. "The Movement of History in *Our Mutual Friend*." *PMLA* 95 (1980): 487–95.

Partlow, Robert B., Jr., ed. *Dickens the Craftsman: Strategies of Presentation*. Carbondale: Southern Illinois University Press, 1970.

Pearson, Gabriel. "Dickens and His Readers." In *Victorian Literature: Selected Essays*, edited by Robert O. Preyer, 146–58. New York: Harper Torchbooks, 1966.

———. "Towards a Reading of *Dombey and Son*." In *The Modern English Novel: The Reader, the Writer and the Work*, edited by Gabriel Josipovici, 54–76. New York: Barnes & Noble, 1976.

Pratt, Branwen Bailey. "Dickens and Father: Notes on the Family Romance." *Hartford Studies in Literature* 8 (1976): 4–22.

———. "Dickens and Freedom: Young Bailey in *Martin Chuzzlewit*." *Nineteenth-Century Fiction* 30 (1975): 185–99.

Praz, Mario. "Charles Dickens." In *The Hero in Eclipse in Victorian Fiction*, translated by Angus Davidson. London: Oxford University Press, 1956.

Price, Martin, ed. *Dickens: A Collection of Critical Essays*. Englewood Cliffs, N.J.: Prentice-Hall, 1967.

Qualls, Barry V. *The Secular Pilgrims of Victorian Fiction: The Novel as Book of Life*. Cambridge: Cambridge University Press, 1982.

Quirk, Randolph. "Some Observations on the Language of Dickens." *Review of English Literature* 2 (1961): 20–21.

Ragussis, Michael. "The Ghostly Signs of *Bleak House*." *Nineteenth-Century Fiction* 34 (1979): 253–80.

Rignall, J. M. "Dickens and the Catastrophic Continuum of History in *A Tale of Two Cities*." *ELH* 51 (1984): 575–87.

Rogers, Philip. "The Dynamics of Time in *The Old Curiosity Shop*." *Nineteenth-Century Fiction* 28 (1973): 127–44.

Rubin, Stan S. "Spectator and Spectacle: Narrative Evasion and Narrative Voice in *Pickwick Papers*." *The Journal of Narrative Technique* 6, no. 3 (1976): 188–203.

Sadoff, Dianne F. "Storytelling and the Figure of the Father in *Little Dorrit*." *PMLA* 95 (1980): 234–45.

Sanders, Andrew. *Charles Dickens Resurrectionist*. London: Macmillan, 1982.

Schwarzbach, F. W. *Dickens and the City*. London: Athlone, 1979.

Scott, P. J. M. *Reality and Comic Confidence in Charles Dickens*. London: Macmillan, 1979.

Serlen, Ellen. "The Two Worlds of *Bleak House*." *ELH* 43 (1976): 551–66.

Showalter, Elaine. "Guilt, Authority, and the Shadows of *Little Dorrit*." *Nineteenth-Century Fiction* 34 (1979): 20–40.

Slater, Michael, ed. *Dickens 1970: Centenary Essays*. London: Chapman & Hall, 1970.

Solomon, Pearl Chester. *Dickens and Melville in Their Time*. New York: Columbia University Press, 1975.

Spilka, Mark. "*David Copperfield* as Psychological Fiction." *Critical Quarterly* 1 (Winter 1959): 292–301.

———. *Dickens and Kafka: A Mutual Interpretation*. London: Dennis Dobson, 1963.

Steele, Peter. "Dickens and the Grotesque." *Quadrant* 17 (March–April 1973): 15–23.

Steig, Michael. "The Central Action of *The Old Curiosity Shop* or Little Nell Revisited Again." *Literature and Psychology* 15, no. 3 (1965): 163–70.

———. *Dickens and Phiz*. Bloomington: Indiana University Press, 1978.

Steig, Michael, and F. A. C. Wilson. "Hortense vs. Bucket: The Ambiguity of Order in *Bleak House*." *Modern Language Quarterly* 33 (1972): 289–99.

Stewart, Garrett. *Dickens and the Trials of Imagination*. Cambridge: Harvard University Press, 1974.

Stoehr, Taylor. *Dickens: The Dreamer's Stance*. Ithaca: Cornell University Press, 1965.

Stone, Donald D. *The Romantic Impulse in Victorian Fiction*. Cambridge: Harvard University Press, 1980.

Stone, Harry. *Dickens and the Invisible World: Fairy Tales, Fantasy, and Novel-Making*. Bloomington: Indiana University Press, 1979.

———. "Dickens, Cruikshank, and Fairy Tales." In *George Cruikshank: A Revaluation*, edited by Robert L. Patten. Princeton: Princeton University Library, 1974.

———. "Fire, Hand, and Gate: Dickens' *Great Expectations*." *The Kenyon Review* 24 (1962): 662–91.

———. "The Novel as Fairy Tale: Dickens' *Dombey and Son*." *English Studies* 47 (1966): 1–27.

Sucksmith, Harvey Peter. *The Narrative Art of Charles Dickens: The Rhetoric of Sympathy and Irony in His Novels*. Oxford: Clarendon, 1970.

Thomas, Deborah A. *Dickens and the Short Story*. Philadelphia: University of Pennsylvania Press, 1982.

Thurley, Geoffrey. *The Dickens Myth: Its Genesis and Structure*. London: Routledge & Kegan Paul, 1976.

Tillotson, Kathleen. "New Readings in *Dombey & Son*." In *Imagined Worlds: Essays on Some English Novels and Novelists in Honour of John Butt*, edited by Maynard Mack and Ian Gregor, 173–82. London: Methuen, 1968.

———. *Novels of the Eighteen-Forties*. London: Oxford University Press, 1961.

———. "Oliver Twist." In *Essays and Studies 1959*. London: John Murray, 1959.

Trilling, Lionel. *The Opposing Self*. New York: Viking, 1955.

Van Amerongen, J. B. *The Actor in Dickens: A Study of the Histrionic and Dramatic Elements in the Novelist's Life and Works*. London: Cecil Palmer, 1926.

Van Ghent, Dorothy. "The Dickens World: A View from Todgers's." In *The Dickens Critics*, edited by George H. Ford and Lauriat Lane, Jr. Ithaca: Cornell University Press, 1961.

———. *The English Novel: Form and Function*. New York: Harper Torchbooks, 1953.

Vogel, Jane. *Allegory in Dickens*. University: University of Alabama Press, 1977.

Watt, Ian, ed. *The Victorian Novel: Modern Essays in Criticism*. New York: Oxford University Press, 1971.

Weinstein, Philip M. *The Semantics of Desire: Changing Models of Identity from Dickens to Joyce*. Princeton: Princeton University Press, 1984.

Welsh, Alexander. *The City of Dickens*. Oxford: Clarendon, 1971.

Westburg, Barry. *The Confessional Fictions of Charles Dickens*. Dekalb: Northern Illinois University Press, 1977.

Williams, Raymond. "Social Criticism in Dickens: Some Problems of Method and Approach." *Critical Quarterly* 6 (1964): 214–27.

Wilson, Angus. Introduction to *Oliver Twist*. Harmondsworth: Penguin, 1966.

———. *The World of Charles Dickens*. New York: Viking, 1970.

Wilson, Edmund. "Dickens: The Two Scrooges." In *The Wound and the Bow: Seven Studies in Literature*. London: W. H. Allen, 1952.

Wilt, Judith. "Confusion and Consciousness in Dickens's Esther." *Nineteenth-Century Fiction* 32 (1977): 285–309.

Wing, George. *Dickens*. Edinburgh: Oliver & Boyd, 1969.

Winters, Warrington. "Dickens and the Psychology of Dreams." *PMLA* 63 (1948): 984–1006.

Yeazell, Ruth Bernard. "Podsnappery, Sexuality, and the English Novel." *Critical Inquiry* 9 (1982): 339–57.

Zwerdling, Alex. "Esther Summerson Rehabilitated." *PMLA* 88 (1973): 429–39.

Acknowledgments

"The Dark World of *Oliver Twist*" (originally entitled "*Oliver Twist*") by J. Hillis Miller from *Charles Dickens: The world of His Novels* by J. Hillis Miller, © 1958 by the President and Fellows of Harvard college, © 1986 by J. Hillis Miller. Reprinted by permission of Harvard University Press.

"Dickens and the Comedy of Humors" by Northrop Frye from *Experience in the Novel: Selected Papers from the English Institute*, edited by Roy Harvey Pearce, © 1968 by Columbia University Press. Reprinted by permission of the author and the publisher.

"The Demons of History in Dickens's *Tale*" by Robert Alter from *Novel: A Forum on Fictoin* 2, no. 2 (Winter 1969), © 1969 by Novel, Inc. Reprinted by permission.

"The Creation of Consciousness and Dickens's Vision of the City" (originally entitled "Charles Dickens") by Raymond Williams from *The English Novel: From Dickens to Lawrence* by Raymond Williams, © 1970 by Raymond Williams. Reprinted by permission of the author and Chatto of Windus Ltd.

"Language into Structure: Pickwick Revisited" by Steven Marcus from *Daedalus: Journal of the American Academy of Arts and Sciences*, "Myth, Sumbol, and Culture," 101, no. 1 (Winter 1972), Cambridge, MA. © 1972 by the American Academy of Arts and Sciences. Reprinted by permission.

"*A Christmas Carol*: 'Giving Nursery Tales a Higher Form' " (originally entitled "The Christmas Books: 'Giving Nursery Tales a Higher Form' ") by Harry Stone from *Dickens and the Invisible World: Fairy Tales, Fantasy, and Novel-Making* by Harry Stone, © 1979 by Harry Stone. Reprinted by permission of the author and Indiana University Press.

"Plot and the Point of Reversal" (originally entitled "Plot and the Point of Reversal: Dickens and Poe") by Robert L. Caserio from *Plot, Story, and the Novel: From Dickens and Poe to the Modern Period* by Robert L. Caserio, © 1979 by Princeton University Press. Reprinted by permission.

"Language Engenders: *David Copperfield* and *Great Expectations*" (originally entitled "Charles Dickens: Authors of Being") by Dianne F. Sadoff from

Monsters of Affection: Dickens, Eliot and Bronte on Fatherhood by Dianne F. Sadoff, © 1982 by the Johns Hopkins University Press. Reprinted by permission.

"Discipline in Different Voices: Bureaucracy, Police, Family, and *Bleak House*" by D. A. Miller from *Representations* 1, no. 1 (February 1983), © 1983 by the Regents of the University of California. Reprinted by permission of the author and the Regents. The notes have been omitted.

"Monsters of Metonymy: *Hard Times* and Knowing the Working Class" by Stephen J. Spector from *ELH* 51, no. 2 (Summer 1984), © 1984 by the Johns Hopkins University Press. Reprinted by permission of the publisher.

"Homophobia, Misogyny, and Capital: The Example of *Our Mutual Friend*" by Eve Kosofsky Sedgwick from *Between Men: English Literature and Male Homosexual Desire* by Eve Kosofsky Sedgwick, © 1985 by Columbia University Press. Reprinted by permission.

"Dickens's *Great Expectations*: The Motive for Moral Masochism" by Shuli Barzilai from *American Imago* 42, no. 1 (Spring 1985), © 1985 by the Association for Applied Psychoanalysis, Inc., Brooklyn, N.Y. Reprinted by permission.

"The Dickensian 'No Thoroughfare' " originally entitled "Dialectical Images: Benjamin/ Dickens/Freud") by Ned Lukacher from *Primal Scenes: Literature, Philosophy, Psychoanalysis* by Ned Lukacher, © 1986 by Cornell University. Reprinted by permission of Cornell University Press.

"Getting and Having: Some Versions of Possession in *Little Dorrit*" by Jeff Nunokawa, © 1987 by Jeff Nunokawa. Published for the first time in this volume. Printed by permission.

Index